THE GOTHAM LIBRARY
OF THE NEW YORK UNIVERSITY PRESS

The Gotham Library is a series of original works and critical studies. Devoted to significant works and major authors and to literary topics of enduring importance, Gotham Library texts offer the best in literature and criticism.

Comparative and Foreign Language Literature:
Robert J. Clements, Editor

Comparative and English Language Literature:
James W. Tuttleton, Editor

Man and His Myths

Tennyson's *Idylls of the King*
in Critical Context

William E. Buckler

New York University Press
New York *and* London
1984

Library of Congress Cataloging in Publication Data

Buckler, William Earl
Man and his myths.

(Gotham library of the New York University Press)
Includes index.
1. Tennyson, Alfred Tennyson, Baron, 1809–1892. Idylls of the king. 2. Arthurian romances—History and criticism. 3. Myth in literature. I. Title.
PR5560.B8 1984   821C.8   84-8430
ISBN 0-8147-1059-X

For
Once and Future Members of My Family
John, Joe, Lorraine

Contents

Preface

In *Man and His Myths: Tennyson's "Idylls of the King" in Critical Context*, I have tried to give students a fresh way of looking at the poem, a judicious representation of the ways in which other commentators have perceived it over the last thirty years, and a sampling of some of the issues upon which critical debate is likely to be ongoing. The pleasure of literary study itself has been my chief motive, but I have also entertained the hope that the book would give focus to the critical status of its subject and supply, especially to young scholar-critics, encouragement and direction for their own analytical, interpretive, and evaluative endeavors.

I have attempted to be as nonpolemical as my goals would allow. Part 1 is the delineation of an attitude or state of mind, not a methodology; it emphasizes what, in my judgment of the record available to us, Tennyson had taken as his imaginative goal and hence the "capacity and sympathy" likely to be most rewarding to the serious, conscientious reader of his poetic text. Part 2 is an extended *explication de texte* and is critically autonomous. It has been many years in the making, and in it I do not contend with other commentators with other critical angles of vision because I did not want to be contentious or to see the overall perspective lost in controversy. Part 3 is also nonpolemical; I have refrained from refereeing the insights and evaluations of my peers and have

ix

allowed them to have their say as entirely as possible in their own words. The ideas (subjects, issues) around which I have organized their comments sometimes overlap and are imperfect in other ways; I hope they will be genuinely useful to many and grossly unfair to none. The essays in Part 4 attempt to clarify and consolidate points that have been suggested, more or less *en passant,* earlier but that could not be developed there without a strong sense of digression (Essays 1 and 2); or they pursue critical arguments on issues that, though crucial, would have ruptured the line of critical development being followed without allowing for adequate attention to the issues themselves.

A different version of Essay 2, "A Precarious Turning: From Medievalism to Homer," appeared in *Browning Institute Studies,* 8 (1980), 85–102. The text I have used throughout is *The Poems of Tennyson,* ed. Christopher Ricks (London: Longman, 1969). References to line numbers of individual idylls are given in parentheses in the text, using the capital initials of each: *CA, GL, MG,* and so forth.

Acknowledgments

The author and publisher are grateful to the following publishers and editors for permission to reprint substantial passages from works published by them. Permissions not specified here for passages included in the text of Part 3 and included in the List of Works Cited (pp. 000–000) were not required. However, acknowledgment of their source is given with genuine gratitude as indicated in the List.

Thomas P. Adler, "The Uses of Knowledge in Tennyson's *Merlin and Vivien*," *Texas Studies in Literature and Language* (1970), University of Texas Press, publisher.

Harold Bloom, *Poetry and Repression*, Yale University Press. Copyright © 1976 by the Yale University Press.

William R. Brashear, *The Living Will: A Study of Tennyson and Nineteenth-Century Subjectivism* (1969), Mouton Publishers (Division of Walter de Gruyter & Co.).

William R. Brashear, "Tennyson's Tragic Vitalism: *Idylls of the King*" (1968), *Victorian Poetry*, John Stasny, editor.

Jerome H. Buckley, *Tennyson: The Growth of a Poet* (1960), Harvard University Press. Reprinted by permission.

Samuel C. Burchell, "Tennyson's 'Allegory in the Distance'" (1953), *PMLA*.

A. Dwight Culler, *The Poetry of Tennyson*, Yale University Press. Copyright © 1977 by the Yale University Press.

John Philip Eggers, "The Weeding of the Garden: Tennyson's Geraint Idylls and *The Mabinogion*" (1966), *Victorian Poetry*, John Stasny, editor.

Edward Engelberg, "The Beast Image in Tennyson's *Idylls of the King*" (1955), *English Literary History*.

Donald S. Hair, *Domestic and Heroic in Tennyson's Poetry* (1981), University of Toronto Press.

Ward Hellstrom, *On the Poems of Tennyson* (1972), University Presses of Florida.

Gerhard Joseph, "The Idea of Mortality in Tennyson's Classical and Arthurian Poems: 'Honor Comes with Mystery'" (1968), *Modern Philology*.

Gerhard Joseph, *Tennysonian Love: The Strange Diagonal*, University of Minnesota Press, Minneapolis. Copyright © 1969 by the University of Minnesota Press.

James R. Kincaid, "Tennyson's 'Gareth and Lynette'" (1972), *Texas Studies in Literature and Language,* University of Texas Press, publisher.

James R. Kincaid, *Tennyson's Major Poems: The Comic and Ironic Patterns,* Yale University Press. Copyright © 1975 by the Yale University Press.

Henry Kozicki, *Tennyson and Clio: History in the Major Poems* (1979), Johns Hopkins University Press.

George P. Landow, "Closing the Frame: Having Faith and Keeping Faith in Tennyson's 'The Passing of Arthur'" (1974), *Bulletin of the John Rylands Library,* Frank Taylor, editor.

Boyd Litzinger, "The Structure of Tennyson's 'The Last Tournament'" (1963), *Victorian Poetry*, John Stasny, editor.

Kerry McSweeney, *Tennyson and Swinburne as Romantic Naturalists* (1981), University of Toronto Press.

Robert Pattison, *Tennyson and Tradition* (1979), Harvard University Press. Reprinted by permission.

Lawrence Poston III, "The Argument of the Geraint-Enid Books in *Idylls of the King*" (1964), *Victorian Poetry*, John Stasny, editor.

Lawrence Poston III, "'Pelleas and Ettarre': Tennyson's 'Troilus'" (1966), *Victorian Poetry*, John Stasny, editor.

F. E. L. Priestley, *Language and Structure in Tennyson's Poetry* (1973), Andre Deutsch.

John D. Rosenberg, *The Fall of Camelot: A Study of Tennyson's "Idylls of the King"* (1973), Harvard University Press. Reprinted with permission.

John D. Rosenberg, "Tennyson and the Landscape of Consciousness" (1974), *Victorian Poetry,* John Stasny, editor.

Clyde de L. Ryals, "*Idylls of the King:* Tennyson's New Realism" (1967), *Victorian Newsletter,* Ward Hellstrom, editor.

Clyde de L. Ryals, "The Moral Paradox of the Hero in *Idylls of the King*" (1963), *English Literary History.*

W. David Shaw, "The Idealist Dilemma in *Idylls of the King*" (1967), *Victorian Poetry,* John Stasny, editor.

W. David Shaw, "*Idylls of the King:* A Dialectical Reading" (1969), *Victorian Poetry,* John Stasny, editor.

W. David Shaw, *Tennyson's Style.* Copyright © 1976 by Cornell University. Used by permission of the publisher, Cornell University Press.

E. Warwick Slinn, "Deception and Artifice in *Idylls of the King*" (1973), *Victorian Poetry,* John Stasny, editor.

Donald Smalley, "A New Look at Tennyson—Especially the *Idylls*" (1962), *Journal of English and Germanic Philology.*

Stanley J. Solomon, "Tennyson's Paradoxical King" (1963), *Victorian Poetry,* John Stasny, editor.

David Staines, "Tennyson's 'The Holy Grail': The Tragedy of Percivale" (1974), *Modern Language Review,* C. J. Rawson, editor, The Modern Humanities Research Association, publisher.

Catherine Barnes Stevenson, "Druids, Bards, and Tennyson's Merlin" (1980), *Victorian Newsletter,* Ward Hellstrom, editor.

Michael G. Sundell, "Spiritual Confusion and Artistic Form in Victorian Poetry" (1971), *Victorian Newsletter,* Ward Hellstrom, editor.

Paul Turner, *Tennyson* (1976), Routledge & Kegan Paul Ltd.

R. B. Wilkenfeld, "Tennyson's Camelot: The Kingdom of Folly" (1968), *University of Toronto Quarterly.*

Part One

A Critical Orientation

A Critical Orientation

The reader who comes to Tennyson's *Idylls of the King* from the reading acts that precede it in the canon knows that it is essential that he position himself in a right relationship to the poem, that he attempt to discover a locus of imaginative apprehensiveness that will make him aesthetically alert and enable him to experience the poem at the deepest possible level. He has been trained by the Tennysonian poetic experience to certain kinds of critical expectation—that he will hear voices, one or many, other than an authorial voice; that however many structural analogues may function more or less visibly in the literary background of the piece, it will move along a cluster of experimental structural coordinates, will be monitored by an essentially new form; that it will not be importunate in the conveyance even of its consciously intended meaning, but will release through a process of imaginative fine-tuning—sometimes under-vocalized, sometimes urgent—infinite possibilities of awareness; that it will be an imaginative experience, not of mind speaking to mind, but of experienced consciousness speaking to experienced consciousness, of *all the poet is* sharing in deep spiritual communion with *all the reader is;* that the infinite awarenesses of the poem will emerge out of the images (actions, emblems, verbal constructs, focusing patterns) "because the thought within the image is so much more than any one interpretation." Fundamental to the aesthetic workability of these and other critical expectations is the reader's role as co-creator of the Tennysonian poetic experience. The reader is led into a new topography of poetic language, symbolic and complexly patterned, and is invited to explore a novel country which, despite its newness, he has strange intimations that he has visited before. What is really new in the experience, he knows from the first verse-paragraph, is the medium of language in which this poetic country is suddenly enabled to exist, along with the attitude, induced by the language, that for the very first time he may come to understand, to know a little better, what in fragmentary ways has been long familiar.

The principal linguistic introduction he is likely to have had to this novel country ("new-old") is Malory; but imaginative note-catching tells him immediately that this is very different poetic terrain from Malory's, that Malory translated even the raw *Stoffen* of a shared fiction into a very different linguistic reality. Malory supplies to the memory some of the fragments that account for the persistent sense of déjà vu that accompanies the reading of this essentially new poem. But even more of that sense comes from the reader's fragmentary familiarity with "all the mighty world" around him—with how people feel and aspire and join fellowships and question and drift away and deceive themselves and role-play and become haughty or humble or lustful or frightened or troubled almost beyond endurance; so that all the generic perceptual experiences he has had about life, many or few, orderly or chaotic, assume a distant or immediate relevance to this new language-world that promises tentatively to give them place at some new level of shared apprehension. Thus the reader bringing to the *Idylls* some sophistication concerning the peculiarities of literary procedure—especially of well-developed Tennysonian literary procedure—and noting uninhibitedly how the poetic text begins its forward motion (leads into itself) perceives that, in this novel poetic country, he is going to both witness and explore, see and interpret, literature made of literature (a Tennyson text made of a Malory and other texts) and literature made of life (Tennyson's, man's generally, and his own); and further, he is going to witness and explore how literature and life meet and merge in those imaginative moments when our whole attention is simultaneously riveted on the two. What the reader brings to the literary text (knowledge of the subject matter, of man in his world, of literary procedure) and the degree of his availability to the text (itself somewhat conditioned by what he brings to his reading of it) will determine in significant ways how he reads it—will monitor the quality of participatory co-creation by which he supplies supplementary scenes of the imagination and provides the poem's artistic unity. An unsophisticated reader will inevitably be an unsophisticated co-creator. But it is a defining characteristic of this particular Tennysonian text, *Idylls of the King,* that it cuts out almost none of its potential co-creators—provides as it were a universal reading act—and becomes thereby a poetic document in ultimate literary relevance, through which novice and sophisticate can alike engender such poet as may exist within them.

This quality of universal availability in an engendering poetic text accounts, further, for the experiential rather than ideological character of *Idylls of the King.* If, like other poets in the symbolist tradition, Tennyson wishes the creative act to affect the reader creatively, then he must avoid substituting *his* interpretation for *their* interpretation, must induce rather than be a revelation. To the degree that the poem were thesis-dominated, it would be imaginatively closed down, illustrative rather than imaginatively generative. Thus the authorial voice of Tennyson is never heard. Each segment of imaginative life is shaped by a narrative voice, specified as in *The Holy Grail* and *The Passing of Arthur* or generically anonymous as in most of the idylls, that is itself an integral dimension of the total narrative accomplishment. Even in the verse-epistle "To the Queen" at the end of the *Idylls,* Tennyson touches lightly, not on the poem's meaning, but on its procedure—"shadowing" the universal contention in man between flesh and spirit and clothing the "idea" of being a man with the "historical" reality of being such. He does not assert eternal Providence nor justify the ways of God to men. He releases, through this "old imperfect tale," itself an emblem of man's best efforts and failures, thousands of rich but inconclusive *aperçus* in a process of sensitizing the imaginative susceptibilities of the reader as a way of inducing in him a capacity to read both literature and life in his own way and to his own ends.

Tennyson was imaginatively removed from dialectics and

equivalencies, from all those structures and one-for-one's by which mind contends with mind and builds gladiatorial constructs having often magnificent and authentic élan. When he used them, he anchored them deep in personality, made them function as formulae of character. Hence he responded in a deeply disconsolate tone to the habitual efforts of readers (specifically critics) to rip images out of imaginative context and speak of them in terms of equivalencies: "They are right, and they are not right. They mean that and they do not. . . . I hate to be tied down to say, '*This* means *that*,' because the thought within the image is much more than any one interpretation."[1] Tennyson was globally aware that, in truly imaginative poetry, *this* never means simply *that*. And as he did not want to "be tied down" to such poetic diminution, we may be reasonably sure that it was part of his aspiration for the reader that, gradually through the imaginative processing of a poem like *Idylls of the King*, he would become less and less inclined to such imaginative reductiveness too—of life as well as literature.

Tennyson was reacting specifically to the Bishop of Ripon's rather circumspect suggestion that the "right" interpretation of the three Queens was as "Faith, Hope and Charity." In another context, he might have applied a different emphasis, deflecting the habitual notion that "this *means* that." "Meaning" is a very complex and subtle object of aesthetic contemplation to the student of Tennyson's poetry. Except in his verse-epistles, such as the "Dedication" preceding *Idylls of the King* and the epistle "To the Queen" with which the poem is "tagged"—graciously versified prose statements—Tennyson's poetry threatens to collapse into poetic meaninglessness (meaning become very drab and prosaic) in direct proportion to the positivism of the critical mentality that bombards it for some apothegmatical significance. "Poetry is like shot-silk with many glancing colours," Hallam records his father as affirming. "Every reader must find his own interpretation according to his ability, and according to his sympathy with the poet."[2] Thus Tennyson found the abstract possibility of absurd excesses of impressionistic solipsism more acceptable as an approach to his poetry than rigid critical monism with a rage for an inevitably reductive meaning.

There were two fundamental reasons for Tennyson's attitude. One was his deep and complex devotion to the integrity and the incomparable significance of poetry in the modern world. The other is a corollary to the first: modern man has an urgent need for transformations which only poetry, in the ordinary course of things, has any chance of effecting on a broad popular base. It is a curious cultural paradox: poetry is moving in the direction of the coterie and the ivory tower in almost direct proportion to the unparalleled need for poetry and poetry's values in the marketplace. That Tennyson found the "palace of art" alternative large and alluring, especially on the eve of coming into his majority as a poet, we cannot reasonably doubt. But it was a troublesome attraction even when most enticing, and he very soon came to see it as a false dilemma. The poet could, by simply undergoing an attitudinal metamorphosis and by managing his craft accordingly, both satisfy his most exquisite inner demands for beauty of form and awareness and reach out to a public that had a large and growing need of him. Homer had done it, as had Leonardo and Michelangelo and Shakespeare; and the modern poet could do it too. It was not an easy or a safe thing for Tennyson to do, and for it he received his share of critical superciliousness from the more doctrinaire poet-critics of three post-Tennysonian generations. On the other hand and at long last, one begins to relish the higher courage and supreme success with which he did it, after all.

But he did not do it through ideas, and Tennyson's hypersensitivity to criticism—that is, to the staple fare of the monthlies and quarterlies—was imaginative rather than personal. He shrank, in his ardor for poetry and poetry's genuine serviceability, from the bald translation into "meaning" that, for the most part, the reviewers subjected his poetry to. In this respect, Tennyson came startlingly close, aesthetically, to the critical apprehensions of Walter Pater, and Pater's Conclusion to *The Renaissance* is fruitfully suggestive, if kept within tactfully critical bounds, of Tennyson's controlling aesthetic attitudes and perceptual concerns in *Idylls of the King*.[3] The poem is pervaded with a strong sense of mutability, with an inversion of the perpetuation myth to which art so customarily dedicates itself, while at the same time *Idylls of the King* attempts to give a sort of fluid permanence to the very awareness of mutability that is the poem's perceptual center. Whether one thinks of Arthur or of the Arthurian dispensation imaged forth by the Round Table, "birth and gesture and death" is a quintessential identification of everything that goes on in the poem. It is the resonant representation of one of "the various forms of enthusiastic activity" which gives both the characters and the reader a "quickened sense of life" for a "given time"—for as long as it lasts in the "quickened, multiplied consciousness." But though real enough at one inestimable level of truth, the representation has only "the solidity with which language invests" it; and the "clear, perpetual outline of face and limb is but an image of ours, under which we group them," with the co-creative assistance of the poet—"a design in a web, the actual threads of which pass out beyond it." It is not the mighty world, but an image of the mighty world and thus both truer than truth and not true at all. For the readers of the poem, as for its central characters, "when reflexion begins to act upon these objects they are dissipated under its influence; the cohesive force seems suspended like a trick of magic," as that same "cohesive force" had been created by a "trick of magic," the indispensable act of poetic faith, ours and theirs. Even after those objects "are dissipated," however, something remains for the reader. Having been to some degree trained by the poetic experience itself to "see in them all that is to be seen in them by the finest senses," to "pass most swiftly from point to point, and be present always at the focus where the greatest number of vital forces unite in their purest energy," we can never again be quite the same because we have become possessed, again in individual degree, of an organically altered availability to imaginative apprehension. The chief impediment to such organic alteration would be the aesthetic slovenliness born of boredom, a succumbing to the rough, habitual, stereotyped response; and one of the usual manifestations of that impediment is the reliance, not on imaginative images, but on naked ideas: "The theory or idea or system which requires of us the sacrifice of any part of this experience, in consideration of some interest into which we cannot enter, or some abstract theory we have not identified with ourselves, or what is only conventional, has no real claim upon us" in our reading of this or any of Tennyson's principal poems. Although Pater turned his musings finally toward narrower conclusions to which Tennyson would perhaps have had limited access, the aesthetic apprehensions of the two writers—their nondoctrinaire aesthetic dispositions and tendencies—are remarkably alike.

When Tennyson makes the reader's "sympathy with the poet" one of the two conditions for interpreting his poems, he implies more than a usual relationship between him and his reader and again suggests the need for a common feeling rather than a cerebral communication. A sympathy for what the poet is trying to do—how, with language, structure, myth, he is trying to open up his own and the reader's consciousness of himself and the world around him—is the fairest interpretation of Tennyson's phrase. And, thus interpreted, it is a matter of great significance. Modification of inherited genres is a defining characteristic of Tennyson's poetry. He was, like the poet of Shelley's *Defence*, both the creator and the creation of his age; and he knew, with Shelley, that poetic structure, however deep its roots in the literary past, must mutate in response to the altered spiritual pressures brought to it by a new and conspicuously different age. This recognition and its effects on imaginative literary structure is one of the most visible literary phenomena of the nineteenth and twentieth centuries and one of the indices to the very measurable difference between this era in letters and any that had preceded it. Tennyson's poetic structures not only mutated inevitably but also were altered by a bold and forthright experimentalism, the awareness of poetic need on the part of Tennyson being advanced far beyond the force for change at the center of the *Zeitgeist* itself. He was bringing together the literary past and the literary future in the transience of the present. What Arthur says to "those great Lords from Rome"—"The old order changeth, yielding place to new" (*CA*, 508)—has conspicuous relevance, not only to the fable, but to the form. "On Malory, on Layamon's *Brut*, on Lady Charlotte Guest's translation of the *Mabinogion*, on the old Chronicles, on old

French Romance, on Celtic folklore, and largely on his own imagination, my father founded his epic. . . ."[4] The "old order" of the matter of Arthur becomes one point on a continuum of measurable change. The formal epic becomes another.

Hallam Tennyson refers repeatedly (and rather casually) to the *Idylls* as an epic: "founded his epic," "earliest fragment of an epic," "the epical King Arthur," the poem's "Epic unity."[5] Tennyson himself, on the other hand, wrote to his American publishers in December 1858, "I wish that you would disabuse your own minds and those of others, as far as you can, of the fancy that I am about an Epic of King Arthur. I should be crazed to attempt such a thing in the heart of the 19th Century."[6] Tennyson's point could not be clearer, and yet Hallam's term is wholly reasonable: the length, prosody, subject matter, stylistic strategies, and divisions of the *Idylls* clearly invite comparison of the poem with the formal epic. Between the two lies a significant truth: as he had moved the matter of Arthur forward, letting it fuel and be fueled by his own imaginative imperatives and those of his age, so Tennyson moved the formal epic forward, letting its classical lineaments be altered by the new aesthetic pressures of a spiritually eclipsed time. It was the inner life that needed new foundations, and thus the journey, of epic proportions but only vaguely epic-like, was into the sanctuarial self. Still, Arthur's world-apprehension has a firm analogy in literary mutation:

> "The old order changeth, yielding place to new,
> And God fulfils himself in many ways,
> Lest one good custom should corrupt the world."
>
> (*PA*, 408–410)

Thus Tennyson set aside the "big raft" of the traditional epic and designed instead "a small vessel, built on fine lines" as "likely to float further down the stream of Time. . . ."[7] Float, that is, into the future; and this brings us to another point on a continuum of measurable change.

That Tennyson was intuitively in touch with the distant future is implicit in every aspect of the manner of *Idylls of the*

King. The very vagueness of the architectural outlines that has so fretted some of its impatient critics is a mark of its poetic genius: the more classical its structure—for example, the more Miltonic—the less available would it have been to a broad popular readership and the more likely that, among professional students of literature, criticism of it would have turned on traditional, genre-oriented lines. Tennyson was in no way attempting to challenge Milton, although he and Milton have many shared concerns, and Milton obviously looms large in the literary background out of which Tennyson, like Keats and Shelley, was trying to invent a new poetic voice. But he did not want the *Idylls* to founder on shrunken, unfruitful comparisons with *Paradise Lost;* so he created a new species of experiential structure out of the epic resources of his literary tradition, moving the matter into a medium of storied verisimilitude, shaped but not imperially structured, having faith that, among sympathetic readers and after some inevitable doctrinaire dissatisfactions, the drift of his structure and the drift of his meaning ultimately would be perceived as aesthetically coherent.

He separated himself, likewise, from the great English allegorist, whom he admired and from whom he had learned: *Idylls of the King* suggests little by way of comparison with *The Faerie Queene,* and the deeply textured, complexly resonant allegory of Spenser is literary ages removed from the "parabolic drift" of Tennyson. The "darke conceit" of Spenser was anchored in very different coordinates of beauty and awareness from those which Tennyson and the future needed to create. Spenser's poem represented, among other richer substances, an elegant intellectualism that Tennyson's age could draw from many sources; it needed something other than that from its poetry. The future, Tennyson seems to have intuited, would be a time of structured deconstruction, of monistic pluralism, in which monolithic historical monuments would have about them a remote archaeological air and where people, drawn into contemporaneity by the exciting multiplicity of their explosive new environment, would be obsessed by an infinity of details. But until human nature itself changed, they would need—and, after some heady turbulence, be available to—some means, some useful processes, for discovering, gradually and without stentorian dogmatism, who they were and what and why they believed; they would need some sense of cosmic order that they could find only in an ordered consciousness quickened by a multiplied imaginative awareness. And to that need he quietly addressed himself through "the dream of man coming into practical life and ruined by one sin."[8] That "one sin," like poetry itself, has "many glancing colours" which flame out in all directions in the characters and episodes of the poem; but that "one sin" is set against the multitudinousness of modern man's concerns, against the confusions of his deconstructed existence, as a poetic way of insinuating into his consciousness the perception that all confusions are essentially one confusion, that the sea that "moans round" him with so "many voices" has in fact but one voice, that he is the one potential coherent of his universe if he can, like Arthur, inscape a self capable of dealing, at least tentatively, with Time.

Arthur is, as Guinevere comes belatedly and after much disaster to recognize, the quintessential microcosm of potential man. He fails, of course, both magnificently and miserably, in the yet unequal battle with all his warring senses; but, however weakened the faith in him—that is, his latter-day faith in himself—he does not die; and his second coming is emblematic of returns to the nth power because every man, at some moment of expectant spiritual equipoise, wants to be ideally good. No one has ever succeeded, of course, despite the efforts of Christian mythmakers to make Christ perfect and of pagan mythmakers to present Prometheus as wholly good. But every man, at least for a fleeting moment on this tableland of contest between the mysteries of birth and death, has a go—always has had and always will have. Even the inexplicable exceptions, represented in the poem by Vivien and her strange fellowship, only prove the general truth by their very moral outlandishness. Thus it was sympathy of a very complex sort that Tennyson asked of a reader of *Idylls of the King*—sympathy with the far-reaching changes he was working on the matter, manner, and meaning of poetry.

To see King Arthur as the "soul" and the Round Table as the "passions and capacities of *a man*" (emphasis added), as Tennyson is reported by James Knowles to have said,[9] is to see the *Idylls* in a severely microcosmic way; and this seems a very useful approach. But the poem has historical coordinates too, existing in a vague frame of mythohistorical time somewhere between the fifth and the thirteenth centuries. The last remnants of imperial Rome are in the process of withdrawing from this untenable outpost of barbarism/civilization, creating an authority vacuum which Arthur for a time successfully fills; and this provides a time alpha for the mythohistorical period in which the central fiction functions. But the book of time, once opened, is never closed. We know that the Arthurian dispensation ends with the results of "that last, dim, weird battle in the west," with Bedivere's recognition that "'the true old times are dead,'" and with Arthur's departure to "the island-valley of Avilion." And we know, too, that the final narration is that of Bedivere, "Told, when the man was no more than a voice/In the white winter of his age, to those/With whom he dwelt, new faces, other minds" (*PA*, 3–5). But we do not know what new sort of era was ushered in, what these "new faces, other minds" were like, what power filled the authority vacuum in turn created by the passing of Arthur. It is clear enough, on Tennyson's own testimony, that it was not another Arthur because, as Hallam Tennyson attests, the poet subscribed to the view of Joseph of Exeter: "The old world knows not his peer, nor will the future show us his equal: he alone towers over other kings, better than the past ones and greater than those that are to be."[10] Obviously, then, the vacuum has not been filled and cannot be until Arthur comes again; and since Tennyson believed in myths, not in fairy tales, in God-like anointings, not in magic wands, Arthur can come again—and again—only in the pages of poems like *Idylls of the King,* in which he returns to each generation of imaginative readers. Time must end with the second coming of Arthur as of Christ, and any interim journey to the world would be a source of false expectation and dismay since he did all he could in time the first time. So the

mythohistorical open-endedness of the piece suggests that
the best that we can hope for (and it is a goodly best) is to deal
with Time in an Arthurian fashion by giving his myth sanctuary in our imaginative selves in the belief that, thus come
again, it will somehow obliquely but organically affect our
"ways with men."

Mythohistorical time is in this manner returned to its microcosmic center in Arthur himself, and historical time becomes a dimension of the metaphoric fiction that enables the
poem to exist. Time as ordinarily perceived is an illusion,
indispensable but ultimately unreal. Like space, it is a mode
of consciousness, a perceptual metaphor, a vehicle of knowledge; like images in poetry, it is a way the sensuous mind has
of validating its existence. Duty requires time and space to
give it definition, and merit is meaningful only in a temporal-
spatial frame. It is not easy of access, this awareness of the
difference between an indispensable appearance and an ultimate reality, the route to the one being, certainly for the
generality of men, by way of the other. Inevitably "man coming into practical life"—man caught up in the toils of daily
living among the all-too-pervasive appearances of mind,
body, earth, air, light, duty, and merit, among the "passions
and capacities of a man"—quite understandably falters and
falls. He is vulnerable to every weakness of perception and
conduct that the knights of the Round Table collectively ex-
hibit and that Merlin embodies pathetically, Guinevere quintessentially. Arthur does not himself succumb to this complex
of vulnerabilities, but neither does he succeed in his mighty
apostolate. Indeed, his failure was inevitable, for a reason—
"one sin"—that few of his associates in this magnificent perceptual adventure ever have the least inkling of.

Arthur has, in the sensuous fiction in which he functions,
the most sophisticated sensuous awareness of anyone in the
mythic world of the poem, an awareness to which he gives
voice in his address to the remnant knighthood at the end of
The Holy Grail, explaining why he would not, even had he
"'seen the sight,'" have sworn the vow (900):

> "Not easily, seeing that the King must guard
> That which he rules, and is but as the hind

To whom a space of land is given to plow.
Who may not wander from the allotted field
Before his work be done; but, being done,
Let visions of the night or of the day
Come, as they will; and many a time they come,
Until this earth he walks on seems not earth,
This light that strikes his eyeball is not light,
This air that smites his forehead is not air
But vision—yea, his very hand and foot—
In moments when he feels he cannot die,
And knows himself no vision to himself,
Nor the high God a vision, nor that One
Who rose again: ye have seen what ye have seen."

                                    (*HG*, 901–915)

It is an extraordinary speech for Arthur to make, there being nothing even roughly like it elsewhere in the poem.

Arthur is brought to this uncharacteristic verbal behavior by the cataclysmic results of the Grail-quest. The whole affair had taken place, for Arthur, in an overwrought ambience of impending doom. He had been summoned away by an "outraged maiden"

Crying on help: for all her shining hair
Was smeared with earth, and either milky arm
Red-rent with hooks of bramble, and all she wore
Torn as a sail that leaves the rope is torn
In tempest. . . .

                                    (*HG*, 209–213)

He had returned with companions, "their arms/Hacked, and their foreheads grimed with smoke, and seared" (*HG*, 264–265), too late to prevent the vow-making, but just in time to see the roofs of Camelot "rolled in thunder-smoke!" and to rush homeward "In horror lest the work of Merlin wrought,/ Dreamlike, should on the sudden vanish, wrapt/In unremorseful folds of rolling fire" (*HG*, 259–261). He had then been faced with the fait accompli of the knights' misguided but sacred vows and had made his dark prophecy of their disastrous results. Through the months occupied in the quest, Arthur has been left with the knights' places vacant at his side; and when the quest is over—"scarce returned a tithe"—and when, "gazing at a barren board,/And a lean order," he has listened patiently to the Grail-quest histories of his chief knights—the self-inflations of Percivale, the flippancies of Gawain, the deep-flowing sadness of Bors, the agonizing jeopardy of Lancelot—Arthur is led to express, in simple but far-reaching terms, a world view that, through innate modesty and the lack of so generative an occasion, he has never before articulated to his knights in this particular language and mode.

What Arthur here shares with his knights, who are themselves enmeshed in varying degrees of ego-definition, inflated or shrunken or numb as a result of their experience in the quest, is who, perceptually, he is, of where he fits in a metaphor of world-apprehensiveness. He, like God and Christ, is a reality, a true truth. He is not a vision or an appearance or a metaphor: he really exists, is a Thing-in-itself. But he is located in an illusion of time and space that is indispensable in that it enables him to do his work, defines duty, makes merit meaningful; but it can also be a grand deception, leading one to confuse, at a fundamental level, appearance with reality, reality with appearance. The brain ("forehead") with which he thinks, the eye with which he verifies, the hand with which he proves three-dimensionally, the foot that gives him carriage and enables him to move about—these are all indispensable illusions in an illusive framework of time and space, appearance rather than reality. The external world, too, that exists in a frame of time and space—earth, light, air—is illusive appearance, not reality. It is a spiritual rather than a religious apprehension that Arthur expresses, even though he does include God and Christ as true truths; and his metaphysical awareness has about it no touch of a theological scheme. He has *feelings* about the immortality of this real self, but his soul-knowledge does not encompass, except by implicitly hopeful analogy, personally eternal life.

But it is crucial that the reader of *Idylls of the King* see this speech of Arthur's, despite its luminously self-evident importance, as atypical, the surfacings of extraordinary spiritual pressures upon him in the practical conduct of his life. He is not a philosopher-king in any abstract sense of that ancient term, and he does not instruct his knights, by habit, in philosophical perception. He expresses, in the most domestic and personal language, an awareness that any reader might have and that, genuinely perceived as a principle of both perception and conduct, might well affect his life in infinitely far-reaching ways; and he expresses it, when sorely tried physically and faced with a fundamental challenge to everything he has fought and worked for, as an irreducible gloss on the subtlest temptation of the spirit of man. No other misdemeanor—not adultery or falsehood or rebellion against rule or jealousy or broken trust—has ever threatened the Arthurian dispensation with a like magnitude.

No one in the poem expresses an acuter understanding of the uses of the sensuous world of man and nature than Arthur, and thus no one else has been able, like Arthur, to translate such an understanding into day-to-day programmatic action—"righting human wrong." But the excitement of Arthur's practical and wholly serviceable awareness is that it looks through its sensuous metaphor, which places a man for a time squarely in his universe and enables him thus to function therein, at a reality beyond sensuous measure. That is the "secret word" that "God hath told the King" and that the knights, credulous but uncomprehending, jubilate in paeans of affirmation at the King's marriage to his Queen. Arthur understands, with a simple clarity that makes him seem austere to those who do not share at least to some degree his singular insight, the true nature of human potential, for he is himself an inscape of that potential.

But despite the crystal-clarity of Arthur's soul-sight, it cannot be spoken of except in paradoxical language. In order to have any genuine access to that potential, man must know that he truly exists, but he cannot know that he truly exists unless he perceives the difference between the appearance of his existence and the reality of his existence, and the only way for the generality of men to cultivate in themselves the capacity for such a perception is to work upward through the sensuous frame to such a fine-tuning of the human spirit that the spirit can look upon itself as the true reality (the true "I") and recognize therewith such other spirit-realities as "the high God" and "that One/Who rose again." Having reached that point of ontological perception, the "I" can then dwell in peace amid the sensuousness of an authentic illusion because to that degree it has dealt with Time and all the other illusive appearances and can put them to the service of others who have not yet discovered an access route to reality and its spiritual peace.

But something so delicate and all-important as this unequivocal apprehension of the authenticity of the spirit of man is not something that even Arthur achieves once and for all and has forever available as a routine daily companion. Its epiphanic moments are real but transitory; they alter one's knowledge of the significance of human life in this world, in this body, but as things in themselves, as spiritual touchstones, they require perpetual renewal of the spirit in its sensuous frame. The analogy with poetic processing is very basic: like poetry, it is a perpetual process of becoming; the images exist in a state to some degree chaotic until the cohering illumination emerges, but the illumination can emerge, except perhaps for the very, very few, only through the conscientious orchestration of the images themselves. On the other hand, after one of those fortunate moments of imaginative/spiritual perspective, one can never, one's life in this world can never, be the same again, because he knows what poetry or he or life in this world is all about. Not abstractly or philosophically or theologically, but poetically and truly.

Clearly, this one but sufficient illumination of Arthur's is closely correlated with the one but sufficient "sin" by which his efforts at "practical life" were "ruined." If the positive energy with which he makes his realm and reigns is centered in perception, a cohering insight, then its neutralization must be centered in misperception, a chaos of misapprehension, which destroys his realm and ends his reign. At the level of "practical life," this will be reflected in a multiplicity of images of behavior—physical, psychological, verbal—and "sin" will often be conceived of at an ordinary moralistic level. But Arthur's crucial perception of the difference between appear-

ance and reality—the central flow in his spiritual/imaginative/
aesthetic life, setting its direction and giving meaning to all
he says and does—envelops all the poem's images and procedures and sensitizes the reader imaginatively to the potential difference between *all* appearances and *all* realities, alerts
him to the poetical need, even when he has yielded most fully
to the sensuous inducements of the poem, "to look through
the insistent, and often grotesque, substance at the thing
signified."[11]

In an imaginative context, sin can never be a simplistic
metaphor, and it is certainly not a simplistic metaphor in
Idylls of the King. The poetic construct, working through a
dense fabric of sensuously apprehended human failures, may
gradually bring the reader's perception of the subject to a
grand and simple, an imaginatively unified, apprehension;
but, like Arthur's epiphanic moments, this apprehension can
never be frozen in time, but will always be returning to solution and requiring, through a thousand refractive images,
perceptual/imaginative renewal. Thus the "one sin" of which
Tennyson speaks cannot be a particular fault like adultery,
however useful adultery may be as an image through which
the sensuous mind can look through to the suprasensuous
reality ultimately suggested. The "one sin" must be indissolu-
bly related to the "inscape of human potential" which is
Arthur, must be the human failure from which all failures
derive. It is only in that sense that *Idylls of the King* is a "moral"
poem, as it is a "perceptual" poem: it creates a magnificent
imaginative fable having many real/symbolic characters working through many mythic story lines toward a nondogmatic
poetic insight into the ultimate *human* perception and the
ultimate idea in which man's moral nature, surfacing perpetually in successes and failures, can be imaginatively and
acceptably rooted. The deeply moving dramatic climax of the
poem in *Guinevere,* where Arthur and his fugitive Queen have
their final generative meeting, turns upon these awarenesses;
and the near-intolerable psychic pain from which Lancelot so
nobly suffers is centered there. But it casts a varied light—
pathetic or tender, jubilant or brutal, ironic or grotesque,
terrifying or pervasively sad—over the individual idylls and

imparts to the poem as a whole "a mellow soberness of tone, more impressive, to our minds, than if the author had drawn up a set of opinions in verse, and sought to instruct the understanding, rather than to communicate the love of beauty to the heart."[12]

Notes

1. Notes to the Eversley edition of *The Works of Alfred Lord Tennyson,* annotated by Alfred Lord Tennyson and edited by Hallam Lord Tennyson (New York: Macmillan, 1908), III (*Idylls of the King*), 442. All references to these notes are to this edition and are given hereafter as Eversley, with volume and page numbers.
2. Eversley, III, 442–443.
3. Walter Pater, Conclusion to *The Renaissance,* in *The Works of Walter Pater,* 10 vols. (London: Macmillan, 1910), I, *passim.*
4. Eversley, III, 436.
5. Eversley, III, 436, 440, 446.
6. Quoted in A. Dwight Culler, *The Poetry of Tennyson* (New Haven: Yale University Press, 1977), pp. 223, 269, n. 5.
7. Eversley, III, 436.
8. Eversley, III, 443.
9. James T. Knowles, "Aspects of Tennyson," *Nineteenth Century,* 33 (January 1893), 181–182.
10. Eversley, III, 444.
11. Thomas Hardy, Preface to *The Dynasts* (London: Macmillan, 1977), p. 7.
12. Arthur Henry Hallam, "On Some Characteristics of Modern Poetry . . ." (review of *Poems, Chiefly Lyrical*), *Englishman's Magazine* (August 1831), as reprinted in *Tennyson: The Critical Heritage,* ed. John D. Jump (New York: Barnes and Noble, 1967), p. 42.

Part Two

A Critical Reading of
Idylls of the King

1.

1869—The Frame

■ *The Coming of Arthur* ■ *The Passing of Arthur*

Tennyson quite frequently employed the device of placing his poems in a poetic frame—a prefatory verse-epistle as with *The Palace of Art*, a Prologue and Epilogue or Conclusion as in *The Princess* and *In Memoriam*, an introductory poetic narrative as in *The Sea-Fairies* and *The Lotus-Eaters*—conditioning, either ironically or suspensefully, the reader's response to the total poetic experience. He uses the device more elaborately in *Idylls of the King* than anywhere else, centering in *The Coming of Arthur* and *The Passing of Arthur* the mysterious circumstances surrounding both his "birth" and his "death" and both the validity and the authenticity of his kingship. Since these two framing narratives were not published until 1869 in company with *The Holy Grail* and *Pelleas and Ettarre*—some forty years after Tennyson had begun to deal poetically with the matter of Arthur and ten years after the first four idylls had been published—we know that, even if by 1855 Tennyson had not "determined upon the final shape of the poem,"[1] by 1869 he had certainly done so. Thus we can fairly expect to find in these two frame-idylls a full indication of the poet's

25

attitude toward his subject matter, of the poetic method he is going to use in dealing with it, and of the perspective that he wants the reader to have on it.

These two frame-idylls counterpoint lightly an unobtrusive linguistic archaicism against a quiet but firm sense of modern relevance, resulting in an attitude of perenniality, a mutability of a metaphorically permanent sort. They have very different tonal qualities, creating subtly different spiritual/imaginative spaces. The first is spoken by a vigorous voice full of the energy of the events themselves, bold with the authority of someone of considerable stature who has been an active participant in an unparalleled adventure, a voice large with expectation (perhaps "the bold Sir Bedivere" himself in his vigorous prime). The last is told by a loyal geriatric voice, sobered by the events but not disconsolate, reviewing with great particularity the last hurrah of the Arthurian realm when he and his King finally stood alone. Here it is explicitly the witnessing of Sir Bedivere that we are privy to, Bedivere the alien "in the white winter of his age." It is a firm, steady voice, never quavering in its vivid recollection of that doubt-ridden, catastrophic day. The speaker does not, like Percivale in narrating *The Holy Grail,* make repeated reference to his own prestige; nor, like Ulysses, inflate himself with ego-petulance over a lost role. He looks back over half a lifetime at that "dolorous day" with the fresh vividness of the last synoptic, still wholly credulous, still wholly loyal, though the events he tells of are death-ridden and grimly sad.

In neither idyll, despite the very real difficulties facing anyone attempting to know exactly what happened—how Arthur really came, how he really passed—is there any equivocal witnessing; each historian believes his chronicle implicitly. But there is no scuttling the difficulties. No one of the versions of Arthur's birth—and hence of his ordinary right of succession as King—is in itself wholly convincing; and his crowning in the midst of contention and clamor and through the craft of Merlin implants unease in him who hears the tale, if not in the anonymous teller. And in the account of the passing, despite Bedivere's "bold" testimony, a precarious balance between belief and disbelief is created: Arthur's own mind is

torn between doubt and belief, and his ruined situation is a
source of fideistic anxiety since nothing fails like failure; the
testimony of Merlin, that Arthur will not die but come again,
is clouded by the memory of Merlin's own world-weariness
and melancholy catastrophe; and Bedivere's credulity, however firm and loyal, is faulted for the reader in some degree
by his very honesty as a narrator. He *did* doubt Arthur's
wisdom about Excalibur repeatedly; he had a momentary
rush of doubt about Arthur's ultimate return ("'but—if he
come no more—,'" 451); and he was not absolutely sure
of the testimony of his senses ("it seemed there came . . .
/Sounds"; he "saw . . ./Or thought he saw," 457–460,
463–465).

Clearly, then, the poet had a non-positivistic, complex, delicate attitude toward his subject. It was a matter of the very
first order of importance—good witnesses had seen it as the
red heart of their life-experience. Indeed, it was an "image of
the mighty world" itself—a concentrated image, not a simplistic one, that must be allowed to reflect the central truth of
the world, including its ugliest warts and its loosest loose-
ends. But being an image of the mighty world, a world hoary
with age and not very much advanced, the work must deal
largely in failed perspectives, attitudes as facts, a multiplicity
of witnessings that are themselves images of existences—people telling other people, in their fashion, who they are. It is
not history, and it is not fairy tale, but something in between—a storied verisimilitude of the present and the future
in somewhat archaically stylized costume. And it is not a mystery. Life is framed by the mysteries of birth and death—
ontological issues to which man has no real ontological access; but life itself is not an insoluble mystery. Life may be
characterized by complex interweavings of good and evil,
confusion and insight, self-awareness and self-abandonment,
varieties of perception and testimony; but life is apprehensi-
ble, and the good life is both knowable and available.

Making this matter of Arthur and its potential levels of
meaning open to a varied readership (themselves an "image
of the mighty world") required the translation of the poet's
attitude toward his subject matter into the method of his

poem. As prologue and epilogue, the two idylls serve very different literary purposes, the first designed to position the reader in an important and appropriate relationship to the reading act about to take place, the second to restore perspective to the massive imaginative experience that he has been through, to break up any frozen concepts he may have developed, to save the poetic structure itself from tragic desolation by restoring, however ambiguously, the quiet expectation that all is not lost, to remind the co-creative reader that he must "find his own interpretation according to his ability, and according to his sympathy with the poet," and to encourage him, through reflection or a fresh reading act, to let Arthur come again by running the poem through his imaginative consciousness once more. But the two idylls are alike as witnessings, the narrations of persons having their own identities and limitations of perception, setting the respective phases of the literary experience into motion as chronicles of events, persons, attitudes, problems, real if relative solutions. Thus the poet, in the most trustworthy imaginative sense, places himself in relationship to the poem in a position analogous to that of the reader, becomes a reader of his own writing act. There are metaphoric or exemplary patternings in both idylls with which the reader may identify—Leodogran's winnowing of varieties of evidence in preparation for his decision, Bedivere's solitary reaffirmation, despite momentary defection, that Arthur is a wholly worthy King—but he is also free to come at all such matters in his own very different way. Thus the reader is on his own to the utmost degree possible in dealing with a poetic text. He simply brings all he is to the poem and attempts to see with uninhibited imaginative clarity its special idiomatic language-world.

Of course, substance is an inseparable part of method in any poem, and especially in *Idylls of the King:* how one achieves insight is itself the most valuable insight. In no playful sense, *manner is meaning* in the poem, and this is one of the respects in which Tennyson simply changed the history of English poetry. One knows from the poetic pieces in the Tennyson canon that he had the deepest aesthetic reasons for moving in this direction in his poetry, but it is fair to assume that his desire to create a universal literary experience in *Idylls of the King* moved him briskly forward in this experimental regard. He was writing for those who could bring to the poem large knowledge of the matter of Arthur and deep understanding of man in his world as well as the most literarily sophisticated awareness of Coleridge's rubric concerning "poetic faith";[2] and he was writing for those who had perhaps never heard of Malory, who had lived narrow lives of routine drudgery, and who liked their fairy tales straight and simple. For both groups and for many gradations in between, Tennyson wanted Arthur and his Round Table to be able, "for a space," to make a realm and reign. The method that he evolved for this very special purpose is the method of the poem as a whole, but it is apparently modeled in *The Coming of Arthur* and can be fruitfully studied there.

The idyll (and thus the poem) begins with a witness (King Leodogran) and the object of his greatest solicitude (his daughter, Guinevere); and then, having placed Guinevere ("the fairest of all flesh on earth") in the position of the text of a medieval exemplum, the narrative moves swiftly away from her and treats of the social background "ere Arthur came." The chief emphasis is a "community" emphasis, on petty kings, wild beasts, heathen hordes, desperate human anguish ("He knew not whither he should turn for aid," 40). It is a world of babes suckled at the teats of wolves and become wolf-men, a barbarous world analogous to that of the prehistoric days of Romulus and Remus, a world of cannibals "Spitting the child" on the "spike that split the mother's heart" (38–39). These heathens are not simply pagans, but heathmen without the barest rudiments of respect for manhood, in themselves or in others. It is a mythic concurrence that Arthur should, in such desperate bestial times, come upon the scene and that Leodogran should hear of him, since he "yet had done no deed of arms" (46); and it is a mythic concurrence expanded to the nth power that this "flower of kings" (*flos regum*) should share the same time-frame as "the fairest of all flesh on earth." Thus it is a time both to magnify men's souls and to try them as men in their magnified state.

Arthur accepts his vocation ("heard the call," 47), and on the threshold of his *rite de passage,* dressed in the simplest vestments of knighthood and before he has taken up arms, he undergoes, bathed anonymously in the "sudden" light of Guinevere's eyes, the transformational illumination that will shape his and, "for a space," the world's destiny. Having completed his service to Leodogran, he returns to put down rebellion among his own Lords and Barons and, through "Travail, and throes and agonies of the life" (75), enters upon a new and practical phase of his illumination:

> "Her father said
> That there between the man and beast they die.
> Shall I not lift her from this land of beasts
> Up to my throne, and side by side with me?
> What happiness to reign a lonely king,
> Vext—O ye stars that shudder over me,
> O earth that soundest hollow under me,
> Vext with waste dreams? for saving I be joined
> To her that is the fairest under heaven,
> I seem as nothing in the mighty world,
> And cannot will my will, nor work my work
> Wholly, nor make myself in mine own realm
> Victor and lord. But were I joined with her,
> Then might we live together as one life,
> And reigning with one will in everything
> Have power on this dark land to lighten it,
> And power on this dead world to make it live."
>   (77–93)

It is an extraordinary soliloquy, full of truth and an impeccable understanding and such cosmic irony that the stars "shudder" and the earth sounds "hollow" beneath him. The short-term future will take many sad turnings, including the total ruination of his realm; and Guinevere will get to "know" who Arthur is only after much misapprehension and misconduct and the most agonizing of spiritual recognitions. Nonetheless, he is quite right: all other transformations are as nothing compared with Guinevere's transformation. Their wills will be joined too late, despite the formal marriage of their bodies, to enable them to "lighten" the "dark land" and make the "dead world" live, except in story and poem, in which their tragic story is the source of perpetual edification. But Arthur's perception is simply true: unless he can purge the subtlest form of "beast" in Guinevere, he has not been tested and proved worthy of being called the best and greatest of all the kings of men. Having inscaped himself, having broken through the "Travail, and throes and agonies of the life" which Guinevere, in her due time, will have to undergo too, Arthur can inscape his world ("the world/Was all so clear about him, that he saw/The smallest rock far on the faintest hill/And even in high day the morning star," 96–99), be victorious in his battles (do his work), and know the difference between the appearance of things ("So like a painted battle the war stood/Silenced, the living quiet as the dead,/And in the heart of Arthur joy was lord," 121–123) and the true reality. It is a stunning paradox, but a wholly coherent perception. It so magnifies Arthur in the sight of Lancelot that Lancelot fights grandly at Arthur's side, thus leading to their swearing "on the field of death a deathless love" (131) and to Arthur's later sending Lancelot ("his warrior whom he loved/And honoured most," 446–447) to bring Guinevere to their wedding. Thus complex irony rolls into complex irony.

Leodogran's conscientious winnowing of the issue of granting Guinevere's hand to Arthur in marriage—besides, as has been suggested, supplying one possible procedural model for the reading of *Idylls of the King*—contributes richly to the poem's complexity of awareness. Leodogran emerges as a masterful and gracious statesman and as a wholly admirable father-king. He knows thoroughly well the depth of his debt to Arthur's service, that Arthur came as a savior in Leodogran's most desperate and anguished need. But he knows, too, that the issue of giving a king's daughter in marriage is too serious a matter to be dealt with simplistically—a small implant of the suggestion that the same daughter will ultimately rise, through her own process of winnowing and an experiential illumination, to a like conscientious grandeur. But he supplies a model for both the reader and Guinevere in a more complex and imaginative way.

Leodogran enacts in miniature a classic ritual of mythmaking. (1) He wants to believe implicitly in the complete authenticity of this savior-king named Arthur. He has seen enough of the bestial, counterfeit life-in-the-raw, dying between predatory man and beast, and has witnessed the extraordinary contrast in this wholly serviceable, high-purposed, radiant young warrior-king. So he actually tries to find, among the turbulent crosscurrents of rumor about Arthur's lineage, grounds for belief, rejoicing at each partial confirmation. (2) He is an astute man, quickly putting into perspective the bumbling ineptitude of his "hoary chamberlain" and the forthright, earthy, circumstantial naturalism of Bedivere. But he is a keenly imaginative man, too, responding fully to the accomplished elegance and strange cogency of Bellicent's witnessing. She is indeed an expert witness, the ultimate synoptic, drawing upon a variety of personal and legendary experiences to provide, at least in broad strokes, a "life of Arthur" and thus give genuine depth to her own firm faith in both the legitimacy and the authenticity of Arthur's kingship. To Leodogran's first question—can Arthur maintain his kingship against such overwhelming odds?—she adduces the eyewitness account of the magical potency he has over his knights with his "simple words of great authority" (260) and his "large, divine, and comfortable words" (267), perhaps some early version of his intimations about the nature of reality and its implications for conduct, resulting in their taking of his vows and the "'momentary likeness of the King'" that flashed over them. She tells, too, of the mighty attestors to his kingship—the "'three fair queens,'" Merlin, and the profound Lady of the Lake—and of Excalibur, symbol of both his invincibility and the basis of that invincibility in his world-apprehension. To Leodogran's second question, only implied—what is Arthur's true lineage?—she recalls how he seemed to appear in answer to her mother's anguished wish that she had a brother to guard her "'"on the rough ways of the world"'" (335) and, as a lad, comforted her in her childish distresses and grew up with her, variously sweet, sad, and stern, and convinced her by even his boyish conduct that "'he would be king'" (357). Bellicent climaxes her narrative with Bleys's account of the mythical coming of Arthur—the basis of those, in Bedivere's account, who "dream he dropt from heaven" (182)—and Merlin's oath, given in solemn serious-ness, that "'Though men may wound him . . . he will not die,/ But pass, again to come'" (420–421). Leodogran's fascination with Bellicent's narrative and his joy in it show how fully attuned he is to the imaginative apprehension necessary to man's availability to myth. (3) He experiences a "miraculous revelation"—that is, all the emblematic experiences he has gone through, together with his need and strong disposition to believe, induce in him, at the unconscious center of his creative being and with unclouded clarity of affirmation, be-lief in Arthur's divine right of kingship, compared to which "the solid earth" and all naturalistic explanations are as noth-ing. Thus Leodogran's ritual of mythmaking, a miniature of one pattern of reader-response to *Idylls of the King*, is fully enacted.

Arthur's wedding to Guinevere takes place in May, when the flowered earth is fairest, and the half-dozen reiterations of the May motif suggest its fundamental symbolic impor-tance. It is Maytime for Arthur, too, of course, in the cycle of a year upon which his life symbolically turns; but for Guinevere, it is a metaphor of the all-enveloping problem. Guinevere is a May figure, a flower child, enamored of the warmth of the sun and the rich sensuous pleasures that "this fair world" offers. She becomes so imprisoned in the May-game of life that, despite all her regal potentiality, she has desperate difficulty seeing through the consequent diminu-tion of her identity—looking through the sensuous frame of appearances to the true reality. It is a mimic life she leads, as the jousts are mimic battles; and she misapprehends Arthur as she misapprehends life, confusing illusion and truth so almost inseparably that it is only at the end (and demise) of *The Round Table* and after worldwide disaster and much per-sonal suffering that she will finally learn that "the highest" can be the "most human too." The life-secret that she lacks is the very one embodied in Arthur, and her alienation from him is symbolic both of her great need and of her barred access to it.

The two songs sung in *The Coming of Arthur*—Merlin's "Rain, rain, and sun! a rainbow in the sky!" and the knighthood's "Blow trumpet, for the world is white with May"—are symbolist strategies, lyrical outcroppings from the narrative text, characteristic of Tennyson. Merlin's "riddling triplets of old time" have an air of gnomic flippancy about them, annoying to those who ask a straight question and think they need a straight answer. They counterpoint mystery with yet greater mystery and thereby insinuate the uncomfortable realization that, if the question has depth, the answer cannot be simple, does not, in the literal sense, exist at all except simplistically and to the literal-minded. Mystery cannot, by definition, be made plain. A man may get older without being wiser even about self-evident truths—daily truths available to the naked eye—because truth has varied appearances, differently perceived by each individual, to whom it may be variously naked truth or symbolic truth, "known" perhaps to one generation in one way and unavailable to the next generation in that same way. Thus truth, like poetry, is "shot-silk with many glancing colours," and every generation must find, in its own way, its own answers. Truth, like the imagination, does not change; but it is ever being clothed in new images and thus forever generating the imaginative apparatus by which it is apprehended. There is a subterranean seriousness about Merlin's riddling lyric jest that has far-reaching relevance to our recognition that the "meaning" in *Idylls of the King* is largely implicit in its "manner."

There is something symbolistically and profoundly sad about the Battle-Hymn of the Arthurian Republic with which the knights celebrate the marriage of the King and Guinevere. Despite the exhilarating martial grandeur of the song, or perhaps because of it, there is a "dark undercurrent woe" flowing through the lyrics for a reader even vaguely familiar with the matter of Arthur. These are young men caught up in but not really comprehending a form of "enthusiastic activity" whose every expectation will be reversed by the narrative curve of the events to follow: the "long night" is coming; Arthur will, in the end, not "rule in Arthur's realm"; they will die, not live, despite the King's divine "secret," which less than a tithe will ever have any inkling of; the lust will live, and the strength will die; and the "mighty" May Sun will be mighty with a vengeance, leading to confusion, doubt, fear, and universal death.

As *Idylls of the King*, then, is an image of the mighty world, so *The Coming of Arthur* is an image of *Idylls of the King*. It is both a fascinating story and a complex, multiply refractive, long-lingering, imaginative inducement to the reader to know something of himself and of this world he will leave so soon.

■

As the closing notes of *The Coming of Arthur* in their most denotative sense give tonal introduction to *Gareth and Lynette*, so *The Passing of Arthur* is introduced tonally by the connotative qualities of the climactic experience of *Guinevere*. In a state of the most acute spiritual and psychic pain, Arthur is thrown back upon his existential self in "agonies of the life" magnified enormously over those he felt in his initiation to love and life. He has lately returned from a failed siege of Lancelot's castle in France, has just left grovelling in the dust her upon whom he had built his world-identity, and is now faced with "this last, dim, weird battle of the west"—the death-image, for the moment, of all his faith, hope, and self-less love.

But it must always be remembered that this is a *literary* event, an *imaginative* experience, in which literature undertakes the utmost responsibility for dealing with life in its intensest manifestation. Arthur's raw spiritual suffering and the horror and chaos of the final battle of almost universal death-dealing in a medium in which value simply cannot function would be intolerable, aesthetically, to most healthy sensibilities. So it must be mediated, not through idea or theme or authorial intrusion, but through form, through the structuring devices by which art magnifies life at a poetically manageable distance.

For this *literary* purpose, Tennyson chose "the bold Sir Bedivere"—"bold in heart and act and word" (*CA*, 175)—and it was the aptest of imaginative choices. Sir Bedivere was the first knighted of the Round Table, and he is Arthur's last living companion among the people of this world. So he plays a typological role, the alpha and the omega of the total poetic experience.

If something emblematic is to be saved from out the chaos to which the Arthurian dispensation has degenerated, Bedivere must be its savior. We, as readers, must be attentive to what Bedivere takes with him from the life of Arthur. We see him, our symbolic surrogate to the degree that we accept him as such, like ourselves "'Among new men, strange faces, other minds'" (406); like us, seeing that "'the true old times are dead'" (397); like us, looking back over a long metaphor of time at these extraordinary events with unparalleled fascination. But the reader must proceed inductively to his interpretation, not only of how Bedivere manages the narrative events, but what, if anything, they do to him.

We have been quietly alerted to look to Bedivere's "heart and act and word" for meaningful signs. The tale itself is harrowing—an elemental experience not intended for the faint of heart or act or word—but harrowing especially to the conscientious teller committed to the truth. Toward this end, Bedivere relates the story as if it were about somebody else, places himself-as-if-not-himself at the center of an action, knowing that the meaning of the events turns upon both his double consciousness of them—then and now—and the events themselves. Formally, then, what we have is a perceiver (Bedivere removed by time and age) perceiving a perceiver (Bedivere at the center of the action) perceiving (Bedivere responding to and being inwardly moved by the action). The complex symbolist richness of the poetic narrative depends, aesthetically, on all these formal elements, including the reader's availability to the perception that all the textual and subtextual, conscious and unconscious, awarenesses of the poem are seeded there by Bedivere's language. Thus when he looks back over the long metaphor of time and tells this particular tale, like the Ancient Mariner, to "new men, strange faces, other minds" (people like us), he is, in a significant way, telling it to himself; and although, as a poem called *The Passing of Arthur,* it represents in one of its aspects the perpetuation motif (the frozen image), it has a fluid, tentative, exploratory quality too, the reader in that sense becoming Bedivere's surrogate eternally. It is a passing on, a making traditional, of Arthur's storied ideal.

In *The Coming of Arthur,* the new King had himself been the comforter, using "'large, divine, and comfortable words'" (267) to reassure his knights, who were "pale," "flushed," or "dazed" from the vows they had taken in the initial impact of Arthur's secret revelation. At the beginning of *The Passing of Arthur,* Bedivere plays the role of comforter. He hears the King moaning out his spiritual distress in near-disconsolate images—the world as the creation of a "lesser god" into which the "High God" has not yet entered, man imprisoned in a fragment of time and powerless "to see it as it is" (20), his own total failure as King, husband, and friend, arriving momentarily, in language echoes from Christ's final hour, at an irreducible minimum of faith: "'Nay—God my Christ—I pass but shall not die'" (28). Then Arthur slips into a nightmarish sleep haunted by the ghost of Gawain, like Dante's carnal sinners, "blown along a wandering wind" and chanting "'hollow, hollow, hollow all delight,'" impregnating the frozen, moonlit world—"a waste and wild"—with shrill wailing. The character of this horrible nightmare is conveyed to Bedivere in Arthur's waking words, confused and inflated, translating his personal foreboding into an all-enveloping cosmic doom. In trying to comfort Arthur—"'O me, my King, let pass whatever will'" (51)—Bedivere stations himself at a point of psychological/spiritual distance. He clings in his comforting to basic naturalistic solidity: they are elves out there, or deceiving lights; you are a great King and are not dying; Gawain has always been like that; you have an important job to do today. But there is a tone of anxiety in his voice ("O me"), and his language has overtones of imaginative availability that overreach psychological naturalism: "glamour of the field," "a golden cloud/For ever," "the ghost is as the man," "the steps of Modred in the west." It is not imaginatively strong, but it is audible. Thus the traces of the mythmaking pattern again begin to emerge—the disposition to believe, imaginative apprehensiveness, and a miraculous happening. Arthur is drawn out of his deepest level of self-harrowing, though the perceptual bases for it remain, and they move toward Arthur's historical labor, the battle.

The description leading up to the battle and of the battle itself counterpoints blank verse of solemn simplicity to rich symbolic imagery. Every verbal gesture contributes to an incremental explosion of terrifying ontological/imaginative awareness. Arthur rises from the bed of the deepest spiritual distress and in company with the remnant of all he is ("his host") moves through the dark night of the soul to a face-to-face encounter with the ultimate, potentially all-devastating truth of human existence—human potential on a collision course with totally dehumanized meaninglessness. He pushes his existential opponent to the ends of the seemingly solid earth, even beyond the illusion of solidity to the "ever-shifting sand" and the "phantom circle of a moaning sea" (86–87)—an elegiac medium of reality in its most surreal manifestation. It is a country of the disturbed consciousness, an outcropping of hell, like the black spots that disturb one's sight from staring into the fireball of the setting sun. The May Sun of a delusive fertility has become the Winter Sun of dormancy and death against whose cosmic forebodings the Druids built Promethean fires. It is residual truth at its lowest ebb tested in the most uncongenial of wastelands.

> Nor ever yet had Arthur fought a fight
> Like this last, dim, weird battle of the west.
> (93–94)

It is a sightless, heartless battle (95–117), all-enveloped and all-penetrated by the chill, "deathwhite mist"—blind, loveless, fearful, chaotic, internecine. Only the "memory hath eyes," reaching beyond total existential confusion to penetratingly ironic "visions out of golden youth" or haunting guilts ("the faces of old ghosts"). It is a pandemonium of sightly sound, like a thunderous cosmic disintegration confounding the eye of body and soul alike, the external crashings having their internal counterpart:

And shouts of heathen and the traitor knights,
Oaths, insult, filth, and monstrous blasphemies,
Sweat, writhings, anguish, labouring of the lungs
In that close mist, and cryings for the light,
Moans of the dying, and voices of the dead.
                                        (113–117)

After this apocalyptic distillation of chaotic human action is over, a great silence follows—"Save for some whisper of the seething seas" (121)—and,

                    when the dolorous day
    Grew drearier toward twilight falling,
                              (122–123)

a "bitter wind" comes out of the hateful North, moving the mist and raising the tide to flow among dead faces, will-less hands, hollow helmets, and shivered brands. The voice that rolls "far along the gloomy shores" (134–135) is the voice of the universe that preceded man's hearing (his coming) and will be there after he is deaf (his passing). On the continuum of language and experience (actually the *language of experience*) along which Arthur is moving in Bedivere's narration, the King reaches the nadir of selfhood:

    "O Bedivere, for on my heart hath fallen
    Confusion, till I know not what I am,
    Nor whence I am, nor whether I be King.
    Behold, I seem but King among the dead."
                              (143–146)

Arthur has recognized the genuine possibility that it is nature, not man, who is timeless, that time may be the reality rather than the appearance, and that man may be in cosmic time no more significant than the minutest insect on the most mutable leaf. Again Bedivere comforts Arthur, assuring him of his own faith, hope, and love, and directing his energies away from self-destructive thought toward action.

The verse-paragraph containing the clipped account of Arthur's single combat with Modred is the turning point of the idyll and the climactic final upturn—severely simple but sufficient—of the poem's overall apprehension. Induced both by the quiet, unwavering affirmations of Bedivere—his faith, hope, and love—and by the opportunity to take decisive action, Arthur clarifies his own consciousness. Although he can still say, "'My house hath been my doom'" (154)—that is, my house of "passions and capacities," being divided against itself, has fallen—Modred is not "'of my house,'" since among all the conspicuous weaknesses and failures of the knights of the Round Table, hate had no place. Pride, covetousness, lust, anger, gluttony, envy, and sloth—but not hate. Only hate could have disowned his Kingship, and to that degree his Kingship is intact. So Arthur recovers faith in his own Kinghood and

> Striking the last stroke with Excalibur,
> Slew him, and all but slain himself, he fell.
>   (168–169)

The remainder of *The Passing of Arthur*, essentially a transplant in *Idylls of the King* of the symbolist *Morte d'Arthur*, is shaped by two episodes—the throwing away of Excalibur and the departure of the King. In both of these episodes, Bedivere moves closer to center stage, and there is a genial irony, sad but sweet, in his telling of his tale. We begin to see that some process has been at work in "the bold Sir Bedivere." He has been sole companion to the King, comforting him, redirecting his thoughts and actions, bearing him in his strong arms to a ruined sanctuary. It has been a conscientious but heady experience, this of sole counselor to the world's greatest King, and it has begun to have its effects. When Arthur instructs him to take and fling Excalibur "'far into the middle mere,'" having said in passing that its fame will be known through song and story, Bedivere replies with a somewhat unctuous boldness:

> "It is not meet, Sir King, to leave thee thus,
> Aidless, alone, and smitten through the helm—
> A little thing may harm a wounded man;
> Yet I thy hest will all perform at full,
> Watch what I see, and lightly bring thee word."
>   (208–212)

There is something boyishly bumptious about it, and this motif is sustained by the slight inflation of his language and by the agile surefootedness with which he undertakes his task, "stepping down/By zigzag paths, and juts of pointed rock" (218–219), as if contrasting the vigor of his manhood with the fragile infirmity of the King. And although he has earlier tutted "'the harmless glamour of the field'" (52) in comforting Arthur, he here falls victim to the "glamour" of the hilt, having "gazed so long/That both his eyes were dazzled as he stood,/This way and that dividing the swift mind . . ." (226–228). Thus Bedivere begins to lose his perceptual precision, and his ego lets seemingly high-minded rationalization take the place of simple fealty as a guide to action, the waterflags, "stiff and dry" and "many-knotted," being a symbolic gloss on the ultimate result of such a course as Bedivere, in a primitive way, has embarked on here. When he returns like a guilty boy to Arthur, he tells half a lie to half a question: to Arthur's query as to what he has *seen* and *heard*, he replies with an irrelevant version only of what he has heard. Arthur, with upbraiding, sends him again upon the mission with an appeal to love, "'As thou art lief and dear'" (248), bidding him specifically to "watch." His romping somewhat subdued, boyishness takes a new direction: in a slight tantrum, he slaps his hands together (out of earshot, of course) and shouts his disagreement, his high-mindedness becoming explicit in an elaborate scholastic syllogism. I know what I'm doing, and he doesn't; I have excellent reasons which he simply does not understand; therefore, I must do this thing despite its offense to obedience, the higher good taking precedence over the lower good. The irony deepens for the moment toward tragic possibilities, Bedivere stressing the importance of future generations' actually *seeing* Excalibur while his own sight is "clouded" by an ego-directed notion ("conceit"). But despite this verbal self-processing, there is still guilt in his stride as he returns to the King and again tells half a lie to half a question.

In his wrath, Arthur points explicitly to the eye-failure of Bedivere: he himself lies "'widowed of the power in his eye/ That bowed the will'"; "'I see thee what thou art'"; "'like a girl/Valuing the giddy pleasure of the eyes'" (290–291, 295–296). Having eyes, Bedivere will not see, or seeing will not truly perceive. And Arthur's seemingly false charges— "lust of gold" and "giddy pleasures"— are in fact perfectly apt. As a result of ego-inflation leading to specious "wit," Bedivere has begun, however lightly, to renew the sensuous mind (lust and frivolous pleasure) that, carried to maddening extremes, had ruined Arthur's realm. Hence Arthur's vow to "'arise and slay thee with my hands'" (300) is seriously meant. But the bold Sir Bedivere—"bold of heart and act and word"— is fully redeemable and, though in a boyish self-parody he closes his eyes until the sword is flung, he sees this "miracle" enveloped by a yet grander miracle that in fact can never be known except through story and song—*his* story and song. Thus, through a fortunate fall that does not end catastrophically, Bedivere learns something of the secret of seeing and becomes thereby a better mythmaker and a more trustworthy narrator.

The final personal tableau before Arthur and Bedivere move to the closing sequence centers on their eyes:

> he half rose,
> Slowly, with pain, reclining on his arm,
> And looking wistfully with wide blue eyes
> As in a picture. Him Sir Bedivere
> Remorsefully regarded through his tears,
> And would have spoken, but he found not words. . . .
>
> (335–340)

The verbal echoes pick up an analogy in Arthur's speech at the end of *The Holy Grail*, and the degree to which Bedivere has gained access to the Arthurian world-apprehension brings him closer to Arthur in the final episode, where they "see" as one—"Then saw they how" (361) and "they were ware" (363). Bedivere has grown from boy to man: "he walked,/Larger than human on the frozen hills" (350–351); according to his capacity, he too has inscaped the world, and, having become master of himself and thereby gained perspective on the world, he has a preternatural awareness of his physical surroundings even in their present frozen state (352–360).

The final episode is poised at a precarious balance between belief and disbelief, miracle and mystery, consolation and distress. There is clearly an inclination on Bedivere's part to identify Arthur with Christ—he creates, pictorially, a Pietà (375–388), addresses Arthur as "'my Lord Arthur'" (395), and compares the time to that of "'the light that led/The holy Elders with the gift of myrrh'" (400–401)—but he never fully concludes the identification. Although Arthur gives full-bodied imaginative existence in inducive language to

> "the island-valley of Avilion;
> Where falls not hail, or rain, or any snow,
> Nor ever wind blows loudly; but it lies
> Deep-meadowed, happy, fair with orchard lawns
> And bowery hollows crowned with summer sea, . . ."
> (427–432)

doubt lingers ("'if indeed I go [For all my mind is clouded with a doubt],'" 425–426), and from the passengers in the barge there

> rose
> A cry that shivered to the tingling stars,
> And, as it were one voice, an agony
> Of lamentation, like a wind that shrills
> All night in a waste land, where no one comes,
> Or hath come, since the making of the world.
> (366–371)

Moreover, the movement of the barge is glossed with a sad, wholly naturalistic image: "like some full-breasted swan/That, fluting a wild carol ere her death,/Ruffles her pure cold plume, and takes the flood/With swarthy webs" (434–437). Set against these exquisite but experientially disquieting images is Arthur's jubilation of prayer as good for the soul and as a mode of distinguishing between man and beast, of celebrating friendship, and of keeping the world in touch with God: "'For so the whole round earth is every way/Bound by gold chains about the feet of God'" (422–423). Bedivere himself has nagging doubts and empirical uncertainty, but presumably he now understands the rightness of Arthur's spiritual instruction, "'Comfort thyself'" (411) and has himself pointed an analogy between his lot and that of the first man leaving his lost paradise ("'I, the last, go forth companionless,/And the days darken round me, and the years'" (404–405), suggestive of at least a vague awareness that the fall has not been wholly unfortunate. And the ritual of climbing, seeing, hearing with which the idyll (and the poem) closes evokes, symbolically and tentatively, positive responses to what has finally happened to Bedivere. He hears a music of jubilee, sees the last dark speck vanish into light, witnesses the new sun of the new year: thus it all starts over again, this time in the renewed imaginative awareness of "the bold Sir Bedivere"—and ourselves.

Notes

1. Kathleen Tillotson says, credibly, that "Tennyson had planned the final shape of his long poem" by 1855, but by "shape" she means something more organizational than textural, that is, variations in tone, distancing, and perspective. See "Tennyson's Serial Poem," *Mid-Victorian Studies* (London: The Athlone Press of the University of London, 1965), p. 90.
2. Coleridge's celebrated formula is "that willing suspension of disbelief for the moment which constitutes poetic faith."

2.

Completing 1869

■ *The Holy Grail* ■ *Pelleas and Ettarre*

The Holy Grail and *Pelleas and Ettarre* are, like *The Coming of Arthur* and *The Passing of Arthur,* the products of the second great concentrated writing act that went into the making of *Idylls of the King.* Like the frame-idylls, they have carefully monitoring narrative psyches, the one specified, the other generically anonymous. *The Holy Grail* contains some of the most subtle and delicately reverberative turnings in the whole poem: the language is thoroughly symbolic, and character, action, image, episode, through the medium of symbolic language, release infinite perceptual possibilities into a grand orchestration, thus internalizing into the idyll itself Arthur's gloss on the strange uncertain happenings of the quest:

> "For every fiery prophet in old times,
> And all the sacred madness of the bard,
> When God made music through them, could but speak
> His music by the framework and the chord. . . ."
>
> (*HG,* 872–875)

But everything is filtered, at one or two removes, through the moral, psychological, aesthetic sensibility of Sir Percivale. That peculiar sensibility, most excitingly apt for creating a medium of closeness and distance in which to suspend the experience of the Grail-quest, is, in *The Holy Grail* as a work of literary imagination, itself the most fascinating event, reinforcing in a very formal way the critical perception that manner is meaning in *Idylls of the King.* The matter of Percivale's sensibility is managed by the poet with the finest tuning, so that there is nothing black-and-white or heavy-handed about it, one slight index being counterpoised by a seemingly corrective index. For example, his somewhat haughty, rigid self-enclosures are balanced against the facts that Arthur speaks permissively of him and that the "old badger" Ambrosius warms himself at the "little fires" of Percivale's limited caring. But even this delicacy of handling has symbolic significance, drawing the reader's attention both to the problem and to its subtlety. The structure of the narrative itself—a one-sided dialogue between two very different human/monastic types—has an almost Jamesian finesse about it. It is a story told, among lacunae of self-delusion, by someone who has, according to his own estimate, been at the center of an extraordinary action to someone who listens attentively, out of love for the teller and some overlap of shared interest, not entirely understanding or believing, but shaping the narrative to a curiously important degree by the questions he asks and the visibly different values which he represents.

But there are teasingly critical nuances implicit even in the narrative setting itself. If the quest for the Holy Grail is to be apprehended principally or wholly in the context of the central significance of the Arthurian world and of the Grail-quest to that world, can a narrator who has dropped out, become fixated in a singular way on the Grail episode, and begun to look upon all men and women "as phantoms" (564–565) be trustworthy? That will depend, of course, upon such refined adjustments as the reader may make for himself, but *The Holy Grail* idyll thus becomes a central metaphor, with its rich poetic implications, of the Tennysonian manner (and meaning) in *Idylls of the King*—the apparently most elusive subject of the poem being narrated by the most elusive method and placing a co-creative burden on the reader to keep the poem artistically unified.

Pelleas and Ettarre requires a diagonally different methodological alertness on the part of the reader. Here the challenge is not to make the strange familiar, but to keep the familiar fresh. *The Holy Grail* seems to be *sui generis* in the poem, though only the metaphor and the ritual are unique, the persona-exposures (both of narrator and of principals in the narration) being fully coherent with the rest of the poem. *Pelleas and Ettarre*, on the other hand, may, for some readers, be threatened by obvious comparisons with such earlier episodes as those of *Gareth and Lynette* and *Balin and Balan,* many of the comparisons being legitimate, since in a long poem that revolves around "one sin" and "one secret," everything must in a sense mirror everything else. But tightening the network of the poem has, in critical practice, sometimes been done at the expense of a recognition at least as important— namely, the distinctiveness of the various characters, actions, images, episodes, narrations of the poem. Truly imaginative apprehensiveness works in opposite ways, as the poem itself several times suggests. It enables us to bring order out of an infinity of details, but that is a doubtfully serviceable process to the degree that it diminishes either the infinity or the details. Tennyson, like Keats and Hopkins and many others, was devoted to perception, not obscurity, to individuation, not to blurred distinctions; and the enveloping inscape or inscapes of his poem assume rather than dismiss the thousands of crisp individual inscapes of which the poem as a whole is an organic unity.

And what is true of individual images, each distinctive in its language context, is even more certainly true of one of the comprehending idylls. The reader brings a great deal of poetical experience to *Pelleas and Ettarre,* but that should enrich the poem, not emasculate it, should give depth and subtlety to a new variety of poetic experience rather than a stereotyped response which confuses one order of similarity with other orders of dissimilitude. Thus *Pelleas and Ettarre* requires of the reader full recognition that, though its actions, characters, and language appear to exert pressure toward comparison, there are subtle differences that make the manner of "Almost the saddest of the Idylls"[1] individual, discrete, solitary in the meaning of aesthetic experience. Between these two idylls, there seems to be a reversal of ironic focus: in *The Holy Grail*, the irony floods Percivale as narrator and becomes a major source of the reader's pleasurable detachment from Percivale's elegant misapprehensions; in *Pelleas and Ettarre*, the reader is himself the object of wry watchings, the question at issue being whether he, in light of his self-satisfaction at seeing through Percivale's "reading" of the Grail episode, can give a better performance than Percivale's in his own reading of *Pelleas and Ettarre*. And this perception gets a startling validation—the two idylls echoing back and forth persistently—when we realize that Pelleas's blindness to the truth about Ettarre (with which we are unavoidably impatient) is a gloss on the older knights' blindness to the truth about the Grail (with which we have been uneasy but temperamentally sympathetic); that the raw sexuality of Pelleas's fable—frank and even brutal in language, incident, and image—has its subtle, deceptive, and even more terrifying counterpart in the psychosexual medium of language, incident, and image in which the Grail-quest is disquietingly suspended; and that Pelleas's Cyrano, Gawain, in whom, for lack of an available alternative, he places his anxious trust, has just come, literarily, from *The Holy Grail*, where he has abandoned the quest for the most self-indulgent reasons and has received the most caustic public lessoning of anyone in the entire poem:

> "Deafer," said the blameless King,
> "Gawain, and blinder unto holy things
> Hope not to make thyself by idle vows,
> Being too blind to have desire to see."
> (*HG*, 865–868)

So Pelleas's untutored blindness counterpoints the jaded blindness of the older knights, who, despite their sophistication in the ways of courtly love, are yet prone to the most devastating self-deception in a different kind of charade of high-mindedness. And perhaps this is why Arthur, who was "hard upon" his knights, loved Pelleas so spontaneously.

■

Tennyson has himself left us some very interesting observations on *The Holy Grail*—observations so rich and familiar and interpretively influential that they require fresh review in the aesthetic context being developed here.

(1)
Faith declines, religion in many turns from practical goodness to the quest after the supernatural and marvellous and selfish religious excitement. Few are those for whom the quest is a source of spiritual strength.[2]

(2)
The Holy Grail is one of the most imaginative of my poems. I have expressed there my strong feeling as to the Reality of the Unseen. The end, where the King speaks of his work and of his visions, is intended to be the summing up of all in the highest note by the highest of men.[3]

(3)
My father looked on this description of Sir Galahad's quest, and on that of Sir Lancelot's, as among the best blank verse he had written. He pointed out the difference between the five versions of the Grail, as seen by the Holy Nun, Sir Galahad, Sir Percivale, Sir Lancelot, Sir Bors, according to their different, their own peculiar natures and circumstances, their selfishness, and the perfection or imperfection of their Christianity. He dwelt on the mystical treatment of every part of his subject, and said the key is to be found in a careful reading of Sir Percivale's visions. He would also call attention to the babbling homely utterances of the village priest Ambrosius as a contrast to the sweeping passages of blank verse that set forth the visions of spiritual enthusiasm.[4]

(4)
Lines 172–173: "Siege perilous" "stands for the spiritual imagination."[5]
293–294: "The king thought that most men ought to do

the duty that lies closest to them, and that to few only is given the true spiritual enthusiasm. Those who have it not ought not to affect it."[6]

361ff.: "The gratification of sensual appetite brings Percivale no content. . . . Nor does wifely love and the love of the family. . . . Nor does wealth, which is worshipt by labour. . . . Nor does glory. . . . Nor does Fame."[7]

491: "It was a time of storm when men could imagine miracles, and so storm is emphasized."[8]

830: "'The lark' in the tower toward the rising sun symbolizes Hope."[9]

It is curious how valuable but essentially nondirective most of these comments are and how instinctively they avoided the imposition of an "intentional fallacy" on our reading of the poem. Two details, themselves less than dark conceits, are explicated—"Siege perilous" as "the spiritual imagination" and "The lark" as Hope—and the most obvious aspect of the allegorical drift of Percivale's quest is suggested; but even these lead more to thoughts of poetic technique and procedure than meaning, the imaginative procedure that gives the poem its character and the reader his poetic experience being unmediated. Even the poet's "strong feeling as to the Reality of the Unseen" is useful as verification rather than guidance toward discovery of the most evanescent perceptual apprehension of the poem, and characterization of Arthur's speech as the "highest note," like the characterization of *The Holy Grail* as "one of the most imaginative" of his poems, challenges the reader to challenge the poet. Otherwise, Tennyson's comments simply position the reader in relationship to the poem—suggesting the ambient moment at which it takes place, drawing attention to the all-pervasive principle that everything that happens is monitored by the "peculiar natures and circumstances" of individuals, emphasizing that the "key is to be found in a careful reading," and reminding the reader to stay in touch with the way in which prosody projects character (varieties of blank verse, including "babbling homely utterances") and images even the most denotative mutate into imaginative significance (storms/miracles). Even off-guard, then, Tennyson did not abuse the integrity of his poem, enriched rather than depleted the autonomy of the reading act itself.

When Tennyson called *Pelleas and Ettarre* "*Almost* the saddest of the Idylls" (emphasis added), he may well have reserved the place of very saddest for *The Holy Grail.* Despite the nimbus, the aura of splendor, in which the Grail has been clothed in both the literary and the popular imagination, it is the center of the most distressful and complex experience rendered in *Idylls of the King,* and the initiation of the quest through irrefragable vows evokes from Arthur his most forthright lamentation: "'Woe is me, my knights,' he cried" (*HG,* 275). And this begins to explain several nuances surrounding the compositional history of *The Holy Grail:* Tennyson's statement that "I doubt whether such a subject . . . could be handled in these days, without incurring a charge of irreverence";[10] his prolonged resistance to the persistent pressure on him to treat the Grail story, especially his wife's pressure to do "her" story;[11] the white heat with which he finally executed it;[12] and his ultimate judgment that it was "one of the most imaginative"[13] of his poems.

The composite term *imaginative irreverence* seems to pinpoint both the stressful problem and the ultimate solution. Tennyson, who penetrated to the heart of issues very early in a perceptual process which often took many years to work its way through the writing act, must have recognized almost from the start that the Grail story, for him, represented spiritual delusion anchored deep in unperceived and unconfessed psychosexual dislocation. Being the most devastating variation on the "one sin" that ruined "man coming into practical life,"[14] it had to be rooted in the sensuous mind at the deepest possible level, appealing to man's obscurest instincts toward infidelity, voluptuousness, and pride. Such a general view of the essential significance of the Grail story was certainly enough in itself to stun popular nerves, though a poet might safely confront general prejudice with a mighty ironic reversal of expectation in such relatively impersonal areas as spiritual infidelity and spiritual pride. Sexuality was obviously more personal, subject to greater misunderstanding, and more dangerous. And yet, the unmistakable psychosexual foundations of the story were indispensable to Tennyson's radical imagination, and if he failed to follow through on this realization, *Idylls of the King* would itself collapse as a work of full imaginative integrity. So what he was faced with was irreverence darkening into desecration, on the one hand, or his major poem disintegrating, on the other. This adds poignancy to his remark, in 1862, that he dared not "set to work for fear of failure, and time lost."[15]

The problem, like the solution, was obviously one of imaginative handling, and although we do not know how he "handled" the problem in his unwritten "poem on Lancelot's quest of the San Graal,"[16] we must assume that that solution, which "altogether slipt out of memory," was abandoned. But he must have thought the solution that he finally adopted a very happy one, since he completed *The Holy Grail* in a great excited burst of creative energy and acknowledged his imaginative satisfaction with it. Only then could he proceed with creating/finishing the frame-idylls and fill in the white spaces that give us our *Idylls of the King*. The imaginative solution that made possible *The Holy Grail* thus represents the poetic breakthrough that enabled Tennyson to complete his major poem.

A relentless but submerged psychosexuality is a very substantial element in that imaginative resolution whereby the poet, in the subtlest possible way, enabled the faulted flesh and the faulted spirit in man to interpenetrate and illuminate each other in a storied orchestration at the center of which is Arthur's cohering and prophetic image "'wandering fires/ Lost in the quagmire!'" (319–320). Those "wandering fires," a vividly visual image of lapping fire-tongues, flare up in all directions, reaching toward a Pentecostal, an Apocalyptic, and a Promethean analogy, but including the "fervent flame of human love" of the Holy Nun (74), the "little fires" that "'Poor men, when yule is cold,/Must be content to sit by'" (612–613), the "heat" that causes the people to "almost burst the barriers" in the vigil-tourney (335–336), the "rosy colours leaping on the wall" of the Nun's cell (120), the "mocking fire" of the remnant "Paynim" (660–673) who scoff at and imprison Sir Bors ("'what other fire than he,/Whereby the blood beats, and the blossom blows,/And the sea rolls, and all the world is warmed?'"), the lightning-fires that ignite the scene of death and decay in which Galahad launches his departure for the "spiritual city" (493–497), the "maddening" heat of Lancelot's quest, the "dying fire of madness in his eyes" (639–640, 765), the "stormy glare, a heat/As from a seventimes-heated furnace" with which he is "Blasted and burnt, and blinded" (839–841)—even the reiterative "Blood-red" of Galahad's vision (473–476), the "unremorseful folds of rolling fire" that threaten Arthur's "Dreamlike" hall (260–261), the wings of Arthur's statue that "flame/At sunrise" (242–243), and the "fiery prophet" of Arthur's interpretive analogy. It is the fire that warms and enlightens man and the fire that consumes him, that ignites both his sensuous mind and his sensuous frame, meeting in a highly fueled metaphor of enveloping sensuousness.

The "quagmire" of Arthur's prophecy is also a multiplied image. It has a topographical center in the "isle of marsh" upon which Joseph of Arimathaea built his lonely church "with wattles from the marsh" (62–63), and the ghostly deceiving marshlights, illusions engendered by gaseous substances of the bog, are a root-image of the "wandering fires." It is a physical place between earth and water in which one struggles with real but infirm elements, everything yielding to sensuous pressure and threatening one with an inextricable situation. But it is a spiritual space too, and the poet's imaginative translation is to a spiritual topography in which there are many varieties of spiritual precariousness, each leading to a deep, self-degrading psychological slough.

The two images of fire and quagmire and the two topographies, physical and spiritual, are brought together in the explosive, surreal, terrifying, visually firm but mysteriously mystical flight of Galahad from a world of death and decay in an apocalyptic firestorm across a gaseous quagmire ("A great black swamp and of an evil smell,/Part black, part whitened with the bones of men," 499–500) on a series of bridges that explode in flame as soon as crossed. It is a theatrical display of epic proportions, with special effects the most fantastic—a thunder of heavenly voices, "silver-shining armour," the Holy Vessel hung aloft, a boat swift as a sea-monster becoming "a living creature clad with wings," arriving at the pearly gates ("And gateways in a glory like one pearl—/No larger, though the goal of all the saints—," 527–528), the eternal home of both Galahad and the Holy Grail! It is literary parody put to magnificent imaginative uses: Galahad, the Holy Grail, and the whole age of miraculous self-deception explode in a metaphor of orgasmic, melodramatic theatricality concerning which Percivale, despite his momentary purgation, has only the slightest, most transient awareness.

But the psychosexual imaginative presence in *The Holy Grail* is so pervasive and unyielding that it can be said to provide the "spiritual medium" in which the poem is suspended. And although Percivale as narrator seems somewhat ambiguously immune to it and Arthur as interpreter remains wholly aloof, these are elements implanted in the total design of the piece and should not blind the reader to its "real presence" in the poem, a presence that is drawn toward the metaphor of transubstantiation by Galahad's testimony that he "'saw the *fiery* face as of a child/That smote itself into the bread, and went'" (466–467, emphasis added). Gawain's low-grade, self-diminishing, obvious, and rather shabby lust, which leads him to the braggadocio of swearing "louder than the rest" (202), to his brothel-like silk pavilion in ruins, and to his half-true but churlish effort to put the blame on Percivale and his sister (855–865), is one type of presence. Lancelot's "strange" love for Guinevere is another, a sort of archaic heritage from the old courtly love tradition, an adulterous love of a bachelor-knight for the wife of his kingly friend, both blameworthy and seemingly fated beyond blame. The Grail-quest launches Lancelot on a ritual of naming and owning and, through potentially disastrous struggle, opening at least a crevice in his imprisoning self-enclosure. But it is psychosexuality in its grandest and most agonized manifestation, and behind it is the loud shriek and wailing of the Queen— "'This madness has come on us for our sins'" (357)—whose rite of recognition and purgation will be less physical but just as tormented.

But it is through the "virgins" of the piece that the psycho-sexual presence gets its most disquieting reinforcements: through the Holy Nun, Galahad, and Percivale, the poem seems to hover ritualistically over a psychological deflowering of the cult of virginity. The Holy Nun's motive for retirement into a convent inevitably brings the psychological factor into dominance over the spiritual, and this is reinforced by her fixated concern with "the strange sound of an adulterous race" (80). Her self-imposed regimen of "prayer and fasting" (96)—monistic if not positively psychotic—is not sanctioned by her ancient confessor but is the result of intense self-gener-ation. And these disquieting implants get a deeply trouble-some magnification in the unmistakable psychosexuality of the hair cutting, sword-belt weaving, symbol implanting, and consummative investiture/divestiture of Galahad:

> "My knight, my love, my knight of heaven,
> O thou, my love, whose love is one with mine,
> I, maiden, round thee, maiden, bind my belt.
> Go forth, for thou shalt see what I have seen,
> And break through all, till one will crown thee king
> Far in the spiritual city:" and as she spake
> She sent the deathless passion in her eyes
> Through him, and made him hers, and laid her mind
> On him, and he believed in her belief.
>
> (157–165)

It is impossible to ignore the overtones of witchery and rav-ishment in this cabalistic ceremony in which defenseless youth, through its own availability, is raped by an embodied psychosis old and desperate in experience, divesting him of his own identity and, in a strange symbolic inversion of the sex act, planting the seed of herself in him. Even if one strips down the rhetoric somewhat, the symbolic event remains in-tact. Thus to Guinevere's loud shriek and wailing must be added, in the overall imaginative experience of *The Holy Grail*, the subliminal anxiety induced by this character, voice, and ceremony.

Galahad himself mutates in his passage from old legends into the context of Tennyson's poem. He does not become,

despite Arthur's reverence at the time of his knightly investiture, quite so "good" as he is "beautiful" (136). There are
multiple overtones of ironic innuendo in Galahad's development through the symbolic language and imagery of the
poem. Percivale himself, in the undercutting way he has,
plants the first innuendo: he "innocently" releases the rumor
that Galahad is a fairy changeling or a bastard son of Lancelot, though tutting the rumor as soon as released with yet
another undercut—"For when was Lancelot wanderingly
lewd?" (148)—that is, lewd perhaps, but hardly promiscuous!
Further, the clear implication is that Galahad sits in "The
Siege perilous," partially at least, to upstage the greatest
mage:

> but he,
> Galahad, when he heard of Merlin's doom,
> Cried, "If I lose myself, I save myself!"
>
> (176–178)

And there is something a bit unpleasant about the way in
which Galahad announces his vision:

> Then Galahad on the sudden, and in a voice
> Shrilling along the hall to Arthur, called,
> "But I, Sir King, saw the Holy Grail,
> I saw the Holy Grail and heard a cry—
> 'O Galahad, O Galahad, follow me.'"
>
> (288–292)

The suddenness, the shrillness, the emphasis on "I," the curious demotion of the King, the repetitiousness, the enlargement from seeing to hearing too—all these elements taken
together cast Galahad in an inflated, morally colder light.
And even if one's sympathy with Percivale is not at high tide,
one can hardly avoid seeing Galahad's treatment of Percivale
when they meet on quest as bumptious superiority: Is that all
you saw? Why, I saw lots more. I see it all the time, and it has
made me quite a conqueror. Indeed, in light of all this, it is
fairly tempting to see Galahad's fleeing along the bridges of
the thousand piers as skipping ahead of firecrackers at his
heels in a state of deflated discomfiture. It would, in a sense,

be fair play and would add a refreshing dimension of horse-play to the sophisticated literary parody.

But Percivale, more than anyone else, is the staid, unimaginative, ambivalent "virgin" of *The Holy Grail*. In fact, his virginity is literally ambivalent, and by his own testimony. When Ambrosius asks him near the beginning about "earthly passion crost," he dismisses it out of hand: "'Nay,' said the knight, 'for no such passion mine'" (29–30). Later, however, when prodded by Ambrosius into telling a part of his story that he had chosen to omit and after the rationalization that "'All men, to one so bound by such a vow,/And women were as phantoms'" (564–565), he confesses to a youthful love—"'all my heart/Went after her with longing'" (581–582)—for a girl who has since grown a rich widow and "'calling me the greatest of all knights,/Embraced me, and so kissed me the first time,/And gave herself and all her wealth to me'" (594–596). He loses his attachment to the quest, stays with her for some indefinite but substantial period of time, and finally, presumably in a fit of renewed conscientiousness, steals away like a thief in the night (606–611).

But even if Percivale is not quite a cad, there is in his peculiar nature a hidden germ of failure that makes him cold, self-enclosed, perpetually protective of his ego, and inconsistent. For example, when Ambrosius innocently refers to the Holy Grail as "'The phantom of a cup,'" Percivale upbraids him sharply: "'Nay, monk! what phantom?' . . ./'The cup, the cup itself, from which our Lord/Drank at the last sad supper with his own'" (44–47); and yet he says later of an incident that had long preceded Ambrosius' faux pas that he had returned to Camelot "'Glad that no phantom vexed me more'" (538–539). And though Ambrosius twice humbly says that the monastery's ancient books tell about Joseph and King Arviragus, but nothing about the Holy Grail, Percivale chooses to ignore him and to cling rigidly to his "legend."

Percivale's stiffness and unavailability are more than once contrasted with Ambrosius' genial, open friendliness—indeed, it is the symbolic mark of their juxtaposition as unequal interlocutors in the idyll. Whereas Percivale cuts the vows and mankind into quite separate parts, Ambrosius speaks lovingly both of married life and of his monkish regimen, at the same time releasing tropes that measure his friend rather harshly:

> "O the pity
> To find thine own first love once more—to hold,
> Hold her a wealthy bride within thine arms,
> Or all but hold, and then—cast her aside,
> Foregoing all her sweetness, like a weed.
> For we that want the warmth of double life,
> We that are plagued with dreams of something sweet
> Beyond all sweetness in a life so rich,—
> Ah, blessèd Lord, I speak too earthlywise. . . ."
>
> (618–626)

Ambrosius has a humble, realistic, reasonably comfortable notion of who he is and is constantly slipping into his genuine human self—"'like an old badger in his earth,/With earth about him everywhere, despite/All fast and penance'" (628–630). Too much talk of miracles makes his head swim, and then he has to go down into the "little thorpe" and touch wood, get involved with all the detailed reality and vibrancy of teapot life far from the madding crowd. His attraction to Percivale is one of enriched simplicity. Like Jocelin of Brakelond in Carlyle's *Past and Present,* he is a curious open-ended fellow with a need for imaginative love. He has found his brethren in the cloister rigid and cold; but this new monk from Arthur's court, "Stamped with the image of the King" (27), so stirs his need for imagination and affection that he "loved him much beyond the rest,/And honoured him, and wrought into his heart/A way by love that wakened love within,/To answer that which came" (9–12). Percivale, as it turns out, has little capacity for either love or imagination, but they are scaled to Ambrosius' need, and he is "'content to sit by little fires'" (613), getting what he can from both love and imagination and keeping both as authentic as they can be in the situation. And if they do not answer directly to the call within, they touch it in glancing ways, and, like the reader, he can take his own counsel of the "meaning" of this highly personalized, richly fabulous tale.

In Percivale as embodied and self-exposed in his narration of *The Holy Grail,* love and imagination meet and are critically measured, and thereby a great flow of life-awareness is potentially released in the reader's quickened, multiplied consciousness. As Percivale is processed through his role as poet-narrator (minstrel, scop), the reader is processed too; and the gulf that gradually widens between the reader and this poet-narrator constitutes the central imaginative impact of the piece. We have already noticed more than one hint of this. The degree of our identification of a minute, obscure Arthurianism in Ambrosius—his sense of self, his earthy realism, his open availability to variations of truth beyond his practiced ken, his need for love, his tendency to "verify" fabulous phenomena coupled with a nonjudgmental permissiveness toward behavior so long as it does not become a locked-in impediment to growth and change, his role as arbitrator of "random squabbles"—creates a slight rift in Percivale's lute, causing us to hear a false note in his Arthurian revisionism. The degree, again, of our perception and acceptance of the explosive imaginative counterblast (the melodramatic, theatrical literary parody) in Percivale's too solemn, too credulous account of Galahad's departure from the world, including the symbolic wet blanket that falls on him immediately thereafter ("'Then fell the floods of heaven drowning the deep,'" 533), widens the rift and lets some rather musty air escape. And false chords have been sounded both by his inconsistency over the "phantom" cup and his rationalized but essentially cowardly behavior toward his deluded ("'the greatest of all knights,'" 594, 602) but generous benefactress.

The ego-inflations of Percivale take both an obvious and a subtler form. He makes a great point throughout of his identification with Galahad—through his sister ("'himself her brother more than I,'" 142), the King's ranging of him "'close/After Sir Galahad'" (307), the spectators' thunderous applause: "'Sir Galahad and Sir Percivale!'" (337)—and the episode with Galahad is the climax of his personal quest's storyline. He also has a sort of "firstness complex," positioning himself out front with a schoolboy eagerness: "'I sware a vow before them all'" (195); to the King's dismayed inquiry, "'I told him what had chanced'" (271). In his self-inflation, he even lectures the King with a "'bold answer'": "'Had thyself been here,/My King, thou wouldst have sworn'" (277–278). But these are all symbolic surfacings, for the reader, of a deep, ironic, undercurrent reality, austere and penetratingly sad: Percivale does not know that he does not know that he exists, is unconsciously trying to fill an identity vacuum with role-playing. Lacking the imaginative/spiritual resources to voyage deep into his sanctuarial self to discover an authentic identity, he tries to fabricate an appearance of one, becoming in the process a persona-*manqué* and, in his role as narrator, a poet-*manqué*.

The process of the dislocation of the self reaches deep into a personal past of which we get only one specific hint, his only love and that a boy-love:

> "The Princess of that castle was the one,
> Brother, and that one only, who had ever
> Made my heart leap; for when I moved of old
> A slender page about her father's hall,
> And she a slender maiden, all my heart
> Went after her with longing: yet we twain
> Had never kissed a kiss, or vowed a vow."
>
> (577–583)

Such a revelation, however fragmentary, invites the individual reader to fill in for himself the white spaces thus induced according to his inclination, but two connected events—Percivale's dark fleeing from his "'own first love once more'" (619) and his exaggerated devotion to his cloistered sister—draw the incident unavoidably into the poem's psychosexual network and make it a part of a submerged patterning. That patterning includes—besides these three revelations and Percivale's persistent identification with Galahad—his monkhood, his characterization of the women of the court as spiritually depletive ("'while women watch/Who wins, who falls; and waste the spiritual strength/Within us, better offered up to Heaven,'" 34–36), and the Madonna-like, domestic mother-figure with the "'dead babe'" (391–400) who appears in one of his quest-visions.

Quiet overtones of an incestuous, androgynous, homoerotic subliminal sexuality are sustained by the characterization, images, and episodes of the poem; but a simpler, more fundamental explanation is that Percivale's sexuality, like that of the speaker in *Maud,* has simply been arrested in early adolescence, traumatized perhaps by some unrevealed incident, and that he is frozen in a past personal time. Unlike the speaker in *Maud,* he lacks the passionate imaginative resource to break out of the imprisoning circle of his mysterious hurt and instead ritualizes self-enclosure. He cannot fully love, but only sublimate devotion; and his imagination, lacking robust spiritual energy, fails in both awareness and motive, clinging to a legend with a fixed and literal rigidity because he is unable to transform it into a living, evolving reality. He needs miracles, and his narration is a failed effort to authenticate a miracle. The Holy Nun is the visionary of the Holy Grail, but Percivale is its propagandist and prophet. It is he who enshrines her in language, creating of her the Holy Virgin in her niche, and he becomes her angelic messenger. It is a role that energizes such imaginative resource as he has and gives him at least the illusion of being real. Although the narrative process which he undergoes in the poem seems to chasten and subdue him (more than the events themselves, since the narration begins well after those events), he still has gained but limited access to the meaning of Arthur or of life: "'So spake the King: I knew not all he meant'" (916) is perhaps the ironic understatement of the whole poem.

Percivale's own visions appear to constitute the nearest approximation to traditional allegory in *Idylls of the King,* and this may have been one technique of the ever-wakeful Tennyson for insinuating his estimate of Percivale's limited capacity through the manner of his poetic narrative. But clearly the poet behind the poet-narrator would have been little inclined, in a "key" sequence in one of his "most imaginative poems," to settle for meanings such as the following as ultimate awareness: "The gratification of sensual appetite brings Percivale no content. . . . Nor does wifely love and the love of family. . . . Nor does wealth, which is worship by labour. . . . Nor does glory. . . . Nor does Fame."[17] A signal of a very different kind is sent out by the echo in Percivale's opening lines concerning his own quest (361–366) of Arthur's epiphanic illumination in the opening idyll.

Arthur has just reached the battlefield after struggling through the profoundest agonies of a virginal love so mighty that it changes the world's aspect and gives his life definition and meaning. Then he inscapes the physical universe:

> the world
> Was all so clear about him, that he saw
> The smallest rock far on the faintest hill,
> And even in high day the morning star.
>
> (*CA*, 96–99)

Percivale, on the other hand, has just departed from a mock battle:

> "And I was lifted up in heart, and thought
> Of all my late-shown prowess in the lists,
> How my strong lance had beaten down the knights,
> So many and famous names; and never yet
> Had heaven appeared so blue, nor earth so green,
> For all my blood danced in me, and I knew
> That I should light upon the Holy Grail."
>
> (361–367)

Whereas Arthur's love-magnification leads him to a new faith and hope in his "'power on this dark land to lighten it,/And power on this dead world to make it live'" (*CA*, 92–93), Percivale's ego-inflation leads him to easy expectation of just one inflation the more. The difference in their apprehensions turns upon the two words "was" (*CA*, 97) and "appeared" (*HG*, 365), the first reflecting Arthur's strong sense of himself and of the imaginative/spiritual difference between appearance and reality, the second reflecting Percivale's mock self engendered by ego-inflation and his failed sense of true imaginative reality. Proceeding from this perception, we can look behind the allegorical equivalencies of Percivale's account of his visions—sensual gratification, domesticity, wealth, glory, fame—and see them as both true and disguises of a more awful existential truth. Being without imaginative love like that of Arthur, he cannot know that double life, life knitted to another through an all-uniting love, is a metaphor of life to the nth power. His imprisonment is in a vicious circle: not knowing he exists, he tries to fabricate an existence through ego-inflation, and that mock reality removes him even further from the possibility of knowing that he exists, in turn intensifying his need for further self-defeating ego-inflation. Thus he moves in a self-contained, volatile medium of alternating fantasy and despair, acutely vulnerable to any deflative influence (Arthur's "dark warning," negative surfacings of memory), creating fragile alternative fantasies out of his own failures of authenticity and having them collapse inevitably into inert spiritual and imaginative dryness (sand) and near fossilizing pain (thorns)—a shrunken self in a disillusive universe. The question of the "'one man of an exceeding age'" (431) in the ruinous city of himself is the one question above all others that Percivale has no capacity to answer: "'Whence and what art thou?'" (435), and the holy hermit's simple diagnosis of Percivale's moral condition—"'O son, thou hast not true humility'" (445)—goes to a yet deeper metaphoric level, beneath the failures of contentment of the allegorical disguises and beneath the manifestations of Percivale's existential inadequacy. Drawing upon the most fundamental article of his living faith, he evolves a stunning metaphor: even God had the humility to become man, and this Percivale has never been able to do.

Counterpointed to Percivale's pathetic diminution is Lancelot's tragic magnification. Lancelot knows that he exists by the very intensity of his pain, but he does not know who he is. He swears the vow in the desperate, maddened hope that somehow it will enable him to "tear asunder" the entwined "twain" of nobility and voluptuous infidelity in his heart and free him from a pain that, because he is "'Our mightiest'" (762, 763), seems to quantify, quintessentially, the torn, divided state "of all the sons of God" (509). It is counterpointed also to Percivale's theatrical account of Galahad's grand melodramatic climax: though thunderous in its elemental psychic violence and in its austere prosodic sublimity, there is no touch about it of gaslight and orange peel, its dense surge of tropes rolling like a sea-swell. So real and terrifyingly precarious is it that the "most holy saint[s]" themselves weep over the doubtful outcome.

It begins with a simple authentic distinction between man and beast: for all that man shares the beast's bestiality, he has in addition his humanness, his moral imperative. He is conscious of an imperious conscientiousness that, however poisoned and polluted, he can never eradicate or escape since it is the source of all his scandal and of all his glory. It is often the source in man of a maddening psychodrama in which one's vision is almost totally obscured and the world without, the physical world, takes on a character of opaque, malign violence.

Ironically, then, Lancelot assumes a distant and oblique Christ role, implicitly undertaking to confront and deal with the maddening moral agony of man. But Lancelot, though he pursues the quest for the Holy Grail in a fairy-tale hope of instant purification, has a nondelusive awareness of his own desperate moral need, and he takes a vow within the vow: he seeks holy counsel and vows to follow the quest according to that counsel. The counsel that he receives from the "'one most holy saint'" (778) is, presumably, the simple counsel of true faith, counterpointing the simple diagnosis by the holy hermit of Percivale's lack of "true humility." It is true faith that surfaces in the voice that Lancelot hears when his struggle is most precarious: "'Doubt not, go forward; if thou doubt, the beasts will tear thee piecemeal.'" The beasts are within him, of course, the two rampant lions being the emblems from Lancelot's own shield; and this begins to give us perspective on Lancelot's "one sin" as well as the "one sin" that ruins "man coming into practical life."

Lancelot's voluptuousness with the Queen has been disguised in his consciousness as infidelity to his King and friend, and the pain that he has long suffered has been keen but tolerable so long as he has been able to hide a truer reality by clinging to this sensuous moral metaphor since it could in part be rationalized in the manner prevalent in the court. But Lancelot's pain, and his corresponding struggle, has been intensified and magnified as he has gradually come to perceive that his infidelity has essentially been, not to the King, but to himself, ontologically moral rather than sensuously moral: in his consciousness, he has settled for a smaller, more shadowy reality of self. So he is embarked at last on a quest of personal authentication, attempting to break through all impediments and to know "'himself no vision to himself'" (913).

And he is indeed sorely tried. Moving in a medium of madness, he suffers existential loneliness, degradation, stark nakedness in the wilderness of a hostile world, and he reaps a cosmic whirlwind in which all sights and sounds and motions are confusions thrice confounded. The elemental fire within him drives him from earth to water propelled by blasts of air that bring him, after a sleepless, dreary, but symbolically creative journey ("Seven days") to "'the enchanted towers of Carbonek'" (810). There he sees an image of himself,

> "A castle like a rock upon a rock,
> With chasm-like portals open to the sea,
> And steps that met the breaker!"
>
> (811–813)

Having passed the ultimate temptation of self-doubt, he enters stripped of all instruments of mock struggle ("'The sword was dashed from out my hand, and fell,'" 823) into a naked hall, it too stripped of all emblems of distracting social ritual (bench, table, painting, shield). In that "quiet house"— his sanctuarial self—he sees "'only the rounded moon/ Through the tall oriel on the rolling sea'" and hears "'Clear as a lark, high o'er me as a lark,/A sweet voice singing in the topmost tower/To the eastward:'" (830–832). Lancelot has achieved his Arthurian moment: he is real.

The rest of his quest story is prophetic: he must climb "'a thousand steps/With pain,'" seeming "'to climb/For ever'" (832–834), hear ambiguous sounds, open strange doors, endure "'a seventimes-heated furnace'" in which he will be "'Blasted and burnt, and blinded'" so fiercely that he will swoon away (840–842); and he must deal with imaginative illusions/realities like the Holy Grail, even amid shapes and presences surreal and terrifying ("'Great angels, awful shapes, and wings and eyes,'" (845). But he now has a real self to build on, a new hope, a true and tried faith; and the reader, himself purged and reinvigorated, can now believe that Lancelot will "die a holy man" (*LE*, 1418).

Thus *The Holy Grail* emerges, not just as one of Tennyson's "most imaginative poems," but as one of the most imaginatively complex and profound poems in English. In it, Tennyson dismantles the metaphoric and fideistic imaginative stereotypes that he had inherited from earlier literary usage, anchors the experience deep in varied coordinates of human nature, and saves from the ruins of his gently relentless imaginative iconoclasm, ironically but unmistakably, the redemption of the order's mightiest knight, Sir Lancelot.

Pelleas embodies the "false dawn" of the Arthurian tragedy: he brings the sunshine "along with him," and his story renews in miniature the overall curve of the tragedy of *The Round Table*. It returns us to a more simply styled fable than that in the thematically climactic *Holy Grail*; but while it begins a narrative rhythm that will be, in Tennyson's ensuing writing acts, employed with variations in such other idylls as *Gareth and Lynette* and *Balin and Balan*,[18] it is paired with *The Holy Grail* and both mirrors its motifs and shows the deep ambient effects of the ruinous experience of the Grail-quest.

Pelleas and Ettarre is a dog-days idyll, moving the summer circus of *The Holy Grail* (symbolically returning upon itself in the time-image of a "twelvemonth and a day," *HG*, 197), into the heats and blown flowers of its fag end. In ironic counterpoise to an inevitability advanced well beyond its prime, it celebrates a "Tournament of Youth" in which the normal expectations are all changed, as if April could hope to flourish in August. The prizes of the tourney, "A golden circlet and a knightly sword" (11), quietly distanced symbols of female/male fulfillment, are won in an atmosphere of spiritual deception and self-delusion, and they bring, not youthful love duets, but grindingly brutal sadomasochistic rituals of mutual destruction. The psychosexual subtleties and refinements of *The Holy Grail* are given a more frankly animalistic anchorage; and the compensation-for-blindness motif of the

Grail-quest (vows sworn because they "'did not see the Holy Thing,'" *HG*, 281, 284–285) is converted to the dramatic overplus-of-virtue convention of which much human tragedy is made.

Except for the ambient moment and the special fiction in which he will become involved (the fated elements of tragedy over which the protagonist has no control), the essential ingredients of Pelleas's tragic doom are seeded in his opening remark:

> "Make me thy knight, because I know, Sir King,
> All that belongs to knighthood, and I love."
>
> (7–8)

Thus the reader, now to a significant degree transformed by the imaginative procedures of *Idylls of the King* and not quite so free as he may have been to be ruled by untutored sentiment and sympathy, is pressed to ask an essentially *literary* question: How much does this rustic Pan, smelling of the fields, really know about knighthood; what and how wisely does he love? The question is stern only from a popular point of view since literature, being a structuring process of the utmost humanistic significance, inevitably makes rules, however permissively, for the most rewarding participation in its procedures. We look at life millions of times in "our way"; the poem invites us, for the moment at least and as a pleasurable experience, to look at life in literature's way. Therefore, while the current of our sympathy for Pelleas—a raw idealistic youth in a hardened, jaded, self-indulgent, and grossly strategic world—may be legitimately strong, we are asked to look at him from an artistic distance and, not wasting ourselves through formless identification with the pathetic strains of his inadequacy, to yield to the sterner stuff of the tragic apprehension in which he is a terrifying protagonist. Only thereby can the simple metaphor of Innocence pulverized by Experience be freed to assume aesthetic complexity and the symbolic episode enabled to invade various interstices of naiveté in all our lives—and some of the hardened crevices too. The imaginative understanding that replaces the grosser forms of praise and blame in literary study should likewise induce maximum access to metaphoric suggestibility.

Pelleas and Ettarre is a double tragedy of far greater complexity than its relatively simple fable seems at first sight to suggest. Both of the principals are complicit in the outcome at a level far subtler than that of the gross fidelity/infidelity matrix of the external story line. They converge from opposite ends of a continuum of belief, he the fanatic, she the agnostic; and, through their sustained contact with each other, they reverse roles. Ettarre actually dies of a love rejected, missed, and finally fixated on:

> her ever-veering fancy turned
> To Pelleas, as the one true knight on earth,
> And only lover; and through her love her life
> Wasted and pined, desiring him in vain.
>
> (483–486)

Nor is this a mechanical eleventh-hour reversal. Ettarre is as much a product of her experience as Pelleas is of his innocence. She has been so disillusioned by the world that she cannot easily believe that worthy love (hence a worthy lover) does or can exist ("'If love there be,'" 300). Hence her exaggerated life-style and behavior are emblems of the restless cynicism of her spirit, practiced and magnified disguises of a forlorn faith. Pelleas as a seriocomic burlesque of the courtly lover—childish amazement, unstylized devotion, stuttering inarticulateness, brute strength, and hayseed imprinted on his every personal gesture—inevitably prompts a burlesque-like response from her in return. The shock to her shrunken subconscious longing forces her either to dismantle her hardened façade suddenly and romantically, a sentimentality which she is far beyond, or to flaunt even more outrageously her self-protective behavior structures. Thus her very first speech is not only linguistically inflated but projects the ritual movements of the sex-act itself:

> "Youth, we are damsels-errant, and we ride,
> Armed as ye see, to tilt against the knights
> There at Caerleon, but have lost our way:
> To right? to left? straight forward? back again?"
>
> (61–64)

Her sluttishness, though behaviorally real, is rooted in her despair of the authenticity of romantically genuine love and a self-protection against vulnerability. But she is not invulnerable, and, in a double irony, Pelleas's very qualities—undeviating devotion through a series of brutal "trials of faith"—both disarm her and leave her to an inextricable tragic plight.

She yields slowly, with a mettlesome grandeur that validates her tragic stature. At the outset of the journey home, she expresses a light conscience-twinge ("'Damsels—and yet I should be shamed to say it—/I cannot bide Sir Baby,'" 182–183), and she later begins to measure unfavorably her "craven" knight-attendants against him ("'ye that scarce are fit to touch,/Far less to bind, your victor,'" 284–285). The breakthrough to a partial realization of the whole truth comes with the high dignity and integrity of Pelleas's parting speech to her. This noble speech releases new perceptions about the possibility of a true him and a true her:

> "Why have I pushed him from me? this man loves,
> If love there be: yet him I loved not. Why?
> I deemed him fool? yea, so? or that in him
> A something—was it nobler than myself?—
> Seemed my reproach? He is not of my kind.
> He could not love me, did he know me well.
> Nay, let him go—and quickly."
>
> (299–305)

It is Pelleas's last stern nobility, leaving the cold sword "athwart their throats" rather than killing her and Gawain in their sleep, that ignites Ettarre's fatal passion for the young knight she has helped to destroy.

Pelleas's emergence through the poem is much more densely textured, and he is the bearer of a symbolism that is many-leveled. Fresh from his "waste islands" (18, 82) and knowing "scarce any" women except his sisters and the "rough wives" of his "barren" lands (83–85), his claim to "'know . . ./All that belongs to knighthood'" forces the reader to conclude that what he knows, he knows from books. And this perception illuminates Pelleas's story in a host of ways. He is following a "bible of knighthood" as a fundamentalist, literally interpreted, literally lived by. He is a tragic variant of Don Quixote, misreading his Ettarre as perseveringly as Don Quixote misreads Dulcinea. He is not self-degraded by the most heinous treatment, allowing himself to be handled by leprous hands and bound like a slave, because, like Don Quixote, he is a true believer, a shining acolyte, in a religion of chivalry, in which these are well-known "trials of faith." His "debate" with Gawain (310–333) is that between a catechist and a revisionist, between one who lives by the book and one who has rewritten the book. To Pelleas's literalism literally acted out, Gawain countercharges defamation of the "brotherhood" and gross ignorance: "'Come, ye know nothing'" (333). And Pelleas's bookish, biblical fundamentalism, itself teasingly ironic, is glossed in a triple irony in the affair of Gawain and Ettarre: the easy prey that this jaunty man of the world can make of the bookish Pelleas; the eminently preferable value-metaphor that Pelleas represents, in spite of and because of his fundamentalism, to that represented by Gawain; and the wry fact that it is because of Pelleas's strict adherence to his knightly code that, despite Gawain's wretched betrayal of trust, he cannot bring himself to kill a sleeping knight.

But there is a deeply tragic element in Pelleas's catechetical fundamentalism too. The reader knows (as the nineteenth century had known) that the collapse of such a literal faith inevitably brings tremendous aftershocks, and the unyielding quality of Pelleas's dogmatic fidelity begins to induce in the reader strains of pity and fear of its inevitable tragic consequences. Pelleas himself strikes the ominous, heartrending note when he says, "'Else must I die through mine unhappiness'" (324). This tragic self-awareness becomes yet more intense and pathetic when, as Pelleas awaits anxiously, after three days of aimlessness and doubt, for Gawain's promised return with his "golden news" (402), the blighted-rose song becomes a persistent presence in his distressed consciousness:

> "A rose, but one, none other rose had I,
> A rose, one rose, and this was wondrous fair,
> One rose, a rose that gladdened earth and sky,

One rose, my rose, that sweetened all my air—
I cared not for the thorns; the thorns were there.

"One rose, a rose to gather by and by,
One rose, a rose, to gather and to wear,
No rose but one—what other rose had I?
One rose, my rose; a rose that will not die,—
He dies who loves it,—if the worm be there."
                                    (391–400)

The insistent, reiterative note of woe in this lyric celebration of a singular but tragically faulted beauty—so entirely apt as a threshold motif for Pelleas's approaching catastrophe—broadens out by its remembered context ("Which Pelleas had heard sung before the Queen,/And seen her sadden listening," 388–389) to suggest an analogy between Guinevere's fundamental dilemma and his own and thus draws together a cluster of deeply resonant metaphoric significances. There can be no more "golden news," for Pelleas or the Queen or the Arthurian world: the dawn is a false dawn. Both Pelleas and Guinevere have adopted too exclusively a faulty life-apprehension, as both have devoted all their spiritual energy to the wrong love object; and the source of the greatest agonies of their respective lives will be the recognition that if there is "A worm within the rose," either of the love object or of the life-apprehension, then the worm is also within the self.

In the recognition soliloquy that follows the staggering revelation of the treachery of Gawain and the falseness of Ettarre which leaves his religion of chivalry in ruins, Pelleas rises to true tragic stature. He indicts the so-solid-seeming world of his youthful *rite de passage* with the most passionate, condemnatory linguistic brutalities: it is a world of whirling harlot dust, hissing snakes, barking foxes, and yelling wolves, "'Black as the harlot's heart—hollow as a skull!'" (459) But he indicts himself too:

"Who yells
Here in the still sweet summer night, but I—
I, the poor Pelleas whom she called her fool?
Fool, beast—he, she, or I? myself most fool;

> Beast too, as lacking human wit—disgraced,
> Dishonoured all for trial of true love—
> Love?—we be all alike: only the King
> Hath made us fools and liars. O noble vows!
> O great and sane and simple race of brutes
> That own no lust because they have no law!
> For why should I have loved her to my shame?
> I loathe her, as I loved her to my shame.
> I never loved her, I but lusted for her—
> Away—"
>
> (463–476)

It is a truly noble speech and saves the idyll as a thoroughly authentic tragedy, its painful but statuesque, biblical language indicating just how far his faith, his trials, and his catastrophe have brought this magnificent youth from the state of untempered strength with which he entered, so lately, the Arthurian world. His indictments of the narrow segment which he has known are vigorous and true; and though his sore distress leads him a bit beyond the just understanding of his own experience, extrapolating it in a generalized indictment of Arthur's failure in language that Dagonet will echo in *The Last Tournament,* it does not blind him to the most painful of justnesses, his own complicity in his downfall. His rituals of dogmatic inflexibility, his self-effacements beyond human reason, have been rooted not only in a canonical text, but in the sensuous, lustful self.

It is important to recognize that Pelleas is not simply besmirching himself in an incontinent torrent of broadside abuse. At the very beginning of the idyll, he had moved in a medium of insistent sexuality. He had ridden toward Caerleon at the hour sacred to the goat god ("Riding at noon," 19), the sun beating "like a strong knight" on this son of Pan from "many a barren isle," making him reel "Almost to falling" (23). He found a beechen grove undergrown with great holly bushes and surrounded by a prospect of high grasses ("open space,/And fern and heath," 27–28) where he "cast himself down" (in the manner of a goat) and "lay/At random looking over the brown earth/Through that green-glooming twilight

of the grove" (30–32). That is, he lay "At random" and looked
"At random"—like a goat, like Pan, and like a goat he dozed.
It is a simple, pagan, natural world, the fern outside the
shade burning like "a living fire of emerald," a floating cloud
making a momentary shadow, a flying bird, a gentle faun;
and within Pelleas, as within the goat god, there are the imperious demands of sexual longing:

> And since he loved all maidens, but no maid
> In special, half-awake he whispered, "Where?
> O where? I love thee, though I know thee not.
> For fair art thou and pure as Guinevere,
> And I will make thee with my spear and sword
> As famous—O my Queen, my Guinevere,
> For I will be thine Arthur when we meet."
>
> (39–45)

This most delicately sketched but firm classical analogue, the
source of an imaginatively importunate and gentle pathos in
the poem, mutates subtly as Pelleas is abruptly awakened by
human chatter and laughter and looks through the eyes and
sensibility of a startled son of Pan at all this stylized strangeness:

> And glancing though the hoary boles, he saw,
> Strange as to some old prophet might have seemed
> A vision hovering on a sea of fire,
> Damsels in divers colours like the cloud
> Of sunset and sunrise, and all of them
> On horses, and the horses richly trapt
> Breast-high in that bright line of bracken stood:
>
> (48–54)

The analogue not only implants an unmistakable sexuality, a
natural lust, in the character of Pelleas; it also suggests why
he is so easily self-deceived about Ettarre's falsified beauty
and so willing to be her goat. Further, it begins to evoke, in
the most oblique but suggestive manner, much richer imaginative possibilities: that each of us is a "son of Pan" attempting, through our various rubrics, to transform our natural
selves, with their ineradicable natural elements, into new or-

ders of fulfillment; that such efforts are inevitably doomed to failure to the degree that we blind ourselves, however high-mindedly, to any aspect of the total reality of ourselves; and that paganism and Arthurianism are not sequential, but archetypal and hence always in a contention of which there can never be, at least in human history, an ultimate resolution.

If Tennyson had ended *Pelleas and Ettarre* at line 509, he would have had a superbly structured, thoroughly authentic classical tragedy: a young man of some magnificence becomes involved in a contest of life and contributes in part, by some ambiguous element in himself, to his own catastrophe; but because of and in final validation of his degree of magnificence, he rises to his catastrophe, reads it justly, and accepts its self-illumination. But just as Pelleas is himself a false dawn, so also would such a classically invigorating tragedy have been a deception of the literary imagination that Tennyson, in *Idylls of the King*, was attempting both to embody and to induce in the reader. It would have been too neat by far, encouraging the imagination to take sanctuary in an imaginative structure that, though invigorating, was yet, by the measure of a larger imaginative apprehensiveness, stereotypical. So having carefully shaped it, he let it take its place in an enveloping context, still intact as a literary structure, but less conspicuous.

The merger of the one into the other is effected through an apocalyptic nightmare—"a dream, that Gawain fired/The hall of Merlin, and the morning star/Reeled in the smoke, brake into flame, and fell" (507–509)—and through the sudden presence of Percivale as the messenger of a yet larger and more devastating tragic perception. Thus Pelleas is moved out of his formally rounded personal tragedy by a cosmic nightmare that, waking, he finds to be true. And the awful revelation at the hands of Percivale has a touch of shabby uncleanliness about it: though Percivale cannot know the background and the dream that make Pelleas so doubly vulnerable ("as with one/Who gets a wound in battle, and the sword/That made it plunges through the wound again," 518–520), he works by banal sarcasm, half-spoken truth, and noncommittal insinuation, rising finally to haughty verbal brutality:

> "The King!" said Percivale.
> "Why then let men couple at once with wolves.
> What! art thou mad?"
>
> (525–527)

The awful cataclysm opened up before him, Pelleas, half man, half goat and battering ram, races through the world making chaos of everything in his path in a fury over falseness, himself so false to his knightly nature that he runs down a cripple begging alms and sees the hall where he was knighted as a "'Black nest of rats'" (544). His clash with Lancelot is shrill with irony: the courtly lover, full for the moment of easy graciousness, warmth, and cosmic serenity, brought into violent collision with a grand youth—unselfed, emasculated, abstractly wrathful—of whose total desolation he has been one symbolic cause. Pelleas is now without faith or hope or love or identity or instrument of service, nameless and swordless; his so ardent progress from "son of Pan" to strict and perfect knight has ended by hurling him into a cosmic chaos of recriminatory self-destruction:

> "I am wrath and shame and hate and evil fame,
> And like a poisonous wind I pass to blast
> And blaze the crime of Lancelot and the Queen."
>
> (556–558)

Lancelot calls him "'weakling'" (570), and Guinevere, who had been his advocate in the early days of the failing courtship of Ettarre, chides him in ignorance of his more than tragic history:

> "O young knight,
> Hath the great heart of knighthood in thee failed
> So far thou canst not bide, unfrowardly,
> A fall from *him?*"
>
> (583–586)

The irony is crushing: the "fall" is lapsarian almost beyond imagining; "the great heart of knighthood" seems a fragile metaphor for the great heart that has burst in Pelleas; though in some grand ontological morality it may be fair to call Pelleas a weakling, Lancelot has not yet, despite his Grail experience, earned the right; and Guinevere's queenly reprimand, though apt at a conventional level, seems somewhat hollow coming from one who has not yet had her own identity crisis and who will even then hardly suffer more, in scale, than the "Travail, and throes and agonies of the life" of young Sir Pelleas of the Isles, for whom it is very doubtful that the sweet morning star, "Pure on the virgin forehead of the dawn" (495), will ever shine again.

Notes

1. Eversley, III, 499.
2. Eversley, III, 487.
3. Eversley, III, 488.
4. Eversley, III, 494–495.
5. Eversley, III, 492.
6. Eversley, III, 493.
7. Eversley, III, 493–494.
8. Eversley, III, 494.
9. Eversley, III, 497.
10. Eversley, III, 441.
11. Hallam Tennyson, *Alfred Lord Tennyson: A Memoir* (New York: Macmillan, 1897), II, 65.
12. *Memoir*, II, 57.
13. See note 3, above.
14. Eversley, III, 443.
15. Eversley, III, 440.
16. Eversley, III, 441.
17. See note 7, above.
18. *Pelleas and Ettarre* was written in 1869, *Gareth and Lynette* in the spring and early summer of 1872, and *Balin and Balan* during 1872–1874. See Sir Charles Tennyson, *Alfred Tennyson* (New York: Macmillan, 1949), pp. 381–382, 404, 484.

3.

Returning to 1859

■ *The Marriage of Geraint* ■ *Geraint and Enid* ■ *Merlin and Vivien* ■ *Lancelot and Elaine* ■ *Guinevere*

One of the great advantages of coming to the 1859 idylls from a close consideration of the compositions that went into the *Holy Grail* volume is the deep reinforcement which the later volume gives to the critical perception that *Idylls of the King* is a literary artifact and that unfailing attention must be given to the whole poem and to its several parts as *literary* structures and procedures, *to literature's way.* And of the numerous and indispensable guidelines that the reader takes from the example of the *Holy Grail* volume, none is of greater aesthetic importance than that each idyll represents the projection into fable and language of a different apprehending consciousness, specified or generically anonymous—an additional and crucial *literary presence* with whom the reader establishes an independently observant relationship and through whose supposing and stating "fact" the "meaning" of the fable is kept in the fluid state of the "manner" of the narration itself. Thus *Idylls of the King* is, in a rather firm sense, an imaginative orchestration of many instruments, a chorus of many voices, a kaleidoscope of many "glancing colours" and patterns. The *Idylls* as a whole contains examples of drama implanted in a narrative fabric—dramatic lyrics, heightened dramatic dialogues, explosively dramatic situations, dramatic soliloquies, dramatic monologues—but it is also a narrative poem suspended in a monodramatic formulation, not in the manner of *The Ring and the Book,* but in a manner analogous to it.

A further central revelation of *Idylls of the King* is the drama of literature itself, that flexuous instrumentality of the human imagination that is ever inventing new formalistic and linguistic adaptations in a heightened effort both to keep proved traditions alive and to renew itself in the endless effort to give "a modern expression to a modern outlook." Being anchored deep in personality, *Idylls of the King* emerges formally out of distinctive personalities and is shaped, not only by subtly graded protagonists at the center of the various fables, but by subtly graded narrators functioning in subtly graded species of narration. Thus Percivale's manner in the Grail-quest narrative so undercuts the inflations of that irresistible but ill-advised adventure that both the narrator and the generic story itself come to exist in a keenly ironic medium engendering in the reader a wry detachment from such ego-fueled spiritual enthusiasms. The narrator of *Pelleas and Ettarre* is himself perhaps a bookish man who has a highly developed awareness of classical tragic formulation, of the temptations inherent in a too rigid application of frozen literary formulae to the impalpable crosscurrents of life in this world, and of the horrendous consequences that can result from a collision of tragic courses so violent that it goes beyond tragedy in the classically formulated sense. *The Passing of Arthur,* an end-tale, is the narration of the last synoptic, who brings to his account a bold, loyal, faulted, representative consciousness of events whose very reality, though empirically witnessed, have a high degree of mystery about them.

The Marriage of Geraint and *Geraint and Enid,* the only two idylls with a continuous story line, institute a more complex deployment of the concept of narrator-consciousness. If we may assume that a single narrator relates both idylls (and the fact that they are the result of the split into two of one original tale is only a part of the evidence), then we have two different literary modes projected by two different perceptual moods of the same character, not unlike the male-female disjointedness that is at the center of the story itself. Both narrations are consciously faulted literarily, the first from a masculine unease in the context of romantic love, the second from a feminine solemnity that spills into melodrama and thematic unction. To use the wholly relevant terminology of the Conclusion of *The Princess, The Marriage of Geraint* is spoken by a male-mocker mood of character, covering its unease in banter and enveloping its narration in mock-heroic, seriocomic burlesque and romantic parody; and *Geraint and Enid* is the work of a female-realist mood of character, investing its contrasting high seriousness in an effort at the "true-heroic—true-sublime" in which the feminine principle—Enid, Psyche, the Soul—achieves a patient, constant, magnified and transformational victory worthy of Cinderella, Griselda, and Psyche herself. The relevance of *The Princess* is structuring in an even more pervasive sense: *The Marriage of Geraint* initiates, literarily, "a strange diagonal" that moves from burlesque toward its solemn, heroic, sublime terminus in *Guinevere,* and *Geraint and Enid* serves to point the direction of that strange literary diagonal.

■

The Marriage of Geraint is a rich, complex literary experience. The romantic parody emerges through a sophisticated riot of language, tumbling toward a very witty species of burlesque and narrative farce; but this is counterpointed against a muted ground tone of seriousness so cautionary that it induces an awareness of the tragic potentialities in the story, despite the high stylistic comedy, moving the narrative into a medium of the comic grotesque. The characterization of Geraint himself uses symbolic gesture at its seemingly most transparent level

to engender for the reader an intricate psychological portrait, the delineation of a broadly representative incarnation
of "man against himself." The far-flung thematic gloss of "the
true and the false" is so deeply internalized, surfacing and
submerging in both solid primitive images and in fragmentary reflections as of a mirror shattered into a thousand
pieces, that it seems to have ultimate imaginative meaning
only in a reader's capacity to order for himself an adequate
artistic unity. The ceremony of investiture has genuine symbolic significance in its own right, but it also lends its symbolism out, drawing the reader's imaginative apprehensiveness
into the circle of a many-layered multiplication of appear-
ance/reality images. Though Enid-Psyche will gain strength
and stature in the ordeal of constancy of *Geraint and Enid,* she
is childish and relatively characterless in the early story line
of *The Marriage of Geraint*—the flashback—playing girlishly
recessive twitterings and flutterings to Geraint-Cupid's
brawny, self-inflating, aggressive mating-call.

But the introduction to *The Marriage of Geraint* (1–144) is
serious enough. It embodies a brief period of narrative time,
a fulcrum, between the story lines of the two idylls, a moment
of interpretive poise in which the personal/historical past and
the personal/historical future meet; and it provides terms by
which past action can be interpreted and future action judged
as it is processed in the narrative of *Geraint and Enid.* Like the
various frames Tennyson frequently uses, it gives a literary
center against which the distinctive narrative manners of the
tales themselves can be normed.

That these idylls have large reference to *Idylls of the King* as
a whole is signalled immediately by the establishment of
Geraint as a Guinevere figure. He is the object of her gratitude and reciprocal service; she colludes with him in his rituals of investiture; and he carries into summer Guinevere's
May motif. But Geraint is not a simple concrete projection of
Guinevere's influence on the Round Table. The interpretive
legitimacy of such a reading, except as an oblique gloss, is
turned aside by Geraint's over-quick reaction to the vaguest
rumors about the Queen and by his own massive individuality as a substantial generic human type.

An Eros/Cupid figure, Geraint tries to create and inhabit with Enid a bower of bliss, a lotus-land, a palace of sensual art, a sexual paradise—a monistic fantasy-world in which he attempts to enshrine her in a blasphemous religion of distrust. He ministers to her with a manliness shrunken to the level of his genitalia, the inevitable effect being that he transforms her, momentarily, into a symbolic, though exclusive, courtesan. Thus his life is "molten down" (60) with sexual fire, the "uxoriousness" that makes him the object of catcalls being specifically bedridden, and his muscular nakedness is phallus-centered:

> the knotted column of his throat,
> The massive square of his heroic breast,
> And arms on which *the standing muscle sloped,*
> As slopes a wild brook o'er a little stone,
> Running too vehemently to break upon it.
>   (74–78, emphasis added)

Even the "force" that he has lost for more generalized manly activities seems concentrated in orgasmic potency: "'all his force/Is melted into mere effeminacy'" (106–107); and though Enid, a Soul figure, loves Geraint's body, she feels entombed in his concentrated sexual strategies and becomes death-obsessed: "'Far better were I laid in the dark earth'" (97).

But Enid is caught between love and "hate" (91) and fear ("'dare not speak,'" 89) and, thus entrapped, induces the ceremony of silence that will make the struggle between "sense" and "soul" so arduous and prolonged and so inevitable as to seem necessary. Her hot tears, like the oil from Psyche's lamp, fall on his naked breast in the progress of her lamentation over their mutual plight, and he awakens to a misconstruction of her closing words, a misconstruction shaped by his own dwarfed inner resources. Thus it is in a spirit of self-pity rather than self-knowledge, of male self-enclosure rooted in an imagined injury to raw male pride, that he masterminds their lacerating journey into the outer-wilderness in lieu of the fidelity of genuine communicative sharing and an effort to clear the wilderness within and let in genuine personal sunlight.

The retrospective story that leads up to this moment of narrative poise (the flashback) establishes immediately a rich symbolic context for the serious undertow of the idyll. It happens at Whitsuntide, the traditional period of baptism, and Arthur is engaged in a ceremony of hunt for a "milky-white" hart, "Taller than all his fellows" (149–150). Guinevere, although she has "petitioned for his leave/To see the hunt" (154–155), has lain late abed "Lost in sweet dreams, and dreaming of her love/For Lancelot, and forgetful of the hunt" (158–159). When she does at last arouse herself and find a station ("on a little knoll") where she hopes to hear the hounds and see them "break covert," she is joined by a jaunty Lothario, Geraint, "wearing neither hunting-dress/Nor weapon, save a golden-hilted brand" (165–166), dressed like a harlequin—"like a dragon-fly/In summer suit and silks of holiday" (172–173), girdled with "A purple scarf, at either end whereof/There swung an apple of the purest gold" (169–170). Their salutation is positively operatic in its heightened ceremoniousness, and they declare their unity of purpose—"to see the hunt,/Not join it" (179–180). Thus we catch a note of stylized buffoonery beginning to counterpoint a serious undertone represented by Cavall's "baying . . . of deepest mouth" (185–186).

The traveling trio—"a knight, lady, and dwarf" (187)—provide the motive of Geraint's service by the insult done the Queen in the person of her single maiden and of Geraint, her single knight, but they also cast the "princely" Geraint in the role of a clown. He suffers insult at the hands of the "vicious" dwarf, including a cut on the cheek that stains his gay raiment, but backtracks to the Queen for reasons that the inflated language in which they are couched makes ring false:

> But he, from his exceeding manfulness
> And pure nobility of temperament,
> Wroth to be wroth at such a worm, refrained
> From even a word. . . .
>
> (211–214)

The humor darkens: Geraint's vulnerability is clearly suggested, and he is "marked" by the character of his offender.

Like Gawain in his pledge of good faith to Pelleas, he promises to return "on the third day" (222); but Geraint couches
his vulnerability to death in such gross and self-regarding
terms that his allusion to the resurrection, and hence to himself as a savior figure, releases overtones of grotesque absurdity. This absurdity is in turn magnified and reinforced by
Guinevere's promise to clothe the bride that he may find on
his journey "'for her bridals like the sun'" (231) and by
Geraint's failure to see an image of himself in the three dark
figures "against the sky" (240).

The spirit in which this discomfited Lothario undertakes
his journey into discovery is as disheveled as his dress—
peevish, fretful, "vext"—a dramatic contrast to the spiritual
inflations motivating the Grail-quest; and the infernal work-
shop at his journey's end is a shabby, eclipsed affair, Vulcan's
grand manufactory reduced to a tedious, surly industrious-
ness. The rude, bad-humored, discourteous inattention turns
the "princely" Geraint's vexation into spleen:

> "A thousand pips eat up your sparrow-hawk!
> Tits, wrens, and all winged nothings peck him dead!
> Ye think the rustic cackle of your bourg
> The murmur of the world! What is it to me?
> O wretched set of sparrows, one and all,
> Who pipe of nothing but of sparrow-hawks!
> Speak, if ye be not like the rest, hawk-mad,
> Where can I get me harbourage for the night?
> And arms, arms, arms to fight my enemy? Speak!"
>   (274–282)

The shrunken world of this dusty little beehive is, despite its
contrast to Geraint's appearance as "one so gay in purple
silks" (284), an image of his own inner dwarfishness, and he
rails against it as one might rail against a most painful self-
reflection. The "arms, arms, arms" for which he calls so
splenetically he will take a long time to recognize after he has
found them, and he as yet is unconscious that his "enemy" is
within. So when he goes, as directed, to Earl Yniol's castle, he
crosses a "dry ravine" (294) which is a correlative of his own
spiritual state.

With Geraint's crossing of the bridge, burlesque and romantic parody invade the narrative, and through a process of heightened deflation the tone becomes melo-operatic. Even the analogous story line moves into a medium of topsy-turviness: Enid is a mélange of Psyche-Cinderella-nightingale and an adolescent on her first date; the cruel mother is a caricature of Goody-Twoshoes who can hardly wait for the better times a-coming; patient Griselda surfaces in the "hoary Earl," who is as slippery as an eel; Geraint, who prides himself on being from the courtly center of the world and is contemptuous of these rattling provincials, is a Prince Charming who falls in love at first sight, fails to tell the whole truth as to why he is there, imposes his will autocratically, and shows himself rather loutish in his appraisals of others, including Enid-Psyche-Cinderella.

It is great literary fun, this riot of language, gesture, false pretense, and subtly debunked fairy tale; and at this precarious level, it is most adeptly managed, romantic sentimentality made to founder on itself through a slight but conspicuous literary exaggeration. Enid-Cinderella is just a soupçon too demure and self-effacing in her stabling, marketing, cooking, serving, and sewing; Geraint's eye roves a bit too pointedly, he is slightly carried away in his desire to "stoop and kiss the tender little thumb" (395), and his "utter courtesy" is a bit too utter (381); the ancient dame carries agreeable self-effacement to the brink of sycophancy; and there is a touch of hilarious impropriety in Earl Yniol's restraining of Geraint by hanging on to his "purple scarf" (377). Further, there is no mistaking the stagy character of the language: "'Whither, fair son?'" "'Hark, by the bird's song ye shall learn the nest.'" "'Well said, true heart.'" "'Thy leave!'" "'O my new mother, be not wroth or grieved/At thy new son.'" The ceremony of language has its correspondence in the ceremony of clothes, and both are manipulated into transparent symbols of melodramatic inflation, romantic parody, and burlesque.

But behind this fabric of false-gesturing, the source of genuine literary humor, there are depths of misperception and equivocation and deception of a truly sobering kind. Enid's bird-song, for example, in addition to the fact that it expresses, ritualistically, sentiments that her family, in its ruined state, only pretend to live by, reflects an ingratiating falsehood in and of itself:

> "Turn, Fortune, turn thy wheel and lower the proud;
> Turn thy wild wheel through sunshine, storm, and
>   cloud;
> Thy wheel and thee we neither love nor hate.
>
> "Turn, Fortune, turn thy wheel with smile or frown;
> With that wild wheel we go not up or down;
> Our hoard is little, but our hearts are great.
>
> "Smile and we smile, the lords of many lands;
> Frown and we smile, the lords of our own hands;
> For man is man and master of his fate.
>
> "Turn, turn thy wheel above the staring crowd;
> Thy wheel and thou are shadows in the cloud;
> Thy wheel and thee we neither love nor hate."
>   (347–358)

The song expresses a touching sentiment that is a perennial source of human reassurance, but its fault lies in its self-congratulatory inducement to moral, aesthetic, spiritual inertia. It is recessive rather than active, stoical rather than contestant. It is a rationalization of the status quo, which in a context of generation/decay can never remain frozen. It makes a virtue of the kind of decay symbolized in the castle and in Earl Yniol and his wife, and it is a discouragement to the kind of inner growth that both Enid and Geraint need, inevitably leading to the agonies of the life through which they will precariously pass.

Enid-Cinderella is caught up in the burlesque medium of the narration, acting out in the exaggerated fashion of romantic parody her first experience as romantic love object:

> but never light and shade
> Coursed one another more on open ground
> Beneath a troubled heaven, than red and pale

> Across the face of Enid hearing her;
> While slowly falling as a scale that falls,
> When weight is added only grain by grain,
> Sank her sweet head upon her gentle breast;
> Nor did she lift an eye nor speak a word,
> Rapt in the fear and in the wonder of it;
> So moving without answer to her rest
> She found no rest, and ever failed to draw
> The quiet night into her blood, but lay
> Contemplating her own unworthiness. . . .
>
> (521–533)

As an Annunciation scene, it is delicately drawn, but with the ancient dame, her of the "frequent smile and nod " (515), acting as the Archangel Gabriel, and Geraint in the role of the fructifying Holy Ghost, it becomes bizarrely disproportionate to its analogue. On the other hand, it shades into Enid-Psyche and suggests that, although the Soul she symbolizes in a distant way is still in a state of fluttering immaturity, there is promise of potential greatness there. The song she sings, even if faulted, is the tenderest and most inspiriting metaphor in her disheveled world, and the voice with which she sings it is as sweet and affective to Geraint as the nightingale is to another. She moves in her faded silk sheath with virginal delicacy, and her dreams have a refined aesthetic imaginativeness that seems to reach toward both the Arabian Nights and Yeats's "Sailing to Byzantium":

> And though she lay dark in the pool, she knew
> That all was bright; that all about were birds
> Of sunny plume in gilded trellis-work;
> That all the turf was rich in plots that looked
> Each like a garnet or a turkis in it;
> And lords and ladies of the high court went
> In silver tissue talking things of state;
> And children of the King in cloth of gold
> Glanced at the doors or gamboled down the walks. . . .
>
> (657–665)

The dream is generated and collapses in her ugly-duckling

anxieties, of course, but even in such a setting the jewel-like quality has genuine and distinctive authenticity.

Enid's mother, though a parody of Cinderella's cruel step-mother, has still her measure of falseness. She has eaten humble pie, but all "unwillingly" (705), and she instructs the bride-to-be in harsh, materialistic reality:

> "For though ye won the prize of fairest fair,
> And though I heard him call you fairest fair,
> Let never maiden think, however fair,
> She is not fairer in new clothes than old."
>   (719–722)

Enid's father, Earl Yniol, despite his protestations, is an arch-flatterer and deceiver. His version of the foulness done him by his nephew and the townspeople is in itself tenuous enough, especially to a reader familiar with his account as given in the *Mabinogion:* "'I had a nephew, the son of my brother, and I took his possessions to myself; and when he came to his strength, he demanded of me his property, but I withheld it from him. So he made war upon me, and wrested from me all that I possessed.'"[1] It is difficult to believe, too, that there is much truth in his story of having sung Geraint's praises to Enid without end. His self-characterization, though credible, is put to self-serving purposes.

> "And I myself sometimes despise myself;
> For I have let men be, and have their way,
> Am much too gentle, have not used my power;
> Nor know I whether I be very base
> Or very manful, whether very wise
> Or very foolish; only this I know,
> That whatsoever evil happen to me,
> I seem to suffer nothing heart or limb,
> But can endure it all most patiently."
>   (465–473)

It is, of course, a translation into life-style of the import of Enid's bird-song, and it calls into question whether a man like Yniol can honestly be said to exist at all.

It all makes a most suitable context for the authentic exposure of Geraint. This gay Lothario, with his "purple scarf" and his two apples "of the purest gold," has been served up with the two things he craves most—flattery of his ego and stimulation of his libido. Thereby he is assured that he really exists, that he is a man. Under the radiance of such a double sun, he expands and becomes *almost* generous (he sets all the terms of his marriage to Enid and in the most unreasonable, nonnegotiable fashion) and *almost* honest (he withholds the truth about the blood-drawing cut administered to him by the dwarf). There is melodramatic "grandeur" in his declamatory declaration:

> "Thy leave!
> Let *me* lay lance in rest, O noble host,
> For this dear child, because I never saw,
> Though having seen all beauties of our time,
> Nor can see elsewhere, anything so fair.
> And if I fall her name will yet remain
> Untarnished as before; but if I live,
> So aid me Heaven when at mine uttermost,
> As I will make her truly my true wife."
>
> (495–503)

It is all very boyish and egotistical and grand and patronizing and ironic, and in it is seeded Geraint's torturous comeuppance. In his dealings with Enid and her family, Geraint is himself a sparrow-hawk; and when he fights the sparrow-hawk in the tourney, he is so evenly matched that only the extra boost to his force generated by the reminder of "'the great insult'" done the Queen (and himself) turns the balance in his favor. And both the punishment he metes out to Edyrn in lieu of taking his life and the trophy that he wins are self-reflective. In the one case, he sends Edyrn to Guinevere as living testimony to his good service and at the same time acts as grand patron to his in-laws; in the other, the silver wand symbolizes his fairy-tale superiority, and the golden sparrow-hawk lays further unction to his physical prowess, including his sexual prowess in his version of the battle of the sexes, and further identifies him with the dissolute phase of the sparrow-hawk.

The ceremony of investiture, in which Geraint again imposes his will, makes high mass out of a high thing. Even though anxiety over her appearance throws Enid back into her Cinderella mentality ("'if he could but tarry a day or two,/ Myself would work eye dim, and finger lame,'" (627–628) and the recovery of the lost gown makes Enid's mother voluble in her benevolent self-conceit, they are both abashed and uncomfortable with Geraint's demand: it arrogates to himself even the most personal decision, as if he would tell a bird of paradise what plumage to wear, "'like that maiden in the tale,/Whom Gwydion made by glamour out of flowers'" (742–743). But Geraint's justification of the act has coordinates that are even more shocking. Being a Guinevere figure himself, he wants to make Enid a Guinevere figure: he wants to "'bind/The two toegther'" (790–791). Thus he seeds one part of their mutual struggle. The other, already hinted at in Geraint's arrogant declaration that he will "'make her truly my true wife'" (503), is that he wants proof positive so that he can "'rest, a rock in ebbs and flows,/Fixt on her faith'" (812–813). Ironically, it is not her faith that is at issue, but his; and when he declares himself "'A prophet certain of my prophecy'" (814), one can hear the tragic fates moving into position.

Geraint's self-administered baptism of pleasure has not been wholly efficacious, so now he must undergo his self-administered baptism of pain.

The text of the medieval exemplum with which *Geraint and Enid* begins sets the narrative tone of the idyll; it will be a moralized tale, a sort of sermon. The speaker makes a sharp division between the rhetorical tone of this literary piece and that of the preceding tale and in so doing focuses unmistakably one sense of the meaning of what we have just read and enlarges the application of that meaning to include us all, some of whom may be inclined to think that, unlike Geraint, "we see as we are seen!" (7) But the "moralized tale" or sermon quickly assumes *literary* character and definition through the manner in which it evolves: it is a species of epic, of domesticated epic, in which, through the metaphor of literary manner, the intensest personal struggles of man and woman are enlarged to epic proportions in an engendering awareness that most of man's grandest schemes and fatal errors are in fact rooted in that harmony or discord between Cupid and Psyche which, in its quotidian manifestations, is between man and woman, husband and wife. Thus the two Geraint-Enid idylls have an androgynous center, the male-female surfacings of a single narrative consciousness; and that narrative consciousness reflects a reversal of sex roles as ordinarily stereotyped; the romantic sentimentality and self-distortion of *The Marriage of Geraint,* with the male protagonist dominant, told by the male-mood; the austere, epical, redemptive, authentic self-recognition, with the female protagonist dominant, told by the female-mood.

The ornate revel of symbolic gesture—word, character, incident, object—which had characterized *The Marriage of Geraint* is here stripped bare almost to nakedness as the reader is spared romantic distraction and induced to watch the austere, relentless simplicity, Homeric in character, with which an elemental human struggle is brought to an even-handed classical resolution. There is a close approximation of the unities of time, place, and action, and metaphoric turbulence subsides into a quiet but visible network of epic similes. The ultimate resolution, to the degree that it will not be jeopardized by external circumstances, is seeded in character from the very beginning and allowed to emerge with careful gradualness as the fiction itself evolves, so that the ultimate transformation is not a sentimental one.

Although the action, or plot, does full Aristotelian duty in advancing the story, it is always clear that a corresponding action is processing itself at a fully internalized level. The reader's imaginative pleasure is enriched by the use of character foils, and the theme of the fortunate fall which is elaborated in the narrative as a whole gets oblique summation and reinforcement from outside the central story line. There is no clutter of symbolism, but action fuels symbolic perception. Reader empathy is gradually induced through an intensification of pity and fear, and the narrative rises step-by-step to a stunning climax through which external antagonists are destroyed and the internal antagonists and tensions dissolve into magnified unity. There is a firm recognition scene in which the knowledge learned from self-imposed agony is fully articulated, and there is a dénouement in which the permanence of the conversional result is wholly assured.

On the other hand, despite all these firm verifications that the author wanted the reader to be unmistakably aware of the epic dimensions of his subject and of the classical epic as a fit analogue for the narrative method used, he was not pretending that this was a genuine epic rather than an idyll, was not inviting serious critical comparison between *Geraint and Enid* and the *Iliad,* for example, though he almost certainly wanted to show that his idylls could reach in all literary directions. Therefore, he dismantled while he built, subverting the epic analogue in the very process of insinuating it. Geraint is a hangdog hero at best, not crafty like Ulysses or volcanic like Achilles, but confused and laggard. His battles are mean affairs, and his braggadocio peevish. Even his near-fatal wound is a "prick," bleeding beneath his armor, of which he himself is hardly conscious. The trials he imposes on Enid—as forward scout, drover, and dummy—are petulant and self-demeaning; and his final act of "heroism"—leaping from coma to conqueror—is enmeshed in such a melodramatic literary context as to be diminshed to a laughably ironic level. Thus the appearance/reality matrix of the idyll is absorbed into and energized by the very literary manner of the piece.

Geraint as a cruel Cupid and Enid as a long-suffering Psyche not only provide a mythic analogue for the idyll, but draw this heightened but ordinary tale of domestic woe—this fictive configuration of representative human experience—into a mythic medium. What they endure, we all endure, in one way or another—"misconceits" and "divisions dire and wry," "horrid shows" and "long-drawn days of blight."[2] One aspect of it is cultural, not only in the male superiority which is a cultural fixation in Geraint's sense of himself, but also in the metropolis-provinces construct which had surfaced repeatedly in Geraint's self-characterization in *The Marriage of Geraint.* Both of these involve glaring contradictions, of

course. As Arthur in his love-epiphany so dramatically illustrates, inequality of the sexes is diminishment of the sexes,
leading not to fulfillment but to devastating sexual battles
and maneuvers in which no one can win; and although
Arthur's own marriage, being grandly prototypical, fails and
ruins his realm, that initial insight of his is not faulted, however faulted the practical realization of it may be. And for the
"sophisticated" urbanite like Geraint (or Hardy's Angel Clare)
to seek a pure virginal daughter of the soil is a conceit seeded
with a bedlam of contradictions: one so romantically sotted is
projecting a fairy-tale mentality that no authentic woman,
however virginal, could sucessfully cope with; he is looking
for something that, because of his own infidelity hang-up, can
never for long be perceived as faithful; he is trying, through a
rigid and mechanical rubric, to gain successful access to a
living, vibrant object; he is imposing his ego, judgmentally,
upon at least half of mankind.

But the awful irony is that one imprisoned in such cultur-
ally endorsed and apparently high-minded self-delusion is,
inevitably, least capable of the self-awareness indispensable
for freedom from his imprisonment, and in this respect recognition of Geraint as a Guinevere figure takes on deepened
importance. Her role as a May figure helps us to understand
the way Geraint is put together, and her queenly stature gives
a degree of dignity and authority to his peculiar sense of self.
In reverse order, the intense trouble which he has breaking
out of his self-delusion, even with the indispensable help of
Enid, hints at the tragic throes which Guinevere, in her magnified state and alone, will have to endure. Such a comparison, besides helping us to generalize the mythic character of
the problem, keeps Geraint in scale as an Everyman figure
and dissipates some of the reader-impatience which his seeming obtuseness and consequent cruelty may provoke. And the
answer to this question—why is Geraint so obtuse?—brings
us to the heart of the illumination centered in the Geraint-
idylls and to a basic imaginative construct pervasively implanted in *Idylls of the King.*

Geraint as a person suffers from an acute deprivation, a
deprivation that makes the mythmaking process essentially

unavailable to him: he has little or no imagination. The other two elements essential to mythmaking are fully available to him: he has a disposition to believe, and he has the good fortune to find a grand miracle of human experience, Enid-Psyche. But his imagination is dwarfed: he is prudent, meticulous, ceremonious, literal, and incompetent. He is so thoroughly locked into the sensuous mind and at such a low-grade level that he can translate nothing except to its lowest and most literal denominator. He dresses like a gay Lothario because in his stereotyped mind that is what a gay Lothario is supposed to look like. He goes upon his quest in Guinevere's service because, despite his vexation, he can hardly conceive of an alternative. When he hears Enid's voice, it is just a voice. He makes a ceremony of hearing Edyrn's name only from Edyrn himself because that is, quite literally, what he has set as his goal. He is totally insensitive to the true characters of Earl Yniol and his wife because he takes them at a quite matter-of-fact level. He is so rigid on the investiture question and so inaccessible to Enid's and her mother's responses to his heartbreaking, wholly unreasonable mandate because that is the way his mind is set. The repeated trope describing his way of looking at Enid "As careful robins eye the delver's toil" (*MG*, 774, *GE*, 431), while it may soften him a bit, makes him sensuously literally short-goal-oriented. His pathetic rage for proof positive leads him to imprison Enid in his private, exclusive brothel in which he is in turn imprisoned as caretaker; and when that strategy fails him, he literally takes her into the wilderness without any notion of where it is all going to lead. When he applies the discipline to Enid, he simply translates quite literally patterns of the past: she goes in front so that, even in these circumstances, he can keep a perpetual eye on her; she is a drover because she was a Cinderella-slave when he met her; he is imperious in making her a dummy because it was as a voice that she had first charmed him. Enid figures as his savior, his eyes and ears and intuitions, because, though he fights a good brawny fight, he is lost in a wilderness that would otherwise destroy him. His saucy threat to strip Limours, whom he has fabricated as her lover, in front of her so that they may eat honestly is a vulgar double entendre (and

one of his brightest moments); and the spendthrift gran-
diosity with which he disposes of small debts with kings' ran-
soms is a measure of his unimaginative cavalier presumption,
as is the formulaic statement with which he justifies it, "'Ye
will be all the wealthier'" (221, 412). The vulgar but humor-
ous efforts of the genial ruffian Earl Doorm to be stylish with
Enid, "like a mighty patron" (643)—offering her food, wine,
his hand in marriage, half of his earldom, and a whorish
costume—gloss the unconscious Geraint in a faithful if somewhat lurid way; and when he gives her a slight slap, "unknightly with flat hand/However lightly" (716–717), the
imagery shows to what a shrunken plight this pathetic, unimaginative, chauvinistic "man against himself" has brought
her. Enid

> Sent forth a sudden sharp and bitter cry,
> As of a wild thing taken in the trap,
> Which sees the trapper coming through the wood.
>
> (721–723)

Recognition that Geraint suffers from imaginative deprivation seems to floodlight his strange, harsh, but basically
nonmalicious ineptness; and it not only softens the reader's
inclination to be peremptory with him, but also moves his
otherwise confusing tale to the center of the imaginative concerns of *Idylls of the King* as a whole. The simplistic manliness
that he embodies is as far removed from the inscape of human potential that Arthur represents as are the eunuch-like
sexlessness of Percivale and the confused lust-sublimation of
Pelleas. So what begins to emerge in an ever-denser fashion is
not an external fabric of symbolism that would perpetually
threaten to harden into allegory, but buried selves underlying symbols; and the symbols thus become, not things in
themselves, but blazings that help us find our way inward
through a forest of delusions to the existential realities from
which they rise. It places characters like Geraint and Percivale
and Pelleas very close to our own sanctuarial selves and in-
clines us to forgo a judgmental response in favor of an expanding awareness that may help us share at a very personal
level some of the redemptive possibilities inherent in such

awareness. We, in varying degrees, like them, in varying degrees, suffer from an inadequately nurtured imagination, a disposition to get caught up in an infinity of details and to give our lives the semblance of order that our nature demands through a cluster of rubrics that, however seemingly or even truly serviceable they may be, stunt us to the degree that we take them for something more than or different from what they in fact are—symbolic surfacings of our more or less imaginatively refreshed central selves. Each of these protagonists is communicant in a form of religion and is loyal to a fault, but it turns out in each case that the ardor with which they pursue their faith bears very little relation to the authenticity of the faith itself in the context of an ideal manhood.

Geraint's recognition speech is perfectly scaled to his nature. It is not romanticized or sentimentalized, and the reader who has come to understand his personal limitations will see it as wholly apt imaginatively:

> "Enid, I have used you worse than that dead man;
> Done you more wrong: we both have undergone
> That trouble which has left me thrice your own;
> Henceforward I will rather die than doubt.
> And here I lay this penance on myself,
> Not, though mine own ears heard you yestermorn—
> You thought me sleeping, but I heard you say,
> I heard you say, that you were no true wife:
> I swear I will not ask your meaning in it:
> I do believe yourself against yourself,
> And will henceforward rather die than doubt."
>
> (734–744)

He repeats prosaically the literal testimony of his ears—"heard you," "heard you say," "heard you say"—and swears not to ask what Enid meant by saying that she was "no true wife," thus imposing again a ritual of silence, this time on himself. Presumably, too, his three-fold indebtedness will include undocumented faith, uninterrupted service, and unbroken silence on the cause of their "trouble." Enid's reaction is our reaction: she "could not say one tender word/She felt so blunt and stupid at the heart" (745–746).

Yet, despite Geraint's gross limitations as a human being, we can believe him when he says, "'I too would still be honest'" (493). His dullness for good is dullness for evil too, and though he has been prosaically unjust, he has been confused and incompetent rather than malicious. As he has floundered into evil, he has floundered into good: he *did* overthrow Edyrn in his ritual of proud self-destruction and set his foot upon him and give him life (846–849). Edyrn the contemptible has become Edyrn the noble at levels of imaginative awareness inaccessible to Geraint, enunciating the apt gloss on them both: gentleness, "when it weds with manhood, makes the man" (866–868). The "effeminacy" that, as a just chiding, had made Geraint so bullish in his outraged stupidity becomes, rightly understood and properly anchored, his salvation. Thus, with a wry ironic smile, we can accept the jubilant caperings of Geraint's "stately horse," with their conscious inflation of Homeric precedent, and Enid's girlish enactment of heavenly jubilation over a repentant sinner. But even Arthur, who is narrowed, as nowhere else in the poem, to a level of moral domestication by the narrative manner of this idyll, points away from Geraint to Edyrn as the quite extraordinary example of a man who has had

> "Both *grace* and *will* to pick the vicious quitch
> Of *blood* and *custom wholly* out of him,
> And make *all* clean, and plant himself *afresh*."
>   (902–904, emphasis added)

■

No character except Arthur himself could be further removed from the stubble-souled Geraint than the Merlin of *Merlin and Vivien;* and Vivien, daughter of death and death's fallen messenger, is a polar opposite to Enid-Psyche, the fragile Soul emergent into practical life. The domestic concern of the Geraint-idylls, including both the husband-wife center and the peripheral activities of setting up a trustworthy civil service at the end of *Geraint and Enid,* are replaced by fairy-lore undiluted by any mockery of the fairy-tale mentality.

Instead of analogues in classical myth (Cupid and Psyche) and in classical narrative (the epic), we have a legend that flows deep into other channels of story and perception, through dark medieval Europe to a time so prehistoric "'that mountains have risen since/With cities on their flanks'" (673–674). It is medieval, a Breton lay, only in its latter-day literary codifications; but the threads "pass out beyond it," and it seems to touch at their imaginative roots those powers and possibilities which outstrip ordinary human understanding and the very intactness of man, an Ur-world of witches and warlocks and wizards called superstitious in our rational, empirical, civilized codes but nonetheless the persistent source of strange surfacings in our consciousness and wholly empirical nightmares in our dreams.

At its most realistic literary level, it is a January-May fabliau common in both the oral and the written traditions of the Middle Ages, but it is archetypal at a far deeper level of subconsciousness: what about those other possibilities that we have made such practiced efforts to submerge, turning their resistant outcroppings into fairy tale and child-lore? What is our rage for the myopia of scientism but a metaphoric hardening against our fears? What if we were to turn the dial of our structured Manichaean way of dealing with good and evil just slightly and try to get perspective, through altered terms, on a different contention, rooted entirely in Nature herself— not a black-and-white world of either-or, but a gray world of either-either and or-or. And how would that process, followed to a genuine conclusion, condition our way of apprehending, upon our return, the world of our traditional perceptual modes? The narrator of *Merlin and Vivien* takes us on such a journey into alternative perception, with a tragic-grotesque result, thereby moving the whole poem along the strange literary diagonal toward the tragic-sublime; and though he relieves our imaginative anxiety slightly through the literary device of consciously heightened melodrama, there is no winking at his fundamentally serious narrative manner.

Implicit in the January-May motif itself is the literary assumption that May will be the victor—that despite and because of his white hairs, January will fall foolish into comic catastrophe. This of course happens in a way, and the final word of the idyll is "'fool.'" Moreover, the fabliau-rooting of the uneven sexual battle draws through the poem a massive barge of explicit sexuality that constitutes one of its pleasurable dimensions, symbolic at both a superficial and a penetrating level. But by altering some of the normal expectations, both of subject-matter and of literary outcome, the poet alerts the reader against his own species of foolishness, guiding him away from a tempting fabliau-trap.

In Malory and "the old *Romance of Merlin*,"[3] Tennyson's chief sources, Merlin is unequivocally the aggressor, a pathetic old lecher relentlessly pursuing Vivien's maidenhead; in Tennyson's poem, Vivien's maidenhead is long gone, taken first perhaps by Zephyr, the blustery west wind ("sown upon the wind," 45), and often thereafter by the western Mark, and the persevering mock-heroic ritual of seduction is Vivien's. This in turn transforms the motive. In the sources, Merlin's lust after Vivien's body makes him throw himself away on her, easily trading his extraordinary sensual magic for the magic of sensual love, upon which he dotes. In the idyll, Vivien comes to Arthur's court with an apostolic zeal to bring back to Mark "'When I have ferreted out their burrowings,/The hearts of all this Order in mine hand—'" (55–56); and having poisoned the courtly wells but failing to tempt Arthur (hoping, at her most inflated ambition, to bring back even "'one curl of Arthur's golden beard,'" 58), she takes Merlin as her goal, "As fancying that her glory would be great/According to his greatness whom she quenched" (215–216). Hence Merlin's relatively simple, straightforward motive in the sources is, in the shift to Vivien as seducer, transformed to something much more complex and ominous, all her ceremony of sensuality being a mere subterfuge. The ultimate literary outcome, the effect upon the reader, is vastly altered too: the comic effect is as transparent as Vivien's sexual deception and is counterpointed against a ground tone that is both pathetic and terrifying, thus producing the tragic grotesque as the center of aesthetic response. The reader's discomfort at a rather profound level over the outcome of the contest—how could this be?—sends him on an exploratory quest, part curious, part anxious.

Merlin is Vivien's aptest antagonist in the Arthurian world. Neither one is a devil figure in any literal or even symbolic sense, but they are both alien, in vastly different degrees, to the ultimate Arthurian effort.[4] Merlin had been grandly serviceable according to his peculiar capacity, free of all conscious malignity, a precursor and enabler; but this capacity has reached its outer limits, and needs have surfaced in the world of Arthur and his Round Table for which Merlin has no magic touch. An ontological gulf has ultimately revealed itself between Arthurianism and Merlinism, and Merlin shows himself vulnerable to self-destructive needs that simply are no temptation to Arthur. That Vivien leaves Arthur untouched and yet is the total undoing of Merlin suggests that she is the supreme gloss on Merlin and thereby enables us to perceive that, despite the vast degrees of difference between them, Merlin and Vivien are of the same tribe and that Arthur is the quintessential representative of a *different order of being*. Although Merlin is not possessed by the "perfect" Hate of Vivien, he does not possess the "perfect" Love of Arthur either, and so, despite all his wizardry, he lacks the ultimate resource to prevent his becoming Vivien's victim. Merlin's "natural magic," to use Matthew Arnold's tropes, does not compensate for his lack of an ontological "moral profundity."[5] He is a child of nature, and it is to nature's womb that he returns, not to an "island-valley of Avilion" to heal him of his "grievous wound."

The images that are implanted in the opening lines of *Merlin and Vivien* are all images of nature—the "storm," the "winds," the "wild woods," the "oak" *like* "a tower of wild masonwork," the seduction (1–5). It is grand, old, and hollow, a world which "the High God" has not entered at an ontologically moral level. It is man's sensual frame but not his real reality; and although its voice is "The voice of days of old and days to be" (*PA*, 135), preceding his coming and existent beyond his passing, it is in itself an order of reality different from that of man. It is to this wholly natural world that both Merlin and Vivien belong, and it is within its grand but limited terms that their contest takes place.

Merlin is measured in the idyll against two other patently comparable figures—the "wandering voice,/A minstrel of

Caerleon" (8–9) at the beginning and the wizard of his own inner legend (553–648)—and this measuring turns upon both the total curve of the narrative and the specific credentials by which Merlin is characterized:

> the most famous man of all those times,
> Merlin, who knew the range of all their arts,
> Had built the King his havens, ships, and halls,
> Was also Bard, and knew the starry heavens;
> The people called him Wizard. . . .
>
> (164–168)

Merlin is the only one of these three who is given a name in the context of the reiterated burden "life and use and name and fame." His fame is also stressed, as is his use, and his life is the central issue of the story as a whole.

But the tonal qualities with which Merlin is described, matter-of-fact and empirical, are very different from the hieratic projection of the minstrel of Caerleon:

> For he that always bare in bitter grudge
> The slights of Arthur and his Table, Mark
> The Cornish King, had heard a wandering voice,
> A minstrel of Caerleon by strong storm
> Blown into shelter at Tintagil, say
> That out of naked knightlike purity
> Sir Lancelot worshipt no unmarried girl
> But the great Queen herself, fought in her name,
> Sware by her—vows like theirs, that high in heaven
> Love most, but neither marry, nor are given
> In marriage, angels of our Lord's report.
>
> (6–16)

This gentle, reverent, imaginative voice introduces a whole new perspective on the Lancelot-Guinevere relationship, and under Vivien's hypocritical questioning, the minstrel translates it "innocently" to encompass a small but distinct subculture "In Arthur's household":

> "Ay, by some few—ay, truly—youths that hold
> It more beseems the perfect virgin knight

To worship woman as true wife beyond
All hopes of gaining, than as maiden girl.
They place their pride in Lancelot and the Queen.
So passionate for an utter purity
Beyond the limit of their bond, are these,
For Arthur bound them not to singleness.
Brave hearts and clean! and yet—God guide them—
    young."

(21–29)

Vivien and Mark react violently to this naïve, high-minded exaggeration of the Arthurian image, and their attack upon it is fueled by their rage against virtue thus magnified beyond endurable reality. But their determination to reduce it to "'That old true filth, and bottom of the well'" (47) does not obscure it as a beautiful imagining that reaches toward an analogy in high heaven and a state of grace that will fail in practical life but is simply unavailable, even in their imaginings, to Mark and Vivien *and Merlin*. His wizardry is nature-bound, and he has no resources whereby to contribute to the purely human struggle with an ontologically discrete morality in which Arthur's household is now engaged. Merlin's keen sense of role-exhaustion—the exhaustion of a great founder who finds himself irrelevant to the delicate coordinates of fruition—is one of the sources of his "great melancholy." He returns from his three-day journey into the hell of his archaic self unrefreshed.

The parallels between Merlin and the wizard of his legend are much closer, though as he himself says laughingly, they are not quite "like" (616). He belongs to the direct line of the "'little glassy-headed hairless man'" (618) and is the inheritor of his "book," the trustee of his wizardry. But Merlin's sense of self has been very different from that of his forefather in the "'great wild.'" Instead of living on grass, avoiding wine, flesh, and every "'sensual wish'" and pursuing single-mindedly his apprehensions of the world of ghosts, learning "'their elemental secrets, powers/And forces'" (630–631), Merlin has lent his energy to Camelot's forms of "enthusiastic activity," and he has drunk wine, loved women, and sung songs. But what he has done, voluntarily, for his King is, in the end, not so very different from what the ancient wizard, "'by force . . . dragged . . . to the King'" (638) did for his: the object of their wizardry lies "'as dead,/And [has] lost all use of life'" (642–643), as does the Camelot of his dark vision. And as the ancient wizard refused his King's "'proffer of the league of golden mines,/The province of the hundred miles of coast,/The palace and the princess'" (644-646), Merlin has no capacity to receive, not being ontologically human, Arthur's "secret," his inscape of human potential. Though built on the grandest scale, Merlin is an Ur-figure and cannot, like Arthur when his work is done, gain access to those "'moments when he feels he cannot die,/And knows himself no vision to himself,/Nor the high God a vision, nor that One/ Who rose again. . .'" (*HG*, 912–915).

Merlin is also measured by Vivien's song (385–396), as he himself shows by quickly contrasting it with the song the knights sang at the wedding of Arthur and Guinevere and by his admission of the effects her song has had on him:

> "But, Vivien, when you sang me that sweet rhyme,
> I felt as though you knew this cursèd charm,
> Were proving it on me, and that I lay
> And felt them slowly ebbing, name and fame."
>
> (432–435)

The song, as a translation of Lancelot's state through Vivien's state to Merlin's state, is rich in the most complex kinds of irony. Vivien, of course, is trying to break down Merlin's resistance to telling her the charm, and she does this through a pretty show of scholastic wit that highlights, not her wit, but her tenderness; hence she is witty enough to suspend wit itself in charm. And though Merlin is not ultimately susceptible at this level, her technique is very affective to this ancient nature-mage:

> And Merlin looked and half believed her true,
> So tender was her voice, so fair her face,
> So sweetly gleamed her eyes behind her tears
> Like sunlight on the plain behind a shower. . . .
>
> (398–401)

But Vivien's strategic use of the song simultaneously draws into its literary affectiveness the reader's keen awareness of the resonances it has had for Lancelot in his soul-rending dilemma of fidelity in collision with fidelity; and the new perspective provided at the beginning of *Merlin and Vivien* by the minstrel of Caerleon has sophisticated that grand moral dilemma to a finely tuned and penetrating level. This in turn makes it all the more crucial as a measuring of Merlin: he has no faith to turn to, since the usefulness that had made his fame purposeful and his name pleasurable has, at least in this cycle of time, exhausted itself. As he had altered the young squire's shield from "'I follow fame'" to "'Rather use than fame,'" so had he shaped his life: "'Use gave me Fame at first, and Fame again/Increasing gave me use. Lo, there my boon!'" (491–492) "'I rather dread,'" he says, "'the loss of use than fame'" (517). Merlin is a half-believer—half-believing Vivien, Arthur, himself; and Vivien's song, with its reiteratred emphasis on the ultimate effects of a faulted faith, induces in him a strong sense of his imprisonment in his own nature, as if she knew and had worked the "cursèd charm" on him. Arthur has been an extraordinary experience in Merlin's life, magnetizing all his talents and enthusiasms. Merlin has not been bookish in the literalist sense of Pelleas, but a book has been at the center of his capacities, the book of nature's magic lore. It is a book of revelation of a different order from Arthur's "book," but it has brought Merlin, in his rituals of dedication, to the end-point of his ontology and allowed him to look, finally in devastating melancholy, at possibilities unavailable to his placement in the mysterious order of things. It is in that spirit of foreshortened magnification that he looks across the unbridgeable ontological gulf and expresses his deep love and admiration for Arthur, one embodied ideal acknowledging the superior magnificence of quite another ideal:

"O true and tender! O my liege and King!
O selfless man and stainless gentleman,
Who wouldst against thine own eye-witness fain
Have all men true and leal, all women pure;
How, in the mouths of base interpreters,

From over-fineness not intelligible
To things with every sense as false and foul
As the poached filth that floods the middle street,
Is thy white blamelessness accounted blame!"

(789–797)

Despite its unequivocal devotion, Merlin's hymn of praise is that of a phenomenologist whose "own eye-witness" perceives that Arthur's truth, tenderness, selflessness, blameless perfection are rooted in something that contradicts empirical eyewitnessing. He does not understand it, and his eulogy has the tone of a lament over a mystery closed to him.

Thus the defeat of Merlin becomes a refined necessity of the poem's warring tensions, and the central critical question is the imaginative aptness of Vivien as the agent of that defeat. Critical perspicacity requires, of course, that all elements be kept in focus, and for this Vivien herself gives the cue in her reference to the closing in of "'fate and craft and folly'" (57).

Fate operates as a cluster. Besides the heightened motivation given Mark and Vivien by the accident of the minstrel's marooning at Tintagel and the crucial depression brought on by Merlin's foresight of his own and his work's end, there is the ambient moment of the court itself—"While all the heathen lay at Arthur's feet,/And no quest came, but all was joust and play" (142–143)—a summertime of full-blown sensuousness when temptation and fantasy have longest rein and snakes go abroad. Moreover, the tittering way in which Vivien's presence is treated at court ("It made the laughter of an afternoon," 161) suggests a condition of moral slovenliness. Guinevere, on whom Vivien is a discreet and distant gloss, is enjoying her sensuous frame as an Edenic May figure—"All glittering like May sunshine on May leaves/In green and gold, and plumed with green" (86–87)—and she and Lancelot are so wrapped up in their courtly diversions that they have lost their circumspection and hardly see the serpent in the flowers. Even Arthur, though "Vext at a rumour . . ./Of some corruption crept among his knights" (151–152), gazes "blankly" on the thing itself and passes by.

Folly, of course, is centered in Merlin, but it is also insinuated in the cultish virginity-in-singleness of a small number of the younger knights; and it is tragically foolish for Lancelot and Guinevere to think that their summer-idyll will last, as Vivien's song poignantly reminds us. So the contest of Vivien's *craft* with Merlin's famous craft (by which, we remember, Arthur was crowned) is enclosed in this combined atmosphere of fate and folly.

Vivien's strength lies in her singleness and fixity of purpose. She sees herself as hate—

> "As Love, if Love be perfect, casts out fear,
> So Hate, if Hate be perfect, casts out fear."
> (40–41)

And though, like Milton's Satan, she has just a flickering awareness of self-deprivation ("'ride, and dream/The mortal dream that never yet was mine,'" 114–115), her apostolic zeal is unwavering. In this she is, in a sense, Arthur's mighty opposite, but her contest is with Merlin, thus preserving the non-Manichaean character of the struggle. We are also led to believe, relatively early, that Vivien will be the victor, and this serves the classical literary purpose of concentrating our attention on the manner of the contest rather than on the story line.

One reason for this belief is Merlin's self-confessed foolishness in telling her of the charm:

> For Merlin once had told her of a charm,
> The which if any wrought on anyone
> With woven paces and with waving arms,
> The man so wrought on ever seemed to lie
> Closed in the four walls of a hollow tower,
> From which was no escape for evermore;
> And none could find that man for evermore,
> Nor could he see but him who wrought the charm
> Coming and going, and he lay as dead
> And lost to life and use and name and fame.
> (203–212)

Vivien, who is also a nature-throw at the lowest level of evolutionary mobility and an imprisoned phenomenologist, perceives immediately the perfection of this particular charm for her purposes. She knows that matter, however manipulated, cannot be destroyed; but she knows, too, that matter can be frozen into inertness and thus be "lost to life and use and name and fame." Moreover, as a phenomenologist, she believes that "Knowledge is of things we see" (*In Memoriam,* Prologue), and the charm promises a way of enclosing men in a hollow perceptual tower, seeing and being seen only by the charmer. Thus not only Merlin but all mankind would be subject to her wizardry if they did not practice eternal vigilance, and Merlin's careless wakelessness in telling her of the charm promises, through poetic justice, that he will pay for it with eternal sleep.

Another reason for believing that Vivien will be victor is contained in the second line of her song: "'Faith and unfaith can ne'er be equal powers'" (386). Merlin's mind, which can hardly doubt his devastating foresight, is yet clouded with a doubt analogous to Arthur's condition in his final hours. He has doubts about who he is, the purpose of his life, the exact nature of the King whom he has served, the love that warms his ancient veins, this kittenish cajoler who has broken up his great melancholy but who has also become complicit, in his "mind-mist," with the great wave, "'Dark in the glass of some presageful mood'" (293), that is about to break over him and his world. Vivien, on the other hand, is the "fair" beginning of another cycle of time and has no such doubts or half-beliefs.

The snake-imagery pervasive in the piece is many-faceted, appealing to both our prurience and our anxiety and showing that our own phenomenological tendencies are hard to keep entirely intact. Most of us have been harmed less by snakes than by any other living creature, and yet most of us share a common human dread of them greater than our dread of any other living thing. They are sexual in the most manifest as well as the most latent way, and they fill us with fascinated disgust. Merlin, on the other hand, being a nature figure himself, feels none of that disgust, but lets Vivien crawl all over him, her "satin-shining" body (222) writhing around his ankles, in his lap, about his neck. In fact, his sensual blood is warmed by her, his self-induced anger freeing him of all fear of her when she leaps from his lap "Stiff as a viper frozen" (843); and we need not blink at the phallic quality of the image since the whole process in which Merlin and Vivien are engaged will end in a thunderous symbolic sexual climax, the "storm" that "was coming" in the opening half-line. Their struggle has keen sexual coordinates, and Merlin, an old goat (276) in a double entendre, is "prurient for a proof" (485) of his "potency."

Throughout, Merlin makes a proper show of "wit," of course, accusing his maligners of using against him the very "wits" he has given them: "'for men sought to prove me vile,/ Because I fain had given them greater wits:/And then did Envy call me Devil's son'" (493–495). But Vivien, not afflicted by Merlin's doubt or Merlin's prurient need, is witty enough to be unwitty ("'these unwitty wandering wits of mine,'" 344). She leads him, through a strategy of witty witlessness, along a continuum of emotions that explode in the sexual act by which he "dies." The orchestration of his emotional intensity begins slowly and builds to the inevitable climax: kitten-like playfulness and girlish petulance induce bemused toler-ance;[6] vampish flattery and transparent devotion beget a skeptical but faintly felt wish for love; ritualized adoration and coy pranks lead to a more cheerful mood and the warmth of gratitude; devoted service and maidenly meekness provoke a sense of obligation and guilt over his earlier misconception; an appeal for unalloyed faith and trust brings about a confes-sion of his own foolishness and of a generic male distrust of women; lyric tenderness beguiles him into an inclination to believe her true and to fall under her charm, restrained by half-indignation at the uxoriousness she is drawing him into; a sudden show of jealousy is matched by a sudden show of macho pride; anger at not being trusted with the one gift she craves brings forth an offer of a substitute gift; a show of bride-like faith and wifely devotion is met with expansive, genial good cheer; disdain for his determination to withhold his gift and a resolution to discover it on her own make him react with patronizing dismissiveness and a retort that what "they say" about her is probably true; self-righteous anger and a one-by-one attack on her maligners stimulate a one-by-one defense of his "friends," climaxing with a hymn of praise to his one "perfect" friend; a scurrilous, generalized attack on the whole lot provokes a haughty withdrawal into self-justification and a spluttered downgrading of her character and her motives; murderous rage followed by a downpour of self-pity over her heroic efforts and devotion, all totally misunderstood and unappreciated, leads to capitulation and a spontaneous offer of solacing shelter in his shielding and soothing arms; a martyr-like acceptance of his refuge, quickly followed by a withdrawal into her loveless integrity unless he gives her the gift as earnest of his love, is met with blanknesses; sudden jeopardy and genuine fright, forcing a hasty retreat into his arms in a wild search for safety, triggers climax, subsidence, defeat.

That the climax is symbolically sexual is so forcefully insinuated that one hesitates to detail the tumultuous patterning. There is striking and "furrowing" and "javelining/With darted spikes." Merlin looks and sees "The tree that shone white-listed through the gloom" (937). Vivien is "dazzled by the livid-flickering fork,/And deafened with the stammering cracks and claps" (939–940). She

> clung to him and hugged him close;
> And called him dear protector in her fright,
> Nor yet forgot her practice in her fright,
> But wrought upon his mood and hugged him close.
> The pale blood of the wizard at her touch
> Took gayer colours, like an opal warmed.
> She blamed herself for telling hearsay tales:
> She shook from fear, and for her fault she wept
> Of petulancy; she called him lord and liege,
> Her seer, her bard, her silver star of eve,
> Her God, her Merlin, the one passionate love
> Of her whole life; and ever overhead
> Bellowed the tempest, and the rotten branch
> Snapt in the rushing of the river-rain

Above them; and in change of glare and gloom
Her eyes and neck glittering went and came;
Till now the storm, its burst of passion spent,
Moaning and calling out of other lands,
Had left the ravaged woodland yet once more
To peace. . . .

(943–962)

For what he has taken, Merlin pays the highest price: "over-talked and overworn," in the subsidence of his passion, Merlin "yielded, told her all the charm, and slept" (963–964). This fervid copulation in "an oak, so hollow, huge and old" (3) in the middle of a tumultuous storm draws the lowest and the highest form of sensual nature into a grotesque but appropriate poetic unity, as the "old order" of nature also "changeth, yielding place to new."

And how does the process followed in *Merlin and Vivien* condition our way of apprehending the world of our traditional perceptual modes? It reminds us that the sensual mind, however gifted, is not an adequate measure of our humanness; that natural magic, be it ever so spectacular, belongs to an order that is ultimately self-enclosed; and that man's moral nature, despite its profound precariousness, is the center of his identity and his hope.

■

Lancelot and Elaine moves the tragic grotesque of *Merlin and Vivien* measurably forward, along our strange literary diagonal, toward the tragic sublime of *Guinevere*. Not only is *Lancelot and Elaine* exquisitely placed in the total poem's structure; it is also narrated by a supremely refined aesthetic consciousness. All of the rough, melodramatically heightened, sexually violent, disquieting naturalistic agony of the Ur-tale of *Merlin and Vivien* is modulated into gracious stylistic nuances of the most delicate sort, as though the gulf separating bestial coupling in the wilds and man's faulted but civilized and potentially noble moral negotiations has been crossed. The reader welcomes his return to a world in which man is the style and man—his values, his self-awarenesses, his pathetic simplicities, his tragic errors—becomes again the renewed center of concern. At the heart of *Lancelot and Elaine* is a bold, wholly serious, and crucially literary subject—the imaginative, moral difference between tragedy and pathos; and the romantic, novelistic tale which enables it is not itself a tragedy, but a grand overture to tragedy—an aesthetic clarification and cleansing of the reader's imaginative and moral perceptions in preparation for the terrible truths about to emerge.

The pathos is centered in Elaine, a strange, fragile woodland flower—"the fair," "the loveable," "the lily maid"—who magnetizes our sympathies at an excruciating level, but whom we misinterpret at our imaginative/moral peril. The total curve of her tenderly pathetic story releases a host of infinitely complex possibilities that seem to sensitize our mechanisms of awareness in the way that only music usually does, and indeed polyphonic counterpoint is a firm analogy for the manner in which her story is poetically processed. At the center of that story is a song of lyric counterpoint—"The Song of Love and Death"—in which Elaine as a child-poetess, lyric songbird, nestling nightingale, distant daughter of Sappho sets melody against melody, theme against theme, structure against structure, wit against willfulness, simplicity against complexity, vowel against vowel, phrase against phrase in the subtlest modulations, a counterpoint resolved through the monotonic sound and theme patterned in the final rhymes of the four stanzas—"I . . . die . . . I . . . die.'"

"Sweet is true love though given in vain, in vain;
And sweet is death who puts an end to pain:
I know not which is sweeter, no, not I.

"Love, art thou sweet? then bitter death must be:
Love, thou art bitter; sweet is death to me.
O Love, if death be sweeter, let me die.

"Sweet love, that seems not made to fade away,
Sweet death, that seems to make us loveless clay,
I know not which is sweeter, no, not I.

"I fain would follow love, if that could be;
I needs must follow death, who calls for me;
Call and I follow, I follow! let me die."

                                    (1000–1011)

This note of monotonic inevitability, though it suggests an appropriate imaginative/moral positioning in relation to her story, makes us imaginatively available to the melodic *contrappunto* in the life of this Anglicized variation on the *Donna di Scalotta*. As a metaphor, she seems to encompass the very perception of Romanticism as strangeness wedded to beauty. She is both fragile and adamantine, inducing a peculiar combination of pity and fear. Though she "lived in fantasy," she is also brutally matter-of-fact, setting up her relentless *either-or* dichotomy and cutting through even the most affectionate efforts to assign blame for her plight:

"Fret not yourself, dear brother, nor be wroth,
Seeing it is no more Sir Lancelot's fault
Not to love me, than it is mine to love
Him of all men who seem to me the highest."

                                    (1067–1070)

She is delicately childlike, wooing her father's indulgence while nestled in his lap, but her willfulness is rooted in the character of *la belle dame sans merci*. She is both a motherless waif and a Wagnerian goddess, a lovelorn adolescent and a Florence Nightingale. Although her fragile humanness is not at issue in her explicit story, she fills the lords and ladies of Camelot with a terrible dread as of the enchanted Fairy Queen, and she completes the singing of her tender, fatal song on the shrill, wailing note of a Banshee's piercing shriek:

High with the last line scaled her voice, and this,
All in a fiery dawning wild with wind
That shook her tower, the brother heard, and thought
With shuddering, "Hark the Phantom of the house
That ever shrieks before a death," and called
The father, and all three in hurry and fear
Ran to her, and lo! the blood-red light of dawn
Flared on her face, she shrilling, "Let me die!"

                                    (1012–1019)

Elaine's fatal monism does not prevent her from being humble and tender; and despite the severely limited world in which she has moved, she has a finely tuned moral taste and rebels against the vulgar efforts of Gawain at ritualistic amorous suaveness. Her youth is no impediment to an absolute integrity, and she bedecks herself equally for love and death:

> "If I be loved, these are my festal robes,
> If not, the victim's flowers before he fall."
> (904–905)

Lancelot does not translate the symbolism of her "favour" which he binds on his helmet, though it has as intense a relevance to his relationship to Guinevere as to Elaine's relationship to him—pearls of pure beauty on a field of passionate sexuality; and her ultimate choice—death through willfulness—is virginal in its intact simplicity. She will be deflowered by Lancelot, as either wife or paramour, or she will be deflowered by death. When faced finally with no choice but the latter, she stages a nuptial funeral worthy of Götterdämmerung—complete with the bed on which she "died/For Lancelot's love" (1110–1111), both bed and body decked with a queen's richness. She has a chariot-bier, a nuptial-funeral barge, a Charon-like ferryman, a love letter, and a lily:

> the dead,
> Oared by the dumb, went upward with the flood—
> In her right hand the lily, in her left
> The letter—all her bright hair streaming down—
> And all the coverlid was cloth of gold
> Drawn to her waist, and she herself in white
> All but her face, and that clear-featured face
> Was lovely, for she did not seem as dead,
> But fast asleep, and lay as though she smiled.
> (1146–1154)

The love letter, which Arthur reads to the awed assemblage, is the tenderest possible petition in a spirit of heartbreaking literalness; and the burial in the richest shrine available is as much nuptial as funereal, "with gorgeous obsequies,/And mass, and rolling music, like a queen" (1324–1325). Her tomb

becomes her nuptial palace in which, through art, her love
for Lancelot is eternalized:

> "Let her tomb
> Be costly, and her image thereupon,
> And let the shield of Lancelot at her feet
> Be carven, and her lily in her hand.
> And let the story of her dolorous voyage
> For all true hearts be blazoned on her tomb
> In letters of gold and azure!"
>
> (1328–1334)

Thus the story of Elaine's simple, fatal love for Lancelot is
forever frozen in images, sad and bittersweet.

This art-perpetuation motif, reminiscent of the lovers in
Keats' *Ode on a Grecian Urn,* is reflective on the idyll as a
whole: *Lancelot and Elaine* is also a perpetuation-piece, freezing in a poetic artifact a blighted moment of human concurrence. Moreover, art is a recurrent reference-point in the
narrative. The most conspicuous illustration of this is the
poem's analogue in *The Lady of Shalott,* in which Tennyson
had earlier explored the art-reality coordinates of awareness,
and the parallels are valid. Elaine is "cursed" with a willful
nature; she withdraws to her "ivory tower," where she fanta-
sizes elaborately; the "case of silk" that she decorates for Lancelot's shield has its counterpart in the Lady's storied tapestry;
it is Lancelot who, here again unintentionally, motivates her
fatal decision; like the Lady, she approaches Camelot in a
mysterious funeral barge; and as Lancelot had in the earlier
poem "mused a little space," in the idyll he "later came and
mused at her" (1260). *The Lady of Shalott,* of course, does not
provide a way of "reading" Elaine's story, the context being
greatly altered and the reverberations much more elaborate;
but it does provide a significant signal that the idyll has a
deep aesthetic rooting.

The romantic novel or romantic narrative poem, of which
the first half of the nineteenth century produced hundreds
of examples, also seems to serve as a literary analogue. There
is the romantic castle, far from the "rich city," to which the
sad nobleman finds his melancholy way; the fair angelic

maiden who becomes desperately enamored of a strange, battle-scarred hero; the quest for a jewel of inestimable value; the motif of the disguised identity; a near-fatal mock-battle; the long lingering of the hero between life and death, with the angelic maiden as his restorative daughter of mercy; the ill-fated love of the woodland beauty for the grand knight pledged to another in a strange unholy way; the violent passion of the great lady with whom he has his fated bond; the sleep-death of the woodland beauty; the sad wisdom learned by the hero about life, women, and himself.

There are recurrent references, in addition to that to Elaine's song-making, to art and art objects: to "painter" (330), "carven work" and "design" (434, 439), "carven flower" (547), "picture" (985), "statue" (1164); and "the great diamond in the diamond jousts" (31) upon which the story turns is the highest object of the jeweler's art and has a legendary immortality as an indestructible artifact.

But the aesthetic rooting of the idyll manifests itself in an even more significant way in its painterly quality. *Lancelot and Elaine* is so rich in poetic paintings that it must be called the most *picturesque* of the idylls in the special sense of that term in nineteenth-century aesthetics. Noteworthy examples can be found in lines 347–354, 390–394, 402–410, 427–442, 477–488, 1146–1154. These verbal pictures, drawn by rather strict analogy with canvas paintings, momentarily frame a scene and draw the eye's attention to it with such a quick particularity that a new authority is given to the eye, and we get closer to the experience than a fluid impression would bring us:

> she drew
> Nearer and stood. He looked, and more amazed
> Than if seven men had set upon him, saw
> The maiden standing in the dewy light.
> He had not dreamed she was so beautiful.
> Then came on him a sort of sacred fear,
> For silent, though she greeted him, she stood
> Rapt on his face as if it were a God's.
>
> (347–354)

Time is momentarily suspended, and we see him seeing her seeing. Our understanding of their juxtaposition in the idyll as a whole is suddenly and immeasurably deepened. Then the momentary freezing of time merges again in the fluidity of the narrative.

Even an action-painting internalizes its action in a frame, and we suddenly comprehend Lancelot's grandeur in the jousts as no mere assertiveness could make us do. In this instance, it is a painting reinforced by a painting, a picture framed by a picture:

> They couched their spears and pricked their steeds,
>   and thus,
> Their plumes driven backward by the wind they made
> In moving, all together down upon him
> Bare, as a wild wave in the wide North-sea,
> Green-glimmering toward the summit, bears, with all
> Its stormy crests that smoke against the skies,
> Down on a bark, and overbears the bark,
> And him that helms it, so they overbore
> Sir Lancelot and his charger, and a spear
> Down-glancing lamed the charger, and a spear
> Pricked sharply his own cuirass, and the head
> Pierced through his side, and there snapped, and
>   remained.
>
> (477–488)

This pattern of crisp pictorial suspension and quick reimmersion in the narrative flow seems to be consciously counterpointed to the hard, indestructible solidity both of the immortal diamond and of the ornate mausoleum in which Elaine is entombed and thus to engender an awareness about the appropriate relationship of art to life. Art—at its best the quintessence of man's formal awarenesses—necessarily freezes time and threatens to induce a false perceptual reality. Art frees itself from time when it releases in its devotees the capacity to perceive even art *sub specie aeternitatis*, the frozen image being only the most immediately conspicuous dimension of art (*art as artifact*); art's latent capacity to release psychic motion, to trigger inexhaustible possibilities, to make thinking men think (Carlyle) and intelligent men more intelligent (Arnold), is its essential character (*art as an embodiment of the soul's becomings*).

Elaine's efforts, however exquisite, to freeze reality, to make of life a simple fine art, are centered in a delicate and enchanting fantasy, but they are ultimately fantastical. As Lancelot's effort to hide his true self under the pretext of "'joust[ing] unknown of all, and learn[ing]/If his old prowess were in aught decayed'" (581–582) is judged "fantastical" by Arthur, so Elaine's ritual of setting up a rigid, indestructible dichotomy between love and death in which love is imaged in such a personal but frozen way is human and romantic and doom-fixated and horrifying, like the beautiful imagining of the young knights who are "'So passionate for an utter purity/Beyond the limit of their bond'" (*MV*, 26–27). It is reductive of life, a fantasy that something so grand and turbulent and rich in possibilities for both good and evil (say, Lancelot) can be brought down to the measure of the willful illusions of a tender adolescent with no experience of life's large realities and no capacity to negotiate outward beyond her frozen immature personal structures (say, Elaine).

Elaine is a slight Edenic figure frozen, like a diamond, in a paradise of simplicity who chooses to die rather than to grow up and wend her way, like the first humans, into the trials and tribulations and successes of an ontologically moral life; and though we may sympathize with her at the level of the keenest pain, we must finally draw back and see her as pathetic and morally shrunken and horrifying because to the degree that we yield to her life-art illusion, we are in danger of shrinking too. Hers is a species of monistically aesthetic Romanticism current, not only in the nineteenth century, but archetypally; and in the hands of any but a first-rate imagination—one that comprehends both beauty and truth through a large and resonant knowledge of life—it subjects life to a fatally faulted beauty and a fatally faulted apprehension of life's truth. Art is not philosophy, and beauty is not excluded from the young; but an art that slips into pathos in the guise of tragedy and tries to make pathos ingratiatingly beautiful has not only ignored the terrifying purgative truth of an authentic tragic apprehension, but has also crippled man's one indispensable resource for working out for himself "a supreme Dénouement"—namely, a nurtured and purified imagination.

Against the Romantic, aesthetic pathos of Elaine is set the "terrible beauty" of the classical, life-scarred, authentic, precarious tragic poise of Lancelot. Indeed, Elaine's pathetic incompetence in dealing with life that turns so desperately and fixedly to Lancelot may be symbolically fueled by inadequacy's subconscious yearning for self-fulfillment—pathos aspiring to be tragedy's wife or paramour. Lancelot declines, because he must, Elaine's pathetic pleadings, though he understands her incredible beauty, the self-imprisoning nature of her fixation, the incomparable quality of service rendered him by her, the unparalleled devotion of her love, through which he attains an altered view of womankind. Even the recurrent motif of the-might-have-been is not necessarily sentimental, since his nature wedded to her nature at a perfect moment in personal time could in truth have scaled their destinies differently. But that synchronization did not in fact take place, and Lancelot, as he himself knows, is simply not free to leap from a tragic entanglement into an alternative fantasy.

And yet, their different but mingled pain is not wasted: Lancelot emerges from all the associated experiences of Elaine with a more realistic understanding of his own personal plight and with a firmer resolution to take moral action. Although he does not fall into the romantic trough of dying through willfulness, a variation on that theme finds its tragic counterpart in his austerely articulated will to die if he fails at self-purgation. It is Lancelot's longest and most crucial language-exercise in self-placement; and while it does not complete the tragic curve, it brings Lancelot center-stage as a protagonist fully capable of a tragic grandeur that, whatever the configuration of catastrophe, cannot whimper and fail:

> "Ah simple heart and sweet,
> Ye loved me, damsel, surely with a love
> Far tenderer than my Queen's. Pray for thy soul?

Ay, that will I. Farewell too—now at last—
Farewell, fair lily. 'Jealousy in love?'
Not rather dead love's harsh heir, jealous pride?
Queen, if I grant the jealousy as of love,
May not your crescent fear for name and fame
Speak, as it waxes, of a love that wanes?
Why did the King dwell on my name to me?
Mine own name shames me, seeming a reproach,
Lancelot, whom the Lady of the Lake
Caught from his mother's arms—the wondrous one
Who passes through the vision of the night—
She chanted snatches of mysterious hymns
Heard on the winding waters, eve and morn
She kissed me saying, 'Thou art fair, my child,
As a king's son,' and often in her arms
She bare me, pacing on the dusky mere.
Would she had drowned me in it, where'er it be!
For what am I? what profits me my name
Of greatest knight? I fought for it, and have it:
Pleasure to have it, none; to lose it, pain;
Now grown a part of me: but what use in it?
To make men worse by making my sin known?
Or sin seem less, the sinner seeming great?
Alas for Arthur's greatest knight, a man
Not after Arthur's heart! I needs must break
These bonds that so defame me: not without
She wills it: would I, if she willed it? nay,
Who knows? but if I would not, then may God,
I pray him, send a sudden Angel down
To seize me by the hair and bear me far,
And fling me deep in that forgotten mere,
Among the tumbled fragments of the hills."

                                        (1382–1416)

This speech is the closest Lancelot is brought in *Idylls of the King* to the great recognition speech of Guinevere, when she makes her imaginative/moral breakthrough as Arthur departs in tragic gloom to the "last, dim, weird battle of the west" (*PA*, 94). Hence, it is here if anywhere that we must look for the ultimate tragic patterning of Lancelot.

The veiled allusion to Marlowe's Faustus—Lancelot's prayer, if he fails, for the anonymity of Faustus' drop of water in the great ocean—guides our search. Lancelot's self-awareness emerges out of his vivid consciousness of two contrasting images—that of the simple, sweet, tender, pure "fair lily" Elaine, which induces him to prayer and spiritual humility, and that of the jealous, harsh, majestically proud Guinevere, which distances him somewhat from his love-delusion and leads him to a threshold recognition that she is self-deceived in naming her late passionate turbulence. This in turn enables him to center on himself—his origins, his aspirations—and to begin, in an oblique manner appropriate to his present state and to his great nature, to allow patterns of his true self-lineaments to surface lightly.

If we assume for the moment that the Lady of the Lake is not literally a *deus ex machina* but a metaphor of self-shaping, then Lancelot becomes, from earliest boyhood, a lonely motherless child (like Elaine, like Guinevere) who filled the vacuousness of his life with dreams of personal grandeur, saying to himself in his homeless walks along "the dusky mere" some equivalent to "'Thou art fair, my child,/As a king's son.'" Thus as Elaine became fixated on love, Lancelot became fixated on greatness. He was not trivial like Gawain or evil like Modred or gross like Mark. Indeed, his ambition for greatness brought him, by the most gracious accident, into the service of Arthur and magnified it a hundredfold, giving it a ritual of supreme purpose that blended easily with its benign high-mindedness. Still, it was rooted in pride, in personal ambition, in ego-fantasy, and an aspect of it, though he was not in fact a "king's son," was to fill the role of a "king's son."

When he was sent as a king's emissary to bring home a king's daughter for a king's queen, she looked favorably upon him, and he was able to fulfill, at a close but discreet distance, his fantasy of being a "king's son" with his own queen—a king-*manqué* with a queen-*manqué*. He has long been troubled by this fantastic violation of fealty to the true King, but he has been the victim of his own myth, of the dream out of which he has created a seemingly indispensable reality, and so the war within him between truth and fantasy has been a drawn battle, troubling enough but indecisive, deflowering his name, his greatness, his peace of mind, but not moving him to the greater grandeur of letting the fantasy go and settling for the naked truth. Now the strange experience of Elaine has, at one deeply affective level, clarified his understanding of the deadly character of fantasy and moved him, at least momentarily, into a new medium of perceptual clarity in which his own variation on her *either-or* construct becomes operative: he *either* "'must break/These bonds that so defame'" him *or*, God willing, die. But even with his new perceptual clarity, Lancelot is not, like Elaine, an innocent child in fantasy-land; and so he knows that he may fail in the breaking of the bonds. Though Guinevere's love for him is waning, she may not be able to *will* him his freedom; and even if she does, he may not have the *will* to take it. Thus Elaine's willfulness, like every aspect of her story, modulates into the metaphors of the narrative as a whole.

Lancelot is brought only to a point of tragic poise, full tragic realization being saved for the last idyll on our strange literary diagonal, *Guinevere*. But that tragic poise is the result of the most careful imaginative pacing. Lancelot's fantasy about being a "king's son" has its correspondence in Arthur's youthful self-crowning, in the "trackless realms of Lyonnesse" (35), when his heart tells him, "'Lo, thou likewise shalt be King'" (55); and the gothic, abhorrent circumstances surrounding the diamonds for which Lancelot all too successfully competes introduce from the beginning a dark ominous foreboding. It thus seems poetically inevitable that his ambiguous ritual of the diamond jousts (ornaments of a king's crown lost in fratricide) will collapse in its moment of fulfillment. Lancelot's misinterpretation of Guinevere's visual gesture and his lie to Arthur about his ancient wound are emblematic of both his misvision and his delicate self-deception; and that he is, as a result of these subtle flaws, on the brink of downfall is suggested by the inflated unction with which he rationalizes his and Guinevere's relationship:

> "But now my loyal worship is allowed
> Of all men: many a bard, without offence,

Has linked our names together in his lay,
Lancelot, the flower of bravery, Guinevere,
The pearl of beauty: and our knights at feast
Have pledged us in this union, while the King
Would listen smiling."

(110–116)

Guinevere's haughty reply, mirroring a mood of simmering, subterranean grandeur, projects both her anger at Arthur for not prizing her enough and her unacknowledged guilt at not having sufficiently prized him; and she protests her love for a different order of person (namely, Lancelot), like the lady in the play, a bit too much:

"Arthur, my lord, Arthur, the faultless King,
That passionate perfection, my good lord—
But who can gaze upon the Sun in heaven?
He never spake word of reproach to me,
He never had a glimpse of mine untruth,
He cares not for me: only here today
There gleamed a vague suspicion in his eyes:
Some meddling rogue has tampered with him—else
Rapt in this fancy of his Table Round,
And swearing men to vows impossible,
To make them like himself: but, friend, to me
He is all fault who hath no fault at all:
For who loves me must have a touch of earth;
The low sun makes the colour: I am yours,
Not Arthur's, as ye know, save by the bond."

(121–135)

There is just a touch of psychic grossness in both their speeches, and this stands out boldly in an idyll in which much effort has been spent on utmost delicacy and grace.

Guinevere herself, in her new state of presumptive queenliness, authors the pretext by which Lancelot absents himself from her and thus the jeopardy and perceptual alienation which result: it brings him to Elaine's doorstep, almost gets him killed in the joust, causes the tragedy-queen rage with which she acts out her guilt, ego-trauma, and volcanic inner confusion, and pushes Lancelot to a new level of perceptual awareness that dooms their curious love. This ceremony of anonymity into which she plausibly pushes him has a charade-like quality to it. Guinevere herself unnames him, in a symbolic gesture of de-creation; but he exists so massively that he can hide himself from his clan and from his King as little as he can hide himself from himself. The rage of his kith and kin that brings him down is a double-edged rage—that someone should, despite the disguise, look and act so much like him and that he should try to unself himself (and thus unself them) in this absurd way. So both the greatness and the guilt of his love for Guinevere draw themselves into the symbolic action of the mock battle of the joust and almost destroy him.

And yet, Lancelot's rustication by the Queen at Astolat creates a flow of greatness that runs toward him too. It is a time of ego magnification and romantic inflation, full of admiration for him and talk of glorious battles in places with strange-sounding names (280–316); but it is a time, too, in which we see Lancelot at his true and courteous best, pointing always to his subtlest graces and his impeccable admiration for the King:

> "and on the mount
> Of Badon I myself beheld the King
> Charge at the head of all his Table Round,
> And all his legions crying Christ and him,
> And break them; and I saw him, after, stand
> High on a heap of slain, from spur to plume
> Red as the rising sun with heathen blood,
> And seeing me, with a great voice he cried,
> 'They are broken, they are broken!' for the King,
> However mild he seems at home, nor cares
> For triumph in our mimic wars, the jousts—
> For if his own knight cast him down, he laughs
> Saying, his knights are better men than he—
> Yet in this heathen war the fire of God
> Fills him: I never saw his like: there lives
> No greater leader."
>
> (301–316)

And when he points Arthur out to the young Lavaine at the joust, he says simply

> "in me there dwells
> No greatness, save it be some far-off touch
> Of greatness to know well I am not great:
> There is the man."
>
> (447–450)

Thus it is a time of imaginative refreshment and moral renewal when Lancelot, too, unconsciously turns his affection toward his King, and the crisis in formation between him and Guinevere has at its focal center the best that is in them both. Arthur himself is not so much suspicious as keenly attuned to the atmosphere of hyper-psyched strangeness on the part of both Lancelot and Guinevere, and he functions, properly, from an irrefragable inner faith in them both, perceptive and mildly critical, but not harsh or severe. Only with Gawain is Arthur abrupt, using a very short birch rod. And this is just, since Gawain is measured against all the principals and found grossly wanting, with even Elaine reading him a brisk moral lesson.

Their confrontal speeches toward the end of the idyll show that Lancelot and Guinevere occupy very different spiritual spaces. There is no question of Lancelot's being greater than Guinevere, but he has been at the center of some experiences closed to her that have advanced his soul-processing. There is a new degree of refinement in both his thought and his language, and it adds a significant dimension to his legendary might and bravery, as though his experiences since he saw her last have added measurably to his imaginative/moral sensitivity:

> "Queen,
> Lady, my liege, in whom I have my joy,
> Take, what I had not won except for you,
> These jewels, and make me happy, making them
> An armlet for the roundest arm on earth,
> Or necklace for the neck to which the swan's
> Is tawnier than her cygnet's: these are words:
> Your beauty is your beauty, and I sin

In speaking, yet O grant my worship of it
Words, as we grant grief tears. Such sin in words
Perchance, we both can pardon: but, my Queen,
I hear of rumours flying through your court.
Our bond, as not the bond of man and wife,
Should have in it an absoluter trust
To make up that defect: let rumours be:
When did not rumours fly? these, as I trust
That you trust me in your own nobleness,
I may not well believe that you believe."

(1172–1189)

Guinevere, on the other hand, is outrageous to the point of regal parody. She is haughty, taunting, grandly dismissive, diminishing, self-righteous, patronizing, mock-cordial, cruel, and blasphemous. She is outraged without limit that some-one beneath her could have presumed to take her at less than her full measure. But at the center of her volubility, despite the cutting use to which she puts it, is a true acknowledg-ment:

"I for you
This many a year have done despite and wrong
To one whom ever in my heart of hearts
I did acknowledge nobler."

(1201–1204)

That is the acknowledgment, we realize, that she must one day make fullheartedly, and her performance here shows us both that she can ultimately make that acknowledgment and that she will have to pass through the most torturous identity crisis imaginable on her journey to it.

At the end of her royal tirade, she makes a supreme sym-bolic gesture:

Saying which she seized,
And, through the casement standing wide for heat,
Flung them, and down they flashed, and smote the
stream.
Then from the smitten surface flashed, as it were,
Diamonds to meet them, and they past away.

Then while Lancelot leant, in half disdain
At love, life, all things, on the window ledge,
Close underneath his eyes, and right across
Where these had fallen, slowly passed the barge
Whereon the lily maid of Astolat
Lay smiling, like a star in blackest night.

(1225–1235)

Thus their three fates come together in a magnificent operatic crescendo. Guinevere rejects the emblems of their nine-year mock marriage. With that rejection go the diamond symbols of Lancelot's fantasy of being a "king's son"; and perspective is given to its transient reality-unreality by the reflection of their reflection in the water, as a comparable perspective had been rendered for the Lady of Shalott ("From the bank and from the river/He flashed into the crystal mirror," 105–106). As Lancelot watches in chastened recognition, Elaine in her nuptial-funeral barge passes, "smiling, like a star in blackest night." Everything suddenly explodes in a concatenation of mirroring and contrasting symbols that orchestrates a grand imaginative illumination that defies ultimate closure: the heat of the sun, the heat of wrath with its brutal sexual overtones, the spectator as both multivisionary and protagonist, the casement as picture frame of art-reality, the river of life, the river of death, the watery reality of an indestructible reality that is only an appearance of another reality that has no lasting reality, the Arabian Nights quality of the "star in blackest night," the Elizabethanism of nuptial love as nuptial dying, and suffusing it all the Mona Lisa-like smile of Elaine, both infinitely fascinating and beyond positive comprehension.

Such rich imaginative delicacy is a defining characteristic of *Lancelot and Elaine:* it is like an art-jeweler's masterpiece, placing a large and incomparably precious diamond (the severe tragic apprehension) in a rich, inexhaustibly beautiful, illusively simple setting so that every turning to the light releases an explosion of aesthetic illuminations and refractions that are in turn absorbed by the new explosion released by the next turning to the light.

■

Guinevere is unremittingly severe by comparison. The classical unities are imposed with utmost severity: the focus is never removed from the issue of Guinevere's self-recognition; the events all take place in a single room of the nunnery at Almesbury; the action is completed in approximately the amount of time it takes to read the idyll itself. A further unity of atmosphere is engendered by the heavy opaque mist, made luminescent by "a moon unseen albeit at full" (6), which clings to the autumn earth like a mort-cloth. The flashbacks and reminiscences necessary to give the central action proper depth and scale are all kept within a strict rubric of relevance, and there is little or no use of diverting symbolism. The narrator throughout prefers his action to himself, and that action is enabled to exist in the literary structure as it had existed imaginatively in nature.[7] Camelot, with all its colorful pomp and luxuriant trappings, is replaced by the blank convent walls at Almesbury, and the heightened courtly conventions and repartee are reduced to the running chatter of a garrulous little novice. Even Guinevere's name is left behind, and she is distinguished only by the beauty, grace, and power of her person.

Centered heavily in the consciousness of the Queen, *Guinevere* is in a crucial way monitored by memory, and the flashbacks and reminiscences give us an indispensable clue to the precariousness of her situation even after she has sought sanctuary at Almesbury and to the authenticiy of Arthur's farewell speech in enabling her to gain insight worthy of a great tragic heroine. As a woman of genuine stature, she cannot be trivially self-deceived, and so we need to understand the precise character of her self-deception—of why, after "many a week" of residence at the nunnery, she has not sought "for housel or for shrift" (147)—that is, for confession (shrift) and communion (housel)—even though she thinks she is repentant:

> "But help me, heaven, for surely I repent.
> For what is true repentance but in thought—
> Not even in inmost thought to think again

The sins that made the past so pleasant to us:
And I have sworn never to see him more,
To see him more."

(370–375)

It is reasonable to assume that the background narrative provided by the idyll itself represents the incidents that Guinevere has turned over and over in her mind during her many weeks of sanctuary; thus they represent the metaphors by which she has been trying to sort things out. These begin with Modred's camouflaged efforts to gather information confirmatory of the rumors rife in the court and her laughing-shuddering realization ("half-foresaw," 58) that "the subtle beast" (Modred, her own guilt) would eventually track her down and that "hers/Would be for evermore a name of scorn" (60). This threat to her ego polluted the atmosphere of her life, making her guilt-ridden in the face of Modred (as in a mirror) and haunted—night and day, waking and sleeping—by images of guilt and "a vague spiritual fear" (70) that made her hold her breath in fright. She was also possessed in her sleep by an awful repetitive nightmare:

> for then she seemed to stand
On some vast plain before a setting sun,
And from the sun there swiftly made at her
A ghastly something, and its shadow flew
Before it, till it touched her, and she turned—
When lo! her own, that broadening from her feet,
And blackening, swallowed all the land, and in it
Far cities burnt, and with a cry she woke.

(75–82)

Her nightmare has a strong resemblance to Percivale's quest-visions and suggests, especially in her dream-identity with Helen of Troy as incendiary of the civilized world, a lack of "true humility," as do her increasing paranoia around Arthur and members of her household. This is sufficient to motivate her to urge Lancelot's departure for France, but not sufficient to keep them from procrastinating and enjoying their frequent meetings (a euphemism for sexual pleasure: "still they met and met," 93). When they do have their farewell lovemaking ("Stammering and staring," 101), of course, it is "'Too late, too late!'" and they are forced to leave and part by being caught flagrante delicto. Guinevere's reaction is one of ego compounded: she is "'shamed for ever'" (110), and she insists on the priority of her shame (118–119). But this has a touch of nobleness about it, too, as does her recognition that hiding with Lancelot in France is no solution: "'Would God that thou couldst hide me from myself!'" (117). This, in addition to a vague "glimmering" that "'the crimes and frailties of the court'" (135) will wreak some havoc in the realm, is the state in which Guinevere takes sanctuary—with an ego in shambles but with no real understanding of the genuine nature of her "sin" or of its ruinous consequences.

With an irony that is both delicate and devastating, it is the simple, garrulous, foolish-wise novice who prepares the way for Guinevere's consciousness breakthrough later in the night. Having preserved her anonymity, she cannot haughtily break it even when the discomfort is keenest; so she is hoisted on her own petard, the novice being induced to grand judgments by the very stateliness of her anonymous companion. When the rumor spreads that Modred has usurped the realm and that Arthur is waging war on Lancelot, Guinevere's level of regret is still ego-centered—"'With what a hate the people and the King/Must hate me'" (155–156)—and when she seeks relief in tears brought about by the novice's song of the foolish virgins, they are bitter tears indeed, tears of anxiety over lost hope:

> "Late, late, so late! and dark the night and chill!
> Late, late, so late! but we can enter still.
> Too late, too late! ye cannot enter now.
>
> "No light had we: for that we do repent;
> And learning this, the bridegroom will relent.
> Too late, too late! ye cannot enter now.
>
> "No light: so late! and dark and chill the night!
> O let us in, that we may find the light!
> Too late, too late! ye cannot enter now.

"Have we not heard the bridegroom is so sweet?
O let us in, though late, to kiss his feet!
No, no, too late! ye cannot enter now.

(166–177)

Played lightly against Matthew's parable of the foolish virgins
(xxv 1–13) and Herrick's "To the Virgins to Make Much of
Time," this exquisite dramatic lyric—both a dramatic dialogue and a dialogue of the mind with itself—both unveils
Guinevere's precarious position and offers her some stern
insights.

The rosebuds that she had been so eager to gather have
now all blown and left her with a crown of thorns. Her
glorious May sun has set, and she is left only with the cold
borrowed light of a mist-enshrouded autumnal moon. Although she has in fact married, it has not been a marriage
of true minds; and having lost her "prime," she has been
tempted, through pleasurable habit, to "forever tarry." Her
youth is gone, her blood colder, and now the "worse and
worst/Times" are upon her. The light she lived by has turned
to darkness, and she cannot know that the light that she
blinded herself to will ever again, even for a moment, be
offered to her. The stern insights are all recognitions of the
humblest kind—that, despite the luxuriance of her former
state and the haughtiness of her sense of self, she has been
unenlightened; that the "bridegroom" has not in fact been
"cold,/High, self-contained, and passionless" (402–403), but
generous, trusting, and forgiving—"so sweet"; that to "kiss
the feet" of the "highest and most human too" (644) is aspiration, not self-degradation. Thus the little song takes on deep-
ening but simultaneous layers of resonance—that of the
simple novice who has memorized it, that of the distressed
Queen who hears it, and that of the reader who expands it.

Guinevere's weeping signals a new level of availability to
imaginative/moral instruction, not a too-easy transformation,
and that instruction is staged, through the dramatic irony
inherent in the situation, in such a way as to push her through
self-defense toward self-illumination.

First the novice celebrates the joys of a simple, humble

station in life and then goes on to characterize the heavy responsibilities of greatness, where there can be no secrets, even the manner of coping with private grief becoming a public trust. Guinevere attempts to finger Modred as the villain so that she can identify with the feelings of the realm, but the novice fingers Guinevere instead as the source of ruin and a disgrace to womankind. Guinevere then attempts to turn the edge of the novice's direct hit by picking up a minor motif—that of "signs and miracles and wonders"—as a way of dismissing the novice's authority on such a subject. But the defensive ploy collapses in a most delicate, tender way. The novice's "authority" is not that of an empirical, scientific eyewitness but that of a witness to her own reverence and childlike faith in what her father, himself a noble, canonical knight, told her of his own magnified experiences when he came out of waste Lyonnesse into the pristine Arthurian world—bright and fanciful and fresh, an animistic fairyland atmosphere of benevolence and joy, beauty and simple faith. Guinevere's defense then deepens toward sarcasm: if they were so smart, why weren't they smart enough to foresee the present catastrophe? They were, of course, and here the novice turns for her authority to the hieratic figure of the poet-prophet—the "bard" of high emprise and personal bravery and mystery and the "life of Arthur," an evangelist who draws together the fragments of many versions and celebrates a central truth of human potential. There is the inevitable mystery of origins and ultimate destinies, and the prophetic downfall is implicit in the construct itself: ideal manhood closed in real man is doomed both to rise and to fall.

The novice interprets the "scripture" literally and applies it to the present catastrophe. At this point, Guinevere is overcome by a fresh rush of paranoia and lowers her head in silence, while the little novice rides her garrulity to a catechetical question: who is nobler, Lancelot or Arthur? The Queen, though this question gets very close to the red heart of her dilemma, equivocates, falling back upon a respectable, conventional truth/cliché equivalent to "the style is the man." The novice quickly explodes the cliché while saving the truth by reversing the proposition: if, then, the man is the style, what a wretch Lancelot must be! Again Guinevere flies into a personal, *ad hominem* attack, but lets the question collapse into a plea for prayer and pity—for both Lancelot and herself. The novice graciously yields the prayer but not the argument: manners need not be morals, as witness the "sinful Queen" and the present great lady herself. It is the "most unkindest cut of all," and Guinevere retreats into inner turbulence that surfaces as outer wrath, imperially dismissing the fragile little conscience-companion-tutor.

What is adumbrated in this carefully scaled dramatic intercourse between the novice and the hidden Queen—which may be viewed, like the song, as either a dramatic dialogue or as a dialogue of the mind with itself—is the imaginative quest for moral truth. Guinevere is not only an individual but a generic metaphor of all those who are trapped in an imperious self-myth, a hardened fabricated identity, which is deeprooted in their nature and which has been reinforced almost beyond the possibility of recognition by a relatively successful life-style that has implicitly prohibited even the slightest dismantling of the fabricated self. She has historically surrounded herself with elaborate and subtle rituals of reinforcement. She has become Queen because it fitted her personal expectation, but she has distanced herself from Arthur because, although he enabled her myth, he threatened it too: she wanted the perquisites of queenship without its ultimate responsibilities. So she has shaped her world, not to the imperative of her potential self, but to the indulgence of her mythic self. For that, the court—where she was habitually told what she wanted to hear—was the perfect setting; and Lancelot—brave, mighty, adulated, and comparably self-deluded—was the perfect companion. That has now gone up in smoke, but Guinevere is such a child morally that she must be returned to the unsophisticated stage of moral fundamentals in which some very basic and seemingly naïve truths—the kinds of truths that Leodogran stood for in their castle-domicile—can again become visible. These would include such truths as simple honesty, obedience, responsibility, non-erotic love, reverence for innate nobility, childlike faith, joy and tenderness, respect for imaginative wisdom, and a disinclination to order reality through intellective wordplay. These are the truths taught by the little novice, and their time together represents a symbolic return for Guinevere to that personal period in her remote past when she was an innocent girl in her father's house.

Only one time-frame remains to be filled in—that between the age of innocence and the age of experience, and this is the burden of lines 375–404. Having dismissed the novice (her alternative self) in stormy wrath, Guinevere subsides into calmer, more generous, more invigorated self-awareness, and her mind turns to the issue of repentance. But the very act of affirming repentance (370–375) induces a train of thought that discredits it:

> And even in saying this,
> Her memory from old habit of the mind
> Went slipping back upon the golden days
> In which she saw him first, when Lancelot came,
> Reputed the best knight and goodliest man,
> Ambassador, to lead her to his lord
> Arthur, and led her forth, and far ahead
> Of his and her retinue moving, they,
> Rapt in sweet talk or lively, all on love
> And sport and tilts and pleasure, (for the time
> Was maytime, and as yet no sin was dreamed,)
> Rode under groves that looked a paradise
> Of blossom, over sheets of hyacinth
> That seemed the heavens upbreaking through the
>   earth,
> And on from hill to hill, and every day
> Beheld at noon in some delicious dale
> The silk pavilions of King Arthur raised
> For brief repast or afternoon repose
> By couriers gone before; and on again,
> Till yet once more ere set of sun they saw
> The Dragon of the great Pendragonship,
> That crowned the state pavilion of the King,
> Blaze by the rushing brook or silent well.

But when the Queen immersed in such a trance,
And moving through the past unconsciously,
Came to that point where first she saw the King
Ride toward her from the city, sighed to find
Her journey done, glanced at him, thought him cold,
High, self-contained, and passionless, not like him,
"Not like my Lancelot"— . . .

(375–404)

It is a crucial sequence, both monitory and purgative, providing an insight (for the reader as well as for Guinevere) into the inadequacy of her repentance and the opportunity to deal with that inadequacy. It represents the classic pattern of her faulted response to life: when matters became too challenging, she retreated into an alternative fantasy, a symbolic garden of Adonis, where she could luxuriate even knowing that it could not long last. It is a prelapsarian time looked at from a postlapsarian vantage point—the moment just before the fall viewed from the moment just before the revelation of the value of the fall, fortunate or devastating. It juxtaposes Guinevere's first and last views of Arthur, and it confronts her with the central and decisive question of her life: what is true greatness in man? Can anyone be an inscape of true human potential, and is that someone Arthur or Lancelot or another?

This final counterpoising of Arthur and Guinevere is the dramatic climax of *Idylls of the King*. The salvation of Guinevere is at stake, but so is the salvation of Tennyson's chief poetic effort. Now Arthur emerges, not as an ideal clustered with saving human remnants, but as a man so fully fleshed, so closed in awful human reality, so poised on the brink of imaginative as well as existential doom that the poem's integrity is complicit in the man's integrity. Everything in the idyll has been a preparation, not only for Guinevere's moment of moral truth, but also for the poet's moment of imaginative truth. Hence Guinevere's imperious need has its counterpart in the reader's imperious need, and they both depend on the poet's manner with Arthur. As she humbles herself on the floor, hiding her stricken face with her "milkwhite arms" (413) and the abundance of golden hair which had been the symbol of her sexuality and upon which her crown had falsely rested, she is both terrified and expectant at this sudden reversal of fate by which her doom will finally be determined. We strike a different posture, watching with sympathetic detachment to see if the poetic imagination will meet the moral challenge. It is Tennyson's most ambitious effort at human decorum literarily rendered.

The tone of voice, the narrator tells us, is "Monotonous and hollow like a Ghost's/Denouncing judgment" (417–418), and this projects the conscientiousness of a man performing a relentless duty in the face of massive world-weariness. He has come from a failed siege of Lancelot's strong castle (a duty thankless to himself), and he goes to meet Modred, beast, heathen, traitor (the duty that spells his doom). The "judgment" that Arthur "denounces" is not judgment issuing in punishment: his wrath that first led him to "'thoughts on that fierce law'" (534) has passed, as has the wrath that had issue in burning tears. They have largely reversed themselves and been transformed into a desire to protect her in her desolate condition and an acknowledgment that her fallen state has not erased a love for her that is seen as ineradicable. The one thing he can do for her is to help her lay a firm foundation in self-knowledge that will enable her to build her future as she may, together with some honest hope that will help draw her toward the future. In short, he can tell her the exact truth and in so doing blend love and honor for a great but fallen woman. And since her self-identity failure has turned largely upon her failure properly to comprehend him and his life's work, he tries to tell her who he is—his feelings, his thoughts, his beliefs, his excitements, his aspirations, his hurts, his need for love. It is all past now, but he rehearses it in an effort to create between them a spiritual union which will help her in the arduous task of selfing herself authentically and will enable him to march to his doom intact.

Arthur does not spare Guinevere one iota of her blame, not wanting her to build false sentiment on false sentiment. But as he gradually processes himself through language, he moves away from the initial tones of bitterness and outlines the simple bases of the Arthurian dispensation—to bring men into a community ever enlarging itself for mutual support and protection against hostile forces; to give the community a simple moral code symbolized by a leader who assumed public responsibility for upholding that code in an exemplary fashion; and to engender the awareness that a pure and faithful love between a man and a woman unites body and soul, and hence daily nurtures soul, as no other experience available to the generality of men can ever do. That, in brief, is Arthurianism, and Guinevere's infidelity is thereby defined. Her faithlessness to a simple, fulfilling ideal has been the result of a faithlessness to herself: she did not think she could, and therefore she did not try. Instead, she used her queenship as authority for asserting the rule of her unexamined, mythic self and thus gave attractive authority to the realm for doing likewise—for considering ideals negligible because not perfectly attainable, for accepting false authority as exemplary, and for abandoning the idea of community to the degree that it interfered with a principle of personal sensuous pleasure. As a result, she herself is fallen, and she has brought the realm down with her, destroying a "'model for the mighty world'" and making havoc of "'the fair beginning of a time'" (462–463). Thus sexuality as such is only a broadly accessible metaphor of the all-encompassing sensuous mind.

Arthur's personal loneliness is pervasive in his speech. Part of himself lies there upon the pavement, and although it represents a life-illusive decade of his life, it is still what, in his early love-epiphany, he thought it was—"the fairest of all flesh on earth." He must leave the flesh, but it is like ripping himself apart to do so. It makes him half glad to die since Guinevere's absence, like her shame, would be a shadow on every place, gesture, and thought. This leads him to his own alternative fantasy, a high imagining beyond the sensuous mind though itself divinely sensuous:

"Perchance, and so thou purify thy soul,
And so thou lean on our fair father Christ,
Hereafter in that world where all are pure
We two may meet before high God, and thou

> Wilt spring to me, and claim me thine, and know
> I am thine husband—not a smaller soul,
> Nor Lancelot, nor another. Leave me that,
> I charge thee, my last hope."
>
> (558–565)

It is an immortal thought born of an immortal mortal need, and it expresses more than the breath upon the neck or the waving of the hands in blessing the archetypal humanness of King Arthur.

Guinevere rises from her suppliant posture, which has changed slightly to enable her to touch Arthur's extremities, in a state of confusion suffused with exhilaration. She falters for a brief second, as though to capture his physical love, but then she rises to the true truth that has flashed upon her. She has been too overwhelmed to utter a word of thanksgiving for her reprieve at the eleventh hour, but she knows that she is now safe from despair. He has not waved a magic wand over her, but he has given her the courage to face reality honestly in a state, not of purification, but of forgiveness:

> "I cannot kill my sin,
> If soul be soul; nor can I kill my shame;
> No, nor by living can I live it down.
> The days will grow to weeks, the weeks to months,
> The months will add themselves and make the years,
> The years will roll into the centuries,
> And mine will ever be a name of scorn.
> I must not dwell on that defeat of fame.
> Let the world be; that is but of the world."
>
> (616–624)

And he has given her hope, hope in which he is himself complicit,

> "left me hope
> That in mine own heart I can live down sin
> And be his mate hereafter in the heavens
> Before high God."
>
> (630–633)

But most of all he has given her insight—into herself, into himself, into moral order:

> "Ah great and gentle lord,
> Who wast, as is the conscience of a saint
> Among his warring senses, to thy knights—
> To whom my false voluptuous pride, that took
> Full easily all impressions from below,
> Would not look up, or half-despised the height
> To which I would not or I could not climb—
> I thought I could not breathe in that fine air
> That pure severity of perfect light—
> I yearned for warmth and colour which I found
> In Lancelot—now I see thee what thou art,
> Thou art the highest and most human too,
> Not Lancelot, nor another."
> (633–645)

False pride had led her sensuous mind into the behavioral metaphors of sensuous indulgence, and a clear recognition of her own false state enables her finally to recognize Arthur as the high alternative reality that was there all the time but which, being self-blinded, she could not see—"'I see thee what thou art.'" But Guinevere's "one sin" has yet larger implications, radiating largely out of the position she has held—namely, it has been a devastating offense to community. This, too, she now recognizes:

> "Ah my God,
> What might I not have made of thy fair world,
> Had I but loved thy highest creature here?
> It was my duty to have loved the highest:
> It surely was my profit had I known:
> It would have been my pleasure had I seen.
> We needs must love the highest when we see it,
> Not Lancelot, nor another."
> (649–656)

Arthur, then, leaves Guinevere in the most favorable realistic moral state available—forgiven, illuminated, and hopeful.

The rest she must do for herself, making such amends as her nature and circumstances will allow. Toward this end, he also leaves her in the perfect place—a small nunnery, symbol of community. So what she can do, she does—lives a life of exemplary true faith, true hope, and true charity, thus gaining authentic authority over herself and, as Abbess, over the community which she humbly, nobly, and conscientiously serves.

And what Tennyson could do, he did—namely, write an exemplary tragedy—severe, sublime, and restorative.

Notes

1. Quoted in *The Poems of Tennyson*, ed. Christopher Ricks (New York: Macmillan, 1969), pp. 1539–40.
2. Thomas Hardy, "The Spell of the Rose" in *Poems of 1912–13*.
3. Eversley, III, 478.
4. Some critics (e.g., Eggers and Rosenberg—see List of Works Cited in Part 3) imply without actually asserting that *Idylls of the King* is Manichaean in its moral antitheses. The moral complexities of the poem and the oblique angles from which moral questions are looked at actually undercut such a polarized view.
5. Arnold is speaking of the ways in which poetry "interprets" the life it is criticizing, and though Tennyson could not have known Arnold's use of the terms when he wrote *Merlin and Vivien*, he is making integral to his exploration of man and his myths an analogous distinction.
6. It is hoped that the following catalogue will show how carefully Tennyson staged Vivien's strategy and how little the old sage's wit serves him in this contest. The medieval debate is transformed into an erotic ego-massage.
7. The allusions here are to Arnold's defense of classical poetry in the Preface to the first edition of his *Poems* (1853), *Guinevere* being a carefully honed example of classical tragedy.

4.

Filling in the White Spaces

■ *The Last Tournament* ■ *Gareth and Lynette* ■ *Balin and Balan*

With the publication of the *Holy Grail* volume in 1869, the controlling conceptions of *Idylls of the King*—insights, structures, narrative manners—had all been turned into poetic compositions, and although the poem was by no means complete, the paradigmatic formulae that would monitor its completion had all surfaced. In place of a classically neat architectonic structure, the poet had chosen a "parabolic drift" through which the *Zeitgeist* itself could be seen symbolically moving. Representative fables—the lightly shepherded but truly refractive tales of generic individuations of invariably fascinating men and women caught up in their respective "Travail, and throes and agonies of the life"—drift through time, reflecting change but resisting simplification of the nature or workings of change, keeping both cause and consequence organic but not simplistic. The very vegetation-rooting of the poem's time-movement, from dormancy to dormancy, deepest winter to deepest winter, concentrates time in such a severe metaphor that it draws attention to itself as metaphor and thereby frees time as an imaginative symbolic awareness to magnify outward, including not only the time roughly encompassed by the fifth-to-the-thirteenth centuries, but all time: inherent in microcosmic time is not exclusive time or interim time but time itself, all time. In place of an authorial voice adjudicating theme, the poet chose a dozen symbolic/apostolic witnesses of distinctly different temperaments or dimensions of temperament to bear witness to the truth of each tale separately according to each narrator's method of perception and narration (his supposing and stating), thus opening up the notion of "meaning" infinitely. The author is placed in a position analogous to that of a countless number of readers who must approach the individual tales and the poem as a whole according to their individual capacity and sympathy for the sort of literary experience offered here. In place of a single genre and a single level of style, the poet chose to create an anthology of genres and a variety of styles. Although the poem is enclosed in frame-tales and the ten inner tales are specially titled (*"The Round Table"*), the functioning of the poem as a whole does not preclude the use of distinctive literary coordinates connecting several idylls dispersed in the final poem's arrangement, and each idyll (with only the partial exception of *The Marriage of Geraint* and *Geraint and Enid*) has a high degree of poetic autonomy, providing a significant poetic experience, if not quite the same experience as that provided by the poem in an enveloping poetic context—as an artifact removed from its architectural setting may retain a distinct if different beauty.

So when, after the publication of the *Holy Grail* volume, Tennyson came to fill in the white spaces necessary for the completion of his epic-non-epic poem, he had a set of controlling conceptions within which he could very comfortably work. During the four or five years immediately following, he divided *Geraint and Enid* into two (1873), and he wrote three new idylls, *The Last Tournament* (written 1870–1871, published 1871), *Gareth and Lynette* (1869–1872, published 1872), and

Balin and Balan (1872–1874, published 1885). The new idylls are widely dispersed in the completed poem, *Gareth and Lynette* placed second, *Balin and Balan* fifth, and *The Last Tournament* tenth, and they alter the pacing of the poem considerably. *Gareth and Lynette* allows the Arthurian dispensation to have a reasonably pristine moment of practical fulfillment before the dark suspicions rooted in *The Marriage of Geraint* begin to work like wormwood at the heart of Arthurianism. *Balin and Balan* transmutes the undertone of "man against himself" in the Geraint-idylls into a full-blown Doppelgänger narrative and brings Vivien on stage both in preparation for *Merlin and Vivien* and in raw exposure of the varied and clever ways in which she takes advantage of another character's stressful plight to work her will. *The Last Tournament* brings the story of Tristram and Isolt, increasingly pervasive in nineteenth-century poetry and music, within the clusters of the poem, both for its own sake and as an appropriate counterpoint to the story of Lancelot and Guinevere. It also provides, as a revenge tragedy, a dramatic genre-counterpoint to the classically severe tragedy of *Guinevere* and an appropriate poetic context for Pelleas, as the Red Knight, to have his violent dénouement and for the collapse of community, both at court and in the realm at large, to get vivid exposure.

But it should be noted that these new idylls form of themselves an inner poetic ring, the beginning, middle, and end of a "little *Idylls of the King*." *Gareth and Lynette* is a sort of handbook of the new knighthood in fresh flower, the old topsy-turvy knight-errantry having been replaced by a central authority, a new sense of community, and a new set of ideals—bravery, courtesy, fidelity. *Balin and Balan* is the new knighthood under severe stress, a house divided against itself, under the most desperate strain from the enemy within and without. *The Last Tournament* represents post-Arthurianism, the new knighthood in an advanced state of individual and community decay, the central authority being an object of ridicule and the new ideals unobserved even in the breach.

And this perception of an inner poetic ring made up of these three idylls, added to the literary diagonal running through the five idylls published as four in 1859, suggests one of the most dynamic dimensions of *Idylls of the King*—that it not only resists easy closure, but also suspends frozen and self-contained structure. It is in a constant process of re-configurating itself, emerging and re-immersing in new ways, just as its images constantly cluster and dissolve. Thus *Idylls of the King*, like the individual idylls, is a poem beyond itself, "a design in a web, the actual threads of which pass out beyond it."[1] It is not only a rich literary experience, but an "image of the mighty world" of literary experience. A "universal reading act" because of the manner in which the poet gives every reader his own degree of access to the poem, according to his individual capacity and sympathy, it also aspires to be, meta-phorically, a universal writing act in that it varies, to the sym-bolic nth degree, the exemplary workings of the literary imagination (insights, structures, narrative manners) and creates access routes to the multiple literary traditions upon which it builds so deftly but unmistakably. It is not in com-petition with any of its sources—Malory, for example, or the *Mabinogion;* rather, it uses them so conspicuously as to estab-lish with them a complicity that draws them into the reader's enlarging literary orbit. It deploys varieties of tragedy, novel-istic romance, Ur-tale, dramatic lyric, the comic and the seri-ous grotesque, for example, as ways of expanding the reader's literary consciousness by showing how pleasurable such imaginative structures can be and how inherent and indis-pensable they are in the universal search for perspective on experience. Thus they lead outward both to literature (more of the same in the inexhaustible cumulative traditions of the past, present, and future) and to life (wholly accessible strat-egies for supposing and stating facts, for adding imagination to experience and thus creating a keener edge to our insight and truth-telling). *Idylls of the King* confronts the issue of the relevance of imaginative letters in an increasingly positivistic, drab, unimaginative world by demonstrating in a rich variety of ways that imaginative letters deal with man's most elemen-tary day-to-day concerns as human beings and that those day-to-day concerns are chaotic and meaningless without some degree of imaginative perspective, the most rudimentary order itself being the result of some degree of imagination.

■

The Last Tournament is a revenge tragedy in which the individual rebels against the failure of recognized communal forms to render what he considers to be natural justice and thus exposes himself to the workings of the very violence that communal order was designed to protect him from. The main line of this rebellion is embodied in Tristram; but Pelleas's madness—the violent defiance of the goat god against civilization's genuine failure to deliver its promises—is the ultimate dark gloss on failed justice, psychic and moral chaos, and outrageous revenge. In a wholesale reversal of values, the good man is placed in the role of the wicked man, as Arthur's allusion to Job xv 20–21 suggests:

> "Is it then so well?
> Or mine the blame that oft I seem as he
> Of whom was written, 'A sound is in his ears'?
> The foot that loiters, bidden go,—the glance
> That only seems half-loyal to command,—
> A manner somewhat fallen from reverence—
> Or have I dreamed the bearing of our knights
> Tells of a manhood ever less and lower?
> Or whence the fear lest this my realm, upreared,
> By noble deeds at one with noble vows,
> From flat confusion and brute violences,
> Reel back into the beast, and be no more?"
>
> (114–125)

The emphasis is unmistakably on role-reversal, community, and the conditions and mechanisms of revenge tragedy—"'flat confusion and brute violences.'"

The confusion and violence get their most brutal exposure in the Pelleas–Red Knight module of the tale, but through all the vulgar shabbiness inherent in the aesthetic form of the revenge tragedy, the most disquieting undertones of pathos and irony, themselves bitter and violent, persist in surfacing. Pelleas's capacity for riotous cruelty had already been seeded in the incident of running down the cripple soliciting alms in *Pelleas and Ettarre,* and this is aggravated almost beyond endurance by his behavior to the churl tending swine:

> his visage ribbed
> From ear to ear with dogwhip-weals, his nose
> Bridge-broken, one eye out, and one hand off,
> And one with shattered fingers dangling lame,
> (57–60)

"sputtering through the hedge of splintered teeth" (65). We almost laugh in pure self-defense. But to the degree that we begin to suspect that the Red Knight is Pelleas (which the poem itself nowhere specifically validates, though Tennyson has affirmed it),[2] our memory of the excruciating pathos of his earlier story casts a wry light over his rather shabby, unimaginative, mock-Lucifer proclamation of his "'Round Table in the North,'" so consistent with the rigid literalism that broke his boyish-mannish spirit in the first place. Still, he was rawly victimized by the communal order which he had joined in such good faith and honored against such odds. Though he has leaped from whiteness to blackness, what he says of the community against which he has become the revengeful rebel is, in a conspicuous degree, true; and this tug between various species of outrage-in-collision is inherent in the aesthetic character of revenge tragedy. The remembered pathos that infiltrates our response to the ugly brutality of the Red Knight turns to irony of the most shattering sort when the community, in the person of the young, raw, neophyte knights, takes its revenge on the rebel against community. The Red Knight Pelleas has fallen, drunk, face-forward:

> then the knights, who watched him, roared
> And shouted and leapt down upon the fallen;
> There trampled out his face from being known,
> And sank his head in mire, and slimed themselves:
> Nor heard the King for their own cries, but sprang
> Through open doors, and swording right and left

Men, women, on their sodden faces, hurled
The tables over and the wines, and slew
Till all the rafters rang with woman-yells,
And all the pavement streamed with massacre:
Then, echoing yell with yell, they fired the tower. . . .
                                            (467–477)

Justice wrought through violence is itself unjust, and unless we would make a hero-martyr of the outrageous rebel, there seems no place left to look for justice; so pain is "lord," not only in Arthur, but also in the reader.

In the narrative structure of *The Last Tournament,* these events have taken place simultaneously with a dream of Tristram's in which the two Isolts struggle at the edge of a foreign land over Tristram's trophy of the Tournament of Dead Innocence. Isolt of Britain grasps the "ruby-chain" so hard that her hand turns red, and Isolt of Brittany points the moral:

            "Look, her hand is red!
These be no rubies, this is frozen blood,
And melts within her hand—her hand is hot
With ill desires, but this I gave thee, look
Is all as cool and white as any flower."
                                            (411–415)

Just before he wakens, Tristram hears "a rush of eagle's wings, and then/A whimpering of the spirit of the child,/ Because the twain had spoiled her carcanet" (416–418). The placing of Tristram through the device of this metaphoric simultaneity, and through both the fact that he sleeps and the dream-symbols that surface in his sleep, returns the community-focus of the idyll to a barometric center in which we can explore the more quotidian conditions in which the violent extremes represented by the actions of Pelleas and the young knights are implicit.

The last-ditch struggle between the two Isolts is not a simple struggle of passion with purity, but of two imperial cohabitants of the sensuous mind by which the very spirit of innocence ("the spirit of the child") is spoiled if not actually slain. Those two cohabitants are passionate desire and passionate self-righteousness, by which the action imperially desired is justified by Homo sapiens' most imperial secular and secularizing talent, natural reason. Thus "The best [Guinevere, Lancelot] lack all conviction, while the worst [Pelleas, the young knights]/Are full of passionate intensity."[3] Tristram stands between, the natural man in whom the moment of self-inflationary idealism was misapprehended and therefore did not take permanent root but who therefore sees himself as experienced in such matters and capable of being fair and analytical and detached, taking stock of all things by the measure of the hunter and the harper and the rover.

He is Sir Tristram of the Woods, a civilized beast, who sees himself as practiced in life, with more than enough prowess for civilized socializing, civilized lovemaking, and civilized survival. He has lingering remnant intimations of "something far more deeply interfused," but his "inner" eye has been made "dull" by strenuous practice of his "outer eye" (366), and to the degree that he recognizes the fact, his habitual answer has become—so what? The truth is, of course, that he is more competent as an animal than as a man, and the touches of semisophisticated vulgarity about him are designed to correct any tendency on our part to idealize him, while at the same time not demolishing him. He is a failed Orpheus figure; and although he does not indulge in the special rituals that got Orpheus torn to pieces by the Thracian women, he does enrage the women at the tournament through a violation of the code by which the fairest one present was to be awarded the prize, and had he looked backward at the end, Mark would not have "clove[n] him through the brain" (748).

It is a symbolic act since "the brain" is at the center of the community rot of *The Last Tournament,* as a broken, bizarre sort of simulated debate leading nowhere is its chief narrative formula. What we actually have is not intellectual discourse but implicitly or explicitly defined states of being confronting each other in the guise of arguments. Guinevere rationalizes her distaste for the ruby carcanet by suggesting that Arthur make it "a tourney-prize" (32); and when Arthur inquires about the diamonds she has thrown into the river, she answers with a lie (they "Slid" from her hand), a diversion, and a *non sequitur* ("'rosier luck will go/With these rich jewels, seeing that they came/Not from the skeleton of a brother-slayer,/But the sweet body of a maiden babe,'" 45–48). Lancelot replies to Arthur's question "'is it well?'" concerning his service as surrogate-umpire of the Tournament of Dead Innocence with a no/yes; and he conducts the tournament without regard to cause and consequence. Lancelot projects his own shrieking discomfort into a fantasy of death-struggle with Tristram (178–181), and he asks Tristram the victor a surly question that has at least as much applicability to himself:

> "Hast thou won?
> Art thou the purest, brother? See, the hand
> Wherewith thou takest this, is red!"
> (191–193)

Tristram's reply is just about as argumentatively sequential as "Get off my back, brother!"

This formula of two quite different states of being staring at each other across an unbridgeable perceptual gulf, disguised as debate, is most poignantly and dramatically deployed in the confrontation between Dagonet, the fool, and Tristram, the man of natural reason, as Tristram himself ironically suggests, "'I am but a fool to reason with a fool—'" (271). The heart (little Dagonet) has its reasons that the reason (Tristram) knows not of. Tristram has a patronizing attitude toward Dagonet, considering him the witless toy or plaything of the court. Gawain, perhaps in mock celebration of Dagonet's older reputation for smuttiness, had made him mock knight; but it was Arthur who made him court jester, and thereafter Dagonet became totally heart-loyal to the King. So here in the King's absence and all unlike Lancelot, he plays, with the privileges of a cracked brain, an authentic Arthur-surrogate. He does what he does in full faith and pride to be just what he is—King Arthur's fool.

The morning of Dagonet's solitary dance follows the Bacchic revel with which the day of Dead Innocence was concluded, a revel that reached such a peak of sensual, riotous vulgarity that Guinevere had broken it up and gone, pain lord in her bosom, to bed. So this little gargoyle-knight dances to a different tune, to "a silent music up in heaven" (349), music made by the star called "the harp of Arthur" (333) which only he, "Arthur and the angels hear" (350). It is a suprasensuous sight and sound, and access to its loveliness has been Arthur's gift to the fool. Despite his swinelike past, he alone has learned the Arthurian secret:

> "Swine? I have wallowed, I have washed—the world
> Is flesh and shadow—I have had *my* day.
> The dirty nurse, Experience, in her kind
> Hath fouled me—an I wallowed, then I washed—
> I have had *my day* and *my philosophies*—
> And thank the Lord I am King Arthur's fool."
>
>   (315–320, emphasis added)

This is the state of little Dagonet when his solitary dance is interrupted by Tristram, full of *his* day and *his* philosophies.

To Tristram's jovial opener—"'Why skip ye, Sir Fool?'"—Dagonet gives a serious, penetrating answer:

> "Belike for lack of wiser company;
> Or being fool, and seeing too much wit
> Makes the world rotten, why, belike I skip
> To know myself the wisest knight of all."
>
>   (245–248)

Tristram has no notion of what Dagonet is talking about—the difference between wit (reason) and wisdom (faith)—and he attempts to improve upon the situation with "a roundelay." Dagonet lets this sensuous "warbling" pass, as if already waterlogged with it, skipping again only when it stops. To Tristram's reiterated "'Why?'" Dagonet replies with the central brain-image: "'I had liefer twenty years/Skip to the broken music of my brains/Than any broken music thou canst make'" (257–259). Both are bad, but Tristram's "broken music" is worse; and when Dagonet, again to an uncomprehending Tristram, equates harmony with faith and discord with faithlessness—Tristram's broken faith with Isolt of Brittany and

with Arthur—the "witty" Tristram begins to see the drift and
lunges in with a rational rebuttal:

"Fool, I came late, the heathen wars were o'er,
The life had flown, we sware but by the shell—"
(269–270)

It is a rank rationalization, of course, touching only the husk
of the issue, and in a flash of anger Tristram makes an *ad
hominem* attack on Dagonet, recoiling to sing a ditty of the
woods, setting his state of being against Dagonet's—and
Arthur's:

"Free love—free field—we love but while we may:
The woods are hushed, their music is no more:
The leaf is dead, the yearning past away:
New leaf, new life—the days of frost are o'er:
New life, new love, to suit the newer day:
New loves are sweet as those that went before:
Free love—free field—we love but while we may."
(275–281)

What Tristram says is true if man is, however civilized, still
a satyr battening and coupling in the woods with no understanding of or capacity for faithfulness, but it is a music that
Dagonet will not dance to; and when Dagonet simply points
out that such wine eventually runs to mud, Tristram again
indulges in a torrent of *ad hominem* abuse, climaxing in a
"witty" allusion to the gospel according to Matthew: "'For I
have flung thee pearls and find thee swine'" (310). But the
wisdom is Dagonet's, and it is Tristram who is trampling the
pearls into mud. He is the hypocrite taking everybody's inventory but his own; it is he who is equating freedom with
license and making the way broad and easy for himself (Matthew vii).

When Dagonet contrasts those whom Arthur's music at-
tracts with the followers of Orpheus, Tristram leaps to an
identification with Orpheus and a self-blinded misinterpretation of the myth: "'Had such a mastery of his mystery/That
he could harp his wife up out of hell'" (327–328). Could, but

failed to, though Orpheus had a fidelity to Eurydice un-dreamt of by Tristram; and the failure which Tristram blithely ignores had as its root cause a quality—rational curiosity—higher than that embodied in Tristram—rational self-justifi-cation. Hence, Tristram is even a failed Orpheus, piping everything downward toward its lowest common denomina-tor. Still, Dagonet in summing up the cause for the failure of Arthurianism does not entirely abandon the Orpheus-Eurydice myth, expanding the hell image to include the rationalized passion game the knights have played and the resultant false fire that has consumed the Arthurian commu-nity:

> "Ay, and when the land
> Was freed, and the Queen false, ye set yourself
> To babble about him, all to show your wit—
> And whether he were King by courtesy,
> Or King by right—and so went harping down
> The black king's highway, got so far, and grew
> So witty that ye played at ducks and drakes
> With Arthur's vows on the great lake of fire."
>
> (338–345)

Tristram has by now abandoned all effort to contend with the little fool and tries rather to turn the charge of treason back upon him:

> "Lo, fool," he said, "ye talk
> Fool's treason: is the King thy brother fool?"
> Then little Dagonet clapt his hands and shrilled,
> "Ay, ay, my brother fool, the king of fools!
> Conceits himself as God that he can make
> Figs out of thistles, silk from bristles, milk
> From burning spurge, honey from hornet-combs,
> And men from beasts—Long live the king of fools!"
>
> (351–358)

Dagonet's reply is a most delicate rejoinder and a boldly pre-carious balancing by the narrator of the tale. Accused of trea-son by a traitor, Dagonet, in an explosion of gesture ("clapt his hands and shrilled"), turns the implications of Tristram's rationalized morality back upon him in a grand ironic inflation: "You're right, you're right! He *is* a madman like me! Thinks he's God and can do the impossible, trying to reverse nature and get fruit and raiment and child-nurture and sweetness out of things that prick and bind and induce fever and sting, and, madness of madness, thinks he can make men out of beasts like you! God bless him!" It is a stunning climax, full of jubilee and despair, pain and heartrending acceptance of the awful truth, the "terrible beauty," of Arthur. Dagonet dances away, and Tristram, essentially immune to the mad poetry embodied in this experience, rides toward his doom in the west, like Arthur, but in an entirely different psychological, moral state.

Tristram's final contest is a fit emblem of his life—a battle of the sexes—and comes to a horrifying but fit conclusion. As he makes his way toward Tintagel after a long but reasonably pleasant absence, he is filled with the light but troublesome anxieties of a light but habitual deceiver. The narrator is very evenhanded with him—his dull inner eye, his keen outer eye, his animal-like sniffing around old love nests ("beechen-boughs" where the "malkin" or slut has been, "dark in the golden grove," 375, 378, 627), his reflective mind, dulled by his "hunter's eye," functioning at a goatlike level reminiscent of Pelleas in his beechen grove. He wakes from his dream with a shout and sets it aside with a whistle to his horse. When he meets a forlorn woman, he admits to himself that he does not know what he wants and advises her to keep herself pretty, just in case. But the reader has been warned that Tristram will now be caught up in the revenge-tragedy mechanism, the "wretchedness" that the coward Mark has been "devising" (385). Indeed, Mark is the hidden observer of the whole scene between Tristram and Isolt, as we learn from his use at the end of Isolt's phrase at the beginning—"Mark's way" (530, 748); and that he does not strike in the middle of their lovemaking ("and satiated their hearts," 719) adds voyeurism to the ambient sickness of their psychological intercourse.

Isolt's love for Tristram is fueled by her hate for Mark (535–536), the dark fear within clinging with frantic passion to the alter-image without—massive, muscular, tactile, sensuously reassuring and satisfying—and the sexual energy thus generated in turn fuels his passion for her. Thus soul-sickness is at the bottom of it all, and while they taunt each other to near-desperation, they move, as it were irresistibly, toward a sexual climax of would-be cosmic proportions:

"Come, I am hungered and half-angered—meat,
Wine, wine—and I will love thee to the death,
And out beyond into the dream to come."

(713–715)

But they dress it up in a shabby sort of civilized discourse:

"O Sir Knight,
What dame or damsel have ye kneeled to last?"

And Tristram, "Last to my Queen Paramount,
Here now to my Queen Paramount of love
And loveliness—"

(547–551)

This collapses of its inherent phoniness, of course, and they maneuver each other into increasingly violent discord. *You are lovely.* But isn't Guinevere thrice as lovely? *She is beautiful but cold, even perhaps denying Lancelot sexual fulfillment.* Then you are a liar, using their case to persuade me. *What difference does it make, if we are enjoying ourselves? Anyway, did you miss me?* I remember how I hated Isolt of Brittany, wished to be washed upon her shore to chill her bride-kiss. But her worst plague is to have got you. If it weren't for Mark, I'd hate you! *Let her be. I loved the name. She's a thin porridge and will go to a convent.* Well, I'm not and won't, but in the moment after Mark hissed the "good news" of your wedding, I awoke from a swoon crying "'I will flee hence and give myself to God'–/And thou wert lying in thy new leman's arms'" (619–620).

At this point, Tristram makes a remark that is at worst ambiguous, at best graceful, and in any case consistent with his philosphy:

"May God be with thee, sweet, when old and gray,
And past desire!"

(622–623)

But the reference to time throws Isolt into a chaos of emotions, as the hell within momentarily loses its alter-image without. She takes it as a deep personal threat to the future, made painfully present, and launches a tirade of abuse and self-degradation, a torrent of accusation, pleading, lamentation, chaotic contradiction, climaxing in the most ironic prayer-demand that this woman could make to this man:

"I say,
Swear to me thou wilt love me even when old,
Gray-haired, and past desire, and in despair."

(646–648)

It is the despair of one who, clutching frantically at the sensual frame, is brought face-to-face with ravaging time.

Tristram, of course, has no resources with which to deal with emotions like self-rending despair, so he embarks instead upon an elaborate dismantling of Arthurianism and an essay in rational self-justification. He thus brings into focus, at an ordinary analytical level, the "community position" on the Arthurian experience and becomes a spokesman for the skeptical reader who may have many of the same doubts and discomforts. To the degree that one recognizes some of his own intellectual tendencies in Tristram's line of argument, he is provided with an opportunity, not only of argument, but also of character in a dramatic context of passionate extremes, to assess those tendencies afresh.

First, Tristram invokes a series of faulty implicit syllogisms: since we have broken our vows, everybody breaks his vows; since my vow "snapt," it was bound "too strictly"; since I am worse now than I was before swearing, it is because of the swearing. Then he blames his naïveté, a poor innocent from the backwoods who got carried away by the sheer unfamiliar marvel of it all:

"For once—even to the height—I honoured him.
'Man, is he man at all?' methought, when first

> I rode from our rough Lyonnesse, and beheld
> That victor of the Pagan throned in hall—
> His hair, a sun that rayed from off a brow
> Like hillsnow high in heaven, the steel-blue eyes,
> The golden beard that clothed his lips with light—
> Moreover, that weird legend of his birth,
> With Merlin's mystic babble about his end
> Amazed me; then his foot was on a stool
> Shaped as a dragon; he seemed to me no man,
> But Michaël trampling Satan; so I sware
> Being amazed: but this went by—"
>
> (657–669)

That he was a starry-eyed youth bewitched by natural magic, legend, strange wizardry, and Biblical lore seemingly realized in the life may be a fair account of how it was with Tristram, but it becomes faulty to the degree that there is an implication that, as it was with him, so it was with others. That this is the direction in which his thoughts about his personal experience are moving becomes abundantly clear in the way he extrapolates that experience:

> "The vows!
> O ay—the wholesome madness of an hour—
> They served their use, their time; for every knight
> Believed himself a greater than himself,
> And every follower eyed him as a God;
> Till he, being lifted up beyond himself,
> Did mightier deeds than elsewise he had done,
> And so the realm was made; but then their vows—
> First mainly through the sullying of our Queen—
> Began to gall the knighthood, asking whence
> Had Arthur right to bind them to himself?
> Dropt down from heaven? washed up from out the
>   deep?
> They failed to trace him through the flesh and blood
> Of our old kings: whence then? a doubtful lord
> To bind them by inviolable vows,
> Which flesh and blood perforce would violate. . . ."
>
> (669–684)

The susceptible naïf has now become the detached, skeptical historian, culture analyst, psychologist, moral philosopher, diminishing the past, rationalizing the present, and ignoring the future. He suffers from a primitive version of the apex-of-civilization syndrome, the cult of contemporaneousness:

> "For feel this arm of mine—the tide within
> Red with free chase and heather-scented air,
> Pulsing full man; can Arthur make me pure
> As any maiden child? lock up my tongue
> From uttering freely what I freely hear?
> Bind me to one? The wide world laughs at it.
> And worldling of the world am I. . . ."
>
> (685–691)

His day and *his* philosophies have become the measure of the only true reality; and all of his accomplishments—as hunter, harper, and amorous rover—have become sensuous accompaniments to the sensuous mind. Experience has not, in his view, been a "dirty nurse," but a great enlightener; and since reveling is not wallowing, there is no need to wash: innocence, like the "maiden child" we were, is dead. Yesterday's "miracles," like yesterday's loves, are dead leaves of a dead past. That past is not organic with the present, both being literal rather than symbolic, and each new day is wholly sufficient unto itself.

Tristram's plausibility at a primary level is an indispensable dimension of his emblematic serviceability in the poem, but there is a delicate ironic undercurrent that makes his apparent truce with imagination, the posture of a rational empiricist, a genuine imaginative revelation for the reader. What Tristram thinks he is doing, even at such a modest level, is contradicted by the very act of doing it. He is using language, the most organic and symbolic instrument of even natural rational man. The memory upon which he draws to deny the relevance of the past implies that the past is inescapable. The "maiden child" that he claims no longer to be is still a part of what he is, a persistent surfacing in the very consciousness that denies it. The mythic enchantments under whose influence he momentarily, and perhaps falsely, fell and concerning which he tries to be so generous in his impatient dismissiveness were, however explained, real and so affective that they made men appear and act godlike in degree, and of course what has been can and will likely be again. His dreams, however forgettable, suggest that at the center of his subconscious is moral struggle—*homo agonistes*. He uses metaphors to deny the metaphoric levels of truth. Even his infidelity in love implies rationalized confusion rather than lack of faith.

While Tristram is allowed to be who he is—a representative fallible man supposing and stating fact according to his capacity—he is not quite allowed to be who he is not—a spokesman, however representative, for an enclosed, and therefore comfortable, point of view. Even natural, rational man cannot escape the faint remnants of his supranatural, imaginative condition. So when Tristram compares himself negatively to the doomed "'ptarmigan that whitens ere his hour'" (692–693), his trope is an ironically positive self-revelation; and his "'garnet-headed yaffingdale'" (695) mocks, not the vows, but their prodigals. Finally, the inconsistency of his whole philosophy gets a lurid unmasking when Isolt challenges him with her right to act by the same code and charges him to answer:

> He that while she spake,
> Mindful of what he brought to adorn her with,
> The jewels, had let one finger lightly touch
> The warm white apple of her throat, replied,
> "Press this a little closer, sweet, until—"
>
> (708–712)

Tristram's final song is a subtler revelation, drawing into a cluster several symbolic implants of the poem:

> "Ay, ay, O ay—the winds that bend the brier!
> A star in heaven, a star within the mere!
> Ay, ay, O ay—a star was my desire,
> And one was far apart, and one was near:
> Ay, ay, O ay—the winds that bow the grass!
> And one was water and one star was fire,

And one will ever shine and one will pass.
Ay, ay, O ay—the winds that move the mere."
                            (725–732)

There is Dagonet's "star," known as Arthur's harp, that Tristram has heard the legend of but cannot see "'in open day'";
there is the wind and the ruffled/unruffled mere of lines
368–370:

Anon the face, as, when a gust hath blown,
Unruffling waters re-collect the shape
Of one that in them sees himself, returned;

and there is the perspective-in-reflection motif of *Lancelot
and Elaine* (1228–1229). Tristram sings the song as a con-
nubial love-ditty, celebrating the pleasures of love that he has
just enjoyed; but the reiterative "Ay" is an insistent note of
woe, and the winds echo those of the carnal sinner in Dante's
Inferno. The "brier" and "grass" (as opposed, for example, to
Guinevere's "'garden rose/Deep-hued and many-folded'" *BB*,
264–265) suggest a barren wasteland; and the inflated conceit of the star imagery, which defies consistent interpretation, gives the reader perspective (a mirror-image) on Tristram's failure to gain perspective on himself.

After Mark completes the revenge tragedy by cleaving Tristram "through the brain," the reader is left with two remnant
"communities"—the horrifying solitude of Mark and Isolt
and the heartrending companionship of Arthur and Dagonet:

"What art thou?" and the voice about his feet
Sent up an answer, sobbing, "I am thy fool,
And I shall never make thee smile again."
                            (754–756)

■

Gareth and Lynette is the first of the *Round Table* idylls, but it
was the second-last of all the idylls to be written. It is likely,
therefore, that it was conceived by the poet, with almost the
complete composition of his magnum opus laid out before

him, as the foundation piece of all but the frame-idylls themselves. Thus one can fairly expect to find in *Gareth and Lynette,* not only the individual story of a youth passing into manhood, with the qualifications, impediments, and trials thereof, but also a reasonably full elaboration of the ambient culture in which he functions—the nature of that special moment in time through which he moves and by which, however distinctively individual he may be, his success or failure is in part determined. That culture is, in the imaginative fiction of *Idylls of the King,* Arthurian and is embodied in an order called *The Round Table;* hence, in the first of the *Round Table* idylls one looks for an exemplification of what Arthurianism means, of what the special character of this order of men is. Further, since *Gareth and Lynette* is an initiation idyll, its time is prospective; and since time is also organic, it seems likely that the future will be rather fully seeded in the present, certain crucial motifs of the ten idylls of *The Round Table* being implicit in the first. Finally, *Gareth and Lynette* is not only an initiating action but also an initiating literary structure, and its monitorial relevance to the total reading act demands attention.

Gareth is a spring-tide figure, full to the brim of an imperious life-flow. His whole perspective has been shaped in a crucial way by a man named Arthur. His mother, Bellicent, sometimes called Arthur's sister, has spent significant portions of her childhood in his company and remembers him with deep, admiring affection; his father, Lot, has been insurgent against Arthur and now lies moribund in failure; his two older brothers, Gawain and Modred, have become knights in his order. But Gareth is unlike any of the others: his imagination has been ignited and his whole consciousness suffused by the stories he has heard about this fabulous king who makes men free. He, too, wants to be free, and he takes the only route to freedom yet available to him—he translates the objects of his world of domestic seclusion into imaginary adventures of knightly emprise. Being lonely in his advanced youth, he has only himself to place at the center of his imaginary exploits, not arrogantly but inevitably, and this process reinforces a strong sense of self, of personal identity. His sense of self thus enriched brings Gareth into conflict with Bellicent, who, because of her own inner needs as mother, virtual widow, and solitary queen, sees Gareth as still a child with a child's needs for protection and fairy tales, someone to nurture and thereby enter into a compact with, so that her own increasing age will be protected. Gareth, in addition to his lust for life, his surging imagination, his ebullient idealism, his imperious need to align his autonomous self with other life coordinates, has great tenderness for Bellicent and reverences his duty of obedience to her will, though he warns her in oblique, gentle parables of his healthy intuition that age can, even with seemingly high-minded motives, ruin the "fair beginnings" of youth. Bellicent, who invokes the momism motif that persists as an undercurrent threat throughout the idyll, finally yields, but the condition that she sets is the subtlest cut at the very integrity that had forced her to yield: Gareth must, for a twelvemonth and a day, dissemble—enter Camelot through the low door of kitchen service. He accepts, upon reflection, partly because it is his only way out and partly because he recognizes inner resources deeper than those upon which Bellicent had depended to defeat his purpose. Even so, the break cannot be effected in a wholly honorable way: he feels forced by the discomfort in which she has enveloped the idea of his departure to steal away while his mother sleeps.

Another of Gareth's personal characteristics is a strong and protective sense of companionship, of fellowship and community. Hence he faces his great new confirmation of self and makes it organic with his past by taking with him two fellows of his native soil who "had tended on him from his birth" (176), and they travel amid the sights and melodies of spring, "past the time of Easterday" (183), a resurrection motif that is also persistent in the idyll. They feel all the excitement and anxiety of a sacred adventure, and his companions almost panic at the mysterious way the enchanted city of Camelot first reveals itself, real/unreal. But Gareth meets the "glamour" without with the "glamour" within and feels, in the hyperbole of youthful high spirits, that he could out-Merlin Merlin, plunging him into the child-lore of the Arabian Nights.

Poetic justice gives Gareth a chance to test the authenticity of his spirited exaggeration when the ornate symbolism of Arthur's gate, with its inexhaustible configurations of significance, begins to move before their wide-eyed, concentrated stares and Merlin himself appears. Gareth backs a bit into coyness, centering the anxiety in his men rather than in himself, but he puts the question in a well focussed way: is it a mere appearance or a true reality? In other words, am I about to embark upon an authentic vocation or to "follow wandering fires/Lost in the quagmire" (*HG*, 319–320)? Merlin's answer, given in the manner of "the Riddling of the Bards" (280), is one of the crucial illuminations implanted in *Idylls of the King:* both truth and poetry are "like shot-silk with many glancing colours." One can look at the reflection of a ship rather than at the ship, and his truth is turned upside down by another's perceptions. Or one can take a fairy tale for truth, building around it apparent solidities of place and time and manner. Everything appears to be one thing and is another except true truth, real reality itself, and to some even Arthur is only a shadow, their reality being man-made out of solid materials and their fairy tales meaningless. If one is comfortable with his present apprehensions of truth, he should be leery of aspiring to truth at its ultimate level of reality because it will enthrall him in rituals of imperfect perfection, aspirations that can never be totally fulfilled:

> "for the King
> Will bind thee by such vows, as is a shame
> A man should not be bound by, yet the which
> No man can keep. . . ."
>
> (265–268)

These vows, like music, are not matter-of-fact solidities, but imaginative aspirations for which closure, however grand the compass, is a contradiction in terms; being cast for eternity, they cannot bring in time a satisfying sense of completion. And the city, being a mighty poetic image of aspiration, cannot exist except through imaginative aspiration: therefore always building, therefore never finally built, and therefore built forever.

Gareth's angry reaction to Merlin's riddling rises from several sources: his role-playing as protector of his men; the tumbling which the master of imagination gives the neophyte; and the shy but sure guilt that he feels as a deceiver face-to-face with truth severely honed. Merlin confronts the latter two: he gives Gareth a brief lesson in the way truth functions dynamically in poetry—"'Confusion, and illusion, and relation,/Elusion, and occasion, and evasion'" (281–282)—and proves to him that his own proffered reality is but a mock appearance. This insinuates into a deeper level of significance the condition of freedom imposed by Bellicent ("'Our one white lie sits like a little ghost/Here on the threshold of our enterprise,'" 291–292) and promises that it will affect Gareth's tale in all its parts and that the "amends" he is so resolute to make will indeed require persevering resolution.

Our first view of Arthurianism as embodied action is enveloped in a luminous aura by being filtered through Gareth's imagination and generosity of spirit. His fresh, eager eyes go everywhere, and what he sees are industry, purity, health, graciousness, honor, faith, accomplishment, glory, aspiration, and justice. The several vignettes in which Gareth first sees Arthur "delivering doom" (314) have oblique relevance to himself. The first two turn upon age stripping youth of its proper inheritance, and this is a lingering problem (a "half-shadow") of Gareth's. The third, Mark's application for enrollment in the Round Table with cloth of gold and in competition with Tristram, draws Gareth's attention to the symbolism of the shields, among which he sees "The shield of Gawain blazoned rich and bright,/And Modred's blank as death" (408–409), and enables him to hear the King pronounce the vices that stand antipodal to the ideals of Arthurianism: Mark is "'craven—a man of plots,/Craft, poisonous counsels, wayside ambushings—'" (423–424). Mark is, in short, a liar; and Gareth is forced, by the white lie which he accepted from Bellicent, to make application to Arthur in

a shamed false and guilty self. Thus the magnification of
Arthurianism in his eyes has correspondence in the self-
diminution that he feels and that is glossed in its most distasteful extremes by Mark. Again the central importance of
the motif of dissembling is reinforced.

Arthur's acceptance of Gareth's petition to be not-himself
for "A twelve-month and a day" (438) brings youth into further conflict with age. Sir Kay, peevish and suspicious and
wholly lacking in imagination, sees Gareth literally as just
what he says he is and attitudinizes toward him with images of
"a pigeon" and a "hog," linguistically vulgar terms for an
unshorn sheep (hog) who will be his special concern (pigeon).
Lancelot, on the other hand, perceives Gareth's innate nobility and thinks of him in terms of a thoroughbred war-
horse: "'Broad brows and fair, a fluent hair and fine,/High
nose, a nostril large and fine, and hands/Large, fair and
fine!'" (454–456). Lancelot's language, repetitive and somewhat stereotyped, reveals his own imaginative limitations, but
he does become a patron of youth, a sort of director of pos-
tulants, as he will not continue to be in *Pelleas and Ettarre,*
where he is enclosed in personal stress. And Gareth's period
of disguise, through his innate nobility, does have effects
which it might not otherwise have had: it brings into the
kitchen an exemplary obedience, joy, imaginative high-mindedness, athletic competition, and adulation of knightly prowess, and it enables Gareth to learn with the perspective of an
outsider the role and origins and ideals of Arthur and his
Round Table.

When Gareth is relased from his temporary vow as pos-
tulant, he petitions for novice-knighthood with the extraordinary request that he retain his anonymity until he makes a
name for himself. Arthur, though well disposed, instructs
Gareth in the obligations of knighthood—

"utter hardihood, utter gentleness,
And, loving, utter faithfulness in love,
And uttermost obedience to the King."
(542–544)

But he quizzes him about his motive, concerned lest it be rooted in ego-inflation. It is, in fact, a penance by which Gareth hopes to atone for his white lie. Arthur yields, "half-unwillingly" (565), but he appoints Lancelot as director of novices for Gareth, counterpointing Lancelot's anonymity to Gareth's.

Thus Gareth's *rite de passage* is a symbolic selfing, and the trials with which he must cope "'for a day'" (563) are within himself. He must free himself from the Castle Perilous of imprisoned youth and enter manhood. His emergence from his dun-colored robes into "jeweled harness," like the butterfly from the chrysalis, is the beginning of self-discovery, not the end. The wide doorway through which he follows Lynette lacks the cultivated gravity and step-by-step steadiness of the opposite entry through which Arthur passes. The time metaphors with which he must cope—Morning, Noon, Evening, and Night—are stages in his own day. The two sisters are Doppelgänger images of a single self, both of which mirror him. The relentless taunting to which Lynette subjects him constitutes a ritual of penitential self-purification since his collusion even in a white lie smells of mendacity, and he must name it for what it is before he can fitly name himself, seeing it not as a minor thing-in-itself but as an image of its more terrible possibilities. The six caitiffs whom he disperses from an attempt at drowning a noble, loyal baron of the King are, like his own collusion, half-weak, half-cowardly, and the weird dance of death by bog-light on the grotesque mere is a surreal reminder of the decay to which self-deception ultimately leads. The burden "Lead, and I follow" is not only a motto of knightly obedience and perseverance by which the art of leadership is learned, but a penitential refrain by which he seeks to purge the act by which he was drawn into his collusion with a lie. Although, like Cinderella-Phoenix, he will rise from the ashes, he cannot forget that, unlike the Cinderella of the fairy tale, his being in the ashes to begin with was an act of duplicity by a "King's son" (881–882). The gradual reversal of the lead-follow rubric is an internal process as Gareth gradually gains freedom, through amends, from the heavier weight on his tender conscience of his own reversal of appearance/reality.

When Gareth finally comes face-to-face with the "fool's parable," the tone of the narrative changes, and through a new degree of exaggeration, an element of the mock-heroic is introduced which climaxes finally in the comic grotesque of Gareth's horrific battle with Night. The inflated, mock-serious descriptions of the "fools" are one signal; another is Lynette's inciting of his antagonists in the loops of "the serpent river" to degrees of anger. This does not suggest that Gareth's penance for duplicity is not a serious undertaking, but rather that a new form of self-deception—ego-inflation—has been processed by it and has begun to take center stage. Gareth, with his lively but undisciplined imagination, has begun to be enamored of his own invincibility and to lose perspective on the charade in which he is about to be involved. The canticles which Lynette sings after each of the first three contests, while quite lovely in themselves and having a larger significance in the idyll, are, as projections of Gareth's inner feelings, distinctly self-congratulatory:

"O morning star that smilest in the blue,
O star, my morning dream hath proven true,
Smile sweetly, thou! my love hath smiled on me."
                                   (974–976)

"O dewy flowers that open to the sun,
O dewy flowers that close when day is done,
Blow sweetly: twice my love hath smiled on me."
                                   (1040–1042)

"O birds, that warble to the morning sky,
O birds that warble as the day goes by,
Sing sweetly: twice my love hath smiled on me."
                                   (1049–1051)

"O trefoil, sparkling on the rainy plain,
O rainbow with three colours after rain,
Shine sweetly: thrice my love hath smiled on me."
                                   (1130–1132)

That Gareth's self-inflation is indeed at work comes through climactically in his next speech after the last song: "'There rides no knight, not Lancelot, his great self,/Hath force to quell me'" (1153–1154). As if in a replay of Gareth's boyish hyperbole concerning Merlin, Lancelot comes upon the scene with his disguised shield and topples Gareth easily, and the incipient inflation is totally deflated in good-humored laughter that breaks through Gareth's anonymity and restores him to his authentic identity—true prince, true knight.

The motif of age's leathery resistance to youth surfaces again in Gareth's struggle with Evening Star. It is an unknightly struggle, age attempting to strangle youth, and Gareth's situation is a desperate one:

> and his great heart,
> Foredooming all his trouble was in vain,
> Laboured within him, for he seemed as one
> That all in later, sadder age begins
> To war against ill uses of a life,
> But these from all his life arise, and cry,
> "Thou hast made us lords, and canst not put us down!"
> He half despairs. . . .
>
> (1098–1105)

Age is defeated, though in unfair fight; but then the motif surfaces in a subtler way. Lynette turns Bellicent-surrogate and, in a fit of protectiveness, attempts to prevent Gareth's climactic struggle with Night. This is Gareth's deepest-rooted anxiety, and it is unequivocal proof of his full maturity that he rejects mother-jeopardy outright:

> "And wherefore, damsel? tell me all ye know.
> You cannot scare me; nor rough face, or voice,
> Brute bulk of limb, or boundless savagery
> Appal me from the quest."
>
> (1295–1298)

So when youth emerges from the most inflated charade of all, he is a "blooming boy" (1373) "not many a moon [Gareth's] younger" (1380); and when asked why, a fair child, he had challenged Arthur's greatest knight, he says, "'Fair Sir, they bad me do it'" (1382), not dreaming that anyone would survive Morning, Noon, and Evening in "The war of Time against the soul of man" (1168). And if, as the poem suggests, youth has won his battle against age, that battle has been real even if at times comically grotesque. Age, which hates change, is determined not to "go gentle into that good night"; youth, which craves change, is eager to go lusty into that good life. Age, enthroned, refuses to abdicate. Youth is thus faced with some hard choices: to yield and remain a child long past the age of adulthood, a sort of clone of one's parent; to rebel and usurp the throne with violence; or, like Gareth, to escape, even at the price of some temporary compromise, and build on the remnants of one's identity an authentic and trustworthy self.

Arthurianism thus emerges as a grand symbolic opportunity for change—a new "order" in the stricter sense of that term set against an old disordered symbolic knight-errantry and providing men in this world with a new code of value and conduct by which to self themselves authentically. At the heart of the symbol is the idea of order itself, man's craving for a way of constructively organizing his life against the chaos without and within. The particular ordering metaphor of an age or of a group is infinitely variable, but the need in man for order is infinitely constant. "'The old order changeth, yielding place to new,'" says the King in *The Coming of Arthur* (508), and in *The Passing of Arthur*:

> "The old order changeth, yielding place to new,
> And God fulfils himself in many ways,
> Lest one good custom should corrupt the world."
>
> (408–410)

He is not talking about the order of things, but about the orders of men, the structures they adopt to give meaning and potential magnificence to their lives; and he is recognizing that any such structure in an ever-varying Time-Spirit can itself become the source of the corruption which it attempts to treat, the very self-deception from which it would make men free.

Other grand "orders" by which men have attempted to structure and facilitate the good life—for example, those of Benedict of Nursii (480?–543?) and Francis of Assisi (1181?–1226)—are points of reference by which the idea of Arthurianism is clarified. Indeed, the emphasis on the "rules" of the order of the Round Table and the degrees of gladness, joy, and ecstasy that Gareth exemplifies, together with the "canticles" of nature that Lynette sings, suggest rather strongly that Arthurianism is shaped by analogy with the obedience, discipline, fidelity, and service of Benedict wedded to the joy, spiritual exaltation, and love of all God's creatures and creation of Francis, though chastity is replaced by utter faithfulness in love and monastic stability by wide-ranging and militant acts of righting human wrong. Still, the "orders" created by Benedict and Francis are true analogical mirrors of the "order" which Arthur created and of which he speaks.

The glorious affectiveness of such fellowships of conduct ordered on idealistic principles is fully exemplified in the tale of Gareth: it enables him to free himself from bondage and from personal shame and to become, through trial and guided perseverance, true prince, true knight. Gareth, of course, unlike his brothers, is eminently teachable, bringing to the Order of the Round Table qualitites of faith, hope, love, strength, and vocation; and under the refining tutelage of Merlin (imagination), Arthur (ideals), and Lancelot (practice), he succeeds in the rite of creating himself as the beautiful young flower of a strong, gentle, faithful, obedient, serviceable knighthood.

■

Knighthood never again flourishes in the same fresh, gracious way in *Idylls of the King*. This is a pristine moment, and immediately thereafter the order begins the long inevitable process of change. Indeed, there are numerous but lightly sketched foreshadowings, in this rich comedic piece, of motifs which will have an ever-darkening tone in the later literary structures. Gareth's "great Sun of Glory" (22) will become the sun of lustful passion and Vivien's "old sun-worship" that will "'beat the cross to earth, and break the King/And all his Table'" (*BB*, 451–453). Bellicent's "'cloud that settles round [Arthur's] birth'" (128) will become the "'too much wit'" that "'Makes the world rotten'" (*LT*, 246–247). Gareth's unequivocal faith in Arthur's kingliness, radiating outward from the center of his own idealism, will deteriorate as that idealism becomes "summer-wan" and the "dewy flowers" become rank, sensuous, and blown—worldly luxuriance justifying itself through worldly reason. Lynette's "'fool within'" will have many distressing variations, climaxing most dramatically in Vivien's victory over the "fool" in *Merlin*. Gareth's entirely just placing of the proper relationship of Arthur and Lancelot will suffer a devastating reversal in *Balin and Balan*, and his covert departure from Bellicent will surface more distastefully in Percivale's abandonment of his lady in *The Holy Grail*. The Cinderella motif will become grimmer in the Geraint-idylls, and Lynette's harrying of Gareth will, transmuted, have harsher tones in *Geraint and Enid*, more ominous tones in *Merlin and Vivien*, and more relentless and horrifying tones in *Pelleas and Ettarre*. Gareth's impregnable sense of who he is and what he believes will be increasingly distorted or lost as the dissolution of Arthur's world becomes more imminent, a failed sense of it reaching deep into the crises of Guinevere and Lancelot, and being retained in a pure form only by Arthur himself, in a strange form by Galahad, and tangentially by Enid, Dagonet, and Bedivere. Gareth's quest, rooted in clear imaginative reality, is ironically prophetic of the disastrously illusionary Grail-quest, Gareth's departure to the applause of his kitchen peers is in marked contrast to the ego-inflation with which Percivale sets out, and Gareth's simple imaginative fables are very different from the sick quest-visions of Percivale. Gareth's white lie will darken into Lancelot's ominous, confused unselfing in *Lancelot and Elaine* and the desperate ritual of anonymity in which Guinevere attempts to discover hers and Arthur's real identities. Lancelot's supportive role in the youth-age motif of *Gareth and Lynette* will assume a cutting edge of cruelty in *Pelleas and Ettarre*. The fatal identity confusion that will invoke the horrifying catastrophe in *Balin and Balan* is, in the mistaken clash between Gareth and Lancelot, turned graciously and laughingly aside. Though "Arthur's harp" is "summer-wan" (that is, waning toward summer), Gareth, unlike Tristram in *The Last Tournament,* can still see it in open day and, like Dagonet, be moved by its music; but the fact that it is placed "In counter motion to the clouds" (1282) lightly foreshadows the stormy turbulence of the future. *Gareth and Lynette* thus implants in one literary texture a host of motifs that will reappear much altered by very different literary textures.

The matter of literary textures brings us to the final critical issue concerning *Gareth and Lynette*—its monitorial relevance to *Idylls of the King* as a total reading act. *Gareth and Lynette* is the most entirely comedic of the idylls, the alpha of a literary process of which the austerely tragic *Guinevere* is the omega, and the literary diagonal that has been noticed as functioning in the movement of the idylls published as a group in 1859 is extended to include all the idylls of the *Round Table* group, including those of the 1869 volume and the three "white spaces" idylls which the poet wrote last. The poem thus becomes a sort of *Divina Commedia* in reverse, moving from the *Paradiso* of *The Coming of Arthur* and *Gareth and Lynette* to the *Inferno* of *Guinevere* and *The Passing of Arthur,* with the other idylls functioning as an extended *Purgatorio;* and although the analogy should not be taken either literally or rigidly, it does distinguish Tennyson's poem about man in this world from its two most imposing predecessors—*The Divine Comedy* and *Paradise Lost*—as to both its manner and its final positioning of man.

This comedic-tragic literary consciousness is not a light fancy of the poet's but an integral part of the dense fabric of *Gareth and Lynette:* although the poem retains throughout a comedic tone and scale, it is clear that every major aspect of its imaginative world—language, metaphors, parables, setting, protagonist and antagonist, extended trials, catastrophe, recognition, and so forth—implies its opposite and that a significant change here and there could topple the tale into a different literary species. This possibility is implicit in the

characters of the three brothers—Gareth, Gawain, and Modred; and such "companion tales" as *Balin and Balan* and
Pelleas and Ettarre provide counterpoints to the manner of
Gareth and Lynette at least as important as any counterpoints
of meaning. When we combine this mirroring, contrapuntal
presence in the poem with the perception that Lynette and
Lyonors are dimensions of the same self and that they are
metaphoric projections of Gareth's inner reality, then the
possibility begins to emerge that *Idylls of the King* as a whole is,
in an inexhaustibly complex manner, evolved out of a primary Doppelgänger formulation, that at its center is a universal spiritual/psychic landscape summarized in the term "a
man," and that all the confusions are every man's confusions,
the successes and failures common to us all. Thus though we
may, like Gareth, enjoy a conspicuous degree of innocence
and joyous affirmation, every dark possibility in the experience of man is dormant in each of us, and without some such
order as Arthurianism there can be terrible awakenings that
lead out beyond the civilized human imagination.

■

Balin and Balan, the final writing act of *Idylls of the King,* is
such a terrible symbolic awakening. It is a gothic tale set
against the comedic romance of *Gareth and Lynette,* and although the narrator imposes on it a value-structure that attempts to be sad but reassuring, the tale itself breaks through
the fabric of values and tells its own tale of horror. For all his
Gareth-like goodness and attentiveness, Balan cannot civilize
Balin; and since they come from the same womb, either the
argument of natural heritage is totally discounted or the co-
eval nature of gentleness and violence is fully insinuated. The
Doppelgänger formula surfaces in its most explicit and lurid
manifestation, and any tendency we may have had to massage
complacently the question of man's ultimate condition is par-
alyzed by the full implications of the tale.

    The value structure that the narrator attempts to impose
monitors to a degree our reading of the idyll. *Balin and Balan*
carries the theme of debauch in high place to a dark, central

level. The relationship between Lancelot and Guinevere is brought teasingly to the verge of explicitness, and their peculiar natures gain new definition. The passage that relates specifically to Lancelot and Guinevere is crucially important:

Then chanced, one morning, that Sir Balin sat
Close-bowered in that garden nigh the hall.
A walk of roses ran from door to door;
A walk of lilies crost it to the bower:
And down that range of roses the great Queen
Came with slow steps, the morning on her face;
And all in shadow from the counter door
Sir Lancelot as to meet her, then at once,
As if he saw not, glanced aside, and paced
The long white walk of lilies toward the bower.
Followed the Queen; Sir Balin heard her "Prince,
Art thou so little loyal to thy Queen,
As pass without good morrow to thy Queen?"
To whom Sir Lancelot with his eyes on earth,
"Fain would I still be loyal to the Queen."
"Yea so" she said "but so to pass me by—
So loyal scarce is loyal to thyself,
Whom all men rate the king of courtesy.
Let be: ye stand, fair lord, as in a dream."

Then Lancelot with his hand among the flowers
"Yea—for a dream. Last night methought I saw
That maiden Saint who stands with lily in hand
In yonder shrine. All round her prest the dark,
And all the light upon her silver face
Flowed from the spiritual lily that she held.
Lo! these her emblems drew mine eyes—away:
For see, how perfect-pure! As light a flush
As hardly tints the bosom of the quince
Would mar their charm of stainless maidenhood."

"Sweeter to me" she said "this garden rose
Deep-hued and many-folded! sweeter still
The wild-wood hyacinth and the bloom of May.
Prince, we have ridden before among the flowers
In those fair days—not all so cool as these,

Though season-earlier. Art thou sad? Or sick?
Our noble King will send thee his own leech—
Sick? or for any matter angered at me?"

Then Lancelot lifted his large eyes; they dwelt
Deep-tranced on hers, and could not fall: her hue
Changed at his gaze: so turning side by side
They past, and Balin started from his bower.

(235–275)

Independent of the special effect witnessing this scene has on Balin with his very distinctive problems, aspects of the scene itself are of fundamental importance. It takes place within a highly cultivated garden, as contrasted with the ragged wildness which dominates the larger setting of the idyll. Guinevere makes her approach, the sunlight on her face, through a "range of roses," while Lancelot, emerging from the shadows, paces the "long white walk of lilies." The aggressor in the scene is clearly the Queen, who chides Lancelot with the disloyalty of ignoring her; and the fact that disloyalty is the one charge he would least be guilty of begins to define his dilemma and complicate the meaning of their relationship.

Lancelot explains his strange behavior by recounting, somewhat intensely, his dream of the lily maid, the enshrined Lady of purity. Guinevere, in turn, ignores his problem-defining dream and declares herself on the side of robust passion—"'Deep-hued and many-folded!'" But, ironically, she goes a step further in her preference for the "'Wild-wood hyacinth and the bloom of May,'" a flower commemorating the lover of Apollo upon whose blossom "Woe" is written and which is known as a symbol of mutability even more transient than rosebuds.[4] Their fated fall is implicit in his eyes that "could not fall," and they walk prophetically, like Adam and Eve, "side by side" out of their Edenic garden. Circumstanced as they are, Guinevere and Lancelot can never bring the purity-passion (lily-rose) dichotomy to merger and resolution. He knows this, and despite the complicating imperative of loyalty to the Queen, it enters into both his waking and his sleeping consciousness and colors his view of himself and his world. Guinevere, on the other hand, is so rigidly fixed as a May figure that she seems oblivious to it, and being in a position to demand loyalty, she hardly seems to knit the brows of her soul. Her sense of self and her sense of goal are syllogistic, and the imperial cast which this gives to her problem promises that it will take all the grandeur of a great Queen ever to come to terms with it. The Balin-Balan Doppelgänger narrative is a distant analogue to this.

But there is a prior metaphoric analogy. *Balin and Balan* begins with the story of King Pellam, a disloyal tribute prince who, in mechanic imitation of Arthur, tries to stratify spirituality through an elaborate iconolatry. The result is, even in and of itself, bizarre enough; but it spawns discourtesy, treachery, superstition, and decay—spiritual conditions that are antipodal to the Arthurian pressure and provide an additional dimension by which to gloss the Balin-Balan narrative.

That *Balin and Balan* functions according to the Doppelgänger formula is clear enough: the brothers are housed in the same womb; Balan lays the moods that Balin suffers; Balan goes in search futilely of the treacherous "demon of the woods" who hides and attacks from behind, as Balin struggles, futilely also, with an internal demon that erodes with recognized but unmanageable gusto; the two inadvertently kill each other and die "either locked in either's arm" (620). Balin is the ego of the piece. His cardinal sin, at least at the external level of moral action, is ungovernable rage; but the fact that he clearly recognizes this and, despite his firm resolutions and strenuous efforts, cannot cope suggests an inner inadequacy as the real source of his problem, as does the Doppelgänger formula.

The Pellam analogue glosses part of the problem: Balin simplistically seeks light for his inner darkness from a mechanical talisman—the Queen's "crown-royal upon shield" (196). This, in turn, becomes the focus of the baiting that destroys him—by Garlon and by Vivien. Another part of the problem is that his apprehension of the Arthurian ideal is vague at best. He indicts the King for overprizing "gentleness" (180), contradicts the King when Arthur calls the Queen's emblem "'a shadow's shadow'" (198–204), and takes, not the King, but Lancelot as his model (156–180). Balin's most fundamental flaw is infidelity to himself. His passionate self-depreciation gets its most violent articulation when he is face-to-face with Vivien:

> "here I dwell
> Savage among the savage woods, here die—
> Die: let the wolves' black maws ensepulchre
> Their brother beast, whose anger was his lord."
>
> (478–481)

But throughout self-depreciation is Balin's stock response to difficulty: it is his initial despair and his ultimate destruction. Even his view of the intimacy between Guinevere and Lancelot prompts, not a restructuring of his perceptions, but a torrent of self-abuse:

> "Queen? subject? but I see not what I see.
> Damsel and lover? hear not what I hear.
> My father hath begotten me in his wrath.
> I suffer from the things before me, know,
> Learn nothing; am not worthy to be knight;
> A churl, a clown!"
>
> (276–281)

True access to the Arthurian ideal would perhaps be a genuine corrective to Balin's false values, false models, and self-destruction, but somehow he fails of such access. Instead, his plight is externalized for the most part by a combination of vegetation/animal imagery like that of the world before Arthur felled the trees and slew the beast—a naturalistic, superstitious, nonredemptive landscape. Balin's problem is a distant, primitive analogue to that of Guinevere and Lancelot: he is torn between his savage, demonic nature and his desperate yearning for gentilesse. Valuing prowess over gentleness, he cannot find the inner resources to be gentle. Like Lancelot, he would "'break/[The] bonds that so defame [him]'" (*LE*, 1409–1410), but he cannot because, like Guinevere before her recognition scene, he has no genuine understanding of them.

Vivien's role in *Balin and Balan* is clearly preparatory for *Merlin and Vivien* in the context of *Idylls of the King* as a whole, as Sir Chick is a one-dimensional seeding of the motif to be developed more richly and complexly in the Elaine of *Lancelot and Elaine:*

> "I hold them happy, so they died for love:
> And, Vivien, though ye beat me like your dog,
> I too could die, as now I live, for thee."
>   (570–572)

But the role that she plays in *Balin and Balan,* though relatively brief, has larger and crisper implications even than that projection of her place in the Doppelgänger variant of *Merlin and Vivien.* In her song, she celebrates an apprehension of truth that is, however distasteful to idealistic minds, incontrovertible:

> "The fire of Heaven has killed the barren cold,
> And kindled all the plain and all the wold.
> The new leaf ever pushes off the old.
> The fire of Heaven is not the flame of Hell.
>
> "Old priest, who mumble worship in your quire—
> Old monk and nun, ye scorn the world's desire,
> Yet in your frosty cells ye feel the fire!
> The fire of Heaven is not the flame of Hell.
>
> "The fire of Heaven is on the dusty ways.
> The wayside blossoms open to the blaze.
> The whole wood-world is one full peal of praise.
> The fire of Heaven is not the flame of Hell."
>
> "The fire of Heaven is lord of all things good,
> And starve not thou this fire within thy blood,
> But follow Vivien through the fiery flood!
> The fire of Heaven is not the flame of Hell!"
>   (434–449)

In her refrain, Vivien dislocates a traditional and comfortably judgmental Manichaeism: "'The fire of Heaven is not the flame of Hell'" as simply as Apollo is not Lucifer; and yet it is the worship of Apollo ("'This old sun-worship,'" 451), the most generative force in nature, that has infected the sensuous mind—symbolically in the May-figure Guinevere (266)—and released all those forces that destroy Arthurianism. And even though Vivien fabricates a fable about the incident between Guinevere and Lancelot, that fable does not falsify the truth. The facts of Balin's nature magnified by the imaginative facts of Vivien's natural philosophy incite a highly ritualized action just as consistent in its mythic implication as any act of effulgent reverence:

> his evil spirit upon him leapt,
> He ground his teeth together, sprang with a yell,
> Tore from the branch, and cast on earth, the shield,
> Drove his mailed heel athwart the royal crown,
> Stamped all into defacement, hurled it from him
> Among the forest weeds, and cursed the tale,
> The told-of, and the teller.
>
> (529–535)

It is an ugly act by traditional standards, but it is an authentic act too. Though the outcome is one of defamation rather than of consecration, the process that leads to it is an authentic mythic process: a character of a well-defined sort attempting to cope with a deep internal problem in a fully elaborated cultural context undergoes a sudden illumination that enables him to translate one conception of truth into quite another conception of truth. It is not a matter of judgment, but of apprehension, neither tragic nor pathetic. Its aesthetic effects are gothic, leaving us wide-eyed but comprehending.

It is an indispensable revelation, this final writing act of *Idylls of the King,* and it connects itself with some thoughts that Tennyson had had about *In Memoriam* some twenty years after the publication of the elegy and at roughly the time he was beginning to conceptualize *Balin and Balan.* In his remarks to James Knowles on the occasions of reading *In Memoriam* aloud (1870 and 1871), Tennyson said: "It's too hopeful, this poem, more than I am myself . . . [*sic*] The general way of its being written was so queer that if there were a blank space I would put in a poem . . . [*sic*] I think of adding another to it, a speculative one, bringing out the thoughts of *The Higher Pantheism,* and showing that all the arguments are about as good on one side as the other, and thus throw man back more on the primitive impulses and feelings".[5] *Balin and Balan* would seem to be the other poem that, in the spirit of the thought, Tennyson added at the last hour to *Idylls of the King*. As *Gareth and Lynette* is the most metaphysically hopeful of the idylls, *Balin and Balan* is the most metaphysically despairing. Both protagonists have a keen sense of "I am I," though they are very different I's, and both fulfill their doom. And the way in which the poem dissuades us from judging Balin dissuades us from judging Gareth too. On a larger scale, it removes the rubric of judgment, a traditional device of intellectual closure, from reader-instrumentation in the most fruitful approach to Tennyson's major work. That the poet was genuinely circumspect in his decision to add such a basic clarification of the conception underlying *Idylls of the King* is suggested by the long period of time (1874 to 1885) that he allowed to elapse between the completion and the publication of *Balin and Balan*. But its effects on the poem as a whole are tremendous, stripping *Idylls of the King* of borrowed endorsements at odds with an authentic modernism and freeing purely imaginative apprehension to stand solitary on its own.

Though written last, *Balin and Balan* is placed fourth among the *Round Table* idylls, and it is the first embodiment of the explosive violence that overtakes a number of the secondary knights of the Order—Balin, Pelleas, Tristram. Each of these three is, in the end, grossly unfaithful to the Arthurian ideal, and each dies in a devastating act of gothic horror. But in each case, it is not moral profligacy but perceptual incompetence that lies at the root of their disastrous destinies. Even Tristram's moral meandering is specifically traceable to his dulled inner eye. They lack the imaginative resource to transcend their sensuous selves and to perceive their identity in a reality ultimately independent of things seen. The same principle applies to the other failed figures in the poem. Merlin, for all his natural magic, is imprisoned in an order of nature lower than the ontologically moral; Elaine, though delicately refined, is locked into a diminished view of tolerable human experience that strips man of his most turbulent but grandest potentialities. Ettarre is so deformed by worldly cynicism that even the possibility of authentic imaginative love escapes her perceptual capacity, and the lost love over which she grieves herself to death is at best a deeply suspect human quantity. Even those figures who, while they escape catastrophe, miss grandeur—Geraint and Percivale—suffer most conspicuously from a stunted imagination: they take the letter for the spirit, the form for the substance, and enjoy but a dwarfed survival. On the other hand, those characters in the poem who achieve, however painfully, some degree of success in life—for example, Gareth, Enid, Lancelot, Dagonet, Guinevere, and Bedivere—have the capacity, each according to his character and circumstances, to reach some truce with the sensuously imprisoning self and to emerge, in however slight degree, to a level of selfless serviceability based on inner conversion through imaginative love. The conversions of Lancelot and Guinevere are, of course, the most invigorating because of the largeness of their stature and the precariousness of their state, but in all cases the degree of freedom from confusion, though behavioral in its results, is perceptual in its source.

Galahad and Arthur are, in very different ways, the poem's prototypical perceivers, though Arthur gradually looms so large and Galahad plays so relatively slight a personal role that it seems disproportionate to pair them. Moreover, it is fair to say that Galahad's symbolic integrity emerges from the texture of the *Holy Grail* narrative somewhat jeopardized. Still, he is allowed to stand as an imaginative possibility, precarious as a model for most, but perhaps relevant to the very, very few. If he invokes thoughts of the spiritual imagination, then, despite its effectiveness for him, it is a seductive delusion for most.

Arthur, on the other hand, is not seductive in any ordinary sense of that term. He is "pure, generous, tender, brave, human-hearted,"[6] but not seductive. He is the dominant image in the "dream of man coming into practical life," and he embodies the highest expectations of the wholly human imagination. He inscapes reality in such a simple, august fashion that, momentarily at least, men who see and hear him suddenly have a glimmering of their own potential and swear vows to live up to that potential, to realize that startling, awesomely beautiful perception in all their practical affairs. But their "quickened, multiplied consciousness" does not last. As they become immersed in the infinity of details, the multitudinousness, of daily living, they lose touch with the imaginative affection that fueled their aspirations and begin even to remember it but vaguely and as something different from what it in fact was. They chafe at the vows they made, having forgotten that without the perception the vows are essentially meaningless, that without an authentic, cohering life-awareness, it is impossible to rise above an erosive sense of chaos. Thus Arthur functions as the ordering imagination, the code of conduct that he devises being a derivative behavioral structure—a hierarchy of metaphors—for the maintenance of personal order. Moreover, the degree of success that man does attain will be closely related to the character and quality of the myths that his imagination creates since his myths are an empirical measuring of his visions, and Tennyson was surely right in his judgment that there is "no grander subject"[7] than the myth of which Arthur is the cohering center. He fails, of course, "being simple" (*PA*, 22) in thinking that his insight into reality, however true, is equal to the conversion to the highest purposes of all the passions and capacities of even the most favored members of the human community. But his failure is by no means complete, and until he wholly loses poetic faith, until he is willing to let his world collapse into an infinity of meaningless details, man, like Arthur, knows that the ordering imagination will come again and again and that even if he never enjoys complete success, he will never suffer complete failure.

Notes

1. Walter Pater's Conclusion to *The Renaissance, The Works of Walter Pater*, 10 vols. (London: Macmillan, 1910), I, 234.
2. Eversley, III, 501.
3. William Butler Yeats, *The Second Coming*.

4. See Philip Mayerson, *Classical Mythology in Literature, Art, and Music* (Waltham, Mass.: Xerox College Publishing, 1971), pp. 138–140. Apollo promised "that Hyacinth would be reborn as a flower whose petals would be marked with the god's own words of grief: *Ai Ai,* Greek for Alas!" Milton, in *Lycidas,* speaks of this myth of the "sanguine flower," and Keats's Zephyr, in *Endymion,* "Fondles the flower amid the sobbing rain."
5. Knowles, p. 1982, quoted Ricks, pp. 859–860.
6. Eversley, III, 446.
7. See also Tennyson's phrase "the greatest of all poetical subjects" (Eversley, III, 440).

Part Three

A Critical Profile of
Idylls of the King: 1953–1981

A Critical Profile of
Idylls of the King, 1953–1981

Headnote: Three studies of historical significance are not represented here: Paull Franklin Baum's *Tennyson Sixty Years After* (1948),
F. E. L Priestley's "Tennyson's *Idylls*" (1949), and E. D. H. Johnson's
The Alien Vision of Victorian Poetry (1952). Professor Baum's book has
simply self-destructed. The author had little sympathy with his subject, and though he was acute in identifying issues, he was often
capricious (sometimes wittily vicious) in his treatment of them. Professor Priestley's landmark essay has long since been absorbed into
the conventional wisdom on the poem and has been superseded by
his book, *Language and Structure in Tennyson's Poetry* (1973), which is
cited several times. Professor Johnson's book was a great influence
for good until Tennyson studies came into their own; since then, it
has seldom been referred to.

In order to keep the identification of passages cited as clear and
simple as possible, I have keyed them to the List of Works Cited at
the end of Part 3. All citations (quotations or, occasionally, paraphrases) are given chronologically under a given topic and are
identified by author, title (full or abbreviated), date of publication,
and page number(s), full bibliographical detail being given only in
the List of Works Cited. In the numerous cases where two or more
citations from the same author occur, it may be assumed that, in a
given sequence, the second and subsequent citations from the same

author are from the same work. However, many authors have more than one work to their credit, and to eliminate any possible confusion between or among pieces, I have included the date of publication with all citations.

Occasional interpolations and paraphrases are italicized and enclosed in brackets.

To reduce several thousand pages of analysis and criticism to approximately a hundred pages may have led to some mistaken choices and some misplaced categories. For any such instances of failure, I apologize. It hardly needs to be said that this selection is an introduction to, not a substitute for, a rich critical legacy.

Theme

■ [T]he poem is first of all, like the Shakespearean play, a rich pageant and a colorful panorama with an exciting story of sin and retribution. Beyond this, Tennyson's epic is the symbolic study of a corrupt and decadent society from its rise to its fall, when it dragged down even that perfect prince who formed it. This was the loss of an ideal of perfection which Tennyson tried in vain to show his contemporaries; he is showing them not only what actually is but also what could be. Thus the sin of Guinevere is merely the symbol and not the source of the decline of the Round Table. It is but one of many sins—pride, greed, selfishness. The symbolic progress is seen in the springtime *Coming of Arthur* where the wasteland is again made fruitful with the optimistic words: "The old order changeth, yielding place to new" (the irony of this line when it appears in the last idyll is obvious). In *Gareth and Lynette* the Round Table—the new civilization—is in its flower. But in the two Geraint idylls the sin of Guinevere serves to bring to light the pride of one of her husband's knights. And so the progression goes: the decay of kinship in *Balin and Balan,* of intellect in *Merlin and Vivien,* of virtue in *Lancelot and Elaine,* of religion in *The Holy Grail,* and of honor in *Pelleas and Ettarre,* where the fabric of the *Idylls* is tightened:

The Queen
Look'd hard upon her lover, he on her,
And each foresaw the dolorous day to be;

And all talk died, as in a grove all song
Beneath the shadow of some bird of prey.
Then a long silence came upon the hall,
And Modred thought, 'The time is hard at hand.'
                                                    (591–597)

As each virtue and stability of character collapses the civilization is further doomed. (Samuel C. Burchell, "Tennyson's
'Allegory in the Distance'" [1953], 422.)

■ The *Idylls* then pose a persistent Tennysonian question:
"Have we risen from out the beast, then back into the beast
again?" ("Locksley Hall Sixty Years After"). In order to save
himself man must "Move upward working out the beast,/And
let the ape and tiger die" ("In Memoriam" CXVIII). The
alternative is the vision of the brutish reign over the wasteland which opens and closes the *Idylls*. Tennyson, of course,
recognized that the human and the bestial in man are part of
the contraries that perennially raise havoc by waging the
never ceasing *bellum intestinum*. Always suspicious and fearful
of the Passions, the poet sought a solution in the classical
ideals of "Self-reverence, self-knowledge, self-control"
("Oenone"). In the *Idylls* man rejects or ignores each of these
disciplines and thus dooms himself and his society. This decline of human values and attributes is accompanied by an
ascendancy of the beast image—in volume and proportion—
to serve as both a reminder of our lower nature and a dramatic foreshadowing of the final cataclysm. For the *Idylls* end
with a bang not a whimper amidst the growling and roaring
echoes of fallen man. (Edward Engelberg, "The Beast Image
in Tennyson's *Idylls of the King*" [1955], 292.)

■ Tennyson likewise seems more concerned with the mixed
middle state of human beings than with an inhuman or superhuman sanctity, for he concentrates primary attention
throughout the *Idylls* on the conflicts of troubled imperfect
souls, and he takes care to give his real protagonists, Lancelot
and Guinevere, the sort of close psychological motivation that
neither Galahad nor Arthur requires. He probes Lancelot's
"remorseful pain" at the death of Elaine and at once suggests

that through such suffering, Lancelot will slowly grow in stature until he die "a holy man." And to a full analysis of Guinevere's warring passions he devotes the final and climactic panel of "The Round Table." (Jerome H. Buckley, *Tennyson* [1960], 189.)

■ [T]he *Idylls*, read in proper sequence, builds somewhat like *Troilus* to a tragic denouement, which the temper of a whole civilization rather than the sin of any one individual makes inevitable. The poem no longer presupposes the early-Victorian idea of progress, which rang through "Locksley Hall," but a later and gloomier cyclical view of history. Could Arthur's kingdom remain true to its first principles, could it rise in time of crisis to what Arnold Toynbee would call the moral challenge, it might learn to control its successes and turn to social good its manifold selfish energies. But increasingly committed as it is to the values of expediency, sensuality, and self-interest, it must face its certain doom; there can be no renewal, except in another milieu altogether, for by the fundamental law of being "The old order changeth, yielding place to new." Though few of the Victorians could see the pertinence of the analogy to their own age, Tennyson by the time of "The Holy Grail" and all the later Idylls was wholly persuaded of the soundness of his somber vision and able to write with a deeply felt urgency. His finished poem, itself a city built to music, attains its most compelling resonance in the overtones of his conviction. (Buckley [1960], 193–194.)

■ Tennyson created in the *Idylls* a mirror for the society of his times. We are presented with an ideal king, a warrior for Christ, throwing back the forces of barbarism, and ruling with justice, followed by a people labouring together to procure order and righteousness. There can be little doubt that this was his ideal for the British Empire. This in fact is what he revered in Gordon, who had the terrible zeal of the military missionary, and in Wellington. But the *Idylls* actually indicate not Tennyson's ideal for the Victorians, but his condemnation of them. Arthur's kingdom was destroyed by solid selfishness, as Tennyson feared his own generation were destroying their own law and freedom. We are not able to regard the *Idylls* with that enthusiasm which caused Lady Tennyson to see *Guinevere* as the noblest poem in the language, but we cannot altogether dismiss them. The question is, do they express an understanding of things which is really mediated to us through the poetry, or merely a didactic system easily detached from it? Did Tennyson really grasp and communicate what he intended to communicate? And this is a question not about Tennyson's beliefs but about the substance of the poetry itself. (Valerie Pitt, *Tennyson Laureate* [1962], 188.)

■ The traditional interpretation of the *Idylls* is that Arthur's kingdom falls because of the adulterous relationship between Lancelot and Guinevere. Against such an interpretation I would argue that decay has already set in before there is any mention of their guilt. Sir Kay is as boorish as, perhaps more so than, any of the antagonists to Arthur's cause. He fails in gentleness, courtesy, and obedience to the King; he is but the first we meet who does not live up to his vows. For we see as the *Idylls* progresses that by volitional violation Arthur creates the necessity for emotional dependency: being not themselves but pale facsimiles of the King, his knights must depend more and more on someone or something for emotional satisfaction.

Lancelot's and Guinevere's sin is thus, I believe, not the cause but the symptom of what is wrong in Camelot. Arthur has attempted to take Guinevere completely unto himself, to refashion her according to his conceptions, to make her will his, to set her up as the feminine ideal; and he forces this view of her—that is, Guinevere as the feminine counterpart to the ideal man—on his order. Guinevere is not, however, made of the same metal as the King. A real woman and not an abstract ideal presence, she has all the passion and longing for life of a normal woman. In this world of illusions where, says Merlin, all is "Confusion, and illusion, and relation,/Elusion, and occasion, and evasion" ("Gareth and Lynette," ll. 281–82), Guinevere suffers the same delusions as everybody else. This is made manifestly the case when in "The Coming of Arthur"

Guinevere mistakes Lancelot for the King. It is not surprising, therefore, that even the rumor of an illicit sexual relationship on the part of the Queen is enough to disenchant the knights of the Round Table. They have been forced to believe in an ideal; and when they see that their ideal is merely human after all and subject to the same delusions and faults as real people, they immediately are led to suspect that nothing is true—neither the idea of the Round Table nor their loved ones. (Clyde de L. Ryals, "The Moral Paradox of the Hero . . ." [1963], 58–59.)

■ Tennyson's vision in *Idylls of the King* is, as I said, a vision far different from that reflected in *In Memoriam*. The elegy deals with the search for truth by means of speculation on and contemplation of the transcendental world, and it gives a picture of man knowing himself through transcendental experience. The *Idylls*, however, shows man realizing himself through encounter with earthly experience, and, further, portrays, especially in "The Holy Grail," the inadequacy of transcendental experience as a guide to conduct. Tennyson is here clear that there is no truth for the individual except insofar as he creates it for himself in his actions. Hence the necessity for self-committal and unswerving performance in the demands of that commitment. In contradiction to *In Memoriam* the *Idylls* implies that reality as a thought is never more than a possibility, whereas life properly conceived is concerned only with the instant, which is reality itself. As Tennyson himself said apropos of the poem: "Birth is a mystery and death is a mystery, and in the midst lies the tableland of life, and its struggles and performances" (*Memoir,* II, 127.) In other words, man should act on the known, should focus on the struggles and performances of life and not expend his energies on contemplation of abstractions. As Arthur says to the recently returned Grail knights:

> And some among you held that if the King
> Had seen the sight he would have sworn the vow.
> Not easily, seeing that the King must guard
> That which he rules, and is but as the hind

> To whom a space of land is given to plow,
> Who may not wander from the allotted field
> Before his work be done. . . .
> ("The Holy Grail," ll. 899–905)

In the *Idylls* Tennyson takes into account all the contradictions of existence. The poem represents existence as blossom-
ing in eternity but accomplished in the instant; it portrays
that existence as choice and expectation, risk and gain, life
and death, the past declaring itself in the present; and finally
it shows life as a permanent tension between the finite and
the infinite. The philosophy of the *Idylls* is thus a realism and,
as such, a denial of the transcendentalism of *In Memoriam*.
(Clyde de L. Ryals, "*Idylls of the King:* Tennyson's New Realism" [1967], 7.)

■ It is grander in conception than in execution and as-
suredly wooden in some of its details, but in its totality it
represents a kind of judgment by the poet on his own accomplishment. Its double concern with the relationship between
poet and public, and with the responsibility of the poet to
meet the promptings of his own insight, suggests the tensions
of the earlier poetry. In other words, *Idylls of the King* is not
only about society but about poetry, a fact which, I think, has
been insufficiently acknowledged by his previous critics. My
purpose here is to review the poem with special attention to
the theme of the uses and limitations of the poetic art, and to
show how this may be linked to the more generally discussed
moral theme. (Lawrence Poston III, "The Two Provinces of
Tennyson's 'Idylls'" [1967], 372.)

■ It may be helpful to recall the earlier description in
"Oenone" of Troy, the city built to the music of Apollo's lyre
and destroyed in the war which results from Paris's choice of
Aphrodite. Troy is a symbol of social order, but it is also a
product of the poetic imagination. Camelot appears to serve
an analogous purpose. In the Seer's speech, the figure of the
King is closely associated with his city. The King is real in that
he is without duplicity, he is what he seems; at the same time

he is a shadow because he represents an ideal beyond human achievement. The music of the harmonious social order of Camelot will be silenced, as Vivien's song of "the rift within the lute" promises. But Camelot, like Troy, is a paradoxical symbol of the poet's art as well. It is "never built at all" in the material sense, for it is the product of the imagination; but it is "built forever" in the sense that what is created by the imagination is enduring. The words "built forever" contain a further paradox. Camelot is "built" insofar as it is a completed event in the legendary past, but it is also "built" in the sense of "a-building": it grows continuously throughout the poem as an increasingly complex metaphor for the world created by the poet's imagination. The city thus typifies both permanence and change, the perfection of completed art and the development of the poet's mind. On the moral level, this allegory of "the War of Time against the soul of man" shows Arthur's social order as an attempt to arrest time through the imposition of vows which can never wholly be fulfilled, while such figures as Vivien and Tristram actively coöperate with the forces of change and corruption. On the aesthetic level, however, the poet creates a world not susceptible to "time's revenges." (Poston [1967], 377.)

■ [Merlin's] surrender constitutes a kind of withdrawal into a palace of art; by an ironic twist, he is permanently immobilized when he yields to what is transient, involved *in* time. The surrender is obviously sexual, with the edifying moral that Tennyson's audience may have expected, but it is also the surrender of the responsibilities of prophecy for a delusive beauty. It is a pity that Merlin does not heed the warning implicit in his story of the hart with the golden horns: poetry may expel the beautiful when designed to capture it, and the hunters, like Merlin, allow a crucial moment of decision to escape them. (Poston [1967], 378–379.)

■ To borrow Carlyle's phrase, then, I have been trying to show a few instances of Tennyson's concern throughout the *Idylls* with "two provinces," moral and aesthetic. The moral theme emerges through the surface events of Camelot, the aesthetic theme through the addition of lyric and expository comment. The poem reaches its climax in "The Holy Grail," where the two provinces come perilously close to being disjoined altogether, for the social responsibility of Arthur's knights seems to conflict with their dedication to a spiritual quest independent of the aims of society. With Merlin removed from the stage, we must look to the King himself for some kind of reconciliation since Arthur, as the symbol of union, must speak for the divided world over which he presides. (Poston [1967], 379.)

■ The surface meaning of ["The Holy Grail"] is by no means obscure: only a few are capable of meeting the demands, poetic or spiritual, of the visionary quest. The others, as Arthur puts it, "follow wandering fires/Lost in the quagmire!" In "The Voyage," a poem belonging, like "The Holy Grail," to the 1860's, Tennyson had explored two extreme responses to the quest in the mindless enthusiasm of the crew and the sterile and ultimately self-destructive scorn of the cynic. The range of motives in the idyll is a wider one, and is complicated by other elements. The quest recalls the Seer's description of "the Riddling of the Bards" as "Confusion, and illusion, and relation,/Elusion, and occasion, and evasion." Art is a form of speaking by indirection. It creates an illusory world which is regulated by its own laws, in effect an "evasion" of material reality, and yet it also requires "relation": the awareness of an aesthetic order within the work, and a definable relationship between the work and the reality it portrays. Many of the knights, however, are guilty of illusion and evasion in a different sense; their quest is a substitute for life rather than a meaningful ordering of it. (Poston [1967], 379–380.)

■ [*An implicit question implicit in the "Idylls" is this:* "[H]ow is the idealist to act on the basis of *a priori* categories that have only an accidental relation to external process?" *The basic answer:*]

[B]ecause Arthur cannot find God 'in His ways with men' . . ., Tennyson can resolve the idealist's dilemma only by going beyond exemplary human action and apocalyptic imagery to an undisplaced cycle that is not a commentary on the outside world at all, but a subsuming principle of order, disorder, and human re-creation, which contains the world within itself. . . . The real meaning of Arthur's second coming is that for the spirit he represents there can be no past or future but only a continuing present. Tennyson's Arthurian myth is designed to lead to a recognition scene, a discovery in which we see, not our past legends, but the total cultural form of our present life as it is involved in the same venture of civilizing nature and investing the wasteland with the flesh and blood of our own redeeming vision. (W. David Shaw, "The Idealist Dilemma . . ." [1967], 52–53.)

■ [*In realizing his dialectical vision, Tennyson attempts to resolve certain problems:*]
[H]ow to re-create a vision of human and artistic order as something separate from nature, but "as in effect a second nature." . . . Tennyson tries . . . to show how the idealist's values, in involving themselves in the world outside, do not simply reflect external events, but exist somewhere between the particular example and the universal precept. . . . Instead of building on a natural base, it tends to reverse natural process, and subsume it in specifically human symbols. The symbols celebrate the liberation of the Arthurian Order, the transformation of life itself into that "art" which according to Burke is man's "nature." . . . Tennyson's third and final resolution of the idealist's dilemma is, properly, a form of subsuming and including time, and not itself intrinsically temporal. Like all myths, Tennyson's adaptation of the Arthurian legend employs, in Kenneth Burke's words, "a terminology of quasi-narrative terms for the expressing of relationships that are not intrinsically narrative, temporal, or linear, but 'circular' or 'tautological.'" (Shaw [1967], 44–45.)

■ The motif of the "fool" follows the fortunes of Arthur's realm like a malevolent shadow. It appears in the story of

Geraint who in his "sweet observance and worship," forgets his "promise to the King," "the tilt and tournament," "his glory and his name." In this idyll Tennyson presents a secular version of the absolute behaviour (Geraint "never" leaves his wife) which leads to the fruitless quest for the ideal, and by degrees, to the destruction of the Order. The motif appears in the story of Balin and Balan who fiercely extinguish one another while Vivien sings her infernal ballad. It appears more openly in the idyll of Merlin and Vivien as Tennyson narrates in slow, exhausting detail the wearing down of Merlin's wisdom by the samite-robed seductress. Vivien finally draws from Merlin the charm that places a man always in the power of others, never in his own. (R. B. Wilkenfeld, "Tennyson's Camelot: The Kingdom of Folly" [1968], 286.)

■ The narrative design of "The Last Tournament" reflects Tennyson's concern with the mythology of folly. First he suspends the "nestling" story, the conception of the tournament, the preparation for the tournament, the day of the white tournament, and the night of the red feast between Tristram's twice-stated question, "Why skip ye so, Sir Fool?" Then he actively develops Tristram's journey and dream, Arthur's battle with the Red Knight, and Tristram's encounter with Isolt out of Dagonet's answer to the question. The idyll moves irresistibly through a series of intermediate confrontations (Dagonet and Tristram, Arthur and Lancelot, Arthur and Guinevere, Arthur and Lancelot, Tristram and Lancelot, Tristram and Dagonet, Tristram and Isolt of Brittany, Arthur and the Red Knight, Tristram and Isolt of Ireland) to the ultimate confrontations: Tristram and Mark, Arthur and Dagonet, as folly's brethren meet to recognize their essential nature. (Wilkenfeld [1968], 292.)

■ Dagonet speaks truly. Although the "waving hands" of Vivien are subdued by Arthur's own "waving" hands (as he blesses his errant queen), the three greater Queens and the Lady of the Lake await him as the clinging voice of Dagonet gives way to their shivering cry and the fluting of a "full-breasted" swan's "wild carol." As the complex verbal framework out of which the narrative is built makes abundantly clear, Arthur's realm was populated by fools, and it is no surprise to discover he was, himself, the greatest fool of all. He endured and that was his greatness; he died for his vision and that was his folly. Yet although he has to "pass on and on" and go "from less to less and vanish," it is into "light" that he vanishes. Tennyson was neither an intellectual weakling nor a sentimentalist. The light of the "new sun" bringing in the "new year," illuminates both the triumph and the defeat of the Order—a triumph and defeat stunningly concentrated in the overarching multiplex concept of the "fool." (Wilkenfeld [1968], 294.)

■ The benignity of this universe and its God must somehow encompass the fact of mutability and mortality, of Arthur's death and the disappearance of Excalibur, that Bedivere finds so hard to accept. The conclusion to "The Passing of Arthur" answers Bedivere's doubt with a Christian variation of the Hesperidean "wisdom" and of the understanding that Tithonus had come to by the time of his monologue:

> "The old order changeth, yielding place to new,
> And God fulfills himself in many ways,
> Lest one good custom should corrupt the world."
>
> [ll. 408–10]

This climactic message seems to repeat a Hesperidean notion: it is necessary that Arthur die and that Camelot come to blight, that "kingdoms lapse, and climates change, and races die" ("The Hesperides," l. 46). But the Hesperidean Sisters had celebrated natural mutability because it assured the "bliss of secret smiles" and the smug knowlege of divine uniqueness. The "High God" of the *Idylls,* who beholds the world from beyond and enters it to make it beautiful ("The Passing of Arthur," ll. 16–17), withholds immortality from the world for man's good, as well as his own, lest man come to know the "corruption" of a Tithonus. Furthermore, while the Hesperidean Sisters oversee a random clashing of "wandering waters," the High God of the *Idylls,* "fulfils" himself in a teleology, a controlled evolution wherein man moves progressively toward God as he increasingly adapts the world to express himself in his changing forms and as he evolves to man's apprehensions of him. To retain a single good custom too long would frustrate this process. (Gerhard Joseph, "The Idea of Mortality . . ." [1968], 144.)

■ The lasting significance of the *Idylls of the King* is the comprehensive way in which it outlines the most basic of human tragedies, the personal and social dislocations that arise from man's passion to transcend mutability and mortality." (Gerhard Joseph, *Tennysonian Love* [1969], 187.)

■ Tennyson's lack of confidence in social regeneration by law is evident in this poem. Not that Tennyson thinks social reform by law is ineffectual, but he feels, as Burke has stipulated, that wise men will "apply remedies . . . to the cause of the evil, which are permanent, and not the occasional organs or transitory modes in which they appear." He made the following comment in 1860: "He [the protagonist in 'Maud'] does not cry out against the age as hopelessly bad, but tried to point out where it is bad in order that each individual may do his best to redeem it; as the evils he denounces are individual, only to be cured by each man looking to his own heart" (*Memoir*, I, 468). (Joseph Solomine, Jr., ". . . The Rise, Decline, and Fall of the State" [1969], 115.)

■ But just what are the "values" contained in the vows and the Arthurian civilization? Nowhere are they described beyond the vague and youthful prospects of Gareth to "do the good and right the wrong". What is important is not the content or qualities of these values, but rather the fact that they are part of an illusion raised above the Dionysiac realm to preserve the self. Again and again the impossibility of keeping the vows is emphasized, and not only by Arthur's detractors (see "Gareth and Lynette", ll. 266–267). The vows represent the self's resistance to absorption. In a conventional good-and-evil sense the *Idylls of the King* is not the moral tract that some have made it out to be, and it is difficult to discern just where the so-called "Victorian morality" appears.

Immediately Guinevere's "sin" is called to mind, and the fact that it is always referred to as a "sin". Within the medieval context of the poem it is a "sin". Tennyson in a sense passes judgment on Guinevere but not so much because she did "wrong" as because she betrayed and caused the destruction of the Apollonian illusion, man's last hope. So Arthur, apparently when he first suspects Lancelot in "Lancelot and Elaine", instead of reproaching him or breaking with him, tries to bolster and strengthen him by repeating his name to him:

> Lancelot, my Lancelot, thou in whom I have
> Most joy and most affiance, etc.

Nietzsche's description of the triumph of the Dionysiac tendency perhaps provides the best explanation for the use of sexual promiscuity in the *Idylls:*

> The central concern of such celebrations was, almost universally, a completely sexual promiscuity overriding every form of established tribal law; all the savage urges of the mind were unleashed on those occasions until they reached that paroxysm of lust and cruelty which has always struck me as the "witches' cauldron" *par excellence.*

Nietzsche views promiscuity as the manifestation of the destruction of the illusion and the submission to the voice of Dionysos. Arthur's dream-kingdom can be compared to the Apollonian illusion that Nietzsche found completely triumphant in the heroic ideals of Homer. "Nature often uses illusions of this sort in order to accomplish its real purposes. The true goal is covered over with a phantom." And this illusion is necessary. Nietzsche is perhaps a more accurate psychologist than historian in his conclusion:

> The Greeks were keenly aware of the terrors and horrors of existence; in order to be able to live at all they had to place before them the shining fantasy of the Olympians. Their tremendous distrust of the titanic forces of nature; *Moira,* mercilessly enthroned beyond the knowable world . . . the Greek conquered.

This describes the nature of the dream-kingdom of Camelot, surrounded by the beast that must inevitably absorb it and the wave of doom poised at every moment to fall. While *Idylls of the King* has many different facets and levels of significance, at its core it is the most comprehensive vision of a "subjective poet", more tragic than religious, and beyond good and evil in any conventional sense. (William R. Brashear, *The Living Will* [1969], 151–153.)

■ Abstract. One aspect of the broad theme, intrinsic to *Idylls of the King,* of conflict between appearance and reality is the problem of deception and the concomitant artifice which makes it manifest. In the course of the poem, deception intensifies in ferocity and purpose to become a flaw which destroys both personal integrity and social unity. Lies, rumor, sophistry, role playing, and mirror images (which distort the relative realities of object and reflection) effect a web of irony and paradox which obscures the tissues of reality, rendering truth equivocal and virtually inaccessible to human perception. Analysis reveals the manner in which deceit instigates action and provides a means for characters to educe their various designs. Through the intricacies of anticipation and parallel structuring, and through linking the themes of idealism, "use," belief, identity, and social order, the expediencies of deception contribute coherence and unity to a poem which has often been viewed as fragmentary. (E. Warwick Slinn, "Deception and Artifice. . ." [1973], 1.)

■ Tennyson is asserting through the *Idylls* the primacy of the Unseen, the ultimate reality of the spiritual, which is manifested in a constant succession of phenomena. The phenomena are not merely shadows or illusions; they are "real" in that they are the temporal actualization of the ideal. Man's task is not to pierce through the evil of appearances and brush it aside; it is to recognize the relationship of appearance to an ideal reality which he cannot fully know, and to work in the realm of phenomena towards more complete actualization of the ideal in so far as he knows it. . . . The task is not to be fulfilled by a denial of human nature or of human problems; aesceticism is a retreat. Nor is it to be fulfilled by the search for personal intellectual certainty of the Unseen; this again is a retreat from the real duty. (F. E. L. Priestley, *Language and Structure* . . . [1973], 251–252.)

■ Against the Lucretian spirit Tennyson upholds the Ver-gilian [*i.e., against Lucretius' philosophy of the futility of aspiration, Vergil recognized as man's persistent problem the need to find a reasonable ground for his faith*]. (Priestley [1973], 255.)

■ Arthur's reply makes two important points that once again emphasize the main themes of *The Idylls of the King*. First, he tells his knight to have faith that God is present in history, and that history, even the destruction of the Round Table, has meaning and purpose. In a particularly poignant and courageous assertion of his own faith, Arthur expands upon his words to the Roman lords come for tribute in "The Coming of Arthur", telling Bedivere: "The old order changeth, yielding place to new,/And God fulfils himself in many ways,/Lest one good custom should corrupt the world" (408–10). Earlier, the assertion that since the "old order changeth", he would not render tribute to now impotent Rome, acts to demonstrate that the young Arthur well knows in whom to place faith, and he will not do so in those too weak to keep it. Now in this darkened, lessened time, Arthur's recognition that his own time has passed is his final demonstration of faith in God and His ways. He thus tells Bedivere to comfort himself, bidding him to pray for his king's soul.

> More things are wrought by prayer
> Than this world dreams of. Wherefore, let thy voice
> Rise like a fountain for me night and day.
> For what are men better than sheep or goats
> That nourish a blind life within the brain,
> If, knowing God, they lift not hands of prayer
> Both for themselves and those who call them friend?
> (415–21)

In this most explicit emphasis of the poem's theme of faith, Arthur overtly defines man as the being who is able to pray, as the one being whose nature permits him to have faith. This problem of having and keeping faith which Tennyson investigates continuously throughout the poem is, then, more than a matter of Arthurian times, more than something which concerns man in relation to his religious, personal, and politi-

cal existence alone: faith, the ability to have and keep it, defines the essence of the human. (George P. Landow, "Closing
the Frame" [1974], 439–440.)

■ In essence, "The Passing of Arthur", like the entire poem,
concerns itself with the same problems as *In Memoriam* and
offers much the same solutions. This close resemblance
should remind us that in its earliest form the tale of Arthur's
departure from this earth, like Tennyson's great elegy, was a
direct response to Hallam's death. Both poems not only emphasize man's essential need to believe but also those forces
which make it so difficult for him to do so. Equally important,
they both dramatize the process of authentication by which
individual men reach the state of belief. When I point to
these similarities I am not holding that Bedivere is an allegorical representation of Tennyson, or that King Arthur is
Arthur Hallam, or, for that matter, that Arthur, who is so
frequently and elaborately described in terms of Christ, is
meant to be Him. Rather that Tennyson draws upon these
analogous situations to present what remain his main concerns throughout much of his poetic career: that both men
and their societies must be founded on faith—or, more accurately, on many faiths, on faith between ruler and ruled, man
and woman, worshipper and God; and that such faith, however essential, is necessarily a tenuous, subjective, nonra-
tional matter. *In Memoriam* appears optimistic because its
overall movement shows how one man, Tennyson, achieves
faith after great trials, while *The Idylls of the King* is most
pessimistic because it dramatizes the destruction of an ideal
when men do not keep faith. "The Passing of Arthur", while
making it quite clear how the Round Table failed, yet offers
some cause for hope when it presents the trials, triumphs,
and conversion of the ordinary man, Bedivere. (Landow
[1974], 441–442.)

■ Like Bradley's *Appearance and Reality*, the *Idylls* have the
variety and iridescence of life itself, and its indirection, too.
Both works move among opposites and rejoice in contradic-

tions, but founder on the same paradox: "What seems to us sheer waste is, to a very large extent, the way of the universe." But because Tennyson honestly confronts this paradox, he is able to achieve at the end a powerful consolation. The discovery of the dying Arthur is neither the consolation of the optimist—in this best of all possible worlds, everything is a necessary evil—nor is it the consolation of the pessimist—where everything is bad, it must be good to know the worst. "The Passing of Arthur" combines present despair with distant hope. The saddest and most brooding of Tennyson's endings, it charts the Virgilian abyss, the tears in things. Yet the *Idylls*, as Harold Bloom has finely said of Keats's "Ode to Autumn," end "in an acceptance of process beyond the possibility of grief." Though Arthur learns to fathom, in isolation and among the ruins of time, the fear of oblivion—that powerful undertow of terror flowing deep beneath the surface of every human life—his celebration of death, if rightly understood and pondered, becomes a consecration of remembering. It is precisely this kind of subdued elation that Tennyson achieves in the classical monologues and in *In Memoriam*—indeed, in all his best verse, which is always elegiac, even in prophecy and passion. At such moments, glancing down "cliffs of fall/Frightful, sheer, no-man-fathomed" (Gerard Manley Hopkins, "No worst, there is none," ll. 9–10), Tennyson reflects on the dissolving past. From his crumbling foothold in time he has glimpses of hope, but never loses his fear of quick, precipitate descent. The great enemy for Arthur is not a computer programmed to achieve his annihilation. It is despair, a force that is all the more insidious for being internal and self-generated. But as Arthur masters his despair, he affirms his belief in a power above the doomsday machine: a grace that sanctifies and pre-empts from the forces of darkness the judgment of the last great battle. Arthur's distant hopes owe something to the play of his mind on ultimate abstractions such as virtue and justice, qualities already embodied in his life, which flow into the world from the energies of a mind that can exorcise its fears and morbidity, realizing like the mourner of *In Memoriam* and like the poet of the late elegies the promise of even the most diminished life. (W. David Shaw, *Tennyson's Style* [1976], 221–222.)

■ [W]hereas Browning put himself into the frame and wrote a poem which is essentially about the power of the imagination to extract the pure gold of truth from the crude ore of fact, Tennyson put himself into the middle of the poem and wrote about the failure of the imagination to live up to its poetic ideal. (A. Dwight Culler, *The Poetry of Tennyson* [1977], 241.)

■ The lesson of the *Idylls* therefore would seem to be that a life-denying asceticism is as destructive in its effect as a surrender to sensual passion. While Tennyson's ideal was married love, a tranquil ordering of the senses, in his most moving work he celebrated "a lost or unrealisable love in a personal or legendary past." (Philip Henderson, *Tennyson* [1978], 127.)

■ This new poetic medium Tennyson expected to be no better received than Camelot, and of no longer duration, and yet he must have felt it embodied an epic truth that like Arthur and Camelot "will not die/But pass, again to come" (*Coming of Arthur,,* 421). This enduring truth is compounded of the totality of human thoughts and feelings groping in their imperfection and ignorance toward newer forms in the eternal process, that Tennyson believed not only leads to perfection but already contains it; for the goal of eternal process is but perfect process, and even the present striving toward the goal already embodies in a germinal stage the thing it aims for. In this process, the role of the poet must be the role of King Arthur: the patient and dispassionate craftsman, welding together such diverse and imperfect elements as the time provides, in the knowledge that though the world shaped out of his consciousness and captured in his poetry must pass, it shares in its very transience and diversity the attributes of evolving perfection implanted by the divine poet. . . . (Robert Pattison, *Tennyson and Tradition* [1979], 151.)

■ The state is built on heroic spirit but, as the state develops, a point is reached when it eliminates external challenges and thereby reaches a deadly stasis of peace and rest. According to Hegel, the latter is a "mere *customary life*" that "brings on

natural death. Custom is activity without opposition . . . a
merely external sensuous existence which has ceased to throw
itself enthusiastically into its object. Thus perish individuals,
thus perish peoples by a natural death" through "political
nullity and tedium" (pp. 74–75).

A summary of the *Idylls* will support this Hegelian explanation. Camelot rises in an apocalyptic condition of natural
anarchy when oppositions are very real. Heroes enlist under
Arthur as representative of world spirit bringing historical
form and, microcosmically, they subordinate the "self-will of
caprice and passion" to the higher faculty. Through the vows,
they are reborn to be like Arthur, like their higher selves.
Through this engagement with active providence, Camelot
overcomes the Roman power and establishes its hegemony
over various kingdoms, becoming a universal family with a
wise and powerful head. Happiness is not pursued on the
sensuous level, but rather as a joyous sacrifice and duty. This
unity deteriorates when a time of golden rest and "custom"
arrives, because external challenges have been eliminated
. . . . Heroic passions, being immutable (as was urged with
regard to all Tennysonian heroes, Ulysses especially), begin
to eat inwardly to produce an existence on the level of "self"
(ordinary providence). Now, instead of knights like Gareth,
"free" in perfect service, Geraint wanders self-imprisoned
(although finally saved), Balin maddens and dies in fratricide, and Merlin immobilizes himself in Brittany. Dialectical
variations from the spiritual mean appear in the form of Pellam and Vivien: asceticism and sensuality. The vows, also he-
roically immutable, are transferred to historically destructive
objects: the Grail and women like Ettarre. Camelot produces
its dialectical opposite in Pelleas's Round Table of the North.
The contradictions in the historical condition can be held no
longer and Camelot falls in apocalypse back into the natural
anarchy from whence it arose. (Henry Kozicki, *Tennyson and
Clio* [1979], 117–118.)

■ The unity of Camelot covered in the previous chapter begins to deteriorate, first as a fault (although one that closes) in
the Geraint idylls and then as a widening breach in the Balin

and Balan and the Merlin idylls that follow. The central cause for this growing disintegration is that real external opposition to Camelot's growth has been overcome. The will to continue an indefinite expansion has vanished, as has the disposition to take as significant the relatively minor disturbances within the empire. Accordingly, the knights no longer surrender themslves wholly to Arthur's purpose, and the passions (now without an object) become more and more difficult to control. Sacrifice begins to become painful. There is a rough progression in these five idylls. Soul's increasing inability to control sense is shown by Geraint's mendacious detachment from Arthur and by his purposeless wandering in the wilderness, by Balin's anarchical departure from court into the forest, and by Merlin's self-authorized journey into paralysis in Brittany. Internally, "maudlin and introspective morbidities," as Tennyson characterized irresponsibility (*Memoir*, 1:317), are gaining ascendency over the nobler passions involving historical purpose. (Kozicki [1979], 128.)

■ In Freudian terms, we may see Arthur as the reality principle warring against Vivien as the pleasure principle. Those wholly committed to the one or to the other do not display a schizophrenic agony, but those in whom spirit is struggling in further development are in conflict with themselves. Tennyson suggests this struggle as the Doppelgänger motif noted so often in these idylls. (Kozicki [1979], 131.)

■ In the four idylls before the final debacle—"Lancelot and Elaine," "The Holy Grail," "Pelleas and Ettarre," and "The Last Tournament"—Arthur, the vows, and the state itself become progressively oppressive. As Hegel says, with external dangers eliminated, people begin to sense that, in this struggle, they were "fortifying a position for Right and Order *against themselves.*" Arthur becomes something different at this point, an oppressive "other" rather than the embodiment of the universal self. As a result, the vows are transferred from him to the sensual and then to the ascetic object. (Kozicki [1979], 135.)

■ But, as indicated in the previous chapter, critics find a profusion of causes for Camelot's decline. Arthur, then, as Rosenberg notes, is "never more blind to this complexity than when he concludes his denunciation of Guinevere, 'And all through thee!'." Yet, to deny the primacy of the "sin" is to deny the moral center in history. This center fails when there is a betrayal both of the "righteous King of your heart" (Maurice's words) and of the fealty due the head of state. The temptation to sin is a "test of this loyalty" (Seeley). All follows from this. Passions and evil men can be controlled with will and self-sacrifice, but the slack in golden rest brings "the allowed sin," as Tennyson said, that "poisons the spring of life" (*Memoir*, 2:131). Civilization fails by a loss of nerve that spreads contagiously from the center of power. (Kozicki [1979], 140.)

■ None of the evils that descend on Camelot are inevitable, then, even in the dangerous peace where no real challenges rise to test the will to moral perfectibility. Balin, Merlin, Tristram, Pelleas, and particularly Lancelot and Guinevere, all fall into the "sin" of their own choosing. In the general decline, as Merlin—and presumably Tennyson—tells us, Arthur was made, as Milton said, "Sufficient to have stood, though free to fall." The apple eating and the "sin" alike are acts symbolic of rebellion against this "righteous King of your heart." Guinevere may have fallen in love with Lancelot at first sight (MV 773–75), as Vivien did with Mark (MV 60–61), but no immutable consequences need have followed. In Lancelot's initial devotion to Guinevere and in Arthur's approval of it, presumably we have no condition other than the courtly love that fosters great deeds. Yielding to temptation changes this into the sin, but it need not have. (Kozicki [1979], 141.)

■ Thus, the *Idylls* speaks to a profound irony in human affairs, but there is a Christian heart to the mystery. Seeley wrote of the "paradox" (his word) that "no man is so happy as he who does not aim at happiness . . . men are expected to sacrifice not a part of their happiness, but all of it, for the state." Yet all states pass inexorably into oblivion, through the very agencies that brought them into being. (Kozicki [1979], 143.)

■ The paradox of Camelot's diminution—the *"dialectical nature of the Idea in general"* (as Hegel put it), that "it assumes successive forms which it successively transcends" —is that this change is not so much a metabasis, a reversal of things from good to bad, as a peripeteia in the somewhat ambiguous Aristotelian sense of things becoming their opposites. A situation that seems to be developing in one direction suddenly develops in the reverse direction, through the very forces locked into the inceptive form. The condition of failure seems incipient in the condition of success; indeed, success is but failure in the initial state. Critics have noted transformations and dialectical oppositions in the *Idylls*, but generally they have failed to give credit to the historical faithfulness of the representation. (Kozicki [1979], 144.)

■ Arthur as law and moral idea had held the contradictions of the human condition as a "balance or reconciliation of opposite or discordant qualities," in the words (from Chapter XIV of his *Biographia Literaria*) of one of the idols of the Cambridge Apostles, Samuel Taylor Coleridge. But with the attenuation of control brought about by the lack of challenges, the forces locked into Camelot's inception begin to oscillate in a destructive dialectic. There is first a movement to sensuousness and then a countermetamorphosis that turns the court from eroticism to asceticism. Pellam inaugurated it, in a foreshadowing of the Grail quest. (Kozicki [1979], 146.)

■ Arthur's words after the final battle in Lyonnesse refer to the waves crashing on the shore as "this great voice that shakes the world,/And wastes the narrow realm whereon we move" (PA 139–40). Civilization waxes and wanes, but spirit continues, as Hegel says, "in a variety which is inexhaustible," for God is "Infinite Power . . . Infinite Form . . . Infinite Energy" . . . Hegel's is a proposition Tennyson seemed to subscribe to in 1870 with his remark, "I don't find it difficult to believe in the Infinity of Worlds" (*Memoir*, 2:96). In this succession of historical forms Camelot becomes a martyred sacrifice by which an unknown God "fulfils himself in many ways," simply because "one good custom should corrupt the world." (Kozicki [1979], 149.)

■ The word "use" neatly sums up the theme of the *Idylls,* and use may be seen as the heroic form of the domestic virtues. (Donald S. Hair, *Domestic and Heroic . . .* [1981], 127.)

■ *The Holy Grail, The Coming of Arthur,* and *The Passing of Arthur* (which I propose to call the Holy Grail group) powerfully dramatize epistemological and spiritual issues central to nineteenth- and twentieth-century thought. A line from Merlin's "riddling triplets"—'And truth is this to me, and that to thee'—identifies a major preoccupation of these poems: the impossibility of absolute belief, the relativity of truth to point of view, and the consequent epistemological, religious, and political dilemmas. The relationship of the temporal to the transcendent and the cyclic to the apocalyptic, the quality and kinds of religious experience, and the tension between man's longing for permanence and the inevitability of change are cognate matters which these idylls explore in . . . original and striking ways. . . . [*The critic draws a crucial contrast between this epistemological/spiritual center and the "moral considerations" at the heart of "Gareth and Lynette," the Geraint-Enid idylls, "Merlin and Vivien," "Lancelot and Elaine," and "Guinevere."*] (Kerry McSweeney, *Tennyson and Swinburne . . .* [1981], 99.)

Literary Characteristics: Allegory

■ Even if we believe that Arthur is the Soul and Guinevere the Flesh, there is hardly a true moral allegory in the *Idylls of the King.* What allegory there is is the "allegory in the distance." Tennyson puts it in the background, unobtrusively: it is a suggestion, an allusion—a hint that behind the fall of an ideal man there exist the larger issues of morality and Christianity. The poem is the biography of a wasted civilization, the regret for an ideal that cannot be attained again. Perhaps

this is an oversimplification, the dismissal of a baffling allegory. But in its very confusion, in its auspicious failure as a
moral allegory, we find the *Idylls of the King* not as a unified
poem but as a truly suggestive one, not rooted in one dogmatic principle of Soul versus Body, but a medley of pure and
symbolic narrative—a revelation, a diagnosis and a lament for
modern life in its complexity and its decadence, almost perfectly displayed in the last five of the idylls. (Samuel C. Burchell, "Tennyson's 'Allegory in the Distance,'" [1953], 424.)

■ Though Tennyson resisted a rigid allegorical reading of
his poem, he admitted "a parabolic drift"—which is to say a
symbolism—in his argument. Arthur may be intended as
something more than the simple personification of conscience. Yet he acts only from ethical commitment, and his
behavior consciously sets the standard by which the conduct
of his whole realm is to be governed or, wanting that control,
judged. In the war of Sense and Soul, which is the declared
theme of the *Idylls,* he bears the banner of the Soul. (Jerome
H. Buckley, *Tennyson* [1960], 176–177.)

■ The *Idylls* are primarily allegorical . . . [*Quotes Cleanth
Brooks on Eliot's "The Waste Land" as applying* "with very little
modification" *to the "Idylls":*] "The symbols resist complete
equation with a simple meaning. . . . The poem would un-
doubtedly be 'clearer' if every symbol had one, unequivocal
meaning; but the poem would be thinner, and less honest.
For the poet has not been content to develop a didactic allegory in which the symbols are two-dimensional items adding
up directly to the sum of the general scheme." (F. E. L.
Priestley, *Language and Structure* . . . [1973], 240–241.)

■ The poem, then, is primarily not an allegory, which means
something quite different (*allos*) from what it says, but a parable, which implies, alongside (*para*) a realistic narrative, a
generalizing comment on human life. Thus Arthur's life-cy-
cle (corresponding to one revolution of the mediaeval Wheel
of Fortune) is made to typify a 'cycle of generations', the
historical process by which the human race advances, through

alternating periods of progress and regress, rise and fall. (Paul Turner, *Tennyson* [1976], 151.)

■ Rosenberg argues that we should not call the method of the *Idylls* allegorical at all. I continue to do so because Tennyson did and because his method has clear links with the tradition of allegory, most notably that of the Italian poets of the Trecento and Renaissance. True, it evolves that tradition, using the idyll form as a catalyst, as Rosenberg points out: "Building on the techniques of the classical idyll, with its intensification of mood, its highly allusive texture, its startling juxtapositions, flashbacks, and deliberate discontinuities, Tennyson creates an inclusive psychological landscape in which all the separate consciousnesses in the poem participate and in which each action is bound to all others through symbol, prophecy, or retrospect" (p. 27). This is the traditional ambition of all idyll; to stress it exclusively is in part to ignore formal components that Tennyson also wished to embrace in his *Idylls*. (Robert Pattison, *Tennyson and Tradition* [1979], 171n.)

Literary Characteristics: Epic

■ In effect, the ten poems that constitute "The Round Table" stand as separate panels arranged in orderly progression and framed on the one side by "The Coming of Arthur" and on the other by "The Passing of Arthur." The frame defines the beginning and the end of Arthurian society, and each of the panels marks a stage in its growth or decline. Each of the parts is given an appropriate seasonal setting so that the colors of the background may accent the prevailing temper of the protagonists in the foreground and symbolize the moral condition of the realm itself. The sequence accordingly follows the cycle of the year from the fresh springtime of Arthur's marriage and Gareth's arrival at an uncorrupted Camelot, through a long summer of intense idealisms and hot destructive passions, on to the decadent October of the Last Tournament, the bleak November of Guinevere's repentance, and the winter wasteland of Arthur's defeat. Far from being consistently epical or heroic, the style from idyl to idyl is as variable as the weather. The blank verse is carefully adapted in tone to the shifting subject matter, and there is an intentional difference in texture between the frame and the pictures it encloses: "'The Coming and the Passing of Arthur,'" Tennyson explained, "are simpler and more severe in style, as dealing with the awfulness of Birth and Death." The form of the *Idylls of the King* is, in short, essentially a new one which is neither to be measured nor understood by the standards of the epic. (Jerome H. Buckley, *Tennyson* [1960], 173.)

■ [T]o treat it as an epic, or an epic *manqué*, is to regard the completed *Idylls of the King* in the wrong way. The epic is concerned with heroic action; its focus is on the hero in action. The *Idylls* does not have this as its chief concern, for Arthur is the hero in the background. (Clyde de L. Ryals, *From the Great Deep* [1967], 48.)

■ As well as being a continuation of the tradition of the heroic poem . . . the *Idylls of the King* represents a reactionary alternative to the prevailing forms and purposes of narrative. Not by authorial intent but by virtue of its situation in the nineteenth-century literary milieu, the *Idylls* is—in a more relevant sense than the term is often used—an anti-novel. . . . As its name should remind us, the novel fulfills its function by bringing us the news. . . . In contrast to such a function, Tennyson's *Idylls* does not inform us about and accommodate us to the unfamiliar but champions the cause of conventionally accepted though embattled values. . . . Tennyson . . . taking chivalry seriously by making it stand for the old verities that give order and coherence to the moral life, was being essentially quixotic. The term suggests the measure of his epic's right to our disparagement and praise. (James D. Kissane, *Alfred Tennyson* [1970], 118–119.)

■ The narrative discontinuity in the *Idylls,* as in romance, is itself an important virtue, in that it gives a sense of being in an art gallery, glancing slowly from one "little picture" to another. Even the overlaid seasonal progress in the *Idylls* suggests not so much objective, physical time as the spatial representations of time in medieval tapestry of triptychs. This emphasis on space seems to imply the absence of time, which in turn implies the conquest of time. (James R. Kincaid, *Tennyson's Major Poems* [1975], 151.)

■ Virgil and Milton wrote first pastoral, and then epic. Tennyson, wishing to follow their example, was probably encouraged by the upsurge of interest in Homer which began in the 1840s, became conspicuous by 1857, when a reviewer in *Blackwood's* wrote that Homer was 'in danger of becoming the fashion', and culminated in Matthew Arnold's *On Translating Homer* (1861), the immediate cause of Tennyson's 'Specimen of a Translation of the Iliad in Blank Verse' (1863). The fashion originated in the controversy provoked by Wolf's suggestion (1795) that Homer was not a single poet, but merely the name for a compilation of numerous short poems, preserved by oral recitation, and rather inadequately unified by later editors: a view developed by Lachmann, and attacked by Gladstone in the *Quarterly Review* (1847). The Homer boon resulted in unprecedented numbers of articles on Homer and Homeric translation, and of English versions in a variety of styles and metres. Other products were Clough's mock-Homeric *The Bothic of Tober-na-Fousich* (1848), and Matthew Arnold's 'Sohrab and Rustum' (1853), subtitled 'An Episode', Aristotle's term for self-contained sections of Homeric epic. Bulwer Lytton's *King Arthur: An Epic Poem* (1848–9) tried to cash in on the vogue, but was really mock-Arthurian and quite un-Homeric, being written in the metre of *Venus and Adonis*, and in a flippant style sometimes resembling that of Byron's *Don Juan*, as when Gawaine, about to be roasted and eaten by the goddess Freya, appeals to the Utilitarian criterion: 'THE GREATEST PLEASURE OF THE GREATEST NUMBER.'

Tennyson, of course, wished to write a classical, not a Lyttonian epic. The *Idylls* were to resemble the *Iliad* in relating the fall of a great city and civilization, the *Aeneid* in presenting a hero with a divine, historic mission threatened by the woman that he loves (Dido, Guinevere), and *Paradise Lost* in explaining the loss of ideal happiness through sin and disobedience. (Paul Turner, *Tennyson* [1976], 163.)

■ [*Tennyson was a Victorian Alexandrian who*] rejected the long-winded epic in favor of the highly wrought epyllion. . . . (A. Dwight Culler, *The Poetry of Tennyson* [1977], 233.)

■ *The Idylls of the King* are an Arthurian romance composed of twelve idylls so arranged as to form an allegorical, cyclical epic that, while it deals extensively with morals, is itself morally neutral. Because Tennyson had devoted his career to the manipulation of received forms, using the idyll as his primary mode, it is not surprising to find in the crowning poetic achievement of his life, a poem of Homeric scope, the playful, recombinant generic spirit that had been at work in *The Princess, In Memoriam,* and *Maud.* Nor is it surprising that the fusion of so many different forms and traditions at first bewildered the poem's readers. Tennyson's aim, however, was not to bewilder, but to develop the various formal strains of the *Idylls* in such a way that they would mirror his poem. (Robert Pattison, *Tennyson and Tradition* [1979], 135–136.

■ But Tennyson's epic union of his twelve idylls is not merely a matter of appearance. He not only imitated the length and number of books in the traditional epic, but followed the process that he considered essential to the creation of a new epic: he "invented his verse." Aubrey de Vere once criticized both Homer's and Milton's epics as containing much that was boring, to which Tennyson replied, "Possibly—but there's the charm of Milton's style. He invented his verse—just as Virgil invented his." Such a goal was clearly in the poet's mind when he approached the *Idylls:* to invent a verse form that was faithful to the tradition of epic and could sustain a narrative of some ten thousand lines while preserving the best elements of his own shorter idylls. The solution came in his distinctive pentameter and his original use of the verse paragraph. (Pattison [1979], 140–141.)

■ Nor are the epic qualities of the *Idylls* found only in the technical characteristics of its structure. Like Homer, Vergil, and Spenser, Tennyson embarked upon a national, as well as a universal, theme. He followed the trend in epic that evolved after Homer's heroic, social narratives: Vergil had imported from the idyll into the epic (especially in Book IV of the *Aeneid*) an element of romance and an interest in the erotic, emotional Theocritean world that had been foreign to the Homeric epic. Vergil's Italian descendants, Tasso and Ariosto, further exploited this interest in romance, though they were accused in their own time of violating the classical tradition that in fact they were developing. With Milton this romantic aspect of the epic, rooted in the idyllic examination of emotional and mental states, assumed a thoroughly psychological character: *Paradise Lost* is not so much about the Fall as about the psychology leading to it. Wordsworth's *Prelude* takes this psychological dimension of the epic to its logical conclusion in an examination not of some exterior mentality, but of self. Tennyson's epic steps away from Wordsworth's subjectivity (Tennyson's suspicion of the lyric probably hindered him from an epic undertaking on the lines of *The Prelude*), but he fully embraced and expanded upon the clear drift of epic toward romance and psychology, thus fulfilling the demands of both idyll and epic; the concerns of these two forms had become increasingly alike, till in Tennyson they met. (Perhaps this helps to explain the decline of epic in the modern world: as it developed romantic and psychological interests identical to those treated in shorter forms, it put itself out of business.) The *Idylls* are dominated by romance, both in the literary sense in which Tasso's *Gerusalemma liberata* is a romance and in the more modern sense in which the central affair between Lancelot and Guinevere is "romantic." (Pattison [1979], 143–144.)

■ The *Idylls* are several things at once. They are an epic on a national theme (the one Milton rejected in favor of the Christian epic), but they are also romance, allegory, and idyll; and to perceive the continuity they achieve demands a recognition of all these strains. For instance, although the *Idylls* have epic scope, it is not the Homeric scope of heroic actions, or even the Vergilian scope of historical destiny, but the psychological scope of the extended idyll. The allegorical elements of the *Idylls* are similarly transformed from their traditional Renaissance usages, and the romantic aspects of the poem do not accent adventure, as its sources do, but anticlimax. The curious amalgam of forms that constitutes the *Idylls*, resulting in a romantic epic of idyllic psychology, demanded a substitution of stasis for action, a necessity that neatly fitted Tennyson's view of his subject matter. The presence of many forms heightens the reader's awareness of the subtle and complex nature of the human condition described in the *Idylls*, and the curious lack of decision demonstrated by their characters reflects the poet's conclusion that a world of various forms might also be a world of deadlock, in which the competing forms held one another back from a transcendent truth. (Pattison [1979], 146.)

■ *Idylls of the King* is not the story of a single hero like Ulysses or Aeneas, and hence its twelve parts do not have the narrative continuity of the *Odyssey* or the *Aeneid*. Each idyll is a unit complete in itself, and each of the ten central idylls is about a person or persons around Arthur. These idylls each focus on a particular response or responses to Arthur's kingship, often as realized in the vows, more often as realized (or thought to be realized) in his marriage. There is, then, no continuous narrative line in the *Idylls* as a whole, but neither are the idylls wholly discrete. . . . Tennyson . . . compensates for the narrative discontinuity of the *Idylls* by making each a response to Arthur. Hence the form of the *Idylls* is a romance that is both discontinuous and continuous. (Donald S. Hair, *Domestic and Heroic* . . . [1981], 129).

■ [The *Idylls*] is not an epic, but a series of idylls with some order (about which Tennyson exercised himself considerably), which has something of an overall tragic pattern, though one which is to a fair degree episodic. The units of which the whole is composed fall, in any case, within the category of idylls, as Tennyson himself was rightly aware when he rejected the alternative and stricter title Edmund Lushington suggested, *Epylls of the King,* because he did not like the sound of "Epylls." (Theodore Redpath, "Tennyson and the Literature of Greece and Rome" [1981], 115.)

Literary Characteristics: Unity

■ The "idyl" is strictly a picture of mood, character, or gesture; and each of the Idylls moves through a series of sharply visualized vignettes toward its pictured climax, its moment of revelation. Though a few of the characters recur as links between some of the idyls, the unity of the sequence lies not in action or plot but in theme, imagery, and atmosphere. (Jerome H. Buckley, *Tennyson* [1960], 172–173)

■ However wide and various the critical discussions of its unifying forces, I think it may be generally agreed that the poem has a *rhythmic* structure of ebb and flow which in its external form corresponds to the poem's central subject, the rise and fall of a civilization, that the various idylls suspended between the "Coming" and the "Passing" of Arthur detail the swift decline of the Order from the glory and springtime gaiety of "Gareth and Lynette" to the nadir of the Order's fortunes in "The Last Tournament," and that although in "Guinevere" and "The Passing" the mood is sombre and elegiac, Tennyson develops some sense of a partial recovery from the profound despair and brute violence that mark the tenth idyll. (R. B. Wilkenfeld, "Tennyson's Camelot: The Kingdom of Folly" [1968], 281.)

■ Yet despite its tortuous evolution, the *Idylls* displays a remarkable unity. The germ of the whole, the fragmentary "Morte d'Arthur," drafted in 1833, revised in 1835, and published in 1842, was so instinctually right in tone and design that over a quarter of a century after its first publication Tennyson could incorporate it without change into the still-unfinished *Idylls* of 1869. During the next two decades he continually altered and expanded the design of the larger poem without violating the verbatim integrity of this first-composed but last-in-sequence of the idylls. (John D. Rosenberg, *The Fall of Camelot* [1973], 13.)

■ Tennyson's manipulation of time in the *Idylls* produces an effect akin to that of syncopation in music or, closer to his medium, to departures from regular meter in a line of verse. When the stress falls unexpectedly, it falls with twice the weight. The annual Tournament of Diamonds, spaced over nine years, establishes the normal temporal rhythm of the poem. But in "The Holy Grail," when the knights seek violent escape from the diurnal world to the world of eternity, Tennyson causes time to run amok: the narrative is deliberately discontinuous and kaleidoscopic; lightning and darkness, droughts and floods, replace any recognizable moment of day or year; apocalyptic time—in which all times are simultaneously present—displaces chronological time.

Throughout the *Idylls* leitmotifs of all kinds cut across the linear narrative and connect past and future. "Merlin and Vivien" opens with an impending storm that finally bursts in the closing lines; recurrent images of tempests and waves gather to a climax the storm of warring passions internalized in Merlin and externalized in nature. Before Vivien seduces him, indeed before the "present" in which the idyll is narrated, Merlin has

> walked with dreams and darkness, and he found
> A doom that ever poised itself to fall,
> An ever-moaning battle in the mist,
> World-war of dying flesh against the life.
>
> (188–191)

The wave poised to break symbolizes the seer's prevision of his own doom, but his fall is both a cause and prophecy of the larger fall of the kingdom. And so the dreams and darkness through which he walked later become the clouds of self-doubt that enshroud Arthur at the end; the moaning struggle in the mist foreshadows the last dim battle in the West, when the "wave" of heathen at last engulfs the kingdom, and it reverberates back to the founding, when Arthur pushed back the heathen wave and "made a realm and reigned" (CA, 518). (Rosenberg [1973], 30–31.)

■ [O]ur habitual notions of time undergo a progressive disorientation. As the founding recedes further and further into the past, we become more and more conscious of it in a continuous present, so that Camelot is still being built in our mind's eye as it goes up in flames, just as those flames were present in our imagination even as the city was being built. In some ultimate sense that only the experience of the poem can convey, nothing ever happens only once and everything that happens, happens simultaneously with its opposite. Camelot and the wasteland, music and discord, vows and betrayals, white roses and red, men imitating God and lapsing into beasts, growth and decay, soul and sense, reality and illusion, time and eternity—the whole dialectic of interlocked opposites is held in dynamic equilibrium and the opposites themselves, as Tennyson constantly suggests, are fractured halves of the same identity. Arthur's coming is shadowed with the foreknowledge of his passing, but his passing contains the possibility of a second coming. In this Arthur imitates the course of the symbolic season, which as it revolves toward winter is also approaching spring. Lancelot and Guinevere are marred and marked by their sin, and grow in grace because of it. The ruins of Camelot recall the city in its initial splendor, its fall persuading us of its prior reality. These reciprocal movements of rise and fall are held in perfect poise throughout the *Idylls.* In the beginning we are primarily aware of ascent and at the end, of decline. But both are constantly present, like the recurring pairs of symbols that accompany them. (Rosenberg [1973], 64–65.)

■ The most important unifying image, however, is that of music. It evidently arose from thoughts of the Homeric poet-harper Demodocus, the myth of Orpheus, and musical delights which, in the Charlemagne romances, make Avalon like a paradise for Ogier and for Arthur. In notebooks of Tennyson's Cambridge period, now at Harvard, he copied extracts relating to all these topics, including eighteen lines from the Middle English romance *Sir Orfeo,* and also attempted to draw a flute, a harp, and a violin. Though 'not thought to have an ear for music', he loved Mozart, and at Cambridge 'played himself a little on the flute' (*Memoir,* vol. 1, p. 77). Thus at an early stage the idea of music was associated for him with Arthur, especially as the constellation Lyra was also called 'Arthur's harp' ('Gareth and Lynette', 1281).

To summarize briefly the ubiquitous music symbolism of the *Idylls:* Arthur's attempt to 'manufacture Cosmos out of Chaos' (to adapt Carlyle's metaphor for Tennyson's own poetic attempts in 1844) is seen as the creation of music out of discord, an insubstantial and precarious balance of conflicting forces, which has to be constantly recreated. Thus Camelot (as in the Amphion myth) is 'built To music, therefore never built at all, And therefore built for ever' ('Gareth and Lynette', 272–4). 'Arthur's music' is gradually silenced by such disruptive elements as Vivien, herself the 'little rift within the lute' of her own song ('Merlin and Vivien', 387–90), and Tristram, the 'false harper', who substitutes an ugly music of his own, itself 'broken' when Mark murders him ('The Last Tournament', 260–84, 724–48). In each of the first eleven *Idylls* except 'Geraint and Enid' (which was originally only half of 'Enid', separated from the other half in 1873) there is a song: in 'The Passing of Arthur' the music has ceased, but for the wailing from his barge, as it floats away, 'like some full-breasted swan . . . fluting a wild carol ere her death' (433–40). (Paul Turner, *Tennyson* [1976], 168–169.)

■ [*The individual idylls are both* "narratively self-contained" *and narratively interlocked, the process of interlocking being achieved through* "cyclic strategies, repeated heroic and narrative formulae, and composite characterization." *In addition, the poem has* "a descriptive, a stylistic, and a dramatic unity," *and* "above all, its psychological unity is profound."] (J. M. Gray, *Thro' the Vision of the Night* [1980], 1–2.)

Literary Characteristics: Method or Structure

■ The poet's method is not the way of literary realism, and the philosophy that informs his poem is itself a protest against the tyranny of fact that enslaves the realist. Though the epilogue (no doubt to the amusement of the English Aesthetes) denounced an "Art with poisonous honey stolen from France," the French Symbolists, who were most consistent in their devotion to Tennyson, immediately and quite properly recognized the *Idylls* as an antidote to the positivistic spirit that had invaded nineteenth-century poetry. In the reconstructed Arthurian mythology they found a welcome and spacious release for the poetic imagination from the narrowed materialisms of their own age. (Jerome H. Buckley, *Tennyson* [1960], 192.)

■ It may seem poor sportsmanship to object to an author's taking his opportunity for an eloquent opening and conclusion; but in this instance the heightened phrasing seems definitely misleading. "Built to music" connotes a greater tightness of structure and a more sustained inspiration in style than Tennyson's *Idylls of the King* can really be judged to deliver. The impression of a Tennyson somewhat larger than life-size is conveyed also by Buckley's dropping, in two important instances, into a phrasing that tends to convey prestige by association. The *Idylls*, Buckley informs us, "read in proper sequence, builds somewhat like *Troilus*" (a favorite of Tennyson's among Shakespeare's plays) "to a tragic denouement, which the temper of a whole civilization rather than the sin of any individual makes inevitable." The idea is an inviting one; and the reader, borne along with it, is inclined to believe that Buckley is saying (as he is not really saying—at least not explicitly) that Tennyson's poem resembles *Troilus* not only in the way the plot goes but in creating a truly Shakespearean sweep and intensity. Arthur's kingdom, Buckley observes, if it had been able to "rise in time of crisis to what Arnold Toynbee would call the moral challenge," might have survived its successes for a longer period. The idea is again an attractive one, and we are apt to take in along with it the notion that Buckley has claimed for Tennyson's *Idylls* a veritably Toynbeean conception of the tides and currents of history. At times even the specific statements of the chapter strike one as more highly colored than a dispassionate view of the evidence would warrant. Thus we learn that Tennyson, having freed himself from the standards of "realism" that had operated in the *Enoch Arden* volume, entered upon *The Holy Grail* "with a firm aesthetic control" and "boldly adapted his materials to his own vision, now sharp and coherent, of the Arthurian world." (Donald Smalley, "A New Look at Tennyson . . ." [1962], 353.)

■ In these and other descriptions Tennyson builds up, parallel with the story, with the actual events of the poems, a commentary on their significance. This clearly is the right use for his elaborate descriptions. It was easy enough in the mediaeval setting of the poem to transfer the weight of the detail to heraldic descriptions, to the blazons of shields, the windows in the great hall of Camelot, the symbolic carving on the gates of the city. Nor is it possible to complain that these descriptions are inorganic. Though connected with the action, they do not and are not meant to belong to it; they are, as it were, mirrors in which it is repeated and revealed for what it is. (Valerie Pitt, *Tennyson Laureate* [1962], 211.)

■ In closing I should like to suggest how the interpretation of the *Idylls* which I have set forth helps to explain something about the structure of the individual idylls. In the beginning, in the first of the idylls of "The Round Table," the technique is that of straight-forward narration. "Gareth and Lynette" begins with Gareth's leaving home, establishing himself at Camelot, and going on the quest with Lynette; all of this is presented in chronological sequence. In "The Marriage of Geraint" we find the flash-back technique, a frame enclosing the main story of the idyll. "Geraint and Enid" picks up with the frame and proceeds once again in normal time sequence. "Balin and Balan" is more complex in form: we begin with the refusal of Pellam to send his tribute before we are introduced to the Balin story. "Merlin and Vivien" is more complex still: the idyll opens with Merlin and Vivien at Broceliande, then switches to Vivien at Mark's court, continues with an account of Vivien at Camelot—all this before we get to the story proper. The next five idylls, beginning with "Lancelot and Elaine" and ending with "Guinevere," are structurally very complicated. In these there is little continuous narrative flow; rather, there is constant backing and filling, a disruption of chronological narration.

The reason for the increasing complication in form of the ten idylls constituting "The Round Table" is, I believe, that this complexity symbolizes the frustration of Arthur in working his will and fulfilling his ideals. What we find, especially in "The Holy Grail" and "The Last Tournament," is the decay of the King's order indicated by the "broken music" of the narrative flow. The tensions emanating from the guilt, emotional dependency, and failure of the principal actors in these idylls are thus embodied in the very structure of the poem. (Clyde de L. Ryals, "The Moral Paradox of the Hero . . ." [1963], 68–69.)

■ The paradoxes inherent in *Idylls of the King* lend to the poetry that ambiguity which is sometime felt to be sorely lacking in Tennyson's verse. For the modern reader, Tennyson's reputation as a didactic poet often precludes a disinterested reading of the work. Usually read for his "message" or for his "technical skill," Tennyson is seldom appreciated in the way that every other major English poet is—for the merger of form and content. Because of the paradoxes in the *Idylls,* which in a sense become the form of the poem, we are able to see that Tennyson's habit of mind, in what is perhaps his major poetic endeavor, was to construct ironic and ambiguous situations, particularly around the character of Arthur. Rather than conveying ideas as a primarily "reflective poet" (in T. S. Eliot's term), Tennyson in *Idylls of the King* presents paradoxes which are in themselves meaningful; that is, instead of imposing ideas on the poem in order to enrich the texture, he develops his paradoxes so that the significance of the *Idylls* inheres in the narrative structure itself. (Stanley J. Solomon, "Tennyson's Paradoxical King" [1963], 271.)

■ The interpolated lyrics thus reveal character, they comment on the events and sometimes change them, and they usually point to some symbolic problem underlying the drama. They resemble each other in form, consisting usually of three-line stanzas with an *a-a-b* rhyme scheme, and so invite the reader to link them to each other as well as to the narrative in which each occurs. From Enid's song of Fortune to the novice's song in "Guinevere," the lyrics become increasingly cynical or despairing, and indicate the stages in the kingdom's decline. The shift away from the choral form of the knights' anthem in "The Coming of Arthur" may itself reflect the growing disunity of the kingdom and Tennyson's increasing preoccupation with the private world of his characters, whether that world is characterized by surrender to impulse, as in the cases of Gawain and Tristram, or faithful adherence to the promptings of conscience, as with Enid, Bors, and Percivale. (Lawrence Poston III, "The Two Provinces of Tennyson's 'Idylls'" [1967], 375.)

■ Abstract. The problem of structure in Tennyson's *Idylls of the King* may be resolved by considering the books in pairs and focusing on the Hegelian dialectic which informs them. Analyzing them in this manner requires regrouping the poems and subjecting them to sustained analysis, particularly poems of the first and second half. Such an arrangement reveals an exploration of four pairs of opposing beliefs whose conflicts are temporarily resolved in Arthur. The beliefs and the books which dramatize them are empiricism and idealism ("Gareth and Lynette" and "Balin and Balan"); skepticism and credulity ("Pelleas and Ettarre" and "Geraint and Enid"); sensuality and stoical repression ("Merlin and Vivien" and "Lancelot and Elaine"); atheism and mysticism ("The Last Tournament" and "The Holy Grail"). This reading, which turns on the dialectical law that any result must produce by an inevitable process its own opposite, is faithful to the successive shifts of position that characterize Tennyson's interplay of attitude in other poems. This reading also reveals a philosophical integrity that admits comparison with Hegel and, by implication and extension, with modern phenomenologists. The dialectical method prevents any form of consciousness, including Arthur's own, from closing the circle of conflicts generated by the antecedent forms. If the truth is the whole,

then, as Arthur realizes, it is beyond the reach of any one
individual. (W. David Shaw, ". . . A Dialectical Reading"
[1969], 175.)

■ *The Ring and the Book* and *Idylls of the King* are even more
obviously accretive in organization. Each consists of multiple
versions of essentially the same material. In reiterating information from shifting points of view, Browning and Tennyson
absorb variety in totality while evoking and then discarding
all potential perversions of truth. In *The Ring and the Book*,
Browning strives to create the impression that he omits no
possible interpretation of the central incidents of his murder
story. Since reality comprises the seeming infinity of plausible
appearances as well as the simple integrity of spiritual truth,
we must experience the sentimentality of Other Half-Rome
and the sensuality of Bottini to avoid falsification through
incompleteness. Moreover, to gain the power of looking accurately through the veils of falsehood and partial truth, we
must adopt and then reject the various distorted perspectives
of such men.

Though *Idylls of the King* shows this simultaneous gathering
and winnowing less strikingly, it follows a similar process,
presenting variations on a few essential situations. Through
disparate renderings of such recurrent motifs as feudal responsibility, chivalrous romance, and the knightly quest, Tennyson evokes shifting judgments of the Arthurian world and
its values of fidelity, purity, and aspiration. As the versions
accumulate, the view of human possibilities suggested by the
opening idylls impresses us more and more as childishly optimistic. The accretion of evidence peels away illusion, making the vision of life offered by the beginning of the cycle
seem naïve in its perception of the threats to the Arthurian
ideal of a virtuous order imposed on flesh by spirit. By the
time of *The Passing of Arthur,* only grotesque parodies remain
of the great motifs of feudal servitude and knight-errantry
that throughout have symbolized the attempt to realize this
ideal. First Arthur, despoiled of all his knights save Sir Bedivere, must threaten Bedivere's death to enforce his obedience. Then the King rides Bedivere's shoulders through a

wasteland to his own end. These distorted remnants of chivalrous action embody Tennyson's conclusion that Arthur's
aspirations were impractical but inexplicably worthwhile.

The forms of both *The Ring and the Book* and *Idylls of the
King* also reflect their authors' dialectical concerns. As many
scholars have noted, books two to eleven of Browning's masterpiece form a trio of dialectical triads itself dialectical in
nature. This process leads to the just conclusion enunciated
and dramatized jointly in the Pope's soliloquy and Guido's
second monologue. In a similar but less tidy fashion, Tennyson prepares us for his paradoxical judgment that spiritual
aspiration is foolish yet valuable through a series of contrary
renderings of potentially similar situations. Gareth and Pelleas, for example, both seek to impose their will upon the
world, to gain knighthood and manhood by making reality
conform to their imagination. Whereas Gareth succeeds, Pelleas fails, changing in consequence into the antithesis of his
original vision of himself. The stories of Geraint and Merlin
provide a complementary contrast. Despite relinquishing his
will in favor of chance, Geraint acquires new knowledge that
permits informed and vigorous action. Merlin suffers destruction by the same mistake. Through such opposed narratives, Tennyson works toward the breakdown of the dialectical process represented in "The Passing of Arthur," in which
he portrays a state of antithesis when no synthesis can be
discerned. (Michael G. Sundell, "Spiritual Confusion and Artistic Form in Victorian Poetry" [1971], 5–6.)

■ Beyond the simple allegory, if we may call it that, there is
another ordering concept in the *Idylls of the King* and that is
the pattern of faith triumphing over pride-engendered doubt
through humility, love, and selflessness; and, although Arthur
may die and the order may pass away, and the dream of man
may be ruined by that one sin, still the moral assumptions
reflected in Arthur's recognition of God's purpose in the
changing order of things, and the hopeful indications in the
salvation of Guinevere in this life, and Arthur in the next,
belie the melancholy appearances of the tale itself and suggest rather the mood and spirit which conclude *In Memoriam,*

a poem about another ideal man who passed away and whose passing occasioned the review of the same moral design that I have described here; a man who provided a glimpse of the potential man yet to come through the gradual process of self-fulfilment and self-improvement that the race and all individuals are hopefully engaged upon. . . . (John R. Reed, *Perception and Design* . . . [1971], 138.)

■ Large-scale attempts have recently been made to reinstate, or rather, instate *Idylls of the King* as a large-scale achievement. But a reader may find himself concurring with the claims that the *Idylls* are intricately patterned; that they show a subtle and erudite mastery of their sources; that they are a complex allegory and that they anticipate Jungian psychology;—without being convinced that they do indeed constitute a poetic whole. (Christopher Ricks, *Tennyson* [1972], 267.)

■ There may be some point in a crude list which would indicate where—to one reader at least—the unevenness of achievement is manifest. Of the twelve *Idylls,* three seem to me successful both in style and as wholes: "Merlin and Vivien," "The Holy Grail," and "The Passing of Arthur." Five seem a mixture of the successful and the unsuccessful: "The Coming of Arthur," "Balin and Balan," "Lancelot and Elaine," "The Last Tournament," and "Guinevere." Four seem broadly unsuccessful: "Gareth and Lynette," "The Marriage of Geraint," "Geraint and Enid," and "Pelleas and Ettarre." (Ricks [1972], 268–269.)

■ The central deficiencies of the style are two: that Tennyson has not creatively solved the problem of what the dialogue ought to be in a poem which necessarily embodies archaism; and that he has not creatively solved the problem of accommodating his style (what Arnold called his "curious elaborateness of expression") to the simple exigencies of narrative, of the humble essentials which would permit his story to move. (Ricks [1972], 270–271.)

■ The two kinds of time that I have been discussing—cyclic and apocalyptic—are built into the structure of the *Idylls*. The first is epitomized in the best-known and least understood line of the poem, stated at its opening and repeated like a closing chord at the end: "The old order changeth, yielding place to new" (CA, 508; PA, 408). The line itself constitutes a profoundly ambiguous cycle recapitulating the larger, dynastic cycles of the poem: first Rome, "the slowly-fading mistress of the world" (CA, 504), yields to the barbarians, who are then subdued by Arthur, who in turn yields to the chaos that succeeds him. If the first use of the line seems to promise perpetual renewal, its repetition implies the reverse. For Arthur's "new order" at the opening has become the "old order" at the end, and the order that replaces Arthur is even more barbarous than the one he displaced.

From this cyclic perspective, man's reeling back into the beast is both monstrous and *natural.* The Round Table is founded to arrest this process, and it succeeds only "for a space." The time before and after Arthur, and of all the later idylls except "The Holy Grail," is cyclic time, or time in nature, as opposed to Arthur's time, which is eternity and is always rendered apocalyptically. Of the several intentionally conflicting accounts of Arthur's birth and parentage in "The Coming of Arthur," one is especially relevant here. We learn from Bellicent, who long ago heard from Bleys, the master of Merlin, that Arthur was born on a dismal, storm-tossed night "in which the bounds of heaven and earth were lost" (371). The narrative is deliberately couched in indirection, for Tennyson is handling with great tact the central mystery of the *Idylls,* the dual nature of Arthur, who exists in time and transcends time. This is the moment of his "incarnation," and the storm over Tintagil which obscures the horizon symbolizes the instant when the temporal and the eternal transect. (John D. Rosenberg, *The Fall of Camelot* [1973], 37–38.)

■ Throughout the *Idylls* dreams are the enigmatic mediators of Arthur's reality. Landscapes of the mind unbound by the literalisms of time and place, they at once prophesy and reenact the King's self-doubts in "The Passing of Arthur." The dream of Leodogran in "The Coming of Arthur" figures as a kind of "little apocalypse" foreshadowing Arthur's uncertainties as he surveys the dead strewn about the battlefield.

Leodogran dreams of "a phantom king" hidden in a haze of rolling flames; the shouts of men slaughtering each other and crying out against his rule drown out the King's voice. Suddenly the dream changes, the haze lifts,

> and the solid earth became
> As nothing, but the King stood out in heaven,
> Crowned.
>
> (CA, 441–443)

The two halves of the dream have no logical connection, except as mutually contradictory opposites, and either half may be taken as a valid prophecy of Arthur's fate. That Leodogran chooses to support the King is as arbitrary as Gareth's affirming Arthur's reality even as Camelot disappears in mist before his eyes and Merlin warns that the King, like his city, may be only "a shadow" (GL, 262). Throughout the poem substance and shadow change places, and it is Arthur's peculiarity as a character that the shadow he casts is more real than his substance. Hence it is that in "Guinevere" he is unconvincing in his role as injured husband, but the moment he is back in his true setting—the death-white mists of the Last Battle—he takes on an overwhelming reality. As part of the same paradox, he is absent when the Grail is seen, present in its absence, for the two equivocally "real presences" might be mutually annihilatory. Or perhaps Arthur *is* the Grail and opposes the quest because he is already among them but they know him not. (Rosenberg [1973], 90–91.)

■ The structure of the *Idylls* everywhere mirrors its meaning. Hence in his poem in which shadow and substance continually reverse their meaning, dreams and actions are indistinguishable because ultimately identical. Whether Leodogran dreams the *Idylls of the King* or his dream is an event within it depends entirely upon one's point of view. Throughout the poem dreams and symbols become literalized in events, which in turn generate the dreams and symbols that are enmeshed in the narrative. Tristram's dream in "The Last Tournament" illustrates this principle in a single idyll, just as Leodogran's dream illustrates it in the larger compass of the entire poem. Asleep in the woodland lodge in which he had formerly made love to Isolt, Tristram dreams of presenting her with a ruby necklace, which turns to frozen blood in her hands (412). As Tristram sleeps, the action shifts to the opposite end of the kingdom, where Arthur attacks the Red Knight of the North. But Tristram's dream of blood and guilt continues to color this parallel strand of the narrative, in which Arthur's "blood-red" adversary (442) is slaughtered and his hall rings with the shrieks of his massacred followers. The action then returns to Tristram, but with so deft an interweaving of the two narrative strands that it is as if the dreaming Tristram were awakened by distant shouts from the Red Knight's hall:

> Then, out of Tristram waking, the red dream
> Fled with a shout, and that low lodge returned,
> Mid-forest, and the wind among the boughs.
>
> (486–488)

Two events widely spaced geographically but temporally simultaneous—Tristram's journey westward to Tintagil and Arthur's to the North—are fused in Tristram's dream, which in turn propels the narrative into the future, as Tristram rides from the forest to his impending slaughter at the hands of the shrieking Mark.

A similar fusion of dream and action occurs in the garden scene in "Balin and Balan." Chilled by Lancelot's hesitancy in approaching her, Guinevere rebukes his aloofness with a simile: "ye stand, fair lord, as in a dream" (253). The phrase is at once figurative and literal, for Guinevere's words and the lilies by which Lancelot pauses have reawakened his dream of the previous night, when he saw the Virgin standing "with lily in hand" (255–256). The transition between dream and waking life in the garden continues in "Lancelot and Elaine," where Lancelot's dream of the Virgin materializes in the narrative in the form of the virginal Elaine, who with lily in hand floats past him in death. Finally, the dream is commemorated in an imaginary art that extends beyond the art of the poem itself as Arthur directs that the lily of Elaine be sculpted on her tomb.

As dreams have the power of actualizing themselves in the narrative, so symbols take on a life of their own, momentarily usurping the role of the person or thing they symbolize. Throughout the *Idylls* the worm or serpent bears its traditional significance, and worms within gardens are emblematic of the Fall. But the peculiarly Tennysonian use of the symbol occurs in the last of the garden scenes, in which Modred is half-metamorphosed back into the serpent that he symbolizes. Clothed in green, he "couches" high on the wall of Guinevere's garden, where Lancelot discovers him and, plucking the symbol from the wall, "cast[s] him as a worm upon the way" (G, 35).

The inner temper of the characters continually manifests itself in the outward action of the poem. Lancelot, for example, enters the Tournament of Diamonds as a kind of moral cripple; his spiritual wound becomes palpably physical as his own "kith and kin" (LE, 464), emblematic of his divided, guilt-ridden self, bear down upon him and leave him all but dead upon the field. Lancelot's self-struggle intensifies in "The Holy Grail," where, on the steps of the Grail castle, he is confronted by two great lions that rise "upright like a man" (818) and threaten to tear him to pieces. It is as if the rampant lions emblazoned on his shield have come to furious life. The man and his animate emblem grapple with one another much as Balin struggles to suppress, but finally becomes, the savage heraldic beast painted on his shield.

From the synoptic perspective in which we are now viewing the *Idylls,* character cannot be abstracted from symbol and both have no substance apart from the narrative in which they are embedded. In essence the narrative is a sequence of symbols protracted in time, the symbolism a kind of condensed narration. The story functions like the melody in a game of musical chairs, with the dramatic personae exchanging roles as they move from one position to the next. However outlandish, this image figures in the poem itself as the vacant chair, carved with curious figures, which Merlin made and named "The Siege perilous"; he sits in it and is lost forever, Galahad sits and is saved (HG, 168–178). The story of the novice knight and the scornful lady provides a similar narrative matrix; the young Gareth is formed within it and emerges unscathed, whereas the fledgling Pelleas is destroyed in the identical role. (Rosenberg [1973], 135–137.)

■ The archetype of all relationships in the *Idylls* is the triangle of Arthur-Guinevere-Lancelot, of which the many other triangles are variants. Extending beyond this primal triangle, each of the principals gives rise to secondary characters who are their analogues or antitypes. Thus Arthur is reduplicated in his nephew, Gareth, and, by antithesis, in Gareth's brother, Modred. The mixed potentialities of Guinevere's nature reappear in the false Ettarre and the faithful Enid. Finally, Arthur and Lancelot set the pattern for all fraternal relationships that become fratricidal, as embodied microcosmically in Balin and Balan and macrocosmically in the civil wars that destroy the Round Table. (Rosenberg [1973], 139.)

■ At the heart of Arthur's story is the dual cycle of his coming and promised return. The *Idylls,* incorporating this cycle into its structure, is itself a kind of literary second coming of Arthur, a resurrection in Victorian England of the long sequence of Arthuriads extending back before Malory and forward through Spenser, Dryden, Scott, and Tennyson. The poem takes on the quality of a self-fulfilling prophecy and validates itself, like Scripture, by foretelling in one passage what is fulfilled in the next. Dreams most clearly serve this prophetic function, but the various songs interspersed throughout the *Idylls* also anticipate and symbolize the action. Although formally set off from the narrative by rhyme, the songs are in fact lyric condensations of the idylls in which they appear, like "A Worm within the Rose," which foreshadows Pelleas' discovery of Gawain sleeping with Ettarre among the roses.

This capacity of the *Idylls* to symbolize itself is everywhere apparent. The allegorical figure of Time carved in the hermit's cave (GL, 1166–1170) casts in relief the theme of "Gareth and Lynette" and of the entire poem; so, too, the twelve great windows commemorating Arthur's battles mirror the twelvefold division of the *Idylls* and lend a kind of fictive historicity to the King's victories (HG, 248–250). Like the sculptured effigy of Elaine, works of art within the poem memorialize the work of art that *is* the poem. A final image emblematic of the whole occurs in the very center of the *Idylls,* in Vivien's love song to Merlin. Vivien interrupts her song to remark that it resembles a fair necklace of the Queen's

> That burst in dancing, and the pearls were spilt;
> Some lost, some stolen, some as relics kept.
>   . . . so it is with this rhyme:
> It lives dispersedly in many hands,
> And every minstrel sings it differently.
>   (MV, 450–451, 454–456)

The fair necklace symbolizes the quintessential matter of Arthurian legend. Deformed by time, retold in fragments by countless minstrels, the myth was at length shaped by Tennyson into the perfect circle of the *Idylls.* (Rosenberg [1973], 143–144.)

■ The basic structural pattern . . . is the dramatic movement inherent in the rise and fall of Arthur's kingdom. We can recognize in the total sequence of the twelve idylls a three-part structure very much like that of a drama in three acts. The first four idylls show generally the triumph of good over evil, the establishing of Arthur's order, the victory of truth over falsehood, of life over death.

[Part II] opens with a tremendous impact, the grim and violent *Balin and Balan,* followed at once by the sinister triumph of Vivien over Merlin. . . . [*Merlin and Vivien*] comes at the center, the sixth idyll, and henceforth the movement is towards the catastrophe and the coda. The second half of the middle movement, and of the total poem, abruptly shifts tone and style in *Lancelot and Elaine.* . . . We look back again from death and destruction to the world that was and still might be: Elaine's world is like Gareth's world, certain and serene. The destruction of this world and of Elaine by Lancelot is a human tragedy in itself, full of tragic ironies but also powerful in its reflections and interplay with other themes in the poem. . . . *The Holy Grail* continues this sense of conflict of two worlds, and also by its structure emphasizes the theme of disintegration. We are no longer aware of a cohesive and coherent court, a Round Table. We are instead hearing a succession of individual adventures of individual knights, each pursuing his own quest of the Grail, a quest in which Arthur does not join, and of which he has not approved. . . . The last movement again opens with an idyll of savage and brutal impact, *Pelleas and Ettarre,* a powerfully ironic, distorted counterpart of the *Gareth and Lynette* story. . . . *The Last Tournament* is a mere contest for prizes, a contest in which the most skillful, not the worthiest, wins by cheating as much as by skill. . . . The tournament is an empty form, a shell of ritual and external show from which all meaning and spirit have departed, and the whole idyll is penetrated with deeper and deeper irony.

Guinevere begins the coda with a change of tone. The bitter irony of the two preceding idylls is replaced by a sad, elegiac sense of loss, of waste, of too late redemption. . . . *The Passing of Arthur* moves back to the high symbolic style of the opening, and . . . the whole drama is placed in a cosmic and eternal perspective. Emotion is calmed, then moved in the final lines to hope, as "the new sun rose bringing the new year." (F. E. L. Priestley, *Language and Structure* [1973], 133–135.)

■ Abstract. Among Tennyson's finest achievements are his mythical landscapes that symbolize states of human consciousness. The dreamlike quality of his vision, combined with his ability to see at close range "with preternatural clarity and detail," rendered his dreams more vivid than our realities. The distinction first made by Sir Harold Nicholson and reiterated by T. S. Eliot between the expression of Tennyson's personal experience with violence and alienation and the shallow and hypocritical "public" verse no longer satisfies. As we become more sympathetically aware of the complexities of the Victorian age we become more and more aware of the anxious coexistence of their despair and optimism. *In Memoriam* is intensely personal and yet is the archetypal presentation of the Victorians' "tense dialogue of faith in mortal combat with doubt." Tennyson maintained throughout his career powers of keenest observation combined with an abnormally keen awareness of the anomalous state of man—"a spirit incarnate in matter." Tennyson's characteristic note is one of ambivalence between certainty and doubt, past and present, illusion and reality. He incorporates these dichotomies into a vision which, especially in *In Memoriam* and *Idylls of the King*, constitutes a remarkable poetic achievement. (John D. Rosenberg, "Tennyson and the Landscape of Consciousness" [1974], 303.)

■ "The Passing of Arthur" magnificently closes Tennyson's *Idylls of the King* by recapitulating the motifs, structure, and main concerns of the preceding parts of the poem to dramatize once more the poet's central themes of having faith and keeping faith. At the same time, it closes the frame upon the poem's magical world, preparing us for return to our own. Until this closing section we have found ourselves within Tennyson's version of the world of the Romance, a world characterized by passionately sworn oaths, visions, heroic tests, and sharply resounding clashes of steel on steel. The mist-hidden landscapes, the doubts, and the difficulties in "The Passing of Arthur" prepare us for our return to another, a later, a lesser time, one in which men's perceptions are as limited as their faith. The poet's ability to create in his reader the sense that with this last idyll the great deeds of Arthur's realm recede into the obscuring reaches of time long past strikes a note simultaneously heroic and elegiac; for Tennyson convinces us not only that his characters, like those in all epic and heroic verse, stand larger than life, but also that their passing from the earth should occasion in us a piercing sense of loss. In conveying this conviction that something great, something irreplaceable, has vanished from the world, *The Idylls of the King* sounds that note of bitter yearning for what cannot return with a power that had not appeared in English poetry since the Anglo-Saxon bards. (George P. Landow, "Closing the Frame" [1974], 423.)

■ [T]he poet followed Aristotle's prescription in the *Idylls*. Between his 'beginning' ('The Coming of Arthur') and his 'end' ('The Passing of Arthur') he placed ten *Idylls* under the general title of 'THE ROUND TABLE'. By presenting his 'middle' as a circle, he almost invited the reader to see these *Idylls* as a revolving Wheel of Fortune, on which Arthur is first raised, and then, as in his fearful dream in Malory (XXI, iii), flung down into 'an hideous deep black water', full of 'serpents, and worms, and wild beasts, foul and horrible'. Thus the whole central action is a large-scale *peripeteia* (literally a 'falling round'), and Guinevere, at the end, has her own personal *peripeteia* combined with an *anagnorisis*, when, having rejected Arthur as insufficiently human, she recognizes too late that he, not Lancelot, is the man she loves, because he is 'the highest and most human too' ('Guinevere', 644). 'Tragedy tries to keep within a single revolution of the sun' (*Poetics*, v). Tennyson applies the idea imaginatively to the patterning of his epic. In 'Gareth and Lynette' human life is pictured in terms of a single day, both in the names of the knights to be overcome, 'Morning-Star', 'Noon-Sun', 'Evening Star', and 'Night' or 'Death' (619–23), and in the rock-engravings: 'Phosphorus', 'Meridies', 'Hesperus', 'Nox', 'Mors' (1174–5); and the same symbolism is implied in the structure of the whole poem. In 'The Coming of Arthur' (99) he can see 'even in high-day the morning star'; twilight is falling when the last battle ends, and he dies at midnight. Parallel to the diurnal time-scheme is the annual one already mentioned, beginning on New Year's Day and ending in mid-winter. (Paul Turner, *Tennyson* [1976], 166–167.)

■ The structure, in other words, is apocalyptic rather than elegiac, linear rather than cyclical. (A. Dwight Culler, *The Poetry of Tennyson* [1977], 217.)

■ Tennyson purposely shifted the accent of his originals in a psychological direction, as the idyll form requires and as he had done in *Maud*.

The result of this shift was that sooner or later all the major characters of the *Idylls* came to be depicted in moments of divided mentality, and the study of these mental states, as they affected the process of choice and action, became a central preoccupation of the poem. Tennyson borrowed one of the earliest lines for his Arthurian epic from Vergil's portrait of epic irresolution, when Aeneas is searching for a way to tell Dido he must leave her: "atque animum nunc huc celerem, nunc dividit illuc." Tennyson rendered it, "This way and that dividing the swift mind" (*Passing of Arthur*, 228), to describe Sir Bedivere's hesitation in throwing Arthur's sword. In Malory, Sir Bedivere does not waver; he simply determines not to do as he has been told. But for Tennyson the psychology of the Arthurian tragedy was the essence of the story, and that psychology largely revolved about weak and indecisive minds. Thus the *Idylls* present a series of portraits of the Arthurian characters, not in the process of action, but in the throes of internal debate. (Robert Pattison, *Tennyson and Tradition* [1979], 137.)

■ Nowhere is Tennyson's desire to incorporate various shorter forms into his epic more obvious than in his inclusion in the *Idylls* of a number of rhymed lyrics among the epic blank verse, all set in the iambic line surrounding them, but adding an ominous touch to the idylls in which they appear; as in *In Memoriam*, Tennyson seems not to have trusted the lyric form in its pure state. In *Pelleas and Ettarre* the lyric, like the rose it describes, is a moment of beauty that contains a fatal truth, though the hero is as yet unaware of it. It is a revealing fact that a large proportion of the lyric material in *The Idylls of the King* is sung by Vivien. Tennyson wants to associate the sensuous and apparently simple beauty of the form with the deceptive principle of corruption working to bring down Camelot; and the presence of such a form forces his poetry to become increasingly stylized and complicated in order to mirror the world as infiltrated by the deceptively sweet lyric. (Pattison [1979], 142.)

■ The wave and fire imagery in the *Idylls* (in the paragraph above, "cleanse the common sewer" and "heats that spring and sparkle") actually compose carefully controlled patterns that carry the burden of Camelot's complex peripeteia. Seemingly there is a critical problem, for waves bring both Arthur and inundating barbarism, while fire symbolizes both Arthur and Vivien: the ideal and the real. However, the wave imagery shows a cyclic development that suggests the rise and fall of spiritual effort. The Arthurian wave sweeps over the world and cleanses it but in the process loses its vitality, becomes polluted, and finally flattens and dissipates formlessly—and a new wave gathers power to bring another historical cycle. But fire invests all phases of the cycle with equal power. Fire represents the ever-present balance between the higher and lower passions, those held in use by conscience and those let loose, through a slackening of the will, as eros—and worse. First in historical form, then in formlessness, this energy comes with equal measure as God fulfils himself in many ways. (Henry Kozicki, *Tennyson and Clio* [1979], 129.)

Literary Characteristics: Tragedy

■ The collapse of the Arthurian ideal as reflected in "The Last Tournament" is tragic. There is no personal flaw in Arthur, except perhaps that he has believed too thoroughly in the perfectibility of human nature. But his ideal was a good one; its failure can be laid to human frailty, not to supernatural forces, even though Tennyson may use the Grail to symbolize the quest of the impossible. In the parallel battle stories, Tennyson has given dark expression to the failure of the chivalric ideal; in the antithetical development of Tristram and Dagonet he has heightened this expression, but he has also expressed a hopeful, if ironic, note: if the true knight has made a mockery of Arthur's aspirations the mock knight has fulfilled them. In the end, only the Fool and the King— brother fools, but in the sense employed by St. Francis of Assisi—stand true. If the overall effect of "The Last Tournament" is one of tragic gloom, perhaps it merely reflects the mature Tennyson's sobering judgment: man's idealism may be doomed to failure, but the failure is never absolute. (Boyd Litzinger, "The Structure of Tennyson's 'The Last Tournament'" [1963], 59–60.)

■ Within this ancient tragic form, then [*i.e., birth, growth, ripeness, death, promise of rebirth*], Tennyson's figures are enclosed in mythic time, bound in mystery to questions of being and involvement, evil and justice, the meaning of human history. In the ritual cycle, the splendid rise to greatness and ruinous fall of a world is a poignant drama arousing the most profound of tragic emotions, because of the vision of an un- fathomable pattern of justice, in all the waste and loss. (Henry Kozicki, ". . . as Tragic Drama" [1966], 20.)

■ Arthur's dream-kingdom can be compared to the Apollo- nian illusion that Nietzsche sees as triumphant in the heroic ideals of Homer. And this illusion is necessary. Nietzsche con- cludes.

> The Greeks were keenly aware of the terrors and horrors of existence; in order to be able to live at all they had to place before them the shining fantasy of the Olympians. Their tremendous distrust of the titanic forces of na- ture: *Moira*, mercilessly enthroned beyond the knowable world . . . the Greeks conquered.

This rather closely describes the nature of the dream- kingdom of Camelot, surrounded by the beast that must inev- itably absorb it and the wave of doom poised at every moment to fall. While the *Idylls of the King* has many different facets and levels of significance, at its core it is the comprehensive vision of a "subjective poet," more tragic than religious, and beyond good and evil in any conventional sense. (William R. Brashear, "Tennyson's Tragic Vitalism" [1968], 48–49.)

■ Those who assume that the *Idylls* is or should be tragic are prone to see Arthur as a redeemer who fails; those who as- sume a comic form like to see him as a defective human be- ing. Tennyson clearly insists that Arthur is both hero and human, ideal and real, thus suggesting the inability of either comic or tragic conceptions to give a full explanation. In fact, these classifications appear in the *Idylls* only as a parody. The poem is the most complete expression of ironic art in Tenny- son, perhaps in his time. It manages to attack the substance of each of the other three mythoi: its narrative structure par- odies romance; its tone parodies comedy; its characters, particularly its central hero, parody tragedy. (James R. Kincaid, *Tennyson's Major Poems* [1975], 151.)

■ The death of Arthur confirms no justice, universal or local; the poem ends where *In Memoriam* began: in darkness and uncertainty, without heroism, even without meaning. (Kincaid [1975], 157.)

■ [W]hen the individual idylls are seen as part of a larger structure, the shape of the larger structure is the shape of tragedy. But just as Tennyson avoided the traditional epic of heroism, so he avoided the concept of tragedy which we have inherited from the Greeks. . . . the failure of Camelot is not a failure in Arthur but a failure in the knights' response to Arthur. . . . Arthur's subjects, then, bring about their own downfall, and Arthur's increasing age and ineffectiveness simply reflect the condition of his society.

The central figure in the tragedy is not Arthur but Guinevere, and it is possible to see all other responses to Arthur as types of Guinevere's response. (Donald S. Hair, *Domestic and Heroic* . . . [1981], 137.)

■ *Idylls of the King* is, like *Paradise Lost,* about a fall, and hence it is a tragedy. But, as in Milton's epic, the reader is constantly to see the tragic events of the poem in a context ordered and sustained by Providence. One must not confuse the collapse of one man or one civilization with the collapse of divine purpose. That is the fault of many people in *Pelleas and Ettarre* and in *The Last Tournament.* But others, like Bedivere at the end of *The Passing of Arthur,* recognize a renewal, and the central figures' understanding is still more complex. The tragic hero conventionally comes, as a result of his suffering, to recognize a more comprehensive order than the one that has failed in his own endeavors. Arthur . . . gains such insight in *The Passing of Arthur,* and Guinevere does so in her idyll. But whereas Arthur's insight is concerned with the cycle of generations and civilizations, Guinevere focuses on the change of heart within the individual. The *Guinevere* idyll, then, balances the concern with a change of heart in such figures as Lynette, Edyrn, and Geraint, while Arthur's insight expands the understanding that Leodogran comes to in *The Coming of Arthur.* (Hair [1981], 211–212.)

Man and Nature

■ Throughout the poem the wasteland serves both as setting for personal error, passion, and self-will and as symbol of bewilderment and frustration. Geraint, when confused by his own jealous fears, deserts the city and the court, cries, "To the wilds!" and forces his long-suffering Enid to lead him by "Gray swamps and pools, waste places of the hern,/And wildernesses, perilous paths." Merlin, overcome by a melancholy which his intellect cannot dispel, retreats to "the wild woods of Broceliande," where at last he yields body and soul to the libidinous Vivien as a fierce expressionistic storm rages over "the ravaged woodland." And Lancelot, as often as he is troubled by remorse, seeks release or self-communion amid the bleak amoralities of nature:

> His mood was often like a fiend, and rose
> And drove him into wastes and solitudes
> For agony, who was yet a living soul.

Such imagery appears most effectively in "The Holy Grail," where the wasteland connotes the emptiness of selfish desire, the timely recognition of which may be the prelude to spiritual rebirth. (Jerome H. Buckley, *Tennyson* [1960], 187–188.)

■ In the last analysis, the natural order itself, being subject to decay, undermines the achievement of Arthur. Reasons are given for the breakup of Logres—Merlin's surrendering his wisdom to the mere sensuality of Vivien, Lancelot's betrayal of honour to sensuality—but the imagery of the creeping year which runs all through the poem suggests that, to Tennyson, the mere fact of being in time ensures a downfall of the ideal itself. (Valerie Pitt, *Tennyson Laureate* [1962], 215–216.)

■ Throughout the *Idylls* nature, mirroring man, is at war with itself, ever aspiring to some higher order and ever lapsing into the primal chaos. Like the moral wilderness, the physical wilderness constantly encroaches on the space that Arthur has cleared. The obscure powers of the North are both renegade knights from Arthur's court and aboriginal forces within nature, ever poised to fill the vacuum created by the withdrawal of the King's power. The Manichean struggle between powers of light and darkness, order and disorder, humanity and bestiality, is internalized within the characters and also projected upon the landscapes through which they move. Tangled thickets and orderly gardens, sultry meadows and violent tempests are all extensions of human consciousness, a kind of natural amphitheater in which the moral drama of the poem is enacted.

Tennyson deliberately blurs the distinction between character and setting, just as he blurs the boundaries separating past, present, and future. Despite the thousands of lines of natural description throughout Tennyson's poetry, he is least of all what he is most commonly assumed to be—a purely descriptive poet. There are no "descriptive backgrounds" in the *Idylls,* only foregrounds in which we are at times primarily conscious of a particular character, at times of a particular setting. At first glance this seems like a fancy way of saying there is a good deal of "pathetic fallacy" in the *Idylls,* which of course there is, provided one understands by the term a more than merely fanciful coloring of nature in the light of human emotion. The symbolic season which flowers and fades along with Arthur is probably the most sustained pathetic fallacy in our literature. Some such latent animism is present in all natural description, however sophisticated, and it is so current in our daily speech that we use it unconsciously, as in speaking of threatening weather or calm seas. Yet much of what is commonly dismissed as pathetic fallacy is in fact something quite different. The phrase carries an unfortunate connotation, implying the primary reality of the human subject, whose emotion is "fallaciously" projected upon the external order of nature. In the *Idylls,* however, character is as much an extension of landscape as landscape is of character. In this sense the symbolic season does not imitate Arthur's declining career but Arthur's career imitates the course of the seasons, in whose cycle, as a dying god, he is tragically enmeshed.

Tennyson uses landscape, then, not as a decorative adjunct to character but as the mythopoeic soil in which character is rooted and takes its being. George Santayana has analyzed this use of landscape in an essay in which he defends the pathetic fallacy as the means of recovering the primitive, natural symbolism inherent in all great poetry. Character divorced from its environing landscape, Santayana argues, represents only a "fragmentary unity," for "characters are initially embedded in life, as the gods themselves are originally embedded in Nature." Through landscape the poet restores the "natural confusion" of inner and outer worlds common to ancient modes of experience before the classifying intelligence assigned them to separate spheres. Landscape recalls and consecrates this half-forgotten unity. (John D. Rosenberg, *The Fall of Camelot* [1973], 66–68.)

■ Both the wasteland setting of the final battle and the mist which makes it a nightmare of confusion are Tennyson's additions to Malory. Here as throughout the *Idylls* this master of expressionist landscape surrounds his figures with an external nature symbolizing their inner condition. The poet himself pointed out that "This grim battle in the mist contrasts with Arthur's glorious battle in the *Coming of Arthur,* fought on a bright day when 'he saw the smallest rock far on the faintest hill'". The harmony, the faith, the community with which Arthur and his men act in the first battle raises them above the levels human nature usually reaches: the perception of the senses approaches that of the soul as vision approaches the visionary. When Tennyson implicitly contrasts the preternatural clarity of Arthur's vision in the opening section with his confusion in the last, he is making a statement not only about the way political disorder and death necessarily follow loss of faith, but also about the way an ordering faith, which creates harmony of sense and soul, makes man whole, complete, a being of perfect health. Like

Milton who believed in a time of physical joy and health before the Fall, Tennyson traces the very limitation of our perceptions to breaking faith. Considered from this point of
view, *The Idylls of the King* is seen to be another tale of paradise lost. (George P. Landow, "Closing the Frame," [1974],
434.)

■ [T]rees and woodland serve as compositional elements in
the same way as the Forest of Arden does for Shakespeare, to
convey mood and set scenes for human action. In this respect
Victorian poets and painters are alike. What is particularly
remarkable in Tennyson is that the natural scene reflects
even the human nature of the protagonists of the story. (J. M.
Gray, *Thro' the Vision of the Night* [1980], 75.)

Arthur

■ For Arthur is presented as an ideal figure of supernatural
origin and destination, as the emissary of God, and not as a
realistic and therefore fallible hero. (Jerome H. Buckley,
Tennyson [1960], 175.)

■ But despite his ideal manhood, or perhaps because of it,
Arthur is conspicuously ineffective when brought into dramatic relation with the real men of the Round Table and the
complex tumultuous woman who is his Queen. In his encoun-
ters with the marred goodly Lancelot, he seems almost will-
fully naive; unwavering in his own faith, he is all trustfulness;
he cannot bring himself to believe his best and strongest
knight capable of deception, and he thus cannot begin to
understand the meaning or even the intensity of Lancelot's
recurrent dark "moods" or the "madness" that blurs his vision of the Grail. Likewise in his treatment of Guinevere he
seems woodenly imperceptive. Throughout their last interview his avowed charity scarcely matches his self-approving
inflexible regard for moral justice. As a man of perfect principle, he may indeed be ready to forgive "as Eternal God/
Forgives," but as injured husband, he should hardly make the

equation with divine mercy so explicit, and he certainly need
not rehearse in detail the wrongs done to him and to his
order by the wife cringing at his feet in a remorse which
achieves strange dignity. Fortunately, however, he is seldom
called upon to engage directly in the dramatic action of the
Idylls. His major role is essentially recessive; as King, he is a
shadowy background presence, a legendary hero off fighting
the heathen, or at his own court an aloof voice of command
and judgment, always a rather remote yet available standard
of reference. Even in "The Coming of Arthur" he is more
talked of than actually seen; he is known by his work as the
bringer of civilization to a barbarous people, but his personality is no less a mystery than his origin. (Buckley [1960], 177.)

■ Arthur bears all the marks of a Christianised, but recog-
nisably Carlylean hero. He is a king from nowhere, not king
by recognisable right of birth, but by right of the power in
him, the power laid upon him, which makes the knights acclaim and follow him:

> The King will follow Christ, and we the King
> In whom high God hath breathed a secret thing.

He is a new power in the world and sweeps aside (as Carlyle's
heroes sweep aside) old formulas and outworn prerogatives:
he proves himself by overcoming heathen disorder, and by
conquering the effete remnant of Rome. Gareth answers the
objections to his claim by reiterating that this is he,

> who swept the dust of ruin'd Rome
> From off the threshold of the realm, and crush'd
> The Idolaters and made the people free?
> Who should be King save him who makes us free?

The strong man's strength is his inalienable right to leadership. But it is a leadership laid on him as a task and a duty, not
as a privilege, and Arthur preaches to others the Carlylean
doctrine of active work which he himself follows. Neither he
nor they have the right to leave the allotted task to follow
their own advantage, or even so high and holy a thing as the
Grail:

> The King must guard
> That which he rules, and is but as the hind
> To whom a space of land is given to plow.
> Who may not wander from the allotted field
> Before his work be done.

The final mark of his Carlyleanism is his absolutism. Arthur leads, and what he achieves, and what his knights achieve is gained by their personal allegiance to himself. He

> Bound them by so strait vows to his own self,
> That when they rose, knighted from kneeling, some
> Were pale as at the passing of a ghost,
> Some flush'd, and others dazed, as one who wakes
> Half-blinded at the coming of a light.

They vow:

> To reverence the King, as if he were
> Their conscience, and their conscience as their King.

This is a good deal more than feudal; Arthur's knights are not simply his liege-men; they are men dedicated, through him, to the purpose which he serves. It is important here to remember that Arthur has the status of a symbolic as well as of an actual being: Tennyson is not advocating personal dictatorship. Arthur fulfils the divine purpose of order. He is the symbol of the human spirit, and like it, is no more than an agent. (Valerie Pitt, *Tennyson Laureate* [1962], 185–186.)

■ The ultimate meaning of Tennyson's *Idylls* lies, I believe, in the paradox of Arthur. He set out to found a society based on freedom, but to his sorrow he learned that he could not create a free man. His will simultaneously desired social freedom and social slavery. For a while Arthur is content with self-deception, but in the end he can no longer avoid recognizing his deceptions and the unresolvable paradox of reality. For the imposition of his heroic authority, his will, upon reality meant the denial to others of their own moral responsibility. Arthur stands, finally, in moral terms, as both the hero and the villain of the *Idylls of the King.* (Clyde de L. Ryals, "The Moral Paradox of the Hero . . . " [1963], 67.)

■ In considering Arthur's character as central to the paradoxical meaning of the poem, we must first make some observations about the "realness" or humanity of the King. That
Arthur does not strike all readers as a realistic character is
self-evident. Indeed, many of the knights suspected that
Arthur was supernatural. And Tennyson lets us know early in
the *Idylls* that Arthur will stand as a symbol, not only for the
reader but also for his loyal followers, who very early proclaim him in these terms: "The King will follow Christ, and
we the King,/In whom high God hath breathed a secret
thing" ("The Coming of Arthur," ll. 499–500). Even more
indicative of the symbolic representation of the King is Bellicent's narration of the coming of Arthur—the finding of the
child in the sea by Bleys and Merlin. On the other hand,
Tennyson does not tell us this story directly but instead has
Bellicent narrate it to Leodogran as a rumor about which she
herself may have some reservations. In any case, we are not
aware of widespread knowledge among the populace of
Arthur's origins. (Stanley J. Solomon, "Tennyson's Paradoxical King" [1963], 259.)

■ On the dramatic level, the most compelling paradox results from Arthur's inability to sense the sin and disloyalty of
Lancelot and Guinevere. Oblivious to low deeds in those he
trusts, Arthur is prevented by his innocence of heart from
any suspicion of disloyalty. A reader might take issue with
Tennyson over the need for Arthur's extreme degree of
naïveté. Could not Arthur be the perfect king and still entertain a small suspicion? For Tennyson, the answer is clearly
no; the ideal moral cosmos that the poet has conceived will
not permit a suspicious nature in the King. Even when told
(directly or indirectly, we do not know) of the scandal, Arthur
remains suspicious only temporarily. Not aware of the scandal's influence on the court, Arthur appears to his followers
as either foolish or pathetic. To some of the most cynical
knights he is a hypocrite who pretends not to notice, perhaps
in order to maintain harmony in the kingdom. Innocence is
one of the blameless King's major virtues, but paradoxically
it undermines the confidence of the knights. (Solomon [1963],
262.)

■ In his devotion both to the social order and to the integrity of his own vision, Arthur is more than either prophet or poet. He fails as a dramatic figure because his role demands that he be both a Telemachus and a Ulysses, a spokesman for both Duty and the Beautiful. Yet that very failure demonstrates the reality of a visionary ideal which, Tennyson concedes, can never be fully realized even in the "sacred madness" of the poet's art.

Still, we are left at best with a "larger hope." The ideal may be no mere illusion, but how can it be made relevant to an audience? Even Percivale, who has endured the agony and promise of spiritual rebirth, confesses, "So spake the King; I knew not all he meant." The Laureate's view is skeptical at best. Since poetry is an attempt to describe the indescribable, its communication of divine order is at best partial and transitory, doomed like Arthur's rule to defeat in "the war of Time against the soul of man." (Lawrence Poston III, "The Two Provinces of Tennyson's 'Idylls'" [1967], 380.)

■ [*Arthur is* "a monomaniac" *whose knights are* "emotionally exploited" *by him.*] (Clyde de L. Ryals, *From the Great Deep* [1967], 81.)

■ Arthur . . . is the self embodied, and not simply a symbol of it. It may also be said that he is the will that sustains the Apollonian illusion of "Camelot" or civilization above the Dionysiac chaos, and prevents, as long as possible, the individual from merging back into the beast and being no more. . . . The poem is essentially "vitalistic" and the forces embodied in the other persons are vital rather than allegorical. (William R. Brashear, "Tennyson's Tragic Vitalism" [1968], 31.)

■ [I]t is a truism of Tennysonian criticism that Arthur is least credible as a "real" man. Despite the inconsistencies of the conceptual scheme that readers have noticed, Arthur is still most convincing when he assumes his parabolic role as the Ideal that has been sent to redeem the wilderness of the Real, as the soul that both wars with sense and tries to lift it above itself. (Gerhard Joseph, *Tennysonian Love* [1969], 165.)

■ While Guinevere is Tennyson's most complex evocation of a destructive woman, her very weakness manages to undermine the admiration that Tennyson intends us to have for Arthur either as ideal representative of soul or as long-suffering husband." (Joseph [1969], 169.)

■ While it is possible to believe in the austere grandeur of Arthur, it is difficult to sense the warmth and color that Guinevere, so late in life, attributes to him. When he speaks of his "vast pity that almost makes me die" as he scourges Guinevere in a sustained invective of one hundred and fifty-eight lines; when he will show her "even for thy sake" the sin that she has committed; when he finally forgives her even "as Eternal God forgives," the most sympathetic reader must concede a priggishness that has been the scorn of those who see in Tennyson's Arthurian pageant little more than a representatively obnoxious document of Victorian male chauvinism. (Joseph [1969], 171.)

■ The heart of Arthur's denunciation of Guinevere is that her adultery and its foul example have "spoilt the purpose of my life" (450). Yet we cannot uncritically accept Arthur's judgment in his own case, even though he is obviously closer to the truth than is Vivien's counter-judgment: "Man! is he man at all, who knows and winks?" (MV, 779). Judged by his own high standards, the "blameless King" (MV, 777) is more than once at fault, although his faults are the defects of his virtues, as when he wholly misapprehends Vivien's intentions. Both Vivien and Dagonet call him a fool; they are both right and wrong, and they both mean very different things by the term.

We have only to consider the catastrophic miscarriage of Arthur's designs to realize how heavily Tennyson has hedged his King in ambiguity. The causes of the catastrophe are multiple, and Arthur is never more blind to this complexity than when he concludes his denunciation of Guinevere, "And all through thee!" (490). Under the particular circumstances the charge is cruel; under any circumstances it is simplistic. (John D. Rosenberg, *The Fall of Camelot* [1973], 130–131.)

■ Arthur thus resists the first temptation he faces in this idyll [*The Passing of Arthur*], for he refuses to let the evidence of the limited senses crush the soul's faith. But although he has triumphed over a broad theological doubt, he has yet to face the more specific fear that God has abandoned him. He is in great pain because he knows that although he has had faith and kept faith, his great purpose has come to nought. Because all his trust "in wife and friend" (24), which were the foundation of his rule, have been betrayed—because others have not kept faith with him—his "realm/Reels back into the beast, and is no more" (25–26). Making us think of Christ's plaint on the cross, Arthur exclaims "My God, thou has forgotten me in my death" (27), but immediately after his brief lapse of faith, he pulls himself up short, affirming his belief that God keeps faith with man: "Nay—God my Christ—I pass but shall not die" (28). Thus having surmounted the doubts which result from his perception of the evils of human nature in general and his own betrayals in particular, the King falls asleep and receives what we may term his reward for steadfastness. (George P. Landow, "Closing the Frame" [1974], 429–430.)

■ [W]e can no longer see King Arthur as Gladstone saw him, 'as the great pillar of the moral order, and the resplendent top of human excellence'. He appears too much of a prig for that, too much like any Victorian husband angrily lecturing his erring wife in the last speeches of 'Guinevere', which to the Victorians appeared so sublime. (Philip Henderson, *Tennyson* [1978], 134.)

■ Arthur is the true hero, for he does not suffer from the psychic turmoil born of divided will that surrounds him. This observation may go some way toward defending Arthur from the worst criticism leveled against him: that in his reproach of Guinevere during their last interview in the nunnery he is a self-righteous prig. Arthur's behavior, after all, is a textbook example of the kind of approach twentieth-century psychologists insist is the trademark of mental health: he confronts his problem directly by going to Guinevere; he discharges his anger; and having discharged it he finds room in the cool dispassion left to him to forgive and still to love.

Indeed, Arthur's heroic qualities are a perfect counterpart to the formal qualities Tennyson wished to achieve in the *Idylls.* Arthur, like the form of idyll, is detached, but insightful into the psychology of those around him; yet amid the more traditionally heroic passions and events of the legend, he is the one genuinely epic character. Arthur's posture throughout the *Idylls* is like that of the poet of idylls, overseeing his realm from a distance, and in the framework of the story this comes to bewilder and annoy the larger part of his subjects. But Arthur's posture is only a rendition of Tennyson's own lifelong poetic role as craftsman involved in but detached from his materials, and through Arthur, Tennyson could not only justify his own poetic but proclaim it as a new form of epic vision which, like Arthur's, the world was perhaps not ready to admit. (Robert Pattison, *Tennyson and Tradition* [1979], 149.)

■ [*Arthur's credits as a character are these: he is consistent and sincere; he is* "the wise and decisive ruler"; *he shows compassion toward the young; he has a* "total command of language"; *he is* "accustomed to supreme authority, and wise in the ways of human nature"; *he* "will neither speak any 'slander, no, nor listen to it'"; *he is* "most conscientious" *in performing* "the duties of government"; *his* "spirit emerges" *from the Grail* "trial" *as* "eminently practical, and puts the Grail quest in perspective." "Everything considered," *he lets Guinevere* "off lightly"; *he is capable of feeling the deepest agony of disappointed love and of undergoing* "an agony of doubt and betrayal."] (J. M. Gray, *Thro' the Vision of the Night* [1980], 127–136.)

■ The kind of moral drama we are dealing with [in *Guinevere*] can perhaps be understood best if we compare this scene with a similar scene in book IX of *Paradise Lost.* . . .

However great our sympathy with Adam's unwillingness to abandon Eve to her fate, the poem condemns that sympathy as misplaced, and suggests that Adam's duty was to instruct Eve—in fact, to damn her—and thus bring her to a conviction of sin. But Adam fails in his duty, and becomes just as respon-

sible as Eve for the Fall. Arthur, by way of contrast, does not
fall. Although he is as much in love with his wife as Adam was
with Eve . . . , he does not allow that bond to hinder his better
judgment; he acts correctly by condemning his wife's sin, and
by bringing about repentance in her. (Donald S. Hair, *Domestic
and Heroic . . .* [1981], 216.)

The Coming of Arthur

■ "The Coming of Arthur" opens the *Idylls* by posing its
most crucial general problem: how do we know, what is the
nature of knowledge, what sort of knowledge is authentic? . . . Leodogran appears as the reader's surrogate. . . . He
must determine what truth is and how one arrives at it.
(James R. Kincaid, *Tennyson's Major Poems* [1975], 158.)

■ The superiority of imaginative experience is finally stated
by the last witness. Bellicent, whose testimony is most important because her experience is most direct, [is] least affected
by superficial judgments. . . . (Kincaid [1975], 161.)

■ [*The Coming of Arthur*] does a great deal to define the nature of the spiritual truth with which it is concerned. Though
explicitly a spiritual truth, it can find expression only in the
physical. *Idylls of the King* carefully puts its mystical perceptions into a concrete, even flatly practical frame. The ideal
works through the real; spiritual experience is one with social
experience. (Kincaid [1975], 163.)

■ One way of describing *The Coming of Arthur* is to say that
the idyll presents Leodogran's education, and his experience
is a type of all the experiences of those who must respond to
the mystery of Arthur. (Donald S. Hair, *Domestic and Heroic
. . .* [1981], 131.)

Gareth and Lynette

■ The idyll is a poem of spring in every sense: the opening
image of a flooded river suggests not only the renewing and

abundant powers of youth but specific and crucial spiritual qualities. Gareth sees that despite its apparent abandon the river "dost His will,/The Maker's" (ll. 10–11). He instantly transcends the evidence of his senses with his intuition of the certainty of divine control. Subtly, this opening establishes exactly what is lacking in the later empiricists and exactly what Arthur insists on: an assumption of spirituality.

In order to realize this extrarational faculty, Gareth must overcome many obstacles, the first of which is created by his mother, who "holds me still a child" (l. 15). Like all comic heroes, he must assert his manhood in order to begin his real initiation. The fact that Bellicent's demands are so explicitly sexual—she begs him to consider his impotent father, the "yet warm corpse" (l. 79), who "beside the hearth/Lies like a log, and all but smouldered out!" (ll. 73–74)—simplifies his problem by putting it so bluntly and so clearly. The traditional battle with the father has already been won; he must simply escape from his mother. His later prolonged struggle to overcome Lynette's doubts parallels this first difficult struggle with his mother and suggests that the real test is not presented by knights (or men) at all. His real triumph is over women, reflecting ironically and sadly on the central cause of the later fall: Guinevere, Camelot's Eve. (James R. Kincaid, "Tennyson's 'Gareth and Lynette'") [1972], 666.)

■ [*Gareth and Lynette*] is the exemplum for the opening argument. It does not so much define the values of Camelot as create for us an image of the promise it holds: the union of freedom and order. Above all it is an idyll characterized by simplicity and directness. In Gareth's world, there are no real problems. (James R. Kincaid, *Tennyson's Major Poems* [1975], 165.)

■ In one sense all [*Gareth*] has to do is be young—to assert first the power and then the magnificence of youth. (Kincaid [1975], 168.)

■ The final three-part battle (death turns out not to be a test) recalls Red Cross's three-day fight with the dragon as well as Tennyson's allegorical model, the three-day period from Christ's crucifixion to his resurrection. . . . The final enemy, Death, provides the clearest indication of the comic nature of the idyll. Gareth has just been defeated by Lancelot, suggesting the puncture of his last enemy, Pride, and illustrating the key Christian theme that only those who lose egos can find selves. . . . (Kincaid [1975], 170–171.)

■ The narrative is like a fairy tale and lends itself to allegorical treatment, while the dramatic presents the characters as reacting to one another in a psychologically realistic way. It is easy enough to link a fairy tale and allegory; it is much more difficult to understand Tennyson's linking of a realistic dialogue with symbolism. Yet Gareth's relations with women are pervaded with a comprehensive pattern of symbols, which appear in that third aspect of the idyll form, description. (Donald S. Hair, *Domestic and Heroic* . . . [1981], 145.)

■ Tennyson is far more subtle and complex than his contemporary [*Browning*], as an idyll of this kind, considered thoughtfully, indicates. (Hair [1981], 154.)

The Geraint-Enid Idylls

■ Geraint's excessive jealousy is a kind of madness which anticipates that of Balin and Pelleas. Like Merlin, he walks with dreams and darkness. As Merlin, at the end of "Merlin and Vivien," is "lost to life and use and name and fame," so is Geraint at the beginning "forgetful of his glory and his name." Awakening on a warm summer morning as the light streams through the window, he is deluded by his misinterpretation of Enid's words, "I fear that I am no true wife." The situation anticipates that of Pelleas, who awakes from a sleep in a dark wood and "coming out of gloom/[Is] dazzled by the sudden light." Geraint's misplaced jealousy is nearly as destructive as is Pelleas's misplaced trust, and for both, the light of day is at the outset a blinding rather than an illuminating force. Pelleas discovers the lovers (but by moonlight) and goes mad, suspecting even the fidelity of the king. Geraint is as a man "when his passion masters him." He is as mad to suspect Enid as Pelleas is to suspect the king. Enid can protect him against external ambush and treachery—her vision does service for them both; but his treachery to himself unhorses him. (Lawrence Poston III,, "The Argument of the Geraint-Enid Books . . ." [1964], 272.)

■ It is surely no very original observation to say that throughout the *Idylls* Tennyson often draws an analogy between individual and state. In "The Coming of Arthur," Leodogran's lament that "here between the man and beast we die" initiates a dual theme which runs through the rest of the poem. It is quite literally true that Leodogran's kingdom is plagued by the assaults of heathens and beasts. But it is also true that Arthur's knights have the distinctly human problem of combatting the beast-like in themselves. Balin and Pelleas die in the twilight zone of madness, somewhere between man and beast. Edyrn and Geraint redeem themselves. Edyrn, in Arthur's words, has "weed[ed] all his heart/As I will weed this land before I go." Geraint's recovery is spiritual as well as physical. But the Guinevere who participated in the marriage of Geraint and Enid is not the same queen who confirms it. And Arthur's cleansing of the "bandit hold" is perhaps the last significant political reform in the poem.

The ending of the Geraint-Enid books is, then, a double one, for the analogy of individual and state obtains only so far. Geraint and Edyrn are redeemed, but the kingdom is merely reformed. As *Idylls of the King* progresses, Tennyson more than once turns to this kind of resolution. A lasting social reform becomes increasingly unlikely; redemption remains personal. Lancelot laments his sin at the end of "Lancelot and Elaine," "not knowing he should die a holy man." At the end of "The Holy Grail," Arthur holds out hope for some kind of spiritual and poetic insight which Bors, Lancelot, and Percivale have attained according to their deserts. And Guinevere, "for her good deeds and her pure life," becomes Abbess and thereafter attains a heavenly peace. Man's soul is the battleground of reason and passion; but through private insight, poetic or spiritual, a man existing in loneliness can achieve what his transient society can not. In the troubled resolution of "Geraint and Enid," the Tennyson of the 1850's seems to look across the intervening years of confident mid-Victorian optimism and anticipate the resurgent doubt and despair of the 1880's, when "Balin and Balan" was first made available to his public. (Poston [1964], 275.)

■ Enid's moral truth provides a cluster of images running counter to the destructive forces of nature. She sings not like the rooks, but with a bird's "sweet voice." Her nature is the nature of a garden; her happiness as they ride away from Doorm's castle is better than the first rose blowing in paradise. Her gladness is lasting, like the mist in Eden, and her suffering is not transitory like a summer shower. The weeding of the garden is thus the controlling image of the two Geraint idylls; Arthur says he will weed the land before he goes. But while he is ridding his realm of its vicious quitch, he fails to see its fairest flower being plucked behind his back. (John Philip Eggers, "The Weeding of the Garden" [1966], 50–51.)

■ "The Marriage of Geraint" is an idyllic comedy with some suggestion of turbulence and darkness about its edges; "Geraint and Enid" completes the transition into the world determined by the canons of realism, the world of instability, lapses from grace, doubt. (James R. Kincaid, *Tennyson's Major Poems* [1975], 171.)

■ Through Geraint, Tennyson shows the corrupting force of rational doubt and the ability of man to find and destroy the source of that doubt. . . . Geraint must show that identity is solid, even if that solidity demands vigilance and great struggles. Geraint and Enid live in a world of fluctuations, of slippery movements and deceptions, and they must master that world lest they be caught by it. . . . "The Marriage of Geraint" presents a harmony of sense and spirit, meaning and word. Geraint appears as another Gareth, duplicating Arthur's function and thus proving his divinity. . . . Enid's song on

Fortune, or rather *against* Fortune, is the center of ["The Marriage of Geraint"]. (Kincaid [1975], 173–174.)

■ "Geraint and Enid" shows the limits of hope in an ironic world. (Kincaid [1975], 177.)

Balin and Balan

■ *Balin and Balan* deals not only with the place of women in individual redemption or destruction; it deals as well with women's social role. In the idyll two antithetical but equally degenerate societies, which have rejected the spiritual advance of Arthur's kingdom, are introduced. There is first the spiritually stagnant court of Pellam, which with its emphasis on celibacy, asceticism, idolatrous worship of saints, phony relics, and golden altars, even perhaps a kind of apostolic succession in Pellam's attempt to trace his descent from Joseph of Arimathea, is evocative of the spiritually decadent Rome from which Arthur has freed himself. There is also introduced the spiritually retrogressive kingdom of King Mark, represented by Vivien. Mark's is a beastly and sensual society associated in Vivien's song about sun-worship (434–49) with druidical paganism. Equally degenerate as the two societies are, they are at the same time antithetical, as they represent two extremes. (Ward Hellstrom, *On the Poems of Tennyson* [1972], 115–116.)

■ On the simple narrative level, coincidence and confusion of identity provide a dénouement rich in the pathos of romance. But on a deeper level Balan is not at all mistaken: Balin *is* in fact the wood-demon, the "outer fiend" whom Balan finally lays to rest. We first see the two brothers as mirror images of each other moving in harmony to the music of Arthur's Order. When Balin's violence returns, they split apart and as Balin recedes further into the wilderness, the two selves become progressively alienated. Disjoined by violence, they are rejoined in violence. In the Freudian terms the tale inevitably suggests, repression has failed, and the rational self can control the savage self only by destroying it. The unwitting fratricide is in reality a symbolic suicide. The point is subtly underscored by the actual cause of the brothers' death. Balin's spear pierces Balan's flesh, but Balin is slain by the bestiality within himself, as symbolized by his wearied horse, which fell upon him and "crushed the man/ Inward" (553–554). "My madness all thy life has been thy doom," the dying Balin tells his twin, who answers in echo, "We two were born together, and we die/Together by one doom" (608, 617–618). (John D. Rosenberg, *The Fall of Camelot* [1973], 82–83.)

■ "Balin and Balan" works very well as an inversion of many of the principal themes and values of the Geraint-Enid books. . . . "Balin and Balan" is a poem that deals with unnatural and fatal divisions. The most obvious form of this split, of course, is that between the two brothers, the divorce of the rational and social man from the instinctive and private one. Behind this rupture is the shadow of the rumored separation of Guinevere from Arthur, body from soul. The idyll's emphasis on lying or slander continues the important motif of the *word.* Creation falls apart in a lie, since a lie destroys all coherence and denies the ability of man to create a permanent order. . . . The only alternatives Balin seems to have take him into extremes: unnatural spirituality or unnatural and cynical empiricism. (James R. Kincaid, *Tennyson's Major Poems* [1975], 178–179.)

■ *Balin and Balan* is a sad and ironic poem on the absurd disjunction of things, a disjunction that leaves man no reasonable choices. We are less likely to judge Balin, then, than to judge both the condition of the world that drives him to such wildness and the power of chance that can so easily overcome the best intentions. (Kincaid [1975], 180.)

■ There is a slight but fine ambiguity here [*the ending*]: two children suddenly wake and stare at a world that is blankly staring back at them. All their innocence and trust mean nothing now; they can only promise one another a reunion in heaven. Comedy has been pushed altogether out of the world. (Kincaid [1975], 182.)

■ In "Balin and Balan," the sin is obvious to anyone, like Balin, who wanders about the court. It is even common knowledge in remote castles like Pellam's. Neither the smell of the rose garden nor Lancelot's encounter with Guinevere are sweet to Balin. The court is languorous and its courtesy is becoming precious. No battle alarms ring. The sin causes the deaths of Balin and Balan, for Balin had made the queen's worship (instead of the king's) central to his value system. He maddens when Vivien lies about seeing Lancelot and Guinevere kiss. "Some loyal souls are wrought to madness" under the sin's blight, Tennyson commented (*Memoir,* 2:131). Tennyson had worked the sin well into the *Idylls'* fabric by the time of the Merlin idyll. (Henry Kozicki, *Tennyson and Clio* [1979], 133–134.)

■ [*Though there appear to be two quests,*] as the Idyll proceeds, we begin to realize that the two quests are in fact one, and the brothers are seeking each other. . . . Balin chooses as his model for conduct Lancelot, and as his inspiration the queen, whose crown on his shield is the "golden earnest of a gentler life" (204). In terms of fairy tale, Guinevere is Balin's Sleeping Beauty, and his approach to her symbolizes all that he would awaken in himself. The scene in which he happens to observe Lancelot and Guinevere in the queen's garden is a version of the fairy tale, but it is an ironic version. . . . What he sees and hears is a pattern of divided opposites that is analogous to his own relations with his brother, opposites that ought to complement each other. (Donald S. Hair, *Domestic and Heroic* . . . [1981], 171–172.)

■ *Balin and Balan* . . . was unquestionably placed by Tennyson at the beginning of the middle of his poem because it contains the first concrete illustrations of the two principal forces (both set in motion by causes ultimately traceable to Guinevere's adultery) which bring Arthur's kingdom to ruin: the asceticism instanced by King Pellam, who has made his castle into a sort of Mount Athos, and the unbridled sexuality incarnated in Vivien. But the most important point about *Balin and Balan* is that, unlike the Geraint and Enid idylls which precede it and *Merlin and Vivien* which follows, it is not concerned with ethical exempla or moral conduct. The poem is a psychological romance comparable to those of Tennyson's American contemporary Hawthorne. Its concerns are with psychological necessity, not with conscious virtue. (Kerry McSweeney, *Tennyson and Swinburne* . . . [1981], 103–104.)

■ The self-destructive irrationality latent in Balin, "that chained rage, which ever yelped within," is stimulated by sexuality. . . . [*Vivien's* "fire of heaven" *song, a*] celebration of natural process, equating seasonal fruition with erotic fulfilment, is one of Tennyson's most direct and powerful lyrics, and his most Lawrencian. It may be thought a palinode to "Tears, Idle Tears," the vibrant assertion of the passion of the present in the former answering the enormously poignant evocation of the passion of the past in the latter. In the context of *Balin and Balan*, Vivien's song identifies the sexual and generative energies which, because he is unable to come to terms with them, fuel Balin's self-destructive violences. But we can hardly say there is anything immoral about the song; it is amoral. . . . (McSweeney [1981], 105–106.)

Merlin and Vivien

■ Much of the dichotomy between passion and reason in *Merlin and Vivien* centers on a consideration of the proper limits of knowledge if it is to be used for a worthy purpose, a question which is also central to *Paradise Lost*. When Eve eats of the fruit, she worships it as a source of knowledge and wisdom, not recognizing that the knowledge of evil is a knowledge better left to God and Satan since it can only bring destruction to man. Eve sees in the tree a promise of godhead: "Till dieted by thee I grow mature/In knowledge, as the Gods who all things know" (*PL*, ll. 803–804). The irony is that in attempting to become like God, Adam and Eve become more like animals. The quest for a knowledge that supersedes the limits of what it is really good for man to know goes hand in hand with pride as the basic cause of the Fall. Vivien, too, has a passion for knowledge, and Merlin knows full well that she will misuse the charm to harm those who "babble" for her. Knowledge is either good or bad depending on the motive for which it is used, and the degree of its goodness, in turn, is measured by its reasonableness, that is, by its usefulness to man's spiritual and material development.

In both *Merlin and Vivien* and *Paradise Lost* there is a close connection between excess of knowledge, disorder in the natural world, and human sexuality. Adam eats of the fruit at Eve's bidding, nature feels the effects of the sin, and human lust is born. Just as in *Paradise Lost,* "Sky low'r'd, and muttering Thunder, some sad drops/Wept at completing of the mortal Sin" (*PL,* ll. 1002–3), so, too, it is during a tempestuous thunderstorm that Merlin takes Vivien to him, succumbs to her snares, and reveals the charm to her. Nature echoes Vivien's word "fool" after she has imprisoned Merlin in the hollow oak, robbing him of any further usefulness to the Arthurian order.

Charles Tennyson claims that "the *Idylls* is essentially a religious poem . . . deeply charged with Christian feeling and symbolism." This is true of *Merlin and Vivien* insofar as Tennyson has here re-enacted man's fall from grace. Sin has entered Camelot, and the destruction of Arthur's court will ensue, because Merlin, praised as the first among men for his knowledge and power, chose fleeting love over lasting fame, and Vivien, a re-embodiment of Satan and Eve, exceeded the bounds which right reason imposes upon knowledge in her passion to destroy the good. (Thomas P. Adler, "The Uses of Knowledge . . ." [1970], 1402–1403.)

■ "Merlin and Vivien," as I have suggested, is a poem largely concerned with the psychology of mood. The mind itself is the slave of the emotions, for they govern the nature of its processes. But both should be vassals to an imagination glorified by a high ideal. Merlin, echoing *In Memoriam,* where doubt was to be made vassal to love, declares that fame should "work as vassal to the larger love." The question of mastery is central in this poem, for, in reality, it is the intellectual Merlin who is imprisoned by the emotionally volatile and irresponsible Vivien. But this constraint is half allowed by its victim because conviction is lost. Arthur needs Merlin, as spirit requires mind, but Merlin can no longer live in the Idea as though it were possible. With no indomitable intent, the mind eddies into backwaters of melancholy and sloth, and, entrapped in this unsavory condition, easily finds the whole world lost or tainted. (John R. Reed, *Perception and Design . . .*" [1971], 56.)

■ "Merlin and Vivien" dramatizes Vivien's prophecy in "Balin and Balan" that she will beat the Cross to earth and break the King. Although Merlin knows that Arthur's high purpose will be broken by the worm, his very foreknowledge serves to incapacitate him, even when—perhaps especially when—the worm entwines itself about him in the form of the serpent-temptress Vivien:

> "Great Master, do ye love me?" he was mute.
> And lissome Vivien, holding by his heel,
> Writhed toward him, slided up his knee and sat,
> Behind his ankle twined her hollow feet
> Together, curved an arm about his neck,
> Clung like a snake . . .
>
> (235–240)

Vivien here combines the roles of Eve and Satan. She lusts for Merlin's forbidden knowledge and in grasping his heel, like the serpent in Genesis who bruises man's heel, she brings death into the world. Her affinity with death is especially marked later in the idyll, when Merlin summons the last of his failing powers of resistance and repulses her with the epithet "harlot." The ironically-named *Vivien (vivus:* alive) leaps from his lap "stiff as a viper frozen" and her face momentarily reveals "the bare-grinning skeleton of death" (843–845). An incarnate symbol, Vivien revitalizes the outworn literary convention from which she derives. The *femme fatale* who makes her appearance in Keats's "La Belle Dame

Sans Merci" achieves her most potent realization in Vivien and by the end of the century dwindles into a figure of sado-masochistic jest. (John D. Rosenberg, *The Fall of Camelot* [1973], 114.)

■ "Merlin and Vivien" is less dramatic, more diagnostic, less an image than an analysis of Camelot's fall. What saves the idyll from didacticism is that it is, in the end, a parody of didacticism. . . . There is no conflict of loyalties—all loyalties and values alike are overthrown. (James R. Kincaid, *Tennyson's Major Poems* [1975], 182–183.)

■ The Merlin idyll is the heart of the *Idylls*. It was the first idyll written and shows the self-engulfment of the most powerful figure in the kingdom. But it also required a "pendent," the Balin and Balan idyll, written as a "further introduction to 'Merlin and Vivien'" in 1872 (*Memoir*, 1:121). The two idylls together indicate the vitiation of the will to true freedom—self-surrender to the righteous King. They take the forms of certain developing forces that were present from the beginning but held in check by the will. In the course of this development, it is shown that the ideal is not a balanced opposite of the real and that the ideal is not trans-muted into the real. Rather, the ideal is a controlling order for historical purpose that is lost gradually through the slackening of will that results when external opposition is eliminated. In this "time of golden rest" (MV 140), the first signs of asceticism and sensuality appear to indicate bifurca-tions of spirit. (Henry Kozicki, *Tennyson and Clio* [1979], 132.)

■ But Tennyson also makes clear that Merlin's surrender of his wisdom in the face of his spiritual malaise and physical need is an aesthetic act. Vivien's "sweet rhyme" about the need for absolute faith in love is specifically identified with the charm of woven paces which undermines the individual's social utility. Merlin comments:

> But, Vivien, when you sang me that sweet rhyme,
> I felt as though you knew this cursed charm,

> Were proving it on me, and that I lay
> And felt them slowly ebbing, name and fame.
>
> (ll. 432–435)

The "cursed charm" of which Merlin alone has knowledge was designed to isolate a beautiful woman for the exclusive use and enjoyment of her husband; thus, it is associated with an obsessive devotion to physical beauty and the severing of the bond between the individual and the community. The lure of Vivien's song then is the lure of a sensually pleasing art which, like the charm, captures its listener in a "hollow tower" (perhaps an image of the purely physical body). In yielding to Vivien, Merlin surenders to this kind of art; yet ironically he is *already* the master of such an artistry since he is sole possessor of the charm before he reveals it to Vivien. In a sense, Merlin is destroyed by an aspect of his own artistry— perhaps its "fleshly" side which offers a tempting alternative to the grim rigors of prophetic art—and Vivien may be, as some critics have argued, a projection of a part of Merlin's own aesthetic temperament. (Catherine Barnes Stevenson, "Druids, Bards, and Tennyson's Merlin" [1980], 18.)

■ If the Merlin of 1856 represents the prophetic personality doomed by its own sensibility, the Merlin of the 1869 *Idylls* is a slightly different character—or at least a character who is viewed from a different angle. In "The Holy Grail," for example, we are given another account of Merlin's "loss of himself." Recalling the inception of the Grail quest, Percivale tells of Merlin's creation, which was partly responsible for the Grail mania:

> In our great hall there stood a vacant chair,
> Fashioned by Merlin ere he past away,
> And carven with strange figures; and in and out
> The figures, like a serpent, ran a scroll
> Of letters in a tongue no man could read.
> And Merlin called it "The Siege perilous,"
> Perilous for good and ill; "for there," he said,
> "No man could sit but he should lose himself:"
> And once by misadvertence Merlin sat

> In his own chair, and so was lost; but he,
> Galahad, when he heard of Merlin's doom,
> Cried, "If I lose myself, I save myself!"
>
> (ll. 167–78)

Malory's Merlin fashions the chair but is not destroyed by it; Tennyson's Merlin is here trapped by the precise skills that make him a wizard. Two sets of facts confirm an aesthetic reading of this narrative of Merlin's "fall." First, the "Siege perilous" with its "scroll of letters in a tongue no man can read" resembles in its inscrutability and potential hazardousness the magician's book in "Merlin and Vivien," which is written in a language no man can read (even Merlin can decipher only the marginalia). In addition, the chair, the product of Merlin's ingenuity and special skill, is the agent of his "fall" just as the charm, of which he as a "Mage" alone has knowledge, is the ostensible cause of his "loss of himself." Both the charm and the chair symbolize the esoteric, even lethal, knowledge that the prophet-bard possesses. Algernon Herbert's *Britannia After the Romans* (1836), which Tennyson owned, explicitly connects the "Siege perilous" with the arcane knowledge to which the Druids had access: the seat, he claims, "signifies to us the private belief of the Druidists in a code of astronomy different from that which they published, but one of which they deemed the establishment essential to the secure enthronization of Apollos Belenus." (Stevenson [1980], 19.)

■ The single action of the idyll—Vivien's seduction of Merlin—is . . . not a simple one, though it seems possible to reduce it to an allegory of sense conquering soul, of sensuality and materialism overcoming the intellect and imagination. . . . There are narrative, dramatic, and descriptive sections, and an intercalary song as well. . . . It is important to note that so long as Merlin speaks—that is, so long as the dramatic is dominant—he does not give in to Vivien. At the end, when he does give in, narrative once again is used; we are told about his fall rather than shown it. The failure of the word is thus reflected in the structure of the idyll itself. (Donald S. Hair, *Domestic and Heroic* . . . [1981], 176.)

■ When one steps back a bit from the idyll, it is possible to see it as an ironic reversal of the Sleeping Beauty fairy tale. Instead of the release of energy and vitality by a kiss, energy and vitality are imprisoned by a kiss. The active figure here is female, and she is a villain rather than a heroine; the passive figure is male. . . . The tree is not unlike Sleeping Beauty's castle: "It looked a tower of ivied masonwork" (4). To the charmed man inside, it is "four walls of a hollow tower" (207), and there he "lay as dead" (211)—not actually dead but, like Sleeping Beauty, "lost to life and use and name and fame" (212). This fall is to be repeated again and again as Arthur's society dissolves. (Hair [1981], 180.)

■ On the whole, . . . the vividness of *Merlin and Vivien* is that of melodrama, not of great art. (Kerry McSweeney, *Tennyson and Swinburne* . . . [1981], 100.)

Lancelot and Elaine

■ Lancelot is more typically human, according to Tennyson's usual terms, than any other knight in the poem, for, when confronted with sin, he struggles with it. The very fact that he suffers intensely from his sin is more than the simple Victorian convention of having illicit lovers exist in constant misery. His suffering is an indication of his alert conscience that will not be lulled by verbal enchantments, and yet must strive unendingly against the demons in its own wasteland. Had Merlin possessed this endurance, he might not have failed in his melancholy mood. The narrators of "The Two Voices" and "Locksley Hall" found the metaphor of battle suitable for describing their states of conflict with doubt and evil; the narrator of *Maud,* having settled his internal war, found salvation in an external combat against more than personal enemies. Lancelot, a noble but sinning man, maintains a constant warfare within himself against a mood which is "like a fiend." But the fiend is never triumphant; whereas in "Balin and Balan," moods are no longer *like* fiends, but become fiends in fact which destroy the spirit. (John R. Reed, *Perception and Design* . . . [1971], 84.)

■ The poem ends with Lancelot unsure of how those bonds might be broken, though his very perception of the need signals the onset of the fiercest struggle he has yet endured—the real struggle with himself brought finally to the surface. He has, by inadvertently stepping outside his customary identity, been humbled in the flesh. He has the opportunity to see that the flesh itself is the disguise, the "mortal veil and shattered phantom of that infinite One" ("De Profundis," p. 1283) and that he himself is more than lover or invincible warrior. This is Lancelot's opportunity to see his truest function as a name, a force, a spirit, or a sign—all parts of a larger design and elements of "that infinite One." Being brought low, and weak in the flesh, he has a clearer perception of the ideal he has failed to espouse. Now, the ideal no longer actually attainable, he realizes the true nature of his struggle toward redemption. (Reed [1971], 89.)

■ Elaine's death is really the symbolic culmination of a process of disintegration which is manifested in *Lancelot and Elaine* in many ways. First, for the first time in the *Idylls* the sinful relationship between Lancelot and Guinevere is no longer rumor; it is beyond doubt. Second, because Lancelot is Arthur's greatest knight, whom other knights emulate, knowledge of his taint has more serious social consequences than would that of a lesser knight, and it is important that the taint is now within the kingdom, not without among the heathen, in the court of Mark or Pellam. Third, if at least part of Arthur's virtue lies in the fact that he "honours his own word,/As if it were his God's" (143–44), the process of dissolution is evident, not only in the introduction of Gawain, who tells the truth only when it suits his purpose, but in the lies of Lancelot and Guinevere and their attitude toward those lies—Lancelot's only remorse for a lie to Arthur apparently being that he "lied in vain " (102). Fourth, the kingdom's social purpose breaks down through disobedience and discourtesy. Gawain, vexed at the quest Arthur has given him, not only fails to perform it, but perverts the role of women by giving the quest to Elaine, "the quest/Assigned to her not worthy of it" (819–20). Fifth, there is the loss of the possibility of fruition in the kingdom through Lancelot's rejection of Elaine, who alone could give him "noble issue, sons/Born to the glory of [his] name and fame." The contrast between the "cry of children, Enids and Geraints/Of times to be" with which *Geraint and Enid* concludes and the sterility with which *Lancelot and Elaine* ends marks the progress toward destruction the kingdom has made. Finally, with the loss of Elaine there is no longer any real possibility of women exercising a salutary influence in the kingdom. With Elaine, spirit in the kingdom dies and there is no longer a chance of retarding the acceleration toward a new barbarity. The kingdom is lost. (Ward Hellstrom, *On the Poems of Tennyson* [1972], 121–122.)

■ "Lancelot and Elaine" is a domestic idyll, quite different in scope and manner from the poems surrounding it. (James R. Kincaid, *Tennyson's Major Poems* [1975], 186.)

■ Least of all can Elaine be blamed. The poem is so deliberately plain that explication might be most a matter of pointing out the obvious but for the existence of the now popular notion that Elaine herself at least shares the responsibility for her own doom. (Kincaid [1975], 187.)

■ Elaine is contrasted to the pathetic Guinevere, who simply does not understand. (Kincaid [1975], 189.)

■ Enid's faithfulness is fruitful; Elaine's is arid. Lancelot is not reborn; he simply rejoins his earlier condition: "His honour rooted in dishonour stood,/And faith unfaithful kept him falsely true" (ll. 871–72). These terms are not paradoxical but ironic. For Lancelot, honor is dishonor; loyalty, treachery. (Kincaid [1975], 189–190.)

■ In *Lancelot and Elaine,* each stage of the quest is characterized in a way that is just the opposite of what we should expect. (Donald S. Hair, *Domestic and Heroic . . .* [1981], 181.)

■ Lancelot is a central figure of the *Idylls,* and it could be argued that this poem, like *Paradise Lost,* has a double hero.

Arthur sets the standard of heroism in this poem, as Christ does in Milton's epic, while Lancelot, like Adam, falls but is ultimately redeemed. Its central subject is the love triangle of Lancelot, Guinevere, and Arthur, and its central concern is the conflict within Lancelot himself. (Hair [1981], 181–182.)

The Holy Grail

■ *The Holy Grail* is indeed two poems. One is a carefully worked out homily upon the proper relation of faith or inspiration or vision to good works. For this reading the symbols of the poem serve as subordinate portions of an allegorical framework, and the high point of the piece is the concluding passage in which Arthur pronounces the moral: vision, except in extraordinary cases like Galahad's and possibly Percivale's, should be only an adjunct to good works. It should not preoccupy a good knight or distract him from meaningful constructive labor. This is the poem Tennyson's large middle-class audience must have read and found a noble and satisfying expression of their intimate beliefs. It is throughout its length, with some allowance made for the wealthy bride and the flatness of Ambrosius, a workmanlike poem; but parts of it will continue to register on many readers as they clearly did on Baum and must have done on Nicolson as the product of a Tennyson working much more nearly in the manner of Sir Bors, that "square-cut man and honest," than with the magic of Merlin or the vision of Galahad.

The other poem, which requires judicious skipping or rapid reading over parts of the whole, reaches its highest moments in two great symbolic scenes. In the first, Galahad, having negotiated the hill of a hundred water-courses and left Percivale at the base, traverses an endless black and evil-smelling swamp, part whitened with the bones of men, on bridges that burst into flame as he passes. Entering a boat that thereafter appears (to Percivale's wondering eyes) to transform itself into a living winged creature, Galahad sails off into a blazing, roaring sky to be assumed at last into the spiritual city. In the other scene, Lancelot, after raging in the wasteland striving in vain to pluck his "one sin" from his heart, comes upon a boat half-swallowed in the mounds and ridges of a sea. He drives along the deep with the moon and the stars for seven days until on the seventh night the boat plunges to a stop in the sands beneath the enchanted towers of Carbonek. There, in a room of fire atop a tower of a thousand steps, though "Blasted and burnt and blinded," Lancelot nevertheless beholds the Holy Grail palled in crimson samite and surrounded by "great angels, awful shapes, and wings and eyes." (Donald Smalley, "A New Look at Tennyson . . . " [1962], 356–357.)

■ Essentially, then, the Holy Grail to Tennyson is not an external "thing" to be *discovered*, even a divine "idea", but rather a state of being to be *achieved*. Galahad is not man in the ordinary sense; he is more than man, and consequently we are never allowed to enter his consciousness. Tennyson could not. For Galahad had "lost himself to gain himself", as had Percivale's sister. The Quest was manifestly for them. Arthur will not allow that the Quest is for his other knights because it definitely means the weakening of self and the illusion sustained by the self, and the deposing of the sovereign "will", which is the only "sure", if temporary, defense against the Dionysiac forces, the beast, and the climbing wave that remain perpetually in the background ready to overwhelm the self at its first sign of weakness. Holy selflessness obviously weakens the self as much as submission to the ways of Nature. It is perhaps significant that in "Balin and Balan" King Pellam, the murderous Garlon's father, a former enemy of King Arthur, has taken to the holy and retired life, and indeed epitomizes this kind of life, and yet is described as being a close friend of King Mark. Tennyson thus faces in "The Holy Grail" the problem of trying to reconcile the tragic view of life with the religious view, the former subjective and the latter objective. For the most part, to Arthur, as well as to Tennyson, the intuitions of an external God are too faint or tenuous to risk surrendering the will, which surrender would involve the destruction of the illusory Apollonian realm. Arthur is more a tragic than a religious hero. (William R. Brashear, *The Living Will* [1969], 147.)

■ The Grail quest explores the possibilities for men to reconcile the perplexities of human reality and to perceive a truth unbounded by sensory limits. At the conclusion of "The Holy Grail," Arthur contemplates a time when visions may render all physical substance illusory and remove the distinctions between time and eternity (HG, ll. 906–915). These visions, however, may only be experienced by those, such as Galahad, whose saintly dispositions free them from human inadequacy. Other men are circumscribed by space and time and perceive through earthly senses; the Grail for these, as for Lancelot, is veiled and they must complete their allotted duties on earth before they apprehend divinity or timelessness. Indeed, man, with his frail senses, may find the "pure severity of perfect light" unendurable, as Guinevere did, and therefore prefer the "warmth and colour" which she found in Lancelot (G, ll. 640–643). If man does aspire beyond his human condition, he must first recognize and overcome the deceptions of his own ego. The illusions wrought by selfish desire are symbolized in the successive scenes in Percivale's quest: the gratification of physical appetite in the brook and apple-trees, sexual satisfaction in the gracious woman, material wealth in the jewels, and personal fame in the eulogistic crowd (HG, ll. 379–439). These false visions separate Percivale from the Grail, as all human pride separates man from God, until he acquires humility and renounces self-centered ambition. Yet to relinquish self is to lose purpose and identity on earth, for man's task is inextricably linked with name and fame and use. Hence Arthur's acute disappointment in the Grail quest and the iniquities in disillusionment which frequently follow unmasked deception. The latter is brutally demonstrated in Pelleas' recognition of his illusory love. Blaming Arthur's vows for making him a fool and liar, his despair impels him to complete disintegration and, because denied name and identity through the Round Table's values, he establishes a perverted role in total opposition to the Table. Pelleas' irrational conduct stresses the difficulty man has in sustaining a balanced view of the melange of deception and truth which characterizes human reality. (E. Warwick Slinn, "Deception and Artifice . . . " [1973], 11–12.)

■ *The Holy Grail* does not portray the quest of the Grail as much as it studies the various figures who respond to the Grail. Their responses become the subject-matter of the poem:

> He pointed out the difference between the five visions of the Grail, as seen by the Holy Nun, Sir Galahad, Sir Percivale, Sir Lancelot, Sir Bors, according to their different, their own peculiar natures and circumstances, and the perfection or imperfection of their Christianity. He dwelt on the mystical treatment of every part of his subject, and said the key is to be found in a careful reading of Sir Pervicale's vision and subsequent fall and nineteenth-century temptations. [*Tennyson: A Memoir*, II, 63]

Percivale's vision is the key to the poem, yet it is coloured, rarefied, explained through its contrast with the other four quests. Each vision reflects upon the other visions, and the final commentary, anticipated by the consequences of the quests, is appropriately proclaimed by the King. (David Staines, "Tennyson's 'The Holy Grail'" [1974], 748.)

■ For Percivale, the Grail quest is both beneficial and detrimental; it instils humility in him, yet it removes him from the practical affairs of this world. His new self-awareness lacks proper perspective; he becomes a victim of his own vision. As a victim, he is basically a tragic hero. His capacity to 'be as Arthur' is destroyed by his ultimately selfish 'resolve/To pass away into the quiet life'.

Tennyson's treatment of the Grail story is his study of 'Percivale's vision and subsequent fall and nineteenth-century temptations'. The idyll is Percivale's tragedy, his inability to adapt to his awareness of the limits of human capability. To brand Percivale 'a vain, self-centered, irresponsible knight . . . guilty of the sin of pride' is to overlook Arthur's address:

> '—and ye,
> What are ye? Galahads?—no, nor Percivales'
> (For thus it pleased the King to range me close
> After Sir Galahad).

Though a still somewhat proud Percivale recounts Arthur's comment, the passage does emphasize the high position Percivale merits. A knight second only to Galahad in spiritual perfection, he is the most worthy of those men who are denied the complete vision. By denying him the spiritual realm Malory opened to him, Tennyson makes Percivale a knight related to, but finally separated from, the world where Galahad must live. The offer of an earthly kingdom where 'thou shalt be as Arthur' represents the highest achievement possible for Percivale; his refusal of the offer represents the tragic blindness of a knight who forsakes the world for a calling to which he was never summoned. (Staines [1974], 752.)

■ Percivale, the center of the idyll, becomes the tragic hero, the knight whose high capability for effective rule in this world is unrealized because of his improper response to the Grail; with no support from Malory's account of the quest, Tennyson makes the idyll a tragedy, narrated, most effectively, by the hero who remains unaware of his own tragedy. In the final line, 'So spake the King: I knew not all he meant', Percivale reveals the personal blindness that prevents him from seeing the importance of his own 'allotted field'. He cannot understand the more natural and valid mysticism of his King.

The completion of the Grail idyll permitted Tennyson to return to his general conception of an Arthurian poem and depict further episodes in the story of Camelot. Only a year after he finished the Grail idyll, he published his second quartet of idylls. In view of the long delay in his creation of *The Holy Grail*, the rapidity of his composition of the other idylls in the new volume stands as a final testimony of his personal satisfaction with his unique treatment of the quest of the Holy Grail. (Staines [1974], 755–756.)

■ The poem is the most subtle of Tennyson's exercises in ironic rhetoric. He insists everywhere on the moral and rational framework whose validity he is just as emphatically denying. . . . "The Holy Grail" once again repeats the wasteland motif, the image of elementary inner chaos that one

must conquer. The theme of losing oneself to find a new self
is not at all submerged in this idyll, nor are the means to that
salvation ineffective. Galahad, Bors, and Percivale, perhaps
others, do see the Grail. But now, without a background of
social harmony, salvation acts to make man unfit for social
life. (James R. Kincaid, *Tennyson's Major Poems* [1975],
193–194.)

■ What does it mean that Tennyson is compelled to make of
Percivale a consuming force that devastates everything it en-
counters?

Freud's very problematic final theory of the instincts posits
a group of drives that work toward reducing all tensions to a
zero-point, so as to carry everything living back to an inorganic state. Freud's formulation is difficult, because it suggests that a self-destructive drive back towards origins is a
universal phenomenon. As a theory, Freud's notion here is
frankly daemonic, and related to his dark insight that all repetition phenomena may mask a regressive element in every
human instinct. To account for life's ambivalence towards itself, Freud resorted to a more radical dualism than he had
entertained earlier. The id became the center for represent-
ing every instinctual demand, with none assigned to the ego,
which means that ultimately every desire, whether for power
or for sexual fulfillment, is in some sense linked to the desire
for death. Without pretending to be summarizing the full
complexity of Freud's speculations, I will leave the notion of
the death instincts there, except to note that Freud was compelled to adopt a new formulation in this area, the Nirvana
Principle, which he took from Schopenhauer by way of a
suggestion of the English psychoanalyst Barbara Low.

The Nirvana Principle, introduced in *Beyond the Pleasure
Principle* (1920), is the psyche's drive to reduce all excitation
within itself, whether the origin of the excitation be internal
or external, to the zero-level, or as close to zero as possible. I
have invoked all of this Freudian speculation in order to get
us to the Nirvana Principle, for that is the actuality of Percivale's Quest, despite Percivale's apparent intention and Tennyson's stated and overt intention. Percivale believes he is

questing for the Holy Grail, but in reality he quests for
Schopenhauer's quasi-Buddhistic Nirvana, where desire shall
vanish, the individual self fade away, and quietude replace the
strong poet's search for a stance and word of his own. Percivale, I am suggesting, is as close as Tennyson can come, not
to a return of the repressed, but to an absolute or total fresh-
ening of self-repression. And though *The Holy Grail* is ostensi-
bly a critique of Percivale and an exaltation of Galahad, and
even of the humane and sweet Ambrosius, what any reader is
going to remember is that sublime and terrific destructive
march to the zero-point that is the litany of Percivale's quest.
Reflect even upon the exchange between Ambrosius and Percivale that ends the account of Percivale's ruinous march. Ambrosius cries out, in the name of common humanity:

> "O brother, saving this Sir Galahad,
> Came ye on none but phantoms in your quest,
> No man, no woman?"

> Then Sir Percivale:
> "All men, to one so bound by such a vow,
> And women were as phantoms. . . ."

How shall we read "such a vow"? Only, I think, despite
Tennyson's intentions, as the vow to be a strong poet, whatever the human cost. Percivale, in the deep sense, is Tennyson the poet, unable to get out of or beyond the shadow of
Galahad, the quester who beholds and becomes one with a
strength that resists the Nirvana Principle. I am not propos-
ing any simple equation of Galahad = Keats, but a more
complex formula in which Galahad does represent the High
Romantic quest, and Percivale the belated quest of Victorian
Romanticism. Tennyson was too sublimely repressed a poet
to develop very overtly his ambivalence toward his prime pre-
cursors, and the death of Hallam, who was the great cham-
pion of Keats, augmented the repression. But Tennyson too
was a preternaturally strong poet, and we have seen something of his strength at misprision. The shadow of Keats
never did abandon him wholly, and so the stance of belated-
ness became a kind of second nature for him. But what he

may have lacked in priority of stance, he greatly compensated for in priority of style. He prophesies his true ephebe, the late T. S. Eliot, and time, I am persuaded, will show us how much stronger a poet Tennyson was than Eliot. (Harold Bloom, "Tennyson: In the Shadow of Keats" [1976], 50–52.)

■ The ravishing visions of "The Holy Grail" form the radiant center of the *Idylls*. The identity of lowliness and grandeur, of gloom and exaltation, is a celestial phenomenon that Tennyson accurately portrays in the glorious transformation of earth and nighttime sky. As the great gusts of auroral light are pressed into doctrinal service, the heroic values of saint, seer, and soldier effortlessly fuse in volatile displays of ethereal caprice and earthly power. But celestial ease is eclipsed by "wandering wind[s]" ("The Passing of Arthur," 1. 36); and when the radiant unities recede, dualities of hope and despair, credulity and distrust, continue to spread. In the *Idylls* as a whole, Tennyson even duplicates the careers of his knights—double figures like Gareth and Pelleas, and the brothers Balin and Balan; and he multiplies the main action, the character, and the career of Arthur, who turns out to be a double in himself, a split personality. From the volatile splendor of "The Holy Grail" and the glittering ruin of "The Last Tournament," *Idylls of the King* passes to the somber interrogations of the dying Arthur. In his elusive and modest way, Tennyson seems ignorant of Spenserian allegory: he seldom explicitly relates his Arthurian matter to historical examples and moral precepts. The supernatural occurrences are all things to all men; and we come to feel that the truth is forever hidden, wrapped in "lucid veils" like the Holy Grail, or like Hallam's ghost in *In Memoriam*. The cryptic songs and riddles are to the self-concealing truth of the *Idylls* what the synecdoche of the shell is to the hero's self-regenerating power in *Maud*. An allegorist would show mainly aversion to characters like Guinevere and Lancelot; but by making them extensions of ourselves, Tennyson repudiates the allegorical intelligence, as he would repudiate the intelligence of St. Simeon's God. The God who fulfills himself in many ways does not hate any man, but like Spinoza's God, he does not seem to love any man either. Arthur's secret fear, disclosed in "The Passing of Arthur," that "some lesser god had made the world" (l. 14) alerts the reader to terrors that confirm the unstable nature of the world, always verging on fragmentation and nightmare. Even as Arthur civilizes nature, his failures tell of the failure of man's existence and the failure of his power to exist. (W. David Shaw, *Tennyson's Style* [1976], 218–220.)

■ For the most part, the quest is a case of hysterical religiosity. The nun's making of a sword case for Galahad out of her shorn hair is unsavory, even without the Freudian symbolism; and the "deathless passion in her eyes" and her "My knight, my love, my knight of heaven,/O thou, my love" all too clearly suggest an erotic asceticism. "Holy virgins in their ecstasies," Gawain says sourly. Arthur plainly diagnoses the quest as a "sign to maim this Order which I made" (HG 149–53, 864, 297), yet he rebukes Gawain for his remark and comments on the significance of the events attending the end of an historical cycle: "Blessèd are Bors, Lancelot and Percivale . . . God made music through them" (HG, 870–74). (Henry Kozicki, *Tennyson and Clio* [1979], 146.)

■ But how do these facts influence our reading of Percivale's narrative or how do they alter our retrospective interpretation of Merlin's character as presented in "Merlin and Vivien?" In "The Holy Grail" Merlin seems to "fall" because he willingly immerses himself too completely in his private vision, becomes enraptured by his own artifact. Such a fall is, of course, in keeping with the insistence in this idyll on the dangers of private vision, especially when chosen at the expense of public service. In "Merlin and Vivien," on the other hand, the means of Merlin's "fall" is the charm while the motive seems to be the need for rest and solace in the face of despair. "The Holy Grail" omits the psychological motivation ("misadvertence" is the only cause that Percivale mentions) but clearly identifies Merlin's own artistry as the means of his downfall. In some sense, the later idyll simplifies the task of interpreting Merlin's actions by confirming what is only intimated in "Merlin and Vivien": the bard becomes his own victim when he surrenders totally to the imperatives of his special vision, when he plunges completely into what Tennyson calls "spiritual imagination" (Ricks, p. 1666n.). The effect of Merlin's creation on Galahad and the rest of the Round Table is, then, instructive. When he sits in Merlin's chair, Galahad "loses himself": that is, he casts aside his social self, his personality, to find his spiritual identity through a private quest. By his example, the less worthy knights also seek personal spiritual exaltation and thus precipitate the decline of Arthur's realm; Merlin's loss of himself is but the first domino. Arthur in his speech to Galahad at the idyll's end points to the ultimately private nature of the vision of "fiery prophet in old times,/And all the sacred madness of the bard" (ll. 872–73). As Arthur knows, the experience of a transcendent reality can be only partially and unsatisfactorily communicated within the limitations of the "framework" and the "chord" of the individual. "Divine madness" then, though it may be glorious, is socially disruptive and personally isolating. (Catherine Barnes Stevenson, "Druids, Bards, and Tennyson's Merlin" [1980], 19–20.)

■ In *The Holy Grail,* the irony arises from the use of a narrator with limited understanding, for here and in the next two idylls the central character comes to no such understanding as Lancelot achieves at the end of the seventh idyll. (Donald S. Hair, *Domestic and Heroic . . .* [1981], 181.)

■ The dialogue [*between Percivale and Ambrosius*] is a web of ironies, in which two speakers try to cope with events that neither fully understands. It should not be surprising, then, that the story is full of fits and starts; that the line of the narrative is constantly interrupted by backtracking, explanation, and amplification. Such shifts and changes foreshadow the discontinuous technique of Eliot's *The Wasteland,* for in both poems the discontinuity depends upon the limited understanding revealed by the speakers. (Hair [1981], 191.)

■ Galahad is the hero of Percivale's narrative. In Percivale's view, Galahad, rather than the king, sets the standard of conduct, and Percivale is proud of his association with him. (Hair [1981], 191.)

■ Percivale's account of the quest itself is conventional in that the outer landscape and events mirror his inner experience. (Hair [1981], 195.)

■ [*Arthur's final speech*] is the last and clearly the best word in an idyll that devotes itself to distinguishing different kinds of vision and their sources; and does so with such power and mature psychological insight as to make *The Holy Grail* arguably the richest of the *Idylls.* (Kerry McSweeney, *Tennyson and Swinburne . . .*[1981], 119.)

■ As opposite equals, the hind on the one hand and King Arthur on the other are a Tennysonian version of the Carlylean "Two men I honour and no third" who in *Sartor Resartus* are the peasant toiling for his daily bread and the hero toiling for the bread of life, both of them finding fulfilment in doing the work that lies nearest them. While at the end of the speech King Arthur naturally expresses himself in a Christian idiom, one should not fail to see the kind of experience he describes is by no means traditionally Christian. It is a version of the great Romantic doctrine of "natural supernaturalism" . . ., of living in the present, in the imminent, so fully and unself-consciously that vision, moments of transcendence and experiential immortality (what Arthur calls moments when man feels he cannot die), come as they will— not as a result of quest, but precisely because they are unsought. (McSweeney [1981], 121–122.)

Pelleas and Ettarre

■ The idyll, far from sentimentalizing the "courtly love" ethic, reveals the poverty of the false courtly ideal. [*Like Chaucer's Troilus, Pelleas is* "fortune's fool."] (Lawrence Poston III, "'Pelleas and Ettarre': Tennyson's 'Troilus'" [1966], 199.)

■ [*Tennyson*] dismisses his protagonist much as Shakespeare dismisses his. Totally at the mercy of the irrational passion excited by his recognition that he has made a whore his idol,

Pelleas dashes offstage forever—unless, indeed, he becomes the Red Knight of the following idyll. (Poston [1966], 203.)

■ "Pelleas and Ettarre" excoriates those who idealize what is all too transitory and human. (Poston [1966], 204.)

■ Pelleas is unselfconscious and considers virtue a kind of utensil. He has the proper admiration for what is good, but it is, for him, like a pattern in a lovely tapestry—something taken on trust and trusted in relentlessly. Virtue is a machine whose workings remain unknown, yet seem to operate the better for that ignorance. The paradigm in Pelleas' imagination obscures the flawed reality. He is led not by a spiritual Ideal, but by a material notion. And yet to blame Pelleas for his ignorance or condemn him for his simplicity is unjust and inappropriate; although he is simple and easily duped, his simplicity stems from essential well-meaning. It is a mixed fault, for, were he come to court at better times, when persons were what they seemed, his superficial view of virtue might have been amended. As it is, he lacks the opportunity. In better times even lesser men may be preserved, but in bad times only the finest persevere. And as the roll of disenchanted minor knights increases, the once monumental code proves unsteady, like images in delirium. (John R. Reed, *Perception and Design . . .* [1971], 104.)

■ "Pelleas and Ettarre" is a black parody of the initiation stories that open the *Idylls*. Pelleas himself is the last figure of comic exuberance we hear in the poem: it is almost as if the news had not reached him out there in the wilds. (James R. Kincaid, *Tennyson's Major Poems* [1975], 199.)

■ Finally, in an inversion of Gareth's creation of his own personality, Pelleas specifically renounces his own being: "No name, no name" (l. 553), he shouts to Lancelot. He loses personality and manhood, answering Guinevere's attempt to calm him with a "fierce" eye and a hissing. "I have no sword" (l. 589). He then springs "from the door into the dark" (l. 591). There is now nothing but this dark—and the silence. . . . (Kincaid [1975], 201–202.)

■ [*As the Red Knight*] Pelleas is another murdered innocent, and his reactionary inversion of Camelot is the last cry of the pure in a perverted world. He is so much the antithesis of Arthur's knights and so incapable of disguise that he cannot even stay on a horse long enough to maintain the combat. He falls off in a drunken stupor, whereupon Arthur's men complete the slaughter of innocence. . . . (Kincaid [1975], 203.)

■ [T]he quest in *Pelleas and Ettarre* ironically releases a demon rather than a true knight. Here Tennyson uses (and condemns) the conventions of courtly love, which he fuses ironically with the romance quest." (Donald S. Hair, *Domestic and Heroic* . . . [1981], 181.)

■ Although *Pelleas and Ettarre* was published alongside *The Coming of Arthur, The Passsing of Arthur,* and *The Holy Grail,* Tennyson chose for this idyll the same kind of material that he chose for the idylls published in 1859: it is a story without wonders, and it is told by an anonymous narrator. . . . The entire narrative is pervaded with the conventional situations of courtly love, modified by Tennyson for the purposes of his romance. The first sight of the beloved, for instance, is conventionally described as a vision of a goddess. (Hair [1981], 199–200.)

■ [T]he vows that are the basis of the Order of the Round Table foster the perfection of the individual. When Pelleas denies those vows, he loses his individuality. Instead of finding himself on his quest, as Geraint, for instance, did, he has lost himself. His repeated assertion that "I have no sword" is a confession of his loss of identity as a knight. From Arthur's point of view, the history of Pelleas has come to an end. (Hair [1981], 204.)

■ The subject of *Pelleas and Ettarre,* like that of "Lucretius" . . ., is the destructive power of sexuality, and its form, like that of *Balin and Balan,* is psychological romance, not moral exemplum. (Kerry McSweeney, *Tennyson and Swinburne* . . . [1981], 107.)

■ Pelleas' rite of passage destroys him. He becomes in *The Last Tournament* the demonic immoralist who swears "by the scorpion-worm that twists in hell,/And stings itself to everlasting death." . . . As such, Pelleas is in sharp contrast to Tristram, who is able to accept his sexuality and its relativistic consequences, who is not dazed by but flourishes in the naturalistic warmth of the sun. What Pelleas is shattered by, Tristram celebrates; what makes Pelleas monstrously immoral makes Tristram intelligently amoral. (McSweeney [1981], 108–109.)

The Last Tournament

■ The poem's success, I believe, depends in large measure upon several factors: first, a remarkable unity of tone; secondly, a masterful interweaving of parallel and antithetical threads of narrative; and finally, a skillful use of Dagonet the Fool. For if Dagonet is not the protagonist of "The Last Tournament," he is at least the term of contrast by which the fallen Tristram can be measured. (Boyd Litzinger, "The Structure of Tennyson's 'The Last Tournament'" [1963], 53.)

■ Singled out for attention, the beast imagery in "The Last Tournament" must be seen as a strongly unifying device.
    More important structurally, perhaps, is Tennyson's manipulation of his complex plots. Two of these plots—the winning of the Tournament and Arthur's conquest of the Red Knight—are parallel and lend support to one another after the nature of musical counterpoint; the other two—the degradation of Tristram and the elevation of Dagonet—are antithetical and heighten one another by contrasts. By shifting from one narrative to another, and by a judicious use of the so-called "flashback" technique, Tennyson creates an impression of simultaneous action and reinforces one theme by another.
    The Dagonet-Tristram theme acts as a framework within which the other stories are developed. The poem opens with the meeting of Sir Fool (whom, in lines 1 and 2, significantly,

"Gawain in his mood/Had made mock-knight of Arthur's Table Round") and Sir Tristram, who a day earlier had won the prize in the Tournament. Before we are able to discern the true relationship between these antithetical characters, Tennyson takes us back to the actions which led up to the parallel plots. These plots are not narrated consecutively, but are carefully interwoven, situation and climax counterpointing situation and climax. Thus Tennyson begins the story of the Tournament by narrating the discovery of the nestling child and the ruby carcanet, the proclaiming of the Tournament, and the arming of the knights; but before the Tournament can begin, the next plot is set in motion by the arrival of the disfigured churl, who carries the challenge of the Red Knight to Arthur's court.

Were this interruption a mechanical one, then it were truly blameworthy. But it is not. Tennyson links the two narratives by making the second bear upon the first: in order to meet the Red Knight's challenge, Arthur is forced to turn the conduct of the Tournament over to Lancelot, thus assuring Tristram an uncontested victory in the lists—an important matter, it will be seen—and assuring also the integrity of the poem. (Litzinger [1963], 56–57.)

■ Tristram's worship of natural instinct is one-sided and absurd. Its incongruity lies in its fated incompleteness: "Free love—free field—we love but while we may" ("The Last Tournament," l. 281). If all values are relative, then how can Tristram proclaim the truth of anything, including his own philosphy of relativism? The atheist's freedom to mock everything, if taken seriously, demands universal extension. The skeptic who no longer hears the "silent music up in heaven" knows no limit to his destruction. When Tristram exalts the claims of "flesh and blood" above his "inviolable vows" to God and Arthur he prides himself on his privileged position; he thinks he remains invulnerable above the wreck wrought at the last tournament by the spirit of universal negation. Yet this very immunity to destruction is the atheist's heel of Achilles, for if Tristram cannot renounce his own love for Isolt he cannot renounce everything. The knight who boasts that his love "is not bounded save by love" (l. 698) cannot at the same time proclaim that his love for Arthur was the "madness of an hour" (l. 670). If the atheist who declares "we are not angels here/Nor shall be" (ll. 693–694) cannot negate love he cannot negate all values, and if he cannot negate all values he is not a complete atheist. If Tristram is not a total disbeliever, what happens to his much vaunted freedom of thought? Tennyson's own philosphy is a condemnation of the limited point of view masquerading as total truth. Tristram acknowledges in his love for Isolt what he feels free to disavow in thought. The clash between theory and practice is ironic wherever discerned. Mark's sudden murder of the adulterer is a logical outcome of Tristram's point of view. For if all values, including love, are objects of the atheist's destruction, his own values must obviously be included. (W. David Shaw, ". . . A Dialectical Reading" [1969], 184.)

■ "The Last Tournament" spins out the Tristram-Isolt subplot in sordid counterpoint to Lancelot's and Guinevere's betrayal of Arthur. (Gerhard Joseph, *Tennysonian Love* [1969], 178.)

■ Tennyson's removal of the machinery of fate [*the love potion*] from his Tristram serves to confirm the doctrine of human control that Arthur has defined earlier. . . . Insofar as Arthur's doctrine represents Tennyson's own feelings, the seasonal organicism of the *Idylls,* as Jerome Buckley has suggested, foreshadows Toynbee rather than Spengler. . . . [*i.e.*] individuals . . . are free to shape their destinies. (Joseph [1969], 181.)

■ Tristram amply illustrates the importance of moody pride and self-indulgence in the soul's demise. His disbelief in the vows is conditioned largely by the fact that his own behavior would be inconveniently restricted by them. After all, it was by using the model of Guinevere's sin that he seduced Isolt for his own pleasure. He took his pleasure with her and with Isolt of Brittany, and yet, libertine that he seems to be, he is not willing to allow Isolt the same freedom in love that he enjoys, for he quickly puts an end to their conversation when she entertains a fancy of offering herself to Lancelot, even though it seems no more than a jest. Nor has Tristram's supposed worldly wisdom given him any assurance of firm character, or decided mind, for, in investigating his feelings about the two Isolts, he can only conclude, "'I know not what I would.'" (p. 1718) Like Gawain, his eye seeks its contentment anywhere, yet nowhere does it find fulfilment and certainty. Surely Tristram's ghost, too, will go wailing in the wind, "hollow, hollow, hollow all delight!" (John R. Reed, *Perception and Design . . .* [1971], 117.)

■ Tristram is spokesman for the convenience of doubt. Tristram was once, as Isolt reminds him, a greater man when he had genuine courtesy, but now he has "grown wild beast" himself. (p. 1721) It suits Tristram's purpose, as it did that of the narrator of *Maud,* to judge all men, all vows, by himself and his vows. He failed, and instantly the world was false. So with Pelleas' disenchantment. Again it is a question of mood. When we believe, our behavior follows our belief. The obstacle arises when our belief contends with sensuous drives; should the appetites triumph, for peace of mind we persuade ourselves that our belief was false. (Reed [1971], 118.)

■ Tristram's worldliness, then, is not so adequate as it seems, nor is his doubt so certain as he would have himself believe. His argument, Tennyson suggests, is certainly inadequate. But if proof were needed of the falseness of Tristram's position, it is summed up in his fall. What Tristram has championed is a life of liberty; unprincipled, self-indulgent, uncontrolled. Accordingly, as he hands the symbol of dead innocence to his tainted queen, Mark—the embodiment of this undisciplined, unprincipled existence—strikes him dead. "'Mark's way,'" he says. (p. 1724) Mark's way, indeed. Tristram has here his mortal lesson too late to utilize. What value in his nobility, his prowess, his strength, if there be no rules by which men contend? If he may violate by stealth, then Mark may exterminate him in a similar fashion. By surrendering himself to an anti-code of anarchy and self-indulgence, Tristram has been blinded by his own vanity, for he has failed to realize that this philosphy will operate for all men, and therefore against himself. If one allows that each man's hand is against his neighbor, he should have sense enough to beware his neighbor's hand. Tristram is, in fact, no worldling at all, though Mark is. Tristram is only self-outcast from the camp of virtue. Much as he rails against the vows, he does not truly see all the world consigned to the license he allows himself. He has contempt for Mark, and yet he advocates Mark's way. And, in the end, he has it. Furthermore, the liberty Tristram seeks in freeing himself from the supposed bondage of the vows is only license, which entraps him more surely than hopeful visions would have. He lives from moment to moment, sullen, brutal, and vacillating in nature. His fine qualities are valuable no more, for in a world ungoverned by rules, fine qualities compromised are easily defeated by the most base. Giving up the guidance of the stars, Tristram has plummetted into a swamp of self-concern, unlike Lancelot, who, while bound and confirmed by his one sin, is still capable of "gazing at a star" emblematic of the Ideal, though he continues bewilderedly "marvelling what it" is. (p. 1703) (Reed [1971], 120–121.)

■ The only validity Tristram grants at any time to the vows is a pragmatic one: they served their use. He challenges their permanent validity by a naturalistic argument—Arthur cannot be traced "thro' the flesh and blood/Of our old Kings," i.e., the spiritual values Arthur represents are not derived from the ruling elements of our physical nature. The morality Tristram seeks is one founded on those elements; he is the type of those who talk about making morality conform to the facts of human nature. (F. E. L. Priestley, *Language and Structure in Tennyson's Poetry* [1973], 246.)

■ Although the actions crowded into "The Last Tournament" occupy only a few days, the setting and imagery range widely through all the reaches of the kingdom. The idyll opens with the Fool dancing like a withered leaf before the hall of Camelot, shifts in setting to the woods of Lyonnesse

where Tristram dreams of his two Isolts, to the northern
wastes where Arthur slays the Red Knight, to the west-
ernmost seas surrounding Tintagil, and, with dramatic suddenness, back again to Camelot. As Mark murders Tristram,
the twilit vistas of Tintagil yield to the claustrophobic darkness of Arthur's return "All in a death-dumb autumn-dripping gloom" (750)—to the empty chamber of the Queen. The
line is more than an exercise in the onomatopoeia of decay.
Tristram dies "death-dumb" like a slaughtered animal, and
the Red Knight topples wordless and sodden into the mire.
The "dumbness" of the autumn also symbolizes the silencing
of Arthur's music, first heard at the founding of Camelot,
muted by Vivien's pagan hymn, further fractured into discord by Tristram's song, and now heard only in the muffled
music of the Fool, who greets the returning King with inar-
ticulate sobs. The Fool has been made a mock-knight and in
his folly tries to attune himself to Arthur's Order at a time
when all the true knights have proven false. And so when
Tristram sings of "new life, new love" (279), the Fool chides
him for making false music with Queen Isolt and persists in
dancing "to the broken music of [his] brains" (258), until
at the idyll's end he too has become "death-dumb." The
"autumn-dripping gloom" harks back to the thick rains of the
opening and to the "gloom on gloom" that deepens in Balin
and Pelleas and now overcomes Arthur, who is himself caught
up in the darkening confusion of the realm. (John D. Rosenberg, *The Fall of Camelot* [1973], 88–89.)

■ As a harper, Tristram is an artist, and his verbal altercation
with Dagonet may be seen as a decadent version of the verbal
conflict between Merlin and Vivien. As court entertainer and
Arthur's fool, Dagonet is a comic surrogate for Merlin; less
dignified than Merlin and without Merlin's superior ability as
an artificer, he is still a match for Tristram, who is without
Vivien's intellectual acuity. In the earlier duel, Vivien won
with ominous consequences for Camelot. Here, the victory is
reversed with Merlin's substitute verbally better than Vivien's
successor, but the implications are not reversed, since

Dagonet's character as "mock-knight" and "withered leaf" (LT, ll. 1–4) ironically emphasizes the irreversible decaying of Arthur's realm. Tristram notes that "The glory of our Round Table is no more," and sings of the growth of a new culture: "New life, new love, to suit the newer day" (LT, ll. 189, 279). But he lacks the wit to inspire regeneration, which Dagonet artfully observes in his reference to the Orpheus myth. When Tristram says he has thrown Dagonet pearls and found him swine, the fool retorts that swine and other animals may once have "trooped round" a harper as musical as Tristram, but never a king's fool (LT, ll. 321–324), implying that Tristram's pearls are only fit for swine. Tristram retaliates by twisting the allusion into self-flattery, but Dagonet then inverts the legend by caustically accusing him of harping down (LT, ll. 325–332). Far from raising men's aspirations, Tristram, in his emphasis on the realities of the flesh, indeed pipes men down. His scepticism towards spiritual values and his intellectual limitations bind him (ironically in view of his abhorrence of restrictions) to physical experience. He is incapable even of seducing Isolt intellectually, without force. When she acutely reminds him that she too might love while she may, and consequently reject him for Lancelot, his response is to touch "the warm white apple of her throat"—initially, he was fondling her hands (LT, ll. 596, 621)—and resort to a physical threat (LT, l. 712). Earlier, he endeavors to convince Dagonet of the merit of his artifice (his song had been made in the woods and rung "true as tested gold"—LT, l. 284), but the fool quickly relates his parable of the wine ("the cup was gold, the draught was mud"—LT, l. 298), which is a brilliant analogue for the essence of Tristram's deception, his emphasis on physical surfaces. (E. Warwick Slinn, "Deception and Artifice . . . " [1973], 13–14.)

■ In an ironic world, those who can see seem blind, however, so that Dagonet's wisdom becomes idiocy. He speaks the *word*, but the coherence of language and universe is gone and Dagonet's words emerge as riddles that no one understands. (James R. Kincaid, *Tennyson's Major Poems* [1975], 204.)

■ Tristram is, as he claims himself, a figure of untransformed nature, willing to accept the world, he supposes, just as it is. He completes the collapse of the balance Arthur had once maintained so well. His dream, which, like all dreams in the *Idylls*, is a vision of the dreamer's true self, reveals clearly that destructive imbalance. . . . The climactic scene between Tristram and Isolt demonstrates the impossibility now of permanent values of contracts. (Kincaid [1975], 205.)

■ By the end of *The Last Tournament* the kingdom and the individual alike have gone through the inevitable disintegration to which all nations and all individuals are subject. As the flesh is liable to dissolution, so is the life of the nation. The nation itself must pass, but new nations will be born which will have the potential at least to further the spiritual advance of universal history as Arthur's kingdom has done. Arthur's kingdom cannot be reformed. It has passed inevitably over into a new barbarity, but the individual can be redeemed through repentance. It is here that the nation and the individual part, as the nation has completed its cycle on the lower plane of the natural world where all is cyclical. But though the cycle of the individual is similar on the lower plane, that is, from birth to death, the individual can transcend the cycle through spiritual rebirth. (Robert Pattison, *Tennyson and Tradition* [1979], 131.)

■ The Arthurian wave passes. At the end, Tristram sings of "A star in heaven, a star within the mere!" (LT 726). It is a reflected, cold, and distant fire within a mere flat, like the "dead lake" of *In Memoriam* (16) "That holds the shadow of a lark." On the banks of this "level lake" (PA 359) is the jetsam, like Dagonet, a "mock-knight," a "water-sodden log" (LT 2, 253). Vivien was part of a seemingly inexorable pattern: the "little rat that borest in the dyke/Thy hole by night to let the boundless deep/Down upon far-off cities while they dance." And all "heard and let her be" (MV 110–12, 144), freely let be the hole that, with vigilant inspection, could have been plugged. But a wind is rising, "the winds that move the mere" (LT 732). New waves are gathering upon the deep: "The heathen," that "ever-climbing wave,/Hurled back again so often in empty foam" (LT 92–93) by Arthur. Unchecked, however, the new wave innundates Camelot. The growing savagery of the knights as they attack the unknown Lancelot in the Elaine idyll is given

> as a wild wave in the wide North-sea,
> Green-glimmering toward the summit, bears, with all
> Its stormy crests that smoke against the skies,
> Down on a bark, and overbears the bark,
> And him that helms it.
>
> (LE 480–84)

Tristram represents this new wave of barbarism, and a vigorous wave it is by the strength of the imagery. He repeats Vivien's song: "Free love—free field. . . . New leaf, new life—the days of frost are o'er;/New life, new love . . ." Tristram arrives to hear the tournament crowd, the "voice that billowed round the barriers roar/An ocean-sounding welcome" (LT 275–79, 167–68) to him—and to Camelot. And new fire comes as well, first the "long glories of the winter moon" (a mere reflection of fire) and then, weak and pale, but real, the "new sun rose bringing the new year" (PA 360, 469). (Henry Kozicki, *Tennyson and Clio* [1979], 148–149.)

■ [T]here are two quests in *The Last Tournament,* and the abrupt transitions suggest the confusion of values that characterizes the autumn of the Round Table. Moreover, the quests are framed by the account of Dagonet the fool, and in him we see the mingling of memory and desire that is the basis of the idyll's irony. (Donald S. Hair, *Domestic and Heroic* . . . [1981], 181.)

■ Dagonet . . . identifies folly with doubts about Arthur's kingship, and wisdom (which he ironically calls folly) with insight into the ideals Arthur serves. (Hair [1981], 210.)

■ On the whole Tristram manifests a disinterested and unconditioned vitalism that should not be called immoral or cynical because . . . it does not define itself in opposition to the moral or idealistic. To realize this fully, the reader must learn to distinguish between some of the things Tristram says to Dagonet and Isolt, and what he actually believes. There is no question of insincerity or dissimulation; it is simply a matter of arguing with others in terms which they can understand. . . . That Tristram speaks as he does only because of his interlocutors should not keep us from realizing the shrewdness of his analysis. But we must also realize that he speaks only to convince others: he does not need to convince himself, nor to rationalize his breaking of Arthur's vows. His very physical being negates the ideals of chastity, courtesy, and "sublime repression." (Kerry McSweeney, *Tennyson and Swinburne* . . . [1981], 110–111.)

Guinevere

■ Guinevere's pride hardened her heart against her rightful Lord. She did not believe in him, nor in her proper office. Her concerns were for herself. But when her pleasures are threatened and she admits the necessity to remove herself from the source of her temptation, a temptation that is already tainted more by selfishness than satiation, the struggle for redemption has begun. Guinevere flees to the convent to protect herself; she remains to aid others. She comes to the convent in transports of selfish fear and suspicion; she remains humbly to serve others. The symbolic moment of redemption is the moment when she humbles herself before her proper Lord and throws herself at Arthur's feet. It is her acknowledgment of her sin and her liberation from the concerns of self. Nowhere else in the *Idylls* is the symbolic movement from pride to humility more clearly presented. The tableau having started into action, Guinevere swings toward all that Enid represents, and the slanders of Vivien are reduced to the innocent queries of the little novice in the convent. The still small voice at Guinevere's ear is gradually transformed to one that says "Rejoice! Rejoice!" and hope sanctifies her world once more. (John R. Reed, *Perception and Design* . . . [1971], 76–77.)

■ The kingdom, of course, is irredeemably lost by the time of *Guinevere,* but individual redemption, as I have said, is still possible. Lancelot's redemption does not occur in *Guinevere,* but we are told of it at the end of *Lancelot and Elaine,* where Lancelot in "remorseful pain" is unaware that "he should die a holy man." Guinevere's redemption is similar: she goes through recognition and repentance to salvation. She sees that it was her duty, as it would have been her pleasure and profit, to have loved the highest, yet her pride caused her to look not up but down (635–56). She has come to recognize that Arthur is "the highest and most human too" (644), as he is most spiritual. Though the flesh is necessary, Lancelot and Guinevere have chosen it exclusively and rejected spirit, and that is the sin for which they must repent. Guinevere's salvation comes through her recognition of the primacy of the spirit, her sincere repentance, and her development of the capacity for spiritual love. She therefore finally passes "To where beyond these voices there is peace" (692). (Ward Hellstrom, *On the Poems of Tennyson* [1972], 132–133.)

■ This inner action of regeneration and repentance is the highest form of quest, and the success of that quest here tempers our sense of the tragedy which is playing itself out. (Donald S. Hair, *Domestic and Heroic . . .* [1981], 218.)

■ *Guinevere,* the strongest poem in its group, is full of fine things. (Kerry McSweeney, *Tennyson and Swinburne . . .* [1981], 100.)

The Passing of Arthur

■ The hope for heaven is made both uncertain and generally unreal. What matters is that Arthur has been unable to create heaven on earth. All spiritual values are now so alien and so little a part of man that heaven is more distant than ever. God has retreated altogether from the world, leaving only the mists and confusion that control the final poem in the *Idylls.* (James R. Kincaid, *Tennyson's Major Poems* [1975], 209.)

■ The central ironic narrative, the story of the casting away of Excalibur, is a parable of ignorance and disloyalty and also a deliberate absurdist reduction of tragic grandeur. Instead of a dignified passing, a sustained mood of heroic elegy, we have something like a parody of the *Beowulf* tone. Arthur is reduced to the near ludicrous position of a man unable to get himself buried, haggling with an underling while an audience (i.e. the reader), expecting tragedy, looks on with embarrassment. (Kincaid [1975], 211.)

■ With Arthur's passing, heaven removes itself entirely from the world, and lonely Bedivere is left without comfort. He can only tell his tale to the uncomprehending. This knight who never understood is the only one left to try to re-create Arthur's world out of silence. The *Idylls* trails off dismally, leaving behind the absurd image of Bedivere, telling of magical deeds, disappearing swords, and waving hands to those "new men, strange faces, other minds," who yawn and nudge each other. There are no new beginnings, only the mockery of renewal by a cruel and deceptive nature: "And the new sun rose bringing the new year." (Kincaid [1975], 213.)

■ The breadth and generosity of Tennyson's mind are nowhere more apparent than in his last idyll, "The Passing of Arthur" (1869). Arthur's heroic plainness, as he stoically scrutinizes his own bareness, suppresses none of the attitudes evident in the other idylls: neither the sublimity of "The Holy Grail" nor the disillusion and ruin of "The Last Tournament," neither the elegiac dignity of "Lancelot and Elaine" nor the revulsion and indignity of "Pelleas and Ettarre." Not yet resigned to failure yet charting the pathos of his decline, Arthur is made vividly aware of the fearful toll that heroism exacts. A victim of isolation, of utter personal, moral, and historical aloneness, Arthur withdraws in horror from the unimaginable ruin, the wreckage of his hopes. In a poetry of bleak grandeur, which anticipates the elegies of Tennyson's old age, Arthur records the barrenness of nature, seen now without human power to change. In barely enunciated phrases—"O me!"; "And hollow, hollow, hollow" (l. 37)—

Arthur's dream expresses the nameless weight of depression, a desiccation worse than the ruin that has overtaken Camelot itself. The perfection of "moonlit haze among the hills," like the "lonely city sacked by night" (ll. 42–43), is undone by the misery of the wandering wind, by the whirlings of the birds that "wail their way/From cloud to cloud" (ll. 39–40). These are the whimpers of the king's own voice, the ultimate chill, stupor, and then the letting-go. (W. David Shaw, *Tennyson's Style* [1976], 214.)

■ In a poem that puzzles over nature and fortune, on the small scale of daily living and on the large scale of civilizations and history, it is an unexpected affirmation to have the simple rising of the sun reveal the advent of a new order. There is no idealizing in the coda. Tennyson immediately qualifies the certitude of "saw" by the provisional "Or thought he saw" (ll. 463, 465); and even the sun that "rose bringing the new year" (l. 469) is the neutral sun of the Sermon on the Mount, which God "maketh . . . to arise on the evil and on the good" alike (Matthew 5:45). The cautious advance and retreat are gravely barren. They must be distinguished from the earlier hovering elusiveness, from the piling up of appositions and qualifiers in "The Lotos-Eaters" and "Tithonus" to evoke the mind's pathetic fallacies. The motions backward to the real and the observed from the temptations of the visionary now give an impression of tremendous honesty. The insistent couplings of "clomb" and "climb," "saw" and "saw," the passing "on and on," then going from "less to less" before dissolving, show Bedivere looking harder and harder at the object. Yet the indefinite protraction of three present participles—"Straining," "opening," "bringing" (ll. 464, 466, 469)—as Bedivere stares endlessly into space, seem to suspend the action forever between real and visionary worlds. Arthur's humiliation and defeat, like their medium, the mist and the night, may be dispelled by sunrise. But Tennyson's formula does not dispel, as the mythological dawn of "The Vision of Sin" would have dispelled, Arthur's reason for feeling humiliation and dismay. In his dedication "To the Queen" the narrator makes clear that men must learn to live, like Arthur—or like Bedivere on his Pisgah peak—in a time that is neither the eternal now of their visionary moments nor the miserable, infernal time of the last tournament. It is a double time which, amid misery, contains the promise of happiness and which makes beauty rise out of ugliness—a penultimate moment which both fails to realize "the goal of this great world" ("To the Queen," l. 59) and tends toward it. (Shaw [1976], 217–218.)

■ In *The Coming of Arthur,* there are many characters who respond to the king in a variety of ways. In *The Passing of Arthur* there is only one, Bedivere, and the idyll is, among other things, the account of his education. (Donald S. Hair, *Domestic and Heroic . . .* [1981], 132.)

■ [*Arthur's final speech*] is the central piece of this idyll, and everything leads to it. For Bedivere, it represents instruction in the mysteries that he has confronted but not penetrated; for Arthur, it represents the culmination of his development from a defeated man to a hero wise in the ways in which ideals manifest themselves. . . . Arthur began the idyll by asserting that "in His ways with men I find Him not" (11). He ends by asserting just the opposite. (Hair [1981], 222–223.)

■ [A]t the end of *The Passing of Arthur* the possibility of a recovery of vision and light is neither asserted nor gainsaid; it remains a possibility. But while Tennyson is careful to allow for the possibility, he has nothing to say or show concerning the instrumentality through which the possible vision may be regained. Can it be recovered only apocalyptically, through external agency, as the extraordinary events said to surround Arthur's coming in the first idyll suggest . . .? Or can the vision be recovered in memory through the cyclic (non-apocalyptic) processes of the natural world . . . as the last line of *The Passing of Arthur* allows one to think? Tennyson is characteristically non-specific concerning such questions, for the very good reason that he is not sure. (Kerry McSweeney, *Tennyson and Swinburne . . .* [1981], 118–119).

List of Works Cited

Adler, Thomas P. "The Uses of Knowledge in Tennyson's *Merlin and Vivien. Texas Studies in Literature and Language,* 11 (1970), 1397–1403.

Bloom, Harold. "Tennyson: In the Shadow of Keats," in *Poetry and Repression.* New Haven: Yale University Press, 1976.

Brashear, William R. *The Living Will: A Study of Tennyson and Nineteenth-Century Subjectivism.* The Hague: Mouton, 1969.

——. "Tennyson's Tragic Vitalism: *Idylls of the King.*" *Victorian Poetry,* 6 (1968), 29–49.

Buckley, Jerome H. *Tennyson: The Growth of a Poet.* Cambridge, Mass.: Harvard University Press, 1960.

Burchell, Samuel C. "Tennyson's 'Allegory in the Distance.'" *PMLA,* 68 (1953), 418–424.

Culler, A. Dwight. *The Poetry of Tennyson.* New Haven: Yale University Press, 1977.

Eggers, J. Philip. *King Arthur's Laureate: A Study of Tennyson's "Idylls of the King."* New York: New York University Press, 1971.

——. "The Weeding of the Garden: Tennyson's Geraint Idylls and the *Mabinogion. Victorian Poetry,* 4 (1966), 45–51.

Engelberg, Edward. "The Beast Image in Tennyson's *Idylls of the King.*" *English Literary History,* 22 (1955), 287–292.

Gray, James Martin. *Thro' the Vision of the Night: A Study of Source, Evolution and Structure in Tennyson's "Idylls of the King."* Edinburgh: Edinburgh University Press, 1980.

Hair, Donald S. *Domestic and Heroic in Tennyson's Poetry.* Toronto: University of Toronto Press, 1981.

Hellstrom, Ward. *On the Poems of Tennyson.* Gainesville: University of Florida Press, 1972.

Henderson, Philip. *Tennyson: Poet and Prophet.* London: Routledge and Kegan Paul, 1978.

Joseph, Gerhard. "The Idea of Mortality in Tennyson's Classical and Arthurian Poems: 'Honor Comes with Mystery.'" *Modern Philology,* 66 (1968), 136–145.

——. *Tennysonian Love: The Strange Diagonal.* Minneapolis: University of Minnesota Press, 1969.

Kincaid, James R. "Tennyson's 'Gareth and Lynette.'" *Texas Studies in Literature and Language,* 13 (1972), 663–671.

———. *Tennyson's Major Poems: The Comic and Ironic Patterns.* New Haven: Yale University Press, 1975.

Kissane, James D. *Alfred Tennyson.* New York: Twayne Publishers, 1970.

Kozicki, Henry. *Tennyson and Clio: History in the Major Poems.* Baltimore: Johns Hopkins University Press, 1979.

———. "Tennyson's *Idylls of the King* as Tragic Drama." *Victorian Poetry,* 4 (1966), 15–20.

Landow, George P. "Closing the Frame: Having Faith and Keeping Faith in Tennyson's 'The Passsing of Arthur.'" *Bulletin of the John Rylands Library,* 56 (1974), 423–442.

Litzinger, Boyd. "The Structure of Tennyson's 'The Last Tournament.'" *Victorian Poetry,* 1 (1963), 53–60.

McSweeney, Kerry. *Tennyson and Swinburne as Romantic Naturalists.* Toronto: University of Toronto Press, 1981.

———. "Tennyson's Quarrel with Himself: The Tristram Group of Idylls." *Victorian Poetry,* 15 (1977), 49–59.

Pattison, Robert. *Tennyson and Tradition.* Cambridge, Mass.: Harvard University Press, 1979.

Pitt, Valerie. *Tennyson Laureate.* London: Barrie and Rockliff, 1962.

Poston, Lawrence, III. "The Argument of the Geraint-Enid Books in *Idylls of the King.*" *Victorian Poetry,* 2 (1964), 269–275.

———. "'Pelleas and Ettarre': Tennyson's 'Troilus.'" *Victorian Poetry,* 4 (1966), 199–204.

———. "The Two Provinces of Tennyson's 'Idylls.'" *Criticism,* 9 (1967), 372–382.

Priestley, F. E. L. *Language and Structure in Tennyson's Poetry.* London: Andre Deutsch, 1973.

Redpath, Theodore. "Tennyson and the Literature of Greece and Rome," in *Studies in Tennyson,* ed. Hallam Tennyson. London: Macmillan, 1981.

Reed, John R. *Perception and Design in Tennyson's "Idylls of the King."* Athens: Ohio University Press, 1971.

Ricks, Christopher. *Tennyson.* London: Macmillan, 1972.

Rosenberg, John D. *The Fall of Camelot: A Study of Tennyson's "Idylls of the King."* Cambridge, Mass.: Harvard University Press, 1973.

———. "Tennyson and the Landscape of Consciousness." *Victorian Poetry,* 12 (1974), 303–310.

Ryals, Clyde de L. *From the Great Deep: Essays on "Idylls of the King."* Athens: Ohio University Press, 1967.

———. "*Idylls of the King:* Tennyson's New Realism." *Victorian Newsletter*, 31 (1967), 5–7.

———. "The Moral Paradox of the Hero in *Idylls of the King.*" *English Literary History*, 30 (1963), 53–69.

Shaw, W. David. "The Idealist Dilemma in *Idylls of the King.*" *Victorian Poetry*, 5 (1967), 41–53.

———. "Idylls of the King: A Dialectical Reading." *Victorian Poetry*, 7 (1969), 175–190.

———. *Tennyson's Style.* Ithaca: Cornell University Press, 1976.

Slinn, E. Warwick. "Deception and Artifice in *Idylls of the King.*" *Victorian Poetry*, 11 (1973), 1–14.

Smalley, Donald. "A New Look at Tennyson—Especially the *Idylls.*" *Journal of English and Germanic Philology*, 61 (1962), 349–357.

Solomine, Joseph, Jr. "*Idylls of the King:* The Rise, Decline, and Fall of the State." *The Personalist*, 50 (1969), 105–116.

Solomon, Stanley J. "Tennyson's Paradoxical King." *Victorian Poetry* 1 (1963), 258–271.

Staines, David. "Tennyson's 'The Holy Grail': The Tragedy of Percivale." *Modern Language Review*, 69 (1974), 745–756.

Stevenson, Catherine Barnes. "Druids, Bards, and Tennyson's Merlin." *Victorian Newsletter*, 57 (1980), 14–23.

Sundell, Michael G. "Spiritual Confusion and Artistic Form in Victorian Poetry." *Victorian Newsletter*, 39 (1971), 4–7.

Tennyson, Hallam, ed., *Studies in Tennyson.* London: Macmillan, 1981.

Turner, Paul. *Tennyson.* London: Routledge and Kegan Paul, 1976.

Wilkenfeld, R. B. "Tennyson's Camelot: The Kingdom of Folly." *University of Toronto Quarterly*, 37 (1968), 281–294.

Part Four

Idylls of the King:
Five Essays in Redirection

Essay 1

Dimensions of Narrative:
A Reprise

Meaning is inseparable from manner in *Idylls of the King*. Manner and meaning reciprocate each other so fully that, true to the symbolist tradition to which it in part belongs, the poem rejects discursive thematic implants as simply alien to its nature and insists, through the direct, internal evidence of its unique spiritual constitution, that thought in the ideological sense—moral philosophy, for example—is an inadequate measure of both its poetic character and its poetic purpose. It is the imaginative result of an effort by one of the world's most gifted poet-painters and poet-musicians to wed the symbolist tendency of modern poetry with the epic tendency of ancient poetry, to give the intensely personal, lyric impulse a poetic presence as large as life itself, an epic presence. Tennyson suggests thereby that heroism, action on the grandest human scale, is ultimately centered in the private sanctuarial self, that true epic grandeur has epiphanic roots.

The passage between the symbolist epiphany and the epic was, of course, a narrative passage, and the three dimensions of narrative to which Tennyson gave crucial and all-enveloping attention were, in a phrase from *Balin and Balan,* "the tale,/The told-of, and the teller" (534–535).

301

"The tale"

Like *The Princess, Idylls of the King* moves along "a strange [literary] diagonal." *The Coming of Arthur* and *The Passing of Arthur* are the frame, and they are the most classically epic of the idylls. The canonical voice is most pronounced there; everything coheres around Arthur's role as (spiritually) eponymous hero (the once and future king); the manner is direct and the movement rapid; the traditional subjects of the epic—the epic battle, the epic journey, and the epic foundation—are, though transformed by the imaginative intuition of a new poet, still clearly visible. The classical epic is thus established as the formal literary analogue against which the other narratives, those grouped under *The Round Table*, are to be measured. None of them reaches the epic stature of the frame-idylls, but all are played against it, and, taken together, they constitute a bold integration of the chief structures through which poets in the narrative tradition initiated by Homer have attempted to give imaginative presence to man's struggle with himself, *Idylls of the King* being, for its moment, the omega to Homer's alpha and the result of all the rest.

Gareth and Lynette is the most wholly comedic of the idylls, the beginning of a literary process of which the austerely tragic *Guinevere* is the climax. The human *rite de passage* begins with Gareth, and, faithful to its Arthurian "matter," it is a romantic epic in the guise of a courtly romance. While it retains throughout its comedic tone, it is clear that every aspect of its imaginative world implies its opposite and that a significant change here and there could topple the tale into a different literary species. *The Marriage of Geraint* is a mock-heroic, seriocomic burlesque and parody of the romantic epic; it is a species of the comic grotesque in which Geraint as an Eros/Cupid figure totally misperceives himself and is subjected to a riot of language, gesture, false pretense, and subtly debunked fairy tale. *Geraint and Enid* is an inverted epic, an odyssey in the wilderness of bluntness and stupidity and suffocating literalness, an epic whose resonances are shrunken to the tawdry harrowings of domestic parable. It begins with the text of a medieval *exemplum,* and Cinderella-

Griselda-Psyche is subjected to a trial of faith and endurance that is so humorless that the poet's carefully calculated use of melodrama provides the only wry comic relief, and we are barely prevented from calling down our wrath upon the brutally chauvinistic Geraint by our recognition that he suffers from such animal-like imaginative deprivation that he is morally incompetent and without Enid's protection would simply not survive. *Balin and Balan* is a tale of epic horror, a gothic tale that carries the Geraint-theme of "man against himself" to its tragic-grotesque extremes. It uses the *Doppelgänger* formula to suggest the dark possibilities that are dormant in us all (the tragic dilemma of Lancelot and Guinevere pushed to its grotesque extremes) and that, without some such order as Arthurianism, can invoke terrible awakenings that lead out beyond the civilized human imagination. *Merlin and Vivien*, to which *Balin and Balan* was conceived as an introduction, carries the tragic grotesque into a different stream of story, perhaps into a different ontology. It is a Breton lay; but though it employs the January-May fabliau and the debate formula of medieval literature, it moves away from both Greek classicism and Roman Christianity and employs a legend that flows deep into other channels of story and perception, through dark medieval Europe to a time so prehistoric "'that mountains have arisen since/With cities on their flanks'" (673–674), an Ur-world of witches and warlocks and wizards, called superstitious in our rational, empirical codes, but nonetheless the persistent source of strange surfacings in our consciousness and terrifying nightmares in our dreams. *Lancelot and Elaine* is the longest of the idylls and the most complexly and exquisitely wrought. Its subject is the journey into the sanctuarial self—the dark passage through anonymity into personal authenticity—and its narrative form is that of the romantic verse-novel. It juxtaposes Romantic pathos, ingratiating but morally enervating, and classical tragedy, austere and morally restorative, and brings Lancelot, not to tragic redemption, but to the recognition that, unless he can "break/These bonds that so defame" him, his best hope is that he may be as though he had never been. *The Holy Grail* is a quest-poem in which the spiritual imagination is grossly sentimentalized as a search for the magic wand and the flight from self is revealed, paradoxically, as the chief infidelity to Arthurianism. In the contrast between Percivale's and Lancelot's quests, the epic itself moves in opposite directions—toward impotent ritual, on the one hand, and total existential relevance, on the other: the enticingly deceptive, fail-safe, enclosed allegorical mentality of the Middle Ages yields to the vigorous, agonizing, open-ended and heroic renewal of Homer. *Pelleas and Ettarre* is, like *Gareth and Lynette,* a courtly romance, but it is neither courtly nor romantic. As *Gareth and Lynette* is a comedy containing the seeds of tragedy, *Pelleas and Ettarre* is a tragedy that blows apart. The first 509 lines contain a superbly structured, fully authentic classical tragedy; but then Percivale enters the scene, and a tragic vision becomes a cosmic nightmare. Pelleas, half man, half goat and battering ram, races through the world making chaos of everything in his path in a fury over falseness. *The Last Tournament* is a revenge tragedy in which the rebel against community releases the community's wrath and all order and justice are lost in "'flat confusion and brute violences.'" *Guinevere* is the climactic point toward which our "strange [literary] diagonal" has been leading. It is a classical tragic formulation and, momentarily, a literary recomposition and redemption of the world of *Idylls of the King.*

"The told-of"

A ritual of personal mythmaking constitutes an infrastructure of the narrative histories of the principal characters in *Idylls of the King* and serves as an instrument for measuring them, the quality of their identity myths being our chief index to the quality of their moral insight and hence of their distinctive humanness. The paradigm is established with Leodogran at the beginning of *The Coming of Arthur,* and variations on the paradigm weave a poetic pattern throughout the poem and lift its action into the imaginative significance that distinguishes human capacity from animal passion.

Arthur is the example of human wholeness in *Idylls of the King*—"'the highest and most human too'"—and the identity myths of the other characters reflect various degrees of infidelity to the reality of their existence. Gareth is faulted but survives his identity lie because of a favorable ambience and the vigor of his sense of self; Geraint is a literalist with little notion of who he is—a matinée Lothario whose gifts hardly exceed the grosser requirements of the bordello; Pelleas creates a handbook self in the manner of Don Quixote, a dogmatic self that yields to catastrophe with horrifying after-shocks; Tristram, like man in Pope's *Essay*, is "In doubt to deem himself a god, or beast," and the false dilemma that this creates accounts for the narrative course so-called civilized man's "last tournament" follows—a broken, bizarre, simulated debate that ends inevitably in "'flat confusion and brute violences.'" This creation of false self myths—this betrayal of the reality of personal existence—is the *plot*, or internal apprehension, that underlies the *story*, or external narrative mechanism, of each of the characters in *Idylls of the King;* it is the "one sin" that jeopardizes their lives and, taken together, undoes Arthurianism.

As we learn from Lancelot's recognition speech at the end of *Lancelot and Elaine*, he was, from earliest childhood, a lonely motherless boy who filled the vacuousness of his life with dreams of personal grandeur, saying to himself in his homeless walks along the "dusky mere" some equivalent to "'Thou art fair, my child,/As a king's son.'" Thus as Elaine became fixated on Love, Lancelot became fixated on Greatness. He was not trivial like Gawain, or evil like Modred, or gross like Mark. Indeed, his ambition for greatness brought him, by the most gracious accident, into the service of Arthur and magnified it a hundredfold, giving it a ritual of supreme purpose that blended easily with its benign high-mindedness. Still, it was rooted in pride, in personal ambition, in ego-fantasy, and an aspect of it, though he was not in fact a "king's son," was to fill the role of a "king's son." When he was sent as a king's emissary to bring home a king's daughter to be a king's queen, she looked favorably upon him, and he was able to fulfill, at a close but discrete distance, his fantasy of being a "king's son" with his own queen—a king-*manqué* with a queen-*manqué*. Despite this fantastic violation of fealty to the true King, Lancelot has been the victim of his own myth, of a self-created but seemingly indispensable reality, and though the war between truth and fantasy has been a drawn battle, he has not yet been able to let the fantasy go and settle for the greater grandeur of the true truth.

Guinevere, like the other characters in *Idylls of the King*, is not only an individual, but a generic metaphor of all those who are trapped in an imperious self-myth, a hardened fabricated identity, which is deep-rooted in their nature and which has been reinforced almost beyond the possibility of recognition by a relatively successful life-style that has implicitly prohibited even the slightest dismantling of the fabricated self. She has historically surrounded herself with elaborate and subtle rituals of reinforcement. She has become Queen at a middle distance. Although Arthur enabled her myth, he threatened it too. She wanted the perquisites of queenship without its ultimate responsibilities. So she has shaped her world, not to the imperative of her potential self, but to the indulgence of her mythic self. For that, the court, where she was ceremoniously told what she wanted to hear, was the perfect setting, and Lancelot, brave, mighty, adulated, and comparably self-deluded, was the perfect companion.

"The teller"

Idylls of the King is interspersed with variations on the phrase "as he who told the tale," and this suggests that Tennyson was drawing a distinction between *authority* and *authoriality*, a distinction analogous to that between *plot* and *story* and between narrative as *literary structure* and narrative as simple *fable*. He had good reason to forego authority since the "matter of Arthur" was the subject of a vast literature, and his role was, like Homer's role in the "matter of Troy," that of artist, not inventor. Stories (legends, histories) came into being and maintained themselves because of their inherent truth, and the responsibility of the modern poet, like that of his classical predecessor, was to rediscover that truth and give it shape and accent, an architecture and a voice.

But, as modern critics have discovered and poets have always known, authoriality is itself a complex creative issue for one concerned to give shape and accent to truth in a way that will have both ancient carriage and modern relevance, and Tennyson knew the traps. Under the supreme tutelage of Homer, he was especially alert to the traps of moral dogmatism and rhetorical extravagance, of imprisoning truth in an unrelenting idea-structure and of obscuring truth in an eccentric style, and he avoided both by the ways in which he treated "the teller."

The Holy Grail is one way, and though it is formalistically unique in the poem, the technique of the teller in *The Holy Grail* has pervasive relevance. After a brief canonical introduction, the tale takes the form of a monologue with occasional interruptions. The interruptions are significant, certainly: Ambrosius is a much more Arthurian figure than Percivale is, and his affectionate earthiness both critiques the teller and forces him to deal with flesh-and-blood truths that he would like to ignore. But it is decidedly Percivale's tale, and the Grail-quest is thus suspended in a keen element of ironic distastefulness centered in Percivale himself. He is the most ambiguous of the poem's chief characters, and the more attuned one becomes to that ambiguity, the more spiritually and psychologically blighting it appears to be. Androgynous, incestuous, homoerotic, voyeuristic, all at a subliminal, almost subtextual level, Percivale pollutes everything he touches, like a plague-bearing wind or a poisoned well. He does not perform a single unequivocal act in his whole life-odyssey, *and he does not know it*. He is telling his tale long after the events, and yet he still has no notion of what they meant or mean. He still looks upon women as generically pernicious, still sees men and women as mere "phantoms," is still fixated on the Grail episode despite the devastation it has wrought and despite Arthur's heart-rending lamentation, "'Woe is me, my knights'" (275). He still lacks "'true humility,'" still deals in innuendo, is still an engine of destruction. We are more profoundly affected by reading his tale than he has been by living it or telling it, and this reveals a deep undercurrent reality, austere and penetratingly sad. Percivale does not know that he does not know that he exists. He is desperately trying to fill an identity vacuum with role-playing. Lacking the imaginative-spiritual resources to voyage deep into the sanctuarial self, there to discover an authentic identity, he fabricates an appearance of one and becomes in the process a mere shadow of a man—a grotesquely shrunken self in a universe that is itself a disillusion.

The monologue, Tennyson decided, was the most appropriate way to reveal the perilous deceptiveness of magical guarantees and the awful toll they take in human emasculation, and just as there is some degree of Percivale in us all, an oblique implicit form of the monologue, explicitly used in *The Holy Grail*, has relevance to all the other tellers in *Idylls of the King*, though no other teller, including Bedivere in *The Passing of Arthur*, surfaces in the same formalistic way.

The external narrative difference between *The Holy Grail* and the other idylls is that beween direct and indirect discourse—namely, voice—and the poet's most immediately visible contribution to the stories is that of a canonical voice. *The Passing of Arthur*, we are told, is Bedivere's story, but the idyll as a whole, like *The Holy Grail* in less intrusive fashion, is suspended in voice—not a personal voice, like that of Books I and XII of *The Ring and the Book*, for example, but the voice of a timeless literary tradition, its identifying individual qualities being modified by faint but unmistakable echoes of Homer, Virgil, the Biblical writers, and Milton. It is sober, mellow, and self-effacing, the generic voice of imaginative conscientiousness. Its "faint" but deliberate "Homeric echoes" distinguish its accents from those of Geoffrey of Monmouth, Malory, and the *Mabinogion*, upon which it freely and frankly draws, and it absorbs into its unifying vocal texture the voices of the individual Arthurian protagonists while enabling them to retain, within a necessarily narrow gauge, some personality of style.

Thus, *The Holy Grail* and *The Passing of Arthur*, taken together, define "the teller" of *Idylls of the King*. Each story is conceived as having an individual narrative consciousness;

each narrative consciousness is granted the authority of an eyewitness or synoptic, but his story is profoundly affected by his own sense of self, by the "hidden germ of failure" that works at the center of his being. The poem's multiple consciousnesses are subsumed to a canonical voice that gives them a delicate, nonimperious unity and connects them, with a like delicacy, to man's efforts, through three thousand years, to tell his story.

Essay 2

A Precarious Turning:
From Medievalism to Homer

So little has been said of so much that needs to be said about *Idylls of the King* that the critic is constantly forced back upon the elaboration of essentially elementary concepts and perceptions by the realization that even matters which seem luminously self-evident cannot be assumed to have currency even among Tennysonians. This situation is partly the result, of course, of the masterful imaginative evasiveness into which Tennyson cast the poem—that riddle of the painful earth which defies comprehensive knowledge and yields coherence only to imaginative faith; about which bards themselves can only riddle; and for which the terminus of a study (death) only signals the beginning of a new study (birth). A poet who would dare create an "image of the mighty world" would recognize above all others that no order of thought about it could ever become frozen and conclusive and that the renewal implicit in the prospective myth of Arthur is our only real hope. Like Guinevere's, ours is a fallen condition, and even after much failure and much privileged experience, the best we can hope for is to recognize that "'the highest'" is the "'most human too.'" But the grand imagination of the master poet must not be allowed to cover over the failures of the critic. Even the best critics have failed to recognize the true poetic stature of Tennyson—that he is like Milton, Dante, Virgil, and Homer and must be dealt with as Milton, Dante, Virgil, and Homer have been dealt with. They have labored within a suspicion of rather than a clarified recognition of Tennyson's greatness and have been not only cautious (which is a critical virtue) but timid (which is not). As Churton Collins pointed out almost a century ago, genuine recognition of Tennyson requires that his writings (like those of Milton, Dante, Virgil, and Homer) be "submitted to the ordeal of the minutest critical investigation."[1]

It has long been recognized that, though *Idylls of the King* sends out strong epic signals, it cannot be adequately or appropriately measured by the epic pattern found in Homer. Though epic in scale, it works internally in a way different from the way the *Iliad* and the *Odyssey* work. This difference has been generally identified as the result of a fusion of the cyclic epic of Homer with the little epic or epyllion of Theocritus, a fusion first effected by Virgil and renewed, each in his own fashioning, by Dante, Milton, Tennyson, Pound, Eliot, and others.[2] The cyclic or solar epic, so conspicuous in Tennyson's *Idylls*, is still there, but it has been made to work through the self-contained, relatively short narrative poems called *epyllia*. These epyllia had in turn fused with the Alexandrian *idyllia*—highly wrought "little pictures," "each holding its tiny convex mirror up to nature"[3]—and this enables us to describe how, at the internal level of the individual "little epics," Tennyson's poem works.

This is helpful and moves literary matters a good way forward, but it ends ultimately in ignoring the most imaginative turning that Tennyson gave his central literary inheritance. That final turning, which is a largely unrecognized characteristic of Tennyson and which makes his imaginative credentials so worthy of acclaim, is the return at the very deepest level of this post-Theocritan, post-Virgilian literary development to primary coherence with Homer. He makes full use of the religious ritual and magic to which the little epic was "a deliberate return,"[4] but he makes it coordinate with the "rational and limited social function" of Homer. The magical deep-rootedness which we witness in Elaine, who is the fairy temptress of Lancelot, is in fact resisted by Arthur's greatest knight, and it helps him define and finally heal his torn humanness and rise to a moral conquest that is essentially rational and social. Tristram's dilemma, superficial compared to Lancelot's *as an authentic dilemma*, reflects the autumnal afterglow of Arthurianism in which a victim of magic attempts to give rational justification to his irredeemable state while he plays it out to its horrifying "magical" conclusion. And though Merlin the magician succumbs as inevitably to Vivien as, in its fabliau analogue, January succumbs to the blandishments of May, Guinevere (May) rises in bleak December to a severe rational and social enlightenment that sets aside the magic of her fantasy life and accepts a grand but chastened humanness worthy of Homeric humanity.

Thus, although at its epyllion level *Idylls of the King* seems to be "the tale of the tribe" as distinct from the narrative of individual spiritual conquest exemplified by Homeric epic, at its quintessential level, it is the story of "a man"—of every man—and its ultimate image of human conscientiousness is that of Bedivere standing high and alone, under his "arch of hand" straining his eyes to see and, because he stares into the sunrise, not being sure that what he sees are not simply his own eye-specks. This is an image eminently Homeric, perennially Odyssean, and Tennyson's myth of the return at the subtlest literary level is played out as a return to Homer. So whatever rich use one may make of a post-Theocritan, post-Virgilian Tennyson—complex and *literarily psychological*—the final imaginative turning is back toward Homer.

Further, the individual idylls are not simply idyllian epyllia. As was pointed out in Part II and in the previous essay, the whole poem moves along a strange literary diagonal in which many of the chief structures of Western literature are implanted so that, even though the epyllion is in place, it is played against or counterpointed to an alternative literary structure that may in fact be primary. The argument, being new, bears repetition, and a quick, rather raw catalogue will perhaps illustrate this additional literary dimension of the poem most economically. *The Coming of Arthur* is a pro-legomenon, a frame-tale as to function and a romantic or chivalric epic as to formal literary character. *Gareth and Lynette* is a courtly romance, a *rite de passage,* in which all the obverse of the courtly and the romantic is suspended in comedic tone, though wholly seeded and in full expectation of reversal. *The Marriage of Geraint* is a parody or burlesque of the courtly romance in which the rituals have become mechanical and fantastical and misguided and tasteless and ominous. *Geraint and Enid* is a myth-poem, its analogue being a cruel Cupid and a long-suffering Psyche. It is an inverted epic, formalistically, an odyssey in the wilderness of bluntness and stupidity and suffocating literalness. Its epic resonances are shrunken to the genuine harrowings of domestic parable. *Balin and Balan* is a Doppelgänger tale of the sundered imagination, the Geraint-theme of "man against himself" moved into an ambience of violence and seemingly unavoidable collision. Tragedy is the emergent rubric, but the tragic grotesque is the aesthetic category, touching the terror of the gothic sublime. *Merlin and Vivien* is an Ur-tale, a naturalistic tale of fairy changelings, primitive in its origins, terrifying in its implications. Again tragedy is the rubric, but it is so ontologically displaced that our sense is one of prurient fascination rather than of authentically cathartic pity and fear. *Lancelot and Elaine* also has an Ur-tale quality, and this dyes one coordinate of its courtly love character. Another is its excruciating quality of pathos, by which our capacity to hold onto the stabilizing austerities of the tragic vision—that is, our ultimate faith in humanness—is strenuously tested. We, like Lancelot, are measured, and like Lancelot we survive at a perilous edge. Tragedy and pathos are so weighted and intertwined that we, too, must break the bonds that threaten to defame both literature and life. *The Holy Grail* is a quest poem having analogues in both the epic and the wholly collapsed courtliness of romance. It is a tale of terrifyingly alluring deception, the deception of the sentimentalized spiritual imagination; and we are saved from our temptations by the chillingly ironic narrative manner with which the tale is told. It is a fundamentally *literary* experience for which we have to be eminently grateful, chastened but purged at the subtlest and least comfortable level of our human miracle-mongering. *Pelleas and Ettarre* is a courtly romance wholly brutalized. There is a primitivism to it too, but a primitivism that reaches, not to the dark grots of the Ur-tale, but to the classical groves of Pan. It has a literary analogue in *Don Quixote,* but it mercilessly fractures Don Quixote's idealism and violently tramples the excruciating pathos of *Lancelot and Elaine* by reaching for a brief moment an authentic tragic poise and then blowing tragedy itself to smithereens. *The Last Tournament* is a horrible revenge tragedy on the Roman/Jacobean model, in which the brute violences of a world gone mad with rebellion against community makes pain near-irredeemable lord in the heart of man. *Guinevere* is a classically tragic formulation, a *literary* recomposition of the *literary* world of *Idylls of the King.* *The Passing of Arthur* is an end-tale, the omega of *The Coming's* alpha, an epic of monumental loss at the spongy edges of civilization, with (maybe) just a bare saving remnant of the faith, hope, and love that keeps us, without taking violent revenge on ourselves and our universe, on a precarious course toward our own island valley of Avilion.

And what does all this have to do with Tennysonian medievalism? A great deal, I think, and at a very crucial level, because nothing so conspicuous as the "age of Arthur" can be properly dealt with until one is willing to entertain the possibility at least that Tennyson is doing the wholly unexpected—that, for example, he is critiquing the very Virgilianism of which he has been thought to be an enervated latter-day continuator; that the melancholy that so misled Eliot and Auden is not the ultimate condition but the ultimate strategy of Tennyson's imagination; and that his view of poetry is being subtly but consciously counterpointed to that of the "Virgil of the Middle Ages," Dante. If this should prove to be so—and, once said, its plausibility seems to dilate startlingly—then it gives a wholly new character and coherence to that sudden rush of creativity which Tennyson underwent in the closing months of 1833 and to the fact that Tennyson took a lifetime, an "age," to work out the imaginative implications seeded there, and it finally enables us to make full sense of

Tennyson's assertion that there is more of autobiography in *Ulysses* than in all of *In Memoriam*.

The first thing that we need to notice is that Dante is an imaginative presence in all the important poems seeded here. He is the direct source of *Ulysses;* Tennyson called *In Memoriam* "a kind of *Divina Commedia*"; *Maud*, especially in Part III, uses Beatrice as a clear if evasive analogue; and *Idylls of the King,* both structurally and apprehensively, plays Tennyson's tragedy against Dante's comedy, his *before death* against Dante's *after death.* But more crucial is the fact that Ulysses' speech to Virgil and Dante in Canto XXVI of the *Inferno* has prima facie relevance, not just to Tennyson's brief monodrama, but to the other poems as well:

> "O brothers," said I, "who are come despite
> Ten thousand perils to the West, let none,
> While still our senses hold the vigil slight
> Remaining to us ere our course is run
> Be willing to forgo experience
> Of the unpeopled world beyond the sun.
> Regard your origin—from whom and whence!
> Not to exist like brutes, but made were ye
> To follow virtue and intelligence."[5]

For this "evil counsel," Dante condemned Ulysses; but Tennyson did not, and both the monodramatic model and the precarious but heroic humanness upon which Tennyson's poems turn may well have been extrapolated from this brief speech of Dante's Ulysses. Arthur and Ulysses share the "Ten thousand perils" that brought them "to the West," and Arthur along with Ulysses—that is, conscientious man in all ages—is being reinvested with a portion of that Homericism of which Virgil, Dante, and the Middle Ages had divested him. What we have in Tennyson from 1833 to 1892, certainly from *Ulysses* through *Idylls of the King,* is not the poet of Robson's "dilemma" or of McLuhan's "never able to make up his mind"[6]—the two Tennysons of that uncorrected Romanticism which much modern criticism has adopted—but a poet who, having typed for himself the existential precariousness of man in this world, saw the need to correct while he em-

ployed two millennia of the very richest literary inheritance
and, in that sobering insight that also returns Milton to Homer, to

> "walk this world,
> Yoked in all exercise of noble end,
> And so through those dark gates across the wild
> That no man knows."
> (*The Princess,* VII, 339–42)

Those "dark gates" are also the pillars of Hercules, and "the
wild/That no man knows" is that "wandering western sea"
that leads "beyond the sunset, and the baths/Of all the western stars . . . (*Ulysses,* 60–61).

Thus again we arrive at the unavoidable conclusion that
Tennyson's *Idylls* is supremely literary, not at some Romantic
level of spilt religion or strangeness wedded to beauty, but at
a severely winnowed, truly tragic, classically monitored level.
It is in fact an imaginative literary redemption of man from
the imperious enticements of the metaphor of medievalism,
at whose very center is the devastating quest for the Holy
Grail; of which Galahad, whom the poet moves into a critically ironic imaginative medium, is, with his psychotic nun,
the forlorn best hope; and of which a spiritually, morally,
psychologically depleted Percivale is the ambiguous, unsavory, barometric result. Medievalism is a metaphor of perceptual self-deception absorbed into the basic action of the
poem, and once we get in touch with that basic action, medievalism loses centrality and becomes part of the imaginative
Stoffen, the complex metaphoric materiél, of the poem.
Arthur is a Ulysses retailored in the fabric of time, and his
philosophy of work is Homeric. He loses at the center some
of his Homeric clarity of vision, as do Homer's heroes in their
individual fashions; but the hellish experience of the Grail-
quest (his equivalent journey to the underworld) refreshes his
sight and connects it with that initial intuition or original
inscape by which he had been perceptually liberated from his
most self-torturing "Travail, and throes and agonies of the
life" (*The Coming of Arthur,* 75) and upon which he had built
his determination to "follow virtue and intelligence."

It is not to medievalism, with its grand and grandly faulted myth of man, that the world can turn for fundamental guidance. Medievalism was inevitable and imperious and doomed. It was built on a sublime human enthusiasm that was both irresistible and false, and it spawned human romance and human burlesque, epic endurance and debilitating pathos, self-deception, self-renewal, and self-annihilation. As the quest for the Holy Grail revealed its human despair of humanness at a luridly dissolute symbolic level, so the Order of the Round Table itself, with its analogues in the orders of Benedict of Nursii and Francis of Assisi, became a "good custom" that "corrupt[ed] the world" once individual responsibility was absorbed into a "tale of the tribe," a mechanism (say, even, civilization at its most gracious) substituted for personally motivated, personally performed action. The "tribe" is just as unreal as any other abstraction, be it the Grand Old Man of the anthropomorphic religionists or the generalized and abstracted Man of the utilitarian moralists. Lancelot's weathering of despair is a starkly isolated existential experience, like that of Achilles or Ulysses wrapped in a different fiction and a different fabric of time. Guinevere has her saving breakthrough only after she has stripped herself of all the lifeless mechanicals by which, in the rituals of the tribe, she has entrenched her diminished self in the false pride of (medieval) voluptuousness, and her final recognition of Arthur as "'the highest and most human too'" returns the poem's supreme affirmation to a severely honed classicism. To the degree that post-Renaissance man turns to the Middle Ages for some magical touchstone of redemption, to the degree that the modern man of imagination—say, the poet or the priest—loses sight of the individual in the alluring enticements of the tribe, he will "'follow wandering fires, lost in the quagmire.'" Because to Tennyson as to Homer, the ultimate image of conscientious man is that of one standing high and alone, under his "arch of hand" straining his eyes to see and, because he stares into the sunrise, never being sure that what he sees are not simply his own eye-specks. That, too, is the authentic "Unseen" in whose reality Tennyson tells us he always believed, and man's high humanness will carry him on toward it if he will only remember that he was not made to "'exist like brutes,'" but "'To follow virtue and intelligence.'"

Literature becomes "life at the remove of form and idea," our life distanced to imaginative perspective, in poems like *Idylls of the King* when we see, as Tennyson clearly intended, that all the many characters in the poem are really one character ("a man") and that that character is ourselves: *Tout c'est moi.* This is the supreme unity of action, unity of perception, unity of failure ("one sin") in which the poem is centered; this is what suspends perceptual/moral judgment and induces perceptual/moral awe and the organic response that awe in its turn induces. We are implicated in the poem's every turning, and its ultimate unity is in ourselves. Time and Space are mere modes of consciousness, and our universe cannot cohere around any center but our own: in the metaphor used by Carlyle, unless there is a harmony in ourselves, there can be no harmony in our universe, and neither can "hold together and exist." This is the only source, goal, and significance that any truly distinctive reality can ever have; all else has about it some degree of unreality and therefore some degree of chaos. Until, like Arthur, we discover that we exist, our universe can have no center; and if, like Arthur, we try to lend our discovered selves out, we will of course fail, but we may not fail wholly.

Notes

1. *Illustrations of Tennyson* (London: Chatto & Windus, 1891), p. iv.
2. See, for example, H. M. McLuhan, "Tennyson and the Romantic Epic," in *Critical Essays on the Poetry of Tennyson*, ed. John Killham (New York: Barnes & Noble, 1960), pp. 86–95, and McLuhan's more helpful treatment in his introduction to *Alfred Lord Tennyson: Selected Poetry* (New York: Holt, Rinehart and Winston, 1956), pp. xvi–xxiv.
3. J. W. Mackail, *Lectures on Greek Poetry* (London: Longmans, Green & Co., 1910), p. 219.
4. McLuhan, *Selected Poetry*, p. xviii.
5. Translation by W. W. Robson, in "The Dilemma of Tennyson," *Critical Essays on the Poetry of Tennyson*, ed. Killham, p. 156.
6. *Selected Poetry*, p. xviii. All reference to Tennyson's poetry is to *The Poems of Tennyson*, ed. Christopher Ricks (London: Longman, 1969).

Essay 3

Manner and Meaning:
A Critical Corrective

The efforts of some modern critics to rehabilitate Tennyson's *Idylls* and to make the poem more palatable to contemporary readers, though generally praiseworthy, have sometimes led to critical overstatements that, besides misrepresenting the poem, invite us to admire it on incomplete or false grounds. It is a virtuous fault in the near term, perhaps, but in the long run it does the poem a disservice. As Matthew Arnold observed, the modernization of a classic that ignores some of its defining characteristics reflects but a partial faith in the genuineness of the object's claim to classic status. Professor Ryals's categorical dismissal of the poem's revised but still real and highly relevant epic dimensions is an example of this: "[T]o treat it as an epic, or as an epic *manqué,* is to regard the completed *Idylls of the King* in the wrong way" (see p. 211, above); so, also, is Professor Rosenberg's comparable dismissiveness on the issue of allegory: "The point is not that allegory is simplistic—a patent absurdity—but that the *Idylls* is not an allegory and that those who so read it are forced into simplistic conclusions."[1] Such dogmas attempt to make matters simpler than the crucial issues will allow. Nor is it possible to say, as Rosenberg does in the same context, that "By 'parabolic drift' and 'thought within the image,' Tennyson means precisely what we mean by *symbol*. . . ."

It is certainly true that all allegory is not simplistic, but it is almost certainly true, too, that most modern readers, if left to their own resources, would read even the least simplistic of allegories, Spenser's *The Faerie Queene*, simplistically. Moreover, it is probably true that Tennyson believed that a nineteenth-century audience would virtually have buried a nineteenth-century allegory in simplism. Something had happened to language during the two-and-a-half centuries between Spenser and Tennyson that had changed Spenser's jubilant joy of language into Tennyson's anxious joy of language. Any explanation of this change must be highly speculative, of course, but the change itself is of such fundamental importance to the student of poetry that speculation must be hazarded. Though language itself was throughout the period undergoing constant metamorphosis—standardization, organic growth and decay, dramatic expansion under pressure of a rapidly quantifying knowledge explosion, adaptation to new geographical environments and to new linguistic and political mixes—far more important was the metamorphosis of expectation about language among users of language. Science, reason, history—all the so-called imperatives of modern thought—were exerting enormous pressure on the mind of Western man for an inventory of his world that was real (factual) rather than fanciful. As a result, the depletion of the kind of spiritual soil in which allegory had flourished had been going on long before critics became conscious that allegory no longer had the same appeal and cogency that it had once had. It may even be that *The Faerie Queene* was the climactic harvest of one allegorical tradition as *The Pilgrim's Progress* was that of another, the respective, if not mutually exclusive, spiritual forces that made each possible never again to enjoy a comparable harmony and energy. Although it might simply be argued that no allegorists comparable to Spenser and Bunyan came along in the eighteenth and nineteenth centuries, it seems more likely that no comparable allegorists were possible, the *Zeitgeist* itself having become uncongenial to their peculiar imaginative exhibition. "Does *this* mean *this*, or doesn't it?" was the overwhelming tendency of the modern Western mind, and the ironic result was that Tennyson's pained lament, "I hate to be tied down to say, '*This* means *that*. . . ,'"[2] was a lament over the best, rather than the worst, that could be hoped for in the way of a modern response to allegory.

Tennyson knew this at the creative level, however much he might regret it critically, and so, as he had dismantled the formal epic without actually abandoning it, he dismantled formal allegory while retaining an unyielding remnant of it. He wisely chose not to confront the modern world over the issue of allegory, but he chose, also, not to abandon allegory completely because of the disfavor into which it had fallen. Not only does *this* not mean *that; this* does not mean *this* either, however much it may appear to do so and however determinedly we may try to freeze a particular significance into language and make it so. All things are in that sense unknowable, not simply the unknowables of metaphysics; and an enlarged awareness of that truth is worth, from a poet's point of view, an epical non-epic and an allegorical non-allegory.

The tendency of this argument applies also to the use of symbols and contradicts the unnecessarily categorical assertion that by "'parabolic drift' and 'thought within the image,' Tennyson means precisely what we mean by *symbol,* the antithesis of the reductive, this-for-that equivalence which his commentators had found in the *Idylls*" (22). It is hardly ever judicious to use the word *precisely* in speaking of a Tennyson meaning that one finds "ambiguous," and *reductive* is not "precisely" an antithetical term. It is wrong to characterize Tennyson's remark, "They are right, and they are not right. They mean that and they do not" as "revealingly ambiguous" (21). Tennyson has formulated a classical paradox, not an ambiguity. Ambiguities are revealing of character, not of principle, and, though Tennyson's remark has complex implications, there is nothing confusing about it.[3]

Multiplicity of perception is at the heart of Tennyson's poetry, and *Idylls of the King* is his fullest exploration of multiplicity—moral, aesthetic, cognitive. In attempting to put this vision into place, Tennyson knew that he could not afford to reject categorically any of poetry's proved ways of self-realization since it was as a mirror of human self-imaging that poetry had established its primacy among the arts. Only a poetry wholly aware of itself could hope to be an adequate instrument of self-awareness. Being, in that sense, a universal writing act—a poetic summation of poetry—it sought to be a universal reading act—an introduction to the art and idea of poetry, the "modern expression of a modern outlook" that took, like Arnold, relevance rather than contemporaneity as its criterion of the modern.

The perfect realization of such an aspiration was not only impossible but unthinkable, but to reach in that direction, to see an invisible star and hear an inaudible music, was to give a "framework" and a "chord" to the bard's magnificent madness and to remind the world that "the great vine of *Fable*," despite the counter-illusions fostered by "*Discovery*," still reaches "to every corner under Heaven,/Deep-rooted in the living soil of truth. . . ."[4] It is not a different truth, but since it is looked at from a different viewpoint and with different eyes, both the angle and the vision enable one to entertain quite different possibilities about the truth, possibilities that magnify the spirit in inverse proportion to their positivism.

Tennyson's comment on the "parabolic drift" of the poem and his statement that "the thought within the image is much more than *any* one interpretation" (emphasis added) are relevant to our meaning of *symbol* and suggest Tennyson's imaginative consanguinity with both the French Symbolists and with poets who, like T. S. Eliot, opened modern poetry fully to the French Symbolist current. But they do not constitute a precise overlay of either one. Tennyson used settings, characters, actions, and language as complex and mutually reciprocal symbols in a very modern way, and unless a reader can enter into the endless perceptual resonances generated by the poem's symbols, he is likely to achieve only a severely simplified response to it. On the other hand, even that severely simplified response can be authentically gratifying and is not to be dismissed out of hand as interpretively naïve ("simplistic"), however different it may be from a luxuriant immersion in the poem's complex of symbols. Ideally, the two responses work together, each functioning as both a rein-forcement and a corrective of the other. But they are both there—the austere morality play *and* the rich revel of setting, character, action, and language, the starkness of Sophocles *and* the abundance of Spenser and Shakespeare—and this double presence, once acknowledged, modifies the tendency of some recent critics to be exclusive in their enthusiasm for Tennyson's symbolic textures.

An analogous qualification should be made to the tendency to make Tennyson a symbolist according to the paradigm represented by Mallarmé and Eliot. There is a pervasive pres-ence, an unmistakable visibility, in Tennyson's poetry of the characteristic manner of the Symbolists—the demotion of discursive theme, the promotion of musical theme, concen-tration of image, the use of dramatic painting, evocation and suggestion as the chief means of releasing endless imagina-tive possibilities while resisting closure around *any one* possi-bility—and there seems little question but that Tennyson could have carried these tendencies, which were very natural to him, to a "pure" or complete Symbolist state. But the fact is that he did not do so. He retained the connection with the more explicit moral, "allegorical" tradition of Wordsworth, Milton, and Dante, modified but not abandoned, and thereby signaled his persuasion that a poem should both *be* and *mean,* the poet's responsibility not being to lead people into the garden of either art or belief and leave them there. Like Arnold, Tennyson believed that poetry should be a "complete magister vitae," and although he did not tell his readers what to think or to think in conventional ways, he told them that they must think imaginatively and provided for their stimula-tion dramatic models by which they might break out of thought's drab dead-end and embark upon new and more complete modes of apprehension. It is, as it is in the cases of epic and allegory, a matter of degree, but in that delicate degree rests the true, distinctive, masterful, *and decisive* Ten-nyson, not the old oddity of the "two Tennysons" or the newer, subtler, more ingratiating oddity of the ambiguous Tennyson.[5]

Ambiguity in *Idylls of the King* is itself a crucial issue, and some modern critics seem to take a particular delight in ambiguity. For example, Rosenberg says of Lancelot:

> His love for his king is as absolute as his love for his queen, and it is his tragedy that loyalty to one must be disloyalty to the other:
>
> > The great and guilty love he bare the Queen,
> > In battle with the love he bare his lord,
> > Had marred his face, and marked it ere his time.
> >   (*LE*, 244–246)
>
> The whole force of this passage lies in the juxtaposed "great and guilty": the guilt of the love is indisputable, but so too is its greatness, by which Tennyson means not only intensity but nobility. Indeed, the guilt is a function of the nobility; were it not for Lancelot's nobility, he would feel no guilt, and without the guilt, there would be less nobility." (23)

Such delight in ambiguity would soon strip the world of classical tragedy—would give Oedipus his eyes back and release Antigone from her dungeon tomb. It is not Tennyson who makes Lancelot's love for Guinevere "absolute." Tennyson calls it "great and guilty," not absolute, and later in the idyll, Lancelot treats it as " great and guilty," but not absolute:

> > "I needs must break
> > These bonds that so defame me: not without
> > She wills it: would I, if she willed it? nay,
> > Who knows?"
> >   (*LE*, 1409–1412)

Lancelot clearly does not yield to "These bonds" as one must yield to a recognized absolute; though he does not know that he has the selfless nobility to "break" them (something he will barely learn at Carbonek), he knows that they must be broken and hence that they can be broken. This, too, is the import of Arthur's commentary on Lancelot's account of the motive and experience of his Grail-quest:

> > "'Nay—but thou errest, Lancelot: never yet
> > Could all of true and noble in knight and man

Twine round one sin, whatever it might be,
With such a closeness, but apart there grew,
Save that he were the swine thou spakest of,
Some root of knighthood and pure nobleness;
Whereto see thou, that it may bear its flower.'"
                                    (*HG*, 877–883)

The "root of knighthood and pure nobleness" to which
Arthur refers is what makes the indispensable difference between Lancelot's "love for his king" and "his love for his
queen," and though *absolute* may be too deific a term to apply
even to the former, it certainly has no appropriate application
to the latter.

How one discovers that by "greatness" Tennyson meant
"not only intensity but nobility" is not clear. Arthur distinguishes, in general terms, between what Lancelot is talking
about and "pure nobleness"; Lancelot himself speaks of it as
a defaming love in contrast to his love for Arthur (*LE*,
1408–1409) and begins to see in Guinevere's fury "'dead
love's harsh heir, jealous pride'" (*LE*, 1387); Guinevere speaks
of Arthur as "'one whom ever in my heart of hearts/I did
acknowledge nobler'" than Lancelot (*LE*, 1203–1204). Having
attributed absoluteness and nobility to Lancelot's "great and
guilty" love for the Queen, the critic must rationalize the
guilt, and again is forced back on ambiguity: "were it not for
Lancelot's nobility, he would feel *no guilt*, and without the
guilt, there would be less greatness [i.e., less 'intensity' and
'nobility']" (emphasis added). This, surely, threatens to slip
through ambiguity into moral muddle.

If Lancelot were the "swine" that he and Arthur speak of,
he would feel no guilt, so "without the guilt, there would
[indeed] be less greatness." There would be swinery. Unfor-
tunately, that does not carry us very far toward an understanding of Lancelot's "greatness." Guilt is a measure, not of
one's greatness, but of one's capacity to recognize his own
culpability. Many people feel their guilt so intensely that it
destroys them, and this engenders in those who witness it a
sense of pathos, the pathos being the more suffocating the
grander the alternative to guilt wasted in self-destruction
seems. In fact, Lancelot entertains just such a possibility:

"but if I would not [break these bonds], then may God,
I pray him, send a sudden Angel down
To seize me by the hair and bear me far,
And fling me deep in that forgotten mere,
Among the tumbled fragments of the hills."

(*LE*, 1412–1416)

The true measure of Lancelot's greatness is his capacity to redeem himself from guilt, not his capacity to feel it, and he turns the matter around in the idyll that immediately follows his recognition scene, *The Holy Grail*. He does not achieve the instant purification that, in his near-desperate state, he longs for, even concluding that "'this Quest was not for me'" (*HG*, 849), but, face to face symbolically with his own lions rampant at the entry to Carbonek, he does overcome self-doubt at an irreducible minimum level and begin, on valid terms, the endless journey toward personal holiness. Paradoxically (*not* ambiguously), "this Quest" *was* for him, and the myth of the magic wand is itself redeemed, at the same minimum level, by the deep-rooted authenticity of Lancelot's motive for undertaking it.

Tennyson's great poem is not critically redeemed by a suffocating submersion in Romantic ambiguity, by compromising what is tough but clear through a fatal collusion in the emotional despondency and intellectual violence engendered but purged by the poet's "full look at the Worst."[6] That is to approach tragedy with partial vision, to measure man's greatness by the fact that he perpetually lives on catastrophe's edge plagued by a sense of his own vulnerability. Such a recognition of the precariousness of the human situation is indispensable, of course, but it is not enough. Having stripped reality of its customary delusions, having taken a "full look at the Worst," the poet then poses the climactic question: what, under these circumstances, is "the best consummation possible "?[7] To that question, different people give different answers, and such a multiplicity of perceptions is fully provided for in *Idylls of the King*, but the poem's central parable moves in a *central* direction that man, despite all his wounds—his potentially self-destructive passions and self-dwarfing incapacities, his multiple griefs and recurrent panics into despair—still endorses. Even in a grossly imperfect world that often seems especially inimical to human aspiration, man's duty, man's profit, and man's pleasure are to love "'the highest and most human too.'" It is not Tennyson's parable, and it is not wholly eclipsed even in the day of the cynic. Like the seasons, it has its periods of growth and decay, dormancy and bloom, but man's varied history shows it to be *man's own parable,* his one essential and indestructible self-awareness. It is the faith that fuels all his myths and all the fragile structures he devises for his myths' fulfillment, and until his species completes its tenure in this world, it will not die but forever come again.

This leads us to the issue of the poem's overall import, and here again one can give ambiguity too large and critical a place: "Yet the moral of the *Idylls* is not that men must abide by spiritual values, any more than the moral of *Othello* is that wives should look to their linen. In this sense, the poem is totally without a moral but explores instead the *ambiguous results* of man's quest for such values, and the disastrous effects of abandoning them" (Rosenberg, 24–25, emphasis added). It is not at all clear what is meant by the phrase "In this sense," but it is clear that *Idylls of the King* is in no sense "totally without a moral" and that it is an evasion of the poem's central import to say that it simply "explores . . . ambiguous results," as if it were Tennyson's purpose to infect us all with Lancelot's madness without any hope of sharing in Lancelot's recovery. It is a case of overdrawing one's negatives ("totally without") and underdrawing one's positives ("ambiguous results").

Ambiguity does have a massive presence in the poem, but at the experiential level of character. This is the far-reaching effect of Lancelot's and Guinevere's ambiguous relationship, and it gradually induces an ever-deepening spiritual confusion—like a cataract on the eye of the soul—that climaxes in the "deathwhite mist" of "that last weird battle in the west" when knights "Looked up for heaven, and only saw the mist" and even upon Arthur confusion momentarily fell (*PA*, 29, 95, 112, 143–144). It is an experiential ambiguity that infects the knights until they "know not what" they are, nor "whence" they are, nor "whether" they be knights (adapted from *PA*, 144–145) and almost destroys Guinevere as Guinevere has destroyed the realm. But ambiguity does not infect the poet's imagination: it is his subject matter, not his condition, and he controls it with the implicit, distinctive mastery of a Dante and a Homer, distilling from his myth the relentless moral of human history and rendering the myth itself with history's imperious, often mysterious, inevitability. Hence his moral is not a dogma, but a historical fact, a reading of man's written story, and his prophecy is essentially an assumption of the poetry of the past—only the knowledge into which a soul has been breathed has a future. Though this is not an apothegm, it is a moral, and none of the poem's richness—that is, its thousand reading difficulties—makes its imaginative insight, its "parabolic drift," ambiguous. The voice that Lancelot hears before the "chasm-like portals" of Carbonek warns him about self-destruction when he stands, almost despairing, on its edge: "'Doubt not, go forward; if thou doubt, the beasts/ Will tear thee piecemeal'" (*HG*, 821–822). Though Tennyson, in *Idylls of the King,* brings us to this point too, he does not then add ambiguity to our spiritual depletion and make us "sink in the impossible strife,/And be astray forever."[8]

Notes

1. John D. Rosenberg, *The Fall of Camelot* (Cambridge, Mass.: Harvard University Press, 1973), p. 22. Further references to this book are identified in parentheses in the text. For a counterstatement on allegory, see Pattison (p. 208–210, above). Since the subject of epic is covered in some depth in Part 3 (see 210, above), I do not treat it here.
2. Hallam Tennyson, *Alfred Lord Tennyson: A Memoir* (New York: Macmillan, 1897), II, 123–125.
3. For a different view, see S. C. Burchell, "Tennyson's 'Allegory in the Distance,'" *PMLA*, 68 (1953), 418–424.
4. *Timbuctoo*, ll. 218–221.
5. W. David Shaw raises a similar caution: "[W]ere Victorian contemporaries such as Longfellow, who believed that in the *Idylls* Tennyson had wrought 'rich tapestries worthy to hang by *The Faerie Queene*' . . . any

more mistaken than present-day readers who study the *Idylls* as a Symbolist poem? . . . It is fashionable now to assert the contrary, but in its moral passion, *Idylls of the King* is still closer in spirit to *The Faerie Queene* than to Baudelaire's *Fleurs du mal*." See *Tennyson's Style* (Ithaca: Cornell University Press, 1976), p. 328.

6. Thomas Hardy, *In Tenebris II*.
7. Thomas Hardy, *Apology* to *Late Lyrics and Earlier*.
8. Matthew Arnold, *Empedocles on Etna*, II, 389–390.

Essay 4

Ethics versus Physics:
Man and Nature

The general issue of man's relationship to nature in *Idylls of the King* is central to Tennyson's complex imaginative intuition, to the poetic manner in which he gave it shape and dimension, and to the unique contribution that he hoped to make, through the poem, to modern (i.e., post-Romantic Romantic) man's struggle for self-definition and genuine significance in his universe. Hence, Tennyson's very dependability as a poet, his relevance in Arnold's severe sense of a poet's perennial modernism depending on his relevance, is unavoidably implicit in his handling of the issue of man's place in nature.

Professor Rosenberg begins his chapter on this subject (IV—"*Landscape*") with the most extreme position of any critic of the poem on the issue of the correspondences that Tennyson establishes between man and nature in *Idylls*.[1] For example, he says: "The symbolic season which flowers and fades along with Arthur is probably the most sustained pathetic fallacy in our literature" (67). "Tangled thickets and orderly gardens, sultry meadows and violent tempests are," he says, "all extensions of human consciousness" in a world in which "nature . . . is at war with itself . . ." (66). Arthur is "a dying [nature] god," and his career is "tragically enmeshed" in the cycle of the seasons (67). Accepting Santayana's defense of the pathetic fallacy in *Interpretations of Poetry and Religion*, Rosenberg agrees that, by using landscape in this pathetically fallacious way, "the poet restores the 'natural confusion' of inner and outer worlds common to ancient modes of experience before the classifying intelligence assigned them to separate spheres" (67–68).

Against such "natural confusion," let Darwin's bulldog speak. T. H. Huxley was certainly one of the tough-minded scientific thinkers of his generation who took a professional interest in the subject of "man's place in nature," and he called Tennyson one of "the thought-worn chieftains of the mind" and said of him that he was the only poet since Lucretius "who has taken the trouble to understand the work and tendency of the men of science."[2] One would certainly expect a reluctance to estrange the truth even in the interests of metaphoric impressiveness from such a poet as Huxley describes, especially from a poet who, like Tennyson, not only went to extraordinary pains to be irreproachably precise but also saw one of the grandest myths of human experience (the deity of Jesus Christ) foundering on failed facts. Everything we know about him dictates the conclusion that Tennyson was too serious and wise a poet to erect a major work of the century, one addressing itself at the deepest level to one of the crucial perceptual dilemmas of an intelligent, scientifically literate modern audience, on the "natural confusion" of primitive experience. There were useful lessons to be learned, curious patterns of response to be understood, from a knowledge of and humble respect for primitive "modes of experience," many of which, Tennyson knew, persist in remnant or even pristine modern forms. He himself on occasion reenacted such experiences, even oftener longed for them, and underwent, like the speaker in *Locksley Hall*, great spiritual dilation from the recognition that "Ancient founts of inspiration well through all my fancy yet" (188). However, Tennyson and his readers, like their classical Greek and Hebrew predecessors, belonged to the age of "the classifying intelligence," and there is no evidence that Tennyson ever entertained a serious preference for the "natural confusion" of truly primitive "modes of experience." Despite the absurdity frequently shown in the assumptions, slogans, and actions of the apex-of-civilization advocates among his contemporaries, turning back the psychic clock was neither an option nor an object of Tennyson's world view or of his poetic labors.

There is no serious quarrel about the seasonal framework of *Idylls*. The poet persistently mirrors the drift of the seasons in the movement of his myth, creating, largely by implicit analogy but with varying degrees of unmistakableness, the illusion of perpetual reciprocation and interpenetration between the seasons and the psyches of those brought forward to play their parts in a particular equinox. Details of setting, often minute details, regularly have a symbolic correspondence to the characters' states of mind, sometimes measuring them in a general way, sometimes supplying clues to particular motives and outcomes. In a less specific but highly suggestive way, numerous allusions to earlier vegetation myths enforce an analogy between the highly coded cultural myth of Arthur and the Round Table and various primitive myths built upon worship of the sun and the seasons. This analogy, however, does not imply that the former is to be interpreted according to the details of the latter, but that all things have their rhythms of growth and decay and that the resurrection of the one out of the remnants of the other is a dependable promise of yet another resurrection as like and unlike as these two are to each other.

There is a difference of kind between analogies, illusions of reciprocal interpenetration, and symbolic correspondences, on the one hand, and the "natural confusion" that would result from an acceptance of *Idylls of the King* as "probably the most sustained pathetic fallacy in our literature." *Idylls* is not a "sustained pathetic fallacy"; it does not contain, as expressive of the poet's point of view, a single exemplary pathetic fallacy; and the notions that its thickets, gardens, meadows, and tempests are "all *extensions* of human consciousness" and that Arthur's career is "tragically *enmeshed*" in the cycles of the seasons are not realities of the poem, which is made of sterner stuff. Tennyson was as tough-minded as Huxley, as Huxley knew. Tennyson knew the difference between moral man (ethics) and amoral nature (physics), and he knew the difference between saying that man is at war with himself (a metaphor that almost everybody with some knowledge of man and war can understand) and saying that "nature . . . is at war with itself" (a metaphor that almost nobody with some knowledge of nature and war can understand or accept except as a heightening analogy.) He gave *landscape* a massive presence in his poem as a way of more fully realizing its *inscape*—for refracting, intensifying, and penetrating its essential and discrete subject, *man and his myths*. By so doing he greatly enlarged the reader's sense of both the moral magnitude and the moral intricacy of his myth, extending it outward, seemingly, to the very edges of endless space and endless time and extending it inward to the dreams that lie hidden from consciousness and betoken depths to which we despair of access and which we contemplate with terror. For all its massiveness, however, Tennyson kept careful control over landscape, never sacrificing precision to enlargement and never allowing physics to assume the role of ethics. That, Tennyson knew, would be to abandon the ultimate question to "natural confusion," and that he did not do.

The King's monodramatic self-communing, overheard by Bedivere at the beginning of *The Passing of Arthur* (9–28), is the indispensable passage for clarifying this crucial issue, but it must be read with the same discipline with which it was written. Eggers uses it as the basis for an assertion that "Arthur's utopian ambition rested upon a faith in a lesser god,"[3] and it certainly does not justify saying that. Rosenberg reads it as follows: "Arthur looks back upon the defeat of all his purposes and laments that the world seems to have been made by some lesser god, who 'had not force to shape it as he would'" (66). That is closer, and behind that reading of it is a reflection of Tennyson's awareness that a conflict between God's benevolence and his omnipotence was one of the ways that a man disconsolate over the discrepancy between ideal and real outcomes might use to reconcile, however unsatisfactorily, his despondence and his faith.[4] But it is still not an exact reading of the passage.

"I found Him in the shining of the stars,
I marked Him in the flowering of His fields,
But in His ways with men I find Him not.
I waged His wars, and now I pass and die.
O me! for why is all around us here
As if some lesser god had made the world,
But had not force to shape it as he would,
Till the High God behold it from beyond,
And enter it, and make it beautiful?
Or else as if the world were wholly fair,
But that these eyes of men are dense and dim,
And have not power to see it as it is:
Perchance, because we see not to the close;—
For I, being simple, thought to work His will,
And have but stricken with the sword in vain;
And all whereon I leaned in wife and friend
Is traitor to my peace, and all my realm
Reels back into the beast, and is no more.
My God, thou hast forgotten me in my death:
Nay—God my Christ—I pass but shall not die."

(*PA*, 9–28)

These are the wholly private "moanings of the King" as reported by the poet's official eavesdropper, the last synoptic, and their subject, articulated when Arthur's capacity for inscaping his world seems weakest, is the ultimate relationship of things—nature, man, and God. About nature, there is not the least confusion. Using symbols of utmost distance and permanence ("the stars") and of the utmost closeness and mutability ("the flowering . . . fields"), Arthur declares unequivocally that he "found" ("marked") "the High God" in nature. With equal clarity, Arthur says that he does not "find Him" in "His ways with men," and the rest of his dialogue with himself is an effort to deal with the real center of confusion, man.

First, Arthur frames the dilemma specifically and succinctly: "I waged His wars, and now I pass to die." By every civilized code of honor, of King and conscience, that seems unjust, and so the appearance of divine injustice must be faced. One terrifying possibility ("O me!") is that the hand of the god who made nature so successfully was unequal to the successful making of man, faltered in this higher, more challenging act of creation—was "a lesser god" (than man has assumed) whose "force" (omnipotence) was unequal to his benevolence (to "shape it as he would"). That is not to say, as Rosenberg does, that to Arthur "the world seems to have been made by some lesser god," but that, in confronting the appearance of divine injustice, Arthur momentarily entertains that terrifying possibility. But Arthur does even that as *a condition contrary to fact*—"*As if* some lesser god *had made* the world" (emphasis added)—and then moves immediately to the reconciling perception that, even if that were true, the "High God" would eventually "behold it from beyond,/And enter it, and make it beautiful." Even if it were true, then, it would not abandon the world of man to divine incompetence/injustice forever since a greater God ("the High God"), though presently outside the orbit of human space and time, would see, enter, and redeem man's crooked world.

But the possibility that a lesser god made the world is not the only condition contrary to fact that Arthur entertains; another is that the world of man is "wholly fair" and men misperceive it, their eyes being "dense and dim" and their tenure in the world covering but a fragment of time. In illustration of the plausibility of such a view of man as morally myopic, Arthur cites the collapse into ruin of all his own most precious ideals—conscientiousness in love, friendship, and community service. But this possibility is even more terrifying than the first because it seems to strip man of all sense of goal and make him the victim of the deadening despair that even his rehearsal of the possibility induces for a moment in Arthur himself: "My God, thou hast forgotten me in my death." But it must be remembered that this speculation is *a condition contrary to fact* too, and by presenting Arthur's speculations as such, Tennyson enables the King to vent his inevitable despondency while holding it at the precise perceptual distance at which it can be mastered: "Nay—God my Christ—I pass but shall not die." Like Empedocles, Arthur looks over the edge of the abyss, but, unlike Empedocles, he does not plunge into the crater.

Arthur's metaphor of a lesser god who had adequate power

over the making of nature and inadequate power over the making of man contradicts the notion that man and nature are "extensions" of each other or that their careers are "tragically enmeshed." His second metaphor, of men whose eyes are "dense and dim" and who "have not the power to see [their world] as it is," implies an analogy between man and this lesser god that betokens more than the traditional idea of God's having created man in his own image and likeness, although it includes it: man, like this lesser god, has adequate power over nature and inadequate power over man, and this lesser god, like man, has the capacity fully to perceive physical beauty, but his eyes are "dense and dim" to ethical beauty. However, it is in the arena of ethics that man customarily "'Conceits himself as God,'" as Dagonet says with penetrating irony of Arthur (*LT,* 355), and, like a lesser god, fails of even the best intentions. But even if, like his lesser god, man is inadequate to the austere demands of ethical beauty, seeing ethical ideals but densely and dimly, should he cease to aspire, dismissing imperfectly perceived ideal means as mere pipe dreams and imperfectly perceived ideal ends as mere utopian folly? Not if he is an Arthur because, like the lesser god who is an image of himself, what he fails to do perfectly from lack of force rather than of will the "High God [will] behold . . . from beyond,/And enter it, and make it beautiful." In the meantime, he needs to avoid the "natural confusion" of measuring his moral nature, however obscure, by the standards of the physical world, however clear and beautiful; to accept the wounds of his imperfection, yielding to a power greater than himself the ultimate harmony of things and deriving daily profit and pleasure from undertaking the duty that he does see; and to believe that to pass is not to die because man, like nature but in a way ultimately different in kind, requires endless self-renewals to fulfill the law of his distinct, godlike being.

Notes

1. John D. Rosenberg, *The Fall of Camelot* (Cambridge, Mass.: Harvard University Press, 1973). Further references are given in parentheses in the text.

2. Rosenberg himself (7n.) cites these passages in Jerome H. Buckley's *The Victorian Temper: A Study in Literary Culture* (Cambridge, Mass.: Harvard University Press, 1951), pp. 67, 255.
3. J. Philip Eggers, *King Arthur's Laureate: A Study of Tennyson's "Idylls of the King"* (New York: New York University Press, 1971), p. 67.
4. John Stuart Mill frames the contradiction in *Three Essays in Religion,* and it is one of the options entertained by Hardy's speaker in *Nature's Questioning.*

Essay 5

In Defense of Arthur:
The Moral Imperatives of
Artistic Form

The wasting of heroes and the rehabilitation of villains has been a favorite exercise among popular moralists for some time, and Arthur has certainly had his share of detractors. Insulated against the corrective of the poet's declared purposes by the critical disrepute into which the "intentional fallacy" had fallen, they often made quick work of one of literature's grand fallible heroes and, with a wry inconsistency, even began to claim that Tennyson intended conclusions that they could not possibly have reached except by declaring inadmissible, or by implicitly faulting, the poet's own declarations of intention.

More critically ironic yet is the apparently unredacted assumption that one can demote or even demolish Arthur— "the greatest of all poetical subjects,"[1] "the central dominant figure" upon which the integrity of the poem depends,[2] "*the King*" whose "*Idylls*" these are—and still make extraordinary critical claims for the poem. Thus Clyde de L. Ryals makes the "co-existence and interplay" of "many layers of meaning" the basis for claiming that "*Idylls of the King* [is] a poem of

341

which one never tires"[3] even though, by his analysis, Arthur "learns" chiefly "that the world is impregnable to morality" and "stands, finally, in moral terms, as both the hero and the villain of the *Idylls of the King*."[4] Gerhard Joseph easily concedes "the inconsistencies of the conceptual scheme," finds *our* (as distinct from *his*) admiration for Arthur "either as ideal representative of soul or as long-suffering husband" undermined by Guinevere's "weakness," and, citing Tennyson's failure in the most crucial test of his powers as a dramatic poet, asserts that even "the most sympathetic reader *must* concede a priggishness that has been the scorn of those who see in Tennyson's Arthurian pageant little more than a representatively obnoxious document of Victorian male chauvinism" (see p. 248, above, emphasis added). John Rosenberg, the most rhetorically intense advocate of the poem in this century, seems to find erosion of Arthur's character positively high-minded. He speaks of its "inevitable duality," calls it both a substantive and an aesthetic "dilemma" of the poet, sees Arthur as being always in "double jeopardy," and characterizes Arthur's final speech to Guinevere with such words as "ferocity," "onslaught," "chilling," "shocking," making the Queen writhe "in bestial abasement" and leaving us "as breathless as the man who boasts of his own humility." He says that *Vivien* has taught us not to "uncritically accept Arthur's judgment in his own case"; that he is by no means "blameless," "although his faults are the defects of his virtues"; and that both Vivien and Dagonet are "right and wrong" to "call him a fool." As conclusive evidence of "how heavily Tennyson has hedged his King in ambiguity," he cites the failure of Arthur's purposes and then goes on to say that Arthur's indictment of Guinevere ("'And all through thee!'" [*G*, 490]) is not only "cruel" but "simplistic" and that the "very profusion and variety of evil" in the poem "belie" it. According to Rosenberg, Arthur is "destroyed . . . for the vulnerability of his virtues," and the essence of his tragedy is that his punishment "vastly and inexplicably exceeds" his "crime" of "noble delusion." Despite Arthur's assertion that his "last hope" is that

"We two may meet before high God, and thou
Wilt spring to me, and claim me thine, and know
I am thine husband . . ."

(*G*, 561–563)

and the fact that Guinevere finds redemption by clinging to
that hope, Rosenberg dismisses their marriage as impersonal
and says that what Arthur cannot "survive" is "the loss of 'the
goodliest fellowship of famous knights/Whereof this world
holds record'" (*PA*, 183–184). Arthur emerges, finally, as a
"noble" but deluded fool whose judgment of himself, his
Queen, and his world cannot be trusted and who is deprived
even of the tragic recognition and redemption tendered to
Lancelot and Guinevere.[5]

Arthur has also had his defenders, of course, though the
general tendency has been to assume that Tennyson faltered
rather egregiously in the multifaceted challenge of Arthur.
William Brashear escapes the issue by seeing Arthur and the
other dramatis personae as "vitalistic" rather than symbolic
(p. 247, above). Robert Pattison sees Arthur's freedom "from
the psychic turmoil born of divided will that surrounds him"
as both defining his heroism and rebutting, in part, the
charge that he is "a self-righteous prig" (p. 249, above). By
comparing Arthur's and Guinevere's moral situation with
that of Adam and Eve in Book IX of *Paradise Lost,* Donald
Hair seeks to establish that Arthur succeeds in an austere
moral duty in which Adam had failed (250–251, above).

J. M. Gray has mounted the most elaborate defense of
Arthur of any recent commentator (p. 250, above). But however acceptable one may find Gray's detailed list of Arthur's
credits, one is still faced with the critical problem on which
Browning focused at the end of *The Ring and the Book:*

Why take the artistic way to prove so much?
Because, it is the glory and the good of Art,
That Art remains the one way possible
Of speaking truth, to mouths like mine at least.
How look a brother in the face and say,
"Thy right is wrong, eyes hast thou yet art blind;

Thine ears are stuffed and stopped, despite their
  length:
And, oh, the foolishness thou countest faith!"
Say this as silverly as tongue can troll—
The anger of the man may be endured,
The shrug, the disappointed eyes of him
Are not so bad to bear—but here's the plague
That all this trouble comes of telling truth,
Which truth, by when it reaches him, looks false,
Seems to be just the thing it would supplant,
Nor recognizable by whom it left:
While falsehood would have done the work of truth.
But Art,—wherein man nowise speaks to men,
Only to mankind,—Art may tell a truth
Obliquely, do the thing shall breed the thought,
Nor wrong the thought, missing the mediate word.
So may you paint your picture, twice show truth,
Beyond mere imagery on the wall,—
So, note by note, bring music from your mind,
Deeper than ever e'en Beethoven dived,—
So write a book shall mean beyond the facts,
Suffice the eye and save the soul beside.[6]

Gray has so conceived his defense that he asserts his admiration for an Arthur whom others dislike without apparently perceiving that, for many persons on both sides of the issue, it may be essentially the same Arthur.

Whether one personally likes or dislikes this Arthur is, in and of itself, only tangentially relevant; whether one is *right* in liking or disliking him is the primary literary question.[7] That is the question that challenges the reader who would be critically just to take as circumspect and sympathetic a view of the controlling intuition of the poem as its direct, internal evidence requires and to see the parts in relation to a whole that is shaped by that intuition. He may still find fault with the intuition itself or with its poetic construction, including both the overall architecture and the thousands of individual decisions that, in a poem of epic-like ambition, the poet attempts to make in a manner that will satisfy the most capable of his sympathetic readers. But he will enjoy the positive pleasures of critical conscientiousness in the knowledge that, however fallible his judgment may be, he has not subjected the work of a serious and gifted poet to the caprice of critical peremptoriness or critical neglect.

This subject is a large one: the critical premise and the particular case of Arthur could each be profitably developed at monograph length. All that will be attempted here, however, is a highly selective demonstration of the implications of the critical premise for a judgment of *the artist's Arthur*—that is, the Arthur whom Tennyson has suspended in idea and form, imaginative intuition and imaginative construction.

Above all else, it must be recognized that Arthur's fallibility is not such an elusive perception as to justify hammering his "faults" home with the lawyer-like overkill that has marked some of the commentary. It is the organizing assumption of the poem seeded in Arthur's initial epiphanic dilation over Guinevere—magnificent in its ego-strength and generosity and terrifying in its tragic promise—that leads him in his youthful idealism and inexperience to dream the impossible dream. He can, perhaps, will his will, work his work, and become "'Victor and lord'" in his own "'realm'"—that is, achieve, at a seemingly ideal level, self-conquest. But to extrapolate this conversion of self into an ideal conversion of community, drawing from the intensity of his love-magnification and the sublimity of his ideal of union the "pure, generous, tender, brave, human-hearted"[8] idea that therefore he can "'Have power on this dark land to lighten it,/And power on this dead world to make it live'"(*CA*, 92–93), makes either sentimentality or tragedy inevitable. Every person who has experienced a first love of any grandeur can identify with the young King's feelings of hieratic ardor, but if he has lived long enough, he has gradually learned that, even if he himself has remained faithful, the human community ultimately resists such magic, however glamorous it may have seemed initially, and puts an infinity of obstacles in its way.

From a poet like Tennyson, stern of mind and learned in the best epic and dramatic traditions, we know that matters will work themselves through many literary-experiential variations to their severest tragic conclusion and that only so much of a remnant hope will be saved as classical tragedy allows. What we may not be quite so alert to is Tennyson's keen sensitivity to the sentimental alternative to tragedy which, in the less imaginatively ordered world of daily living, the overwhelming majority opt for and even writers and readers tend to prefer if they possibly can. As a result, tragedy and sentimentality are so persistently played against each other throughout *Idylls of the King* that the tension between them is one of the literary ground tones of the poem, the sentimental alternative to tragic realization being one of the "wandering [emotional] fires" that lead character after character into a precarious or fatal quagmire.

The quest for the Holy Grail is a sentimental journey. Merlin capitulates to sentimentality. Lancelot's romantic search for anonymity, undertaken on the advice of Guinevere, brings him to the verge of death physically and, spiritually, to the temptation of Elaine's fatal pathos that, had he succumbed to it, would have drowned all possibility of salvation in an ocean of sentimentality. Guinevere wraps herself in sentimentality so long and so successfully that it dyes her very sense of self and makes her recognition and redemption at the final hour inextricably dependent on Arthur's austere truth-telling in their last scene together.

In *Lancelot and Elaine,* Tennyson had made the crucial choice between pathos and the tragic vision difficult by presenting "the lily maid of Astolat" in such an ingratiating way that the reader must overcome his habitual inclinations toward sentimentality to hold steady in the morally bracing truth of tragedy. In *Guinevere,* he reverses the reader's challenge by making the very relentlessness with which Arthur perseveres in his moral duty—the equivalent of Oedipus's putting out of his eyes—almost more than the residual sentimentality of the reader can tolerate. Indeed, the *ad hominem* scoffing of many commentators may be a cry of moral pain, like that of the reader who laughs at Little Father Time's genocide-suicide in *Jude the Obscure* because he is unprepared to accept the terrifying truth of the boy's actions or their explanation. But when one fairly considers the alternative—a potentially magnificent woman, "the fairest of all flesh on earth," going to her death tortured to distraction by her inability to find the peace of tragic recognition and acceptance, the grandeur that Arthur has always known to be her birthright pathetically wasted in moral blindness—then one may be driven by poetic necessity, not personally to like the scene or to claim perfection for the two fallible principals who enact it, but to acknowledge that Tennyson, like other poets of the first order, has saved something cathartic and therefore precious from the catastrophe and has spared the reader the horror of hopelessness. Both the poet and his king would thus merit, not vituperation, but the sympathy that understanding brings: the sad wisdom that literary necessity brings is suffered by them as well as by the reader.

There is obviously a contradiction between this insistence on Arthur's fundamental fallibility and the customary notion that he is an "ideal" figure in some superhuman or God-like sense. Obviously, too, such contradictory perceptions lead their respective adherents to reach quite different conclusions on Tennyson's poetic handling of his hero.

According to Jerome Buckley (p. 243–244), "Arthur is presented as an ideal figure of supernatural origin and destination, as the emissary of God, and not as a realistic and therefore fallible hero," and this leads Buckley to perceive Arthur as "conspicuously ineffective" in the drama of the poem—"woodenly imperceptive" toward Guinevere, positively obtuse toward Lancelot, "recessive," "a shadowy background presence." Ryals, too, is uncompromising in his stress on the "ideal" at the expense of the "real." Arthur, he says, "is *exactly* what Tennyson says he is: an ideal man. . . ."[9] Reed characterizes himself as Buckley's propagandist: his goal, he says, is "to promote" Buckley's "views," which he finds "quite sound."[10] By seeing Arthur as "perfect in a scale of values beyond the human," Philip Eggers, who also takes Buckley as his guide, deprives him of any exemplary role in the struggle with the fatality of human experience. In Arthur, "Tennyson sees the possibility of the hero's transcending human failure."[11] Fleshing out his argument, Eggers says that Tennyson makes Arthur "a Christ figure." By this, he means that

Arthur is Tennyson's fictional and metaphoric equivalent of Christ, so idealized in his perfection that he is "beyond tragedy,"[12] and Eggers allows for none of the meticulous and delicate care with which the poet puts a crucial distance between the Christian God-Man and the "Ideal manhood closed in real man" of *Idylls of the King*.

Tennyson was too fine a poet to be heavy-handed on either side of this crucial issue, but even while insisting on the symbolic import of the poem's ingredients, he asserted that "there is no single fact or incident in the *Idylls*, however seemingly mystical, which cannot be explained as without any mystery or allegory whatever."[13] In other words, though the imaginative vitality of *Idylls of the King* is clearly dependent on the richness of its metaphoric or symbolic texture, with each image, incident, and character having meanings that, in Browning's phrase, reach "beyond the facts," it is not necessary to rush to mystical or inflatedly allegorical ("too allegorical") explanations of those meanings. Indeed, the clear implication is that, despite his profound disinclination to place restrictions on any insight that a capable and sympathetic reader might find in his poem, Tennyson felt that some of the perceptions that he himself prized most highly were being deflected or obfuscated by this too-mystical, too-allegorical tendency. A misunderstanding of the central revelation embodied in Arthur would certainly fall into that category.

Two basic questions thus emerge: (1) Are Tennyson's extra-textual characterizations of Arthur—"shadowing Sense at war with Soul,/Ideal manhood closed in real man," ("To the Queen"); "I intended Arthur to represent the Ideal Soul of Man coming into contact with the warring elements of the flesh";[14] "By King Arthur I always meant the soul, and by the Round Table the passions and capacities of a man"[15]—reasonably susceptible to a critical turning that is "without any mystery or allegory whatever"? And (2) What difference does such a critical turning make to our assessment of the character of Arthur and the imaginative integrity of Tennyson's poem?

An affirmative answer to the first question requires that one establish a nonmystical, nonallegorical meaning for the variant phrases with which Tennyson commented on his intent in the portrayal of Arthur. That task is made relatively easy through the poet's own artistic circumspection. In the tradition of Shakespeare, he has planted in the text a translation that carries the authority of the person most qualified by rank and experience to enunciate it:

> "now I see thee what thou art,
> Thou art the highest and most human too,
> Not Lancelot, nor another."
>
> (*G*, 643–645)

Not an infallible "emissary of God" in any extraordinary sense; certainly not "perfect in a scale of values beyond the human"; but "the highest" human being on a comparative scale of human beings that an illumined Guinevere has ever known. "Ideal manhood closed in real man" has as its only authoritative textual translation "'the highest and most human too.'" According to this translation, when we speak of Arthur as an "ideal figure," we should mean simply that he symbolizes the finest idea of the fallen but redeemable creature called man that the conscientious secular imagination of this poet could conceive of—fallible and ever-changing because human, but still very, very fine.

But what of his "supernatural origin and destination"? To assert this as a fact or even as a peculiarly Arthurian possibility is to assert what the poem does not and to literalize in this story one of the universal subjects of man's perpetually unrequited longings. We know as little about the "unfacts" of man's birthing or even of our own births as is known about Arthur's. But there is nothing incredible or even unusual about associating with the event the four elements of fire, air, water, and earth or perceiving it as a strange new beginning, just as there is nothing incredible or even unusual about associating death with a double-pointing myth of the return or perceiving the event as muffled in strange talk of rest, journeying, unearthly wailing, solitariness, rigorous cold, and eventual rebirth. As Matthew Arnold pointed out in *Literature and Dogma*, even Plato was unequal to a really satisfactory idea of immortality, but if one is willing to leave the idea as open as the text of *Idylls of the King* essentially demands, then Tennyson's nonimperious, nondoctrinal representation of man's myth of a hopeful passing, his myth of an eventual return, is a marvelously evocative fusion of aesthetic and hieratic intimations.

The more genuinely human the reader allows Arthur to be—*both* fallible *and* admirable—the more realistic and dramatic he becomes. Like everyone's, Arthur's initial social problem is that of establishing a public role that will enable him to realize a life mission that is inherent in who he knows he is. In seeking a life-companion, he, like many idealistic young men, mythicizes and hence, in the short term, misperceives his choice, just as she, also in the short term, mythicizes and misperceives both him and Lancelot, and the horrid shows, agonies, and "long-drawn days of blight" that ensue are rooted in these identity misperceptions—both his and hers—and their progeny is a whole symbolic generation of identity misperceptions. At the end of life, they finally discover, through catastrophic challenges, who they really are, she a misguided Queen, he a misguided King. They have been misguided about different things, however—she about him and hence about herself, he about the world and the lasting effect he could have on it. But, significantly, he was not misguided about her; though it took catastrophe to prove it, catastrophe proved him right, not wrong, about her. Proof came too late in this cycle of time to reverse the present tragedy, and *this* Arthur and *this* Guinevere must pass into *historical* oblivion. But the *myth* has been born and confirmed by the reconstruction of the only records history has left us. The Arthur and Guinevere *idea* has been reborn and proved viable, and that can never die. So in the cycles of time, the Arthur and Guinevere of corrected vision (the poet's gift to history) may very well have their "new year," and who knows what they then may make of this "fair world"? It is only a hope, of course, but a profoundly educated hope and as dependable as man's endlessly reasserted faith in himself.

We may also begin to discover an alternative explanation of Arthur's so-called recessiveness—his obliviousness to Guinevere's and Lancelot's infidelity, the blankness with which he reacts to Vivien's seductive ploys—and on the basis of it we can perhaps see his "dramatic relation" to the other characters as simply distinctive rather than "conspicuously ineffective."

Arthur is, for a long time, a prisoner of his own gloriously misguided dream. It does have a "fair beginning"—a delusive "false dawn"—and this further fixes in his mind the unrealistic idea (itself a wholly realistic poetic insight) that the impossible dream is in fact possible, that the evanescent appearance is the perfect reality when only a fleeting glimpse of perfection is momentarily imaged there. Like Karshish's Lazarus in Browning's *An Epistle,* Arthur is a man possessed by a heavenly insight, and, like Lazarus, his responses do not follow the quotidian pattern of those not so possessed. He has sworn a deathless love for both Lancelot and Guinevere, and fidelity not only to vows but to vows inextricably interwoven with his aspirations for the world hold him aloof from even that shadow of infidelity, suspicion. In the celebrated incident with Vivien, Arthur is like the unsoiled innocent in many a ribald tale, his blankness to her seductive overture being a source of cynical amusement to the worldly, but ultimately a proof of the innocent's innocence. If it mirrors an aspect of his fallibility and hence his tragedy, it is a token of his worthiness and hence of his triumph too. This is itself a keenly dramatic concept of character, and the poet is to be praised rather than censured for not invalidating Arthur in order to conform to less faithful notions of dramatic propriety.

Tennyson was too shrewd a poet-observer not to realize that Arthur would have his plausible detractors. In fact, he built Arthur's most effective detractors into the poem itself and not only made them in degree credible, but also put the rebuttals to those detractions into curiously faulted hands— Balin growling at Garlon on the eve of stamping the royal crown into defacement and Merlin the seducer in the very act of being seduced. Of course, it might be argued that one of Tennyson's great strategic errors in the conception and execution of *Idylls of the King* was not to be sufficiently forthcoming on the issue of Arthur's foolish innocence in the manner, say, of Dostoevsky's *The Idiot.* His theme allows it, and Arthur's great recognition scene in *The Passing of Arthur* (9–28) frankly says it, "'For I, being simple. . . .'" But that would perhaps have been too great a violation of the tragic traditions of poetry in a poem that very finely measures grades of tragedy, too flippant a divorce from the examples of Homer, Virgil, Spenser, Shakespeare, and Milton. Moreover, the softening of Arthur's character in that way might have seemed to Tennyson a creative coup at the risk of a creative collapse. *That is not this artist's Arthur,* who is every inch a King—talks like one, acts like one, thinks like one, even loves, hurts, grieves, and forgives like one—and one example of impeccable kingliness is not more than the literature of the modern world can bear. Moreover, the very mystique of kingliness, its infinite possibilities for good, is the source of Arthur's "simple" reading of the paradox of human life and the motive equally of his grandeur, his error, the catastrophe to which it leads, the recognition that he reaches, and the hope with which he faces *both* death *and* the future.

To most sympathetic readers, the style of *Idylls of the King* is faultless but not intimidating, the overall simplicity of its manner of discourse challenging any expectation of poetic style that they may have learned from, say, Spenser, Shakespeare, Donne, Dryden, Blake, Keats, and Browning. It is a style that announces that language is going to provide full facility of access, that language is going to be a clear transparency through which to look at the poet's subject. That, of course, is poetry's ultimate illusion, and the pleasure of the illusion combined with the recognition that it is a most delicate and deceptive illusion is a source of one of the first and most sustained aesthetic responses that the poem incites; it announces that, however conspicuously or inconspicuously referential *Idylls of the King* may be in the working out of its art and ideas, it is self-referential in its style and therefore to a degree self-referential, too, in *its way* with art and ideas since their imaginative truth subsists in the poem's style. Tennyson carried the art of concealing his art to a point of rare finish, just as he carried the idea of concealing his ideas in metaphors that do not disclose their inner meaning until one has looked through the apparent substance at the thing signified by it beyond our usual sense of imaginative evasiveness. And until critics of the poem root their conclusions in the artistic soil to which the art and ideas are native and without which they have only an abstract and somewhat unreal existence, readers should look upon them as not only highly provisional, but in many cases perhaps as not what Tennyson meant at all.

Notes

1. "Notes" to the Eversley Edition of *The Works of Alfred Lord Tennyson*, annotated by Alfred Lord Tennyson and edited by Hallam Lord Tennyson (New York: Macmillan, 1908), III (*Idylls of the King*), 440. All references to these notes are to this edition and are given hereafter as Eversley, with volume and page numbers.
2. Eversley, III, 446.
3. Ryals, *From the Great Deep* (Athens: Ohio University Press, 1967), p. 200.
4. Ryals, *From the Great Deep*, pp. 89–90. See also p. 245, above.
5. Above, p. 247, and *The Fall of Camelot* (Cambridge, Mass.: Harvard University Press, 1973), pp. 127–133.
6. F. G. Kenyon, ed. (London, 1910), XII, 837–863.
7. This is the quality of critical conscientiousness that Matthew Arnold found an operating principle of such French critics as Sainte-Beuve and generally ignored by his countrymen.
8. Eversley, III, 446.
9. Ryals, *From the Great Deep*, p. 83, emphasis added.
10. John R. Reed, *Perception and Design in Tennyson's "Idylls of the King"* (Athens: Ohio University Press, 1969), pp. 3, 241–242n.
11. J. Philip Eggers, *King Arthur's Laureate* (New York: New York University Press, 1971), p. 38.
12. *King Arthur's Laureate*, pp. 42, 43.
13. Eversley, III, 442.
14. Eversley, III, 443n.
15. James T. Knowles, "Aspects of Tennyson," *Nineteenth Century*, 33 (January 1893), 181–182.

Index

Headnote: I have attempted to make this index functional while avoiding too rigid a view of how it might function for different users. There are no entries for Tennyson or for *Idylls of the King* since the references would have been so numerous or inclusive as to be meaningless. Arthur, too, was considered to be beyond indexing except for four critical-interpretive sequences in which his character and role are specifically and extensively evaluated; those are indexed. It was assumed that the index could best be used in connection with the "List of Works Cited" (pp. 295–297). Therefore, the names of all the commentators were indexed, but not the titles of their books and articles, which are identified in the notes, as appropriate. Each idyll is indexed, as are all the characters in the poem except Arthur. This often made it necessary to decide whether the real subject to be indexed was a character or an idyll (e.g., Guinevere, or *Guinevere*, Vivien or *Merlin and Vivien*). Though many calls were admittedly quite close, I tried to observe the principles of usefulness and common sense and to achieve reasonable completeness without redundancy.